GERARD MANLEY HOPKINS

GERARD MANLEY HOPKINS

(1844–1889)

A Study of Poetic Idiosyncrasy in Relation to Poetic Tradition

BY

W. H. GARDNER

Volume II

"Fineness, proportion, of feature comes from a moulding force which succeeds in asserting itself over the resistance of cumbersome or restraining matter; the bloom of health comes from the abundance of life, the great vitality within."
(G. M. H., *Further Letters*, p. 159.)

LONDON
OXFORD UNIVERSITY PRESS
NEW YORK TORONTO

Oxford University Press, Amen House, London E.C.4

GLASGOW NEW YORK TORONTO MELBOURNE WELLINGTON
BOMBAY CALCUTTA MADRAS KARACHI LAHORE DACCA
CAPE TOWN SALISBURY NAIROBI IBADAN ACCRA
KUALA LUMPUR HONG KONG

First Published 1949
(by Martin Secker & Warburg)
Reissued 1958
(Oxford University Press)
Reprinted 1961

PRINTED BY LITHOGRAPHY IN BELGIUM
GREGG ASSOCIATES, BRUSSELS

TO

MY MOTHER

ANNIE OXENHAM GARDNER

(1873–1947)

I HUMBLY DEDICATE

THIS VOLUME

PREFACE

CERTAIN constructive suggestions put forward by friendly critics of my first volume chimed so well with my own riper thoughts that I have, as a result, considerably extended the scope of the present complementary work.

Some reviewers of the first volume remarked on the paucity of biographical matter ; but I must repeat that my principal aim is exegesis and criticism, not biography. Nevertheless, in the process of interpretation I have, I believe, omitted very few events or actions of real importance in the life of Hopkins. In the present volume, for instance, an Introduction of some length has been added to provide a more general account of the poet's relationship to his social, cultural, and religious background.

All four chapters in Part I. of the present book have been taken over (with revision) from the original single-volume work which had to be split up owing to the exigences of war-time publication (see Preface to Vol. I.). In a strictly chronological study of the poet's development Chaps. i.—iii. of Vol. II. should be read before Vol. I., Chap. ii. (*The Wreck of the Deutschland*), since they deal in a specialized and historico-critical manner with technical problems underlying the mature poetry of 1876–89. Chronologically, moreover, the last two chapters of Vol. I. may be taken as rounding off the whole story. The last chapter of Vol. II., Part I. records attitudes and judgments which are implicit in Hopkins's total artistic individuality.

The first three chapters of Part II. have grown naturally out of the *one* additional chapter of appreciations promised in the original preface to Vol. I. In these chapters I have attempted to trace Hopkins's development chronologically throughout the finished poems and most important fragments written after *The Deutschland*. Finally, the Epilogue is for me the logical conclusion to all the evidences and arguments brought together in the two volumes.

I am painfully aware of certain shortcomings in my method of presentation ; on the other hand, it has, I am convinced, some important advantages. In the first place, by consulting the Table of Contents or the Index the reader should be able to find quickly what he wants. My total plan should enable anyone to make an intensive and systematic study of the whole or any single part of Hopkins's work as poet and critic. Secondly there is, I think, an advantage in the fact that in these pages Hopkins's poetry and philosophy, with which I am mainly concerned, are not overlaid and obscured by a mass of biographical *trivia*; for such obfuscation is the weakness of most ' critical biographies '. I have long realized that the most competent and sympathetic biography of a poet, in proportion as it is ' domestic ' and ' anecdotal ', almost always tends to belittle him; in many ways it deadens the impact, blurs the clear outline of his unique personality and work; and it is Hopkins's poetry which, for my present purpose at least, is distinctly *multa pars sui*. This does not imply that biographical facts should be suppressed: I merely affirm that such facts should be kept in their place. There are too many people to-day who feel that once they have read the life-story of a poet they know everything about him that really matters.

This, perhaps, is the best place for the announcement that Hopkins's long-lost spiritual diary (or note-book of meditations specifically enjoined by the Jesuit rule) is no longer extant. On October 10, 1945, in reply to my inquiry about this book, the poet's youngest sister, Miss Grace Hopkins (who has since died) wrote me a letter from which I quote the following relevant paragraph:

> " About the *Diary*—on which was written ' *Please do not open this* '—my sister Kate [1] and I considered very earnestly and carefully whether we could allow it to be opened and read by any and every one who was interested in Gerard's life as well as his poems—and we came to the conclusion that we could not do what he requested *might not be done!* I own *I* was the most strongly against the opening it, and so we there and then put it into the fire, without glancing at the contents, and we saw it burnt to ashes. And I feel sure *he* would approve of what we did that day. I hope this will not distress you."

Morally, the position of the Misses Hopkins is unassailable: it is obvious that they acted in perfect good faith. We can see now, however, that the diary should not have been destroyed; it should have been returned to the Society of Jesus, which, according to rules accepted and vows taken by G. M. H., had undoubtedly the first claim on the deceased Jesuit's private and *spiritual* property.

[1] Died 1933.

We cannot of course be sure that this was the only spiritual note-book which Hopkins compiled while a Jesuit ; indeed, such a possibility seems unlikely. As late as January 1947 the Rev. D. A. Bischoff, S.J., from New Haven, U.S.A., discovered at Farm Street, London, a number of new poems and a further 20,000 words of the poet's *Journal*. We have still a hope, therefore, that some at least of Hopkins's most intimate and carefully organized meditations on religion in general and his own soul in particular may yet come to light.

Since my first volume appeared in 1944, Fr. W. A. M. Peters, S.J., has published his interesting critique of Hopkins's poetry. In his Introduction, however, he blames me for not having attempted what he himself set out to do—namely, to prove that almost every stylistic device in Hopkins must be traced to his *purely personal* and *entirely original* concepts of " inscape " and " instress ". All the critics, says Dr. Peters, have failed to see that the word " inscape " represented " something that was not observed by other men, therefore caused a very personal experience, and so was to stand for something not experienced by others, for which consequently there existed no word, because the need for it was never felt." I hope to prove that such a sweeping premise cannot be maintained. Fr. Peters, in rejecting (save for Homer) the powerful and manifold influences of poetic tradition, presents Hopkins as a preternaturally isolated and incredibly original or idiosyncratic poet ; whereas my own purpose is to show how brilliantly he exemplified, as a great and original eclectic, the truth of his own dictum : " the examples of the great masters are the soul of education." If " inscape " is " the very soul of art " and Whistler possessed it, how could Hopkins be the only artist to experience it ? Fr. Peters's examination of *one* aspect of Hopkins's poetry is admirable ; but my own more comprehensive treatment is a necessary corrective to his over-statement. Though my friendly " adversary " dislikes my " subjective " reading of the word *inscape* (*op. cit.*, p. 174), the danger of his own approach is in the suggestion that the whole of Hopkins's vision and method was a complete, portentous and alarming ' subjectivity '.

My grateful acknowledgments are due to all my predecessors in the field of Hopkins criticism, and I am especially indebted to Mr. Humphry House, whose expert knowledge of the poet's early life and early manuscripts was placed at my disposal both

in the preparation of the Third Edition of the *Poems* and in my
revision of the Introduction and Chap. i. of the present volume.
I must also thank Rev. D. A. Bischoff, S.J., for giving me access
to his recent finds and to other facts gleaned by him in his
researches towards the official Jesuit account of G. M. H.'s life
in the Society of Jesus.

For indispensable help in the editing of Hopkins's Welsh
poems, and in my exposition of the Welsh influence generally, I
tender my thanks to Sir H. Idris Bell and his son, Mr. David Bell,
to Mr. T. Parry, M.A., and Mr. M. Harries, B.A., F.R.C.O.
Again I have to thank my friend, Mr. E. L. Hillman, for valuable
critical comment at many stages of the work. Most decisive,
however, in bringing out anything that may be good in this
book have been the frank criticism and generous encouragement
afforded by my publisher, Mr. Roger Senhouse. The book,
moreover, would have been more faulty than it is but for
my wife, whose blunt strictures frequently proved to be the
medium of

"Grace that day grace was wanted."

For kind permission to use copyright material I am indebted
to the Cambridge University Press for extracts from *Greek Lyric
Metre*, by George Thomson ; to Messrs. J. M. Dent & Sons Ltd.,
for excerpts from *Fauré*, by Norman Suckling, to Mr. Edwin
Muir and the Cresset Press for two quotations from *The Present
Age, from* 1918. My greatest obligations are to Mr. Gerard
Hopkins, who represents the poet's family and the Oxford
University Press, and to the Very Rev. M. C. D'Arcy, S.J., the
Jesuit Provincial. Both have at all times shown me the utmost
kindness in giving me access to the Hopkins MSS. which are in
their keeping, and have generously allowed me to quote freely
for purposes of illustration and critical comment. If I have
overlooked any author or publisher whose copyright material I
have quoted I trust that this general acknowledgment of my
indebtedness will suffice.

W. H. GARDNER
February 1948.

University of Natal,
  Pietermaritzburg,
    Natal

CONTENTS

CHAPTER III

CHAPTER IV

PART II : MATURITY AND ACHIEVEMENT

CHAPTER V

PLATES

ABBREVIATIONS

In all footnotes the titles of Hopkins's works will be abbreviated as follows :

Poems.   *Poems of G. M. H.*, Second Edition, 1930.

Poems, Third Edition.   *Poems of G. M. H.*, Third Edition, 1948.

Letters, vol. i.   *The Letters of G. M. H. to Robert Bridges*, 1935.

Letters, vol. ii.   *The Correspondence of G. M. H. and R. W. Dixon*, 1935.

Further Letters.   *Further Letters of G. M. H.*, etc., 1938.

Note-books.   *The Note-books and Papers of G. M. H.*, 1937.

HOPKINS AND HIS BACKGROUND

I

In the opening chapter of our previous volume we said as much about this poet's life and background as seemed necessary, in that context, to ensure a general understanding of the man himself and the main characteristics of his poetry. In subsequent chapters we used *biographia* incidentally and only as they were relevant to the immediate task of exposition or criticism. We shall now attempt to gather up, in one comprehensive survey, facts which could not be handled in our other chapters, but which ought not to be omitted from any study that aims at completeness. Our purpose in this introduction will be to assist the reader in forming his own judgment as to how far Hopkins was moulded by his environment and by the ethos of his age.

Hopkins was not pre-eminently a 'period' writer. Not more than two or three of his poems were directly inspired by events or circumstances which were peculiar to the nineteenth century : his poetry has, in fact, a timeless quality. Still, in his treatment of a number of his themes the impress of his age is apparent. Hence, to obtain a clear picture of the man, and a clear insight into the ultimate meaning and value of his poetry and prose, we must first see him in relation to his domestic, literary, artistic, and religious backgrounds ; at the same time we must reckon with certain diffused influences arising out of the economic and political conditions of Victorian England.

We have already seen how the versatile father and contemplative mother, assisted by artistically gifted aunts and uncles, helped to form the early tastes of Gerard, the eldest of a family of six sons and three daughters. Besides being " a keen student of philosophy, history, and politics ", the mother was a devout Christian. According to Gerard's school-friend, Luxmoore, it was in fulfilment of a promise made to his mother that Hopkins

read daily a small portion of the New Testament ; [1] and although
the father also was, by modern standards, a religious man, it was
probably the mother's influence that was decisive in this direction.
Gerard's later religious intensity seems less remarkable when we
know that his eldest sister, Milicent, became at an early age ' an
outsister at the Margaret Street Home ' and later a full-fledged
Anglican nun.[2]

There were painters and musicians on both sides of the
family. One of the poet's maternal uncles was a landscape
painter of some note in his day. Two of his brothers, Arthur
and Everard, became professional artists, and achieved a competent if not resounding success in the field of magazine and
book illustration.[3] All the brothers had a lively sense of humour ;
the second sister, Kate, was also a " sort of humorist " ; and
we can imagine that the family intercourse must have been
bright with satirical quip and the cultivation of what one of the
brothers, Mr. Lionel Hopkins, once called the " strictly funny ".[4]
None the less the two artists, like the poet-priest himself, pursued
their vocation with a marked earnestness of purpose. There is a
family likeness in the fact that their achievement never quite
fulfilled their early promise, though in the poet's case this must
be qualified : like his own skylark he could hover and sing
at rare altitudes, but he lacked the bird's power of sustained
activity.

From an English mother and a father of Welsh extraction
Gerard inherited certain specifically English and Welsh qualities :
to the Welsh artistic and especially *musical* sensitivity was added
the Englishman's characteristic resourcefulness or ' adaptive '
mastery. Both the English and the Celtic strain were capable of
fostering the poet's response to the beauties of external nature ;

---

[1] *Note-books*, p. 438.   [2] *Ibid.* p. 379.

[3] Arthur (1847–1930) won a gold medal at the R.A. ; was a member and treasurer
of the R.W.S. ; was for twenty-five years on the staff of the *Graphic* and contributed
illustrations to *Punch*. In 1901 he published *Sketches and Skits*. Everard (1860–1928)
held the Slade Scholarship for the whole three years of his studentship under Legros ;
contributed in black-and-white to many magazines, including the *Woman's World*
(edited by Oscar Wilde), the *Illustrated London News*, and *Punch*. In 1910 he illustrated
The Sentimental Journey and published *Lydia*, a novel ; in 1911 he illustrated Tennyson's
The Princess.

[4] *Letters*, vol. i. p. 133. Kate (1856–1933) was skilled in drawing. Besides the
brother, Lionel (b. 1854), there were still, in 1945, two surviving sisters—the eldest,
Milicent (1849–1947) and the youngest, Grace (1858–1946), whom Gerard described
as " musical beyond the common ". She frequently harmonized her brother's songs
(See *Letters*, vol. i. pp. 103, 105, etc.).

but there is evidence that the father was more than normally endowed with this sensibility.

Gerard, while in residence at Balliol from 1863 to 1867, kept a note-book into which he copied poems by Emerson, Miss Smedley, Rossetti, his religious friends Challis and Coles, and others. Among these we find eleven pieces which are all signed " M. H."—the initials of his father, Manley Hopkins. Until 1946, however, the father's authorship of these poems was merely conjectural ; but the discovery last year in the family home of a book of verses called *The Philosopher's Stone*, which was published by Manley Hopkins in 1843,[1] put the matter beyond all doubt, for all the poems signed " M. H. " in Gerard's note-book are in that collection.

The Philosopher's Stone was written before Manley Hopkins had completed his twenty-fifth year. They are the pre-marital bird-trillings of an earnest and cultured man whose real bent was for diplomacy and business ; yet these gracefully turned but on the whole mediocre verses must be taken into account as an essential part of the more gifted son's early literary background.

The title-piece is a longish ballad composed in a vein of moral macabre which emulates many stylistic features of *The Ancient Mariner*, but not the poetry. We quote the conclusion, as this may account for part at least of Gerard's own pre-occupation, in later years, with moral aspects of Death :

> " Gold is dross,—our labour loss,
>   Our robes of byss are rent ;
> The withered crown will soon slide down
>   A skull all bleached and shent.
> Our bitter cry is, ' In vanity
>   Hath all my life been spent ! '

> " The Alchymists rare, are they who prepare
>   For death ere life be done ;
> And by study hard WITHIN THE CHURCHYARD
> IS FOUND THE PHILOSOPHER'S STONE."

---

[1] Its 115 pages contain 51 poems. The publisher was G. W. Nickisson. The book is not in the British Museum catalogue. The dedication is interesting : " To Thomas Hood, Esq.,/These few pages (with his permission) inscribed ; as a slight token of personal friendship, and of admiration for talents which have the peculiar power to beguile care, and have charmed so many hours into mirth and enjoyment, /By his obliged/And sincere Friend/The Author."

A few poems in this book reveal the influence of Wordsworth. *To a Beautiful Child*, for instance, touches on the concept of Nature as an educative power :

> " . . . *thy* book
> Is cliff, and wood, and foaming waterfall ;
> Thy playmates—the wild sheep and birds that call
> Hoarse to the storm ;—thy sport is with the storm
> To wrestle ;—and thy piety to stand
> Musing on things create, and their Creator's hand ! "

Could that beautiful and precocious child have been Gerard himself ? Certainly the idea of ' wrestling with the storm ' was a symbol as prophetic of Gerard's spiritual stress as " musing on things create, and their Creator's hand " was the germinal condition of much of his finest nature-poetry.

A gentlemanly erotic strain in the father is evinced in such titles as *Her Mirror, Her Pillow, Her Sorceries*. In *The Nursery Window* occurs a *motif* which the son developed with singular originality in *Spring* and *The Bugler's First Communion* :

> " Peace to thee, Infancy !—Dear prime
> *Only* of innocence the time."

In *Sonnet* we find a thought which would have pleased Keats and was probably a matter of speculation for the young Gerard :

> " We ask away the poesy of flowers,
> And steal by science from skies, rocks, and birds
> The magic that once pleased our simple sires,—
> And to light wisdom's light, we oft quench fancy's fires."

The diction in " We *ask away* the poesy of flowers " shows a touch of the son's own boldness in the handling of common words ; and in another piece, *The Fairest Flower of Spring*, the miniature beauty of the " Lily of the Vale " is suggested with a delicate, almost Keatsian fancy :

> " Haply to insect ears *of audience fine*
> Those silver bells make music as they swing."

But such felicities are rare. There is too much in the vein of Felicia Hemans and Eliza Cook :

> " My mother loved thee, flower ! And therefore I
> Will love thee in thy prime and withering. . . ."

Gerard too loved to trace the ' scapes ' of a withering flower ;

but although a flower could make him think of the beauty of
Christ, it never evoked the inflated sentiment of

> " And thou must be through life's eternity
>   Unchangingly to me the fairest flower of Spring."

Some of the father's verses, such as *A Child's Loneliness*, are
maudlin and psychologically false. To offset these *A Temperance
Drinking Song* is a brisk and mildly humorous exercise in light
verse. The book contains more variety than quality, and in
view of one of the son's pronounced but strictly controlled
tendencies (to be dealt with later) [1] we note with interest that
the father could not resist the fascination of physical horrors.
The Grave-Digger tells how a peasant was embraced by a headless
corpse ; and in *The Child's Dream* the line

> " I saw his pale hands streaked with blood "

leads up to a climax which overpowered even the innocently
' sadistic ' poet :

> " Quickly their darting eyes were sent
>   Beneath, and there they saw
> O horrible !—most horrible !—
> *   *   *   *   *   *
> *   *   *   *   *   * "

There are surer signs of an adult intelligence in two conventionally Jacobite pieces—*Carisbrooke* and *The Legend : A Cavalier
Song* ; but the real technical *tour de force* is an eighteen-page
poem on John the Baptist, which is all composed (with apologies)
in the irregular measure of Southey's now unreadable epics.

Among the verses from this volume which were anthologized
by Gerard in 1864 and the following year are several which bear
a certain genetic relationship to some of his own mature poems.
One piece called *Clouds*, though devoid of any original handling
of language, does nevertheless show that genuine feeling for the
natural phenomenon which we find on every page of the *Journal*
and also in such poems as *Hurrahing in Harvest* and the *Heraclitean
Fire*.[2] Again, Gerard thought it worth while to copy out a
sonnet beginning " All things grow old—grow old, decay and
change "—a disturbing truism from which he himself sought
relief in the poignant utterance of *Spring and Fall* and *The Leaden
Echo*.[3] Another of these chosen poems, *To a Bird Singing in a*

[1] See below, chapter vi., pp. 320-3.
[2] *Poems*, Nos. 14 and 48.   [3] *Ibid.*, Nos. 31 and 36.

Narrow Street, contains a sentiment which Gerard developed
tersely and theologically in his own sonnet of 1877, *The Caged
Skylark*. The father's sensibility may be gauged by his opening
lines :

> " Bold-hearted captive ! who thy song canst trill
> So blithely in thy darksome cage,—and fill
> The throbbing air around
> With such mellifluous sound,
> Making our bosoms to thy cadence thrill !—
> Hast thou forgot
> All thou hast lost ?—the fields, the open sky,
> The rising sun, the moon's pale majesty ;—
> The leafy bower, where thy airy nest
> Was hung ; and her, thy mate, once so caress'd !
> Carest thou not
> At least, if not for *these*, for liberty ? "

Undoubtedly father and son had much in common. The
walks they took together between 1857 and 1860, both in England
and during their visits to Belgium and Germany, must have
been unusually fruitful in lore and suggestion to the sensitive
and mentally acquisitive boy. As we see in the pleasing
rhythmical ebb and flow of the stanza just quoted, the son could
have learnt from the father many of the traditional graces of
verse-writing ; and when all is said, Manley Hopkins should be
given due credit for the part he played in the making of a
significant poet.

That the father continued to send his own compositions to
Gerard we know from two passages in the letters to Bridges. In
one, dated January 19, 1879, Hopkins says :

> " I enclose some lines by my father called forth by the proposal
> to fell the trees in Well Walk (where Keats and other interesting
> people lived) and printed in some local paper." [1]

Two months later an actual depredation near Oxford called
forth the son's lyrical lament in *Binsey Poplars*.

About the year 1892 Manley Hopkins printed for private
circulation another collection of verses called *Spicilegium Poeticum*
—" the gathering out of the growth of half a century " ; but
artistically there is no growth whatever. As Mr. Humphry
House recently remarked to the present writer, Gerard had
immediately before him an example and warning of what

[1] *Letters*, vol. i. p. 61.

happens to a man who cultivates poetry without the necessary leaven of originality. In the Oxford note-book C. II, in which Hopkins recorded daily his sins and peccadilloes prior to making a ' good confession ', it is set down more than once that the scrupulous son blamed himself for the misdemeanour of " laughing at father ". Manley Hopkins was in some ways a pompous and autocratic Victorian, and Mr. House [1] has revealed the fact that one of the sons, Arthur, was bitterly antagonized ; but there is no reason to believe that the father ever forfeited the respect and affection of his eldest child.

As Consul-General to Hawaii the father was stationed in London, where he was also head of a firm of Average Adjusters. The list of his highly technical publications on shipping law and marine insurance forms a striking contrast with the artistic proclivities of the family as a whole. [2] His professional interest in nautical situations " of doubt, difficulty, and danger " may have predisposed his poet-son to treat, on two occasions, the subject of shipwreck. Against this, however, we must set the possibility that the son inherited from his energetic and versatile father a general and partial aptitude for too many subjects. The son, if not the father, suffered from a tendency to dissipate his vital energies on a number of fascinating avocations which were not germane to his major interests. To his father's little book on the Cardinal Numbers the poet contributed, in 1887, a quaint visual fantasy in illustration of Frank Galton's theories. [3] Such an effort was probably commendable as a token of filial regard ; but that was only one example of his numerous mental diversions. In the mid and late nineteenth century the new developments in philology, archaeology, and the Ruskinian study of atmospheric phenomena aroused much interest among the learned and curious, and Hopkins's learning, considerable as it was, could never keep pace with his curiosity. His lifelong preoccupation with words, his letters to *Nature* on sunsets, his efforts to discover the birthplace of Duns Scotus—these things we can hardly regret. The numerous notes on Egyptology in his letters to

---

[1] Mr. Humphry House is now engaged in writing the full biography of G. M. H.'s early years (1844–1868).

[2] Manley Hopkins (1818–1897) published, in addition to his two books of verse : *A Handbook of Average* (1857) ; *Hawaii : an historical account of the Sandwich Islands* (1862, 1866) ; *A Manual of Marine Insurance* (1867) ; *The Port of Refuge*, or *advice and instructions to the Master-Mariner in situations of doubt, difficulty, and danger* (1873 : 3rd edn. 1888) ; *The Cardinal Numbers* (1887).

[3] *Letters*, vol. i. pp. 294 and 321.

Baillie were probably expedients for maintaining contact with a valued friend.[1] Yet we cannot help wishing that this harassed poet and musican had left his " Egyptian guesses " (" wild and the children of ignorance ")[2] to other minds which were not pregnant with great odes and choral settings.

Gerard's boyhood was both happy and active. He loved to climb a tree and look out at the top, feeling close to the sky. In country rambles he made his younger brothers *taste* the leaves of wild flowers—to discover their intrinsic quality. The most reliable account of his schooldays is that given by his companion, Luxmoore :

> " Skin (Hopkins) . . . was both popular and respected. Tenacious when duty was concerned, he was full of fun, rippling over with jokes and chaff, facile with pencil and pen, with rhyming jibe or cartoon ; good for his size at games and taking his part, but not as we did placing them first." [3]

If the Oedipus-complex is really as general as Freud believed, it would appear in Hopkins's case to have been diverted ; for hatred was directed not against the father but against the man who was *in loco parentis* at Highgate School. As a senior boy, Hopkins had two violent altercations with Dyne, the Headmaster. Of one occasion Hopkins says : " I was driven out of patience and cheeked him wildly, and he blazed into me with his riding-whip." [4] The fierceness of their mutual dislike is still vividly remembered by Mr. Lionel Hopkins.

No doubt this Head was something of a tyrant, and Gerard's sensitive and determined nature had reacted against what he deemed to be injustice. But a schoolboy's " about absolutely nothing " is rarely to be trusted, and the precocious type is often difficult. Whatever the truth here, the remarkable upshot was that Hopkins, instead of developing that strain of rebelliousness, eventually bowed his head to a rule which demanded unquestioning obedience. In compensation, his self-assertiveness was sublimated as artistic idiosyncrasy.

No man of intellect and integrity ever based his religion and philosophy solely upon habits of thought passively acquired from parents, books, or teachers. His direct apprehension of contemporary life plays some part in the shaping of his mind and character, and it may be said of men like Hopkins that

[1] See *Further Letters.*   [2] *Ibid.,* p. 130.
[3] *Note-books,* p. 438.   [4] See *ibid.* pp. 435–40.

their beliefs about the next world are not unrelated to their poorer neighbours' reactions to this one.

By the year of Hopkins's birth, 1844, the old agrarian and pastoral England had been completely changed by that vast ill-organized movement—the Industrial Revolution. Industrialism had already begun to betray the working classes by throwing up rows of mean dwellings, the beginnings of that blight of ugly and insanitary towns which Hopkins deplored in a sonnet and many letters. In those still pleasantly rural suburbs of London where his boyhood was spent—Highgate and Hampstead [1]—the wretchedness of millions who were the victims of ' the inexorable laws of economics ' could not have entered his consciousness ; but as he grew older he became acutely aware of the appalling economic muddle which had been produced by the policy of *laissez-faire*. The conditions prevailing in 1845 are vividly realized in Disraeli's *Sybil*, with its grim picture of social injustice under the sub-title " The Two Nations "—the rich and the poor. Another mirror of the period is Charles Kingsley's *Politics for the People* (1848), in which the author, declaring that the Bible was not just " an opium-dose " for the overworked poor but was mainly intended " to keep the rich in order ", gave Karl Marx the cue for his dubious demagogic slogan—" Religion is the opium of the people ".

Hopkins's childhood was no doubt what is commonly called ' sheltered ' ; but there is evidence that the father, who claimed friendship with the author of *The Song of the Shirt* (1843), was not altogether insensitive to the plight of the working classes. *The Philosopher's Stone*, published in the same year as Hood's poem, contains an earnest prayer-and-exhortation in four stanzas entitled *The Day of Rest*—an expression of genuine sympathy which is adultered, all unconsciously, by a slightly priggish condescension :

> " Oh what a boon, oh what a golden boon
> To all creation is the Sabbath day !—
>
> .   .   .   .   .   .
>
> Scorn not the Poor, if they upon its morn
>   Are sedulously dressed in gay attire ;
> Think of their weekly toils and hardships borne
>   Enough almost to quench their spirit's fire.
> Smile with, *not at* them, then go home and praise
> Him who, in mercy, gave the Sabbath days."

[1] See Hopkins's pencil drawing of " North Road, Highgate, 1862 " (*Note-books*, p. 22).

How these lines would have infuriated the burning reformers ! How different are they in tone and effect from the " toil ; / And wears man's smudge and shares man's smell " passage in *God's Grandeur* ! Stanza 3, however, strikes a more convincing note :

" I would, to Heaven, that all the Poor could doff
  Upon this day, not only labour's weeds,
But with their clouted vestments might put off
  Their care-worn looks, and care-engendering needs ;
That they might feel, at least, one day belonged
By God's own gift to them, whom man had wronged."

The next thought was by no means as Pecksniffian as, to some minds, it may now appear :

" And would that they, with Sunday clothes, might don
  New garments for the mind, too soiled with sin ;
And robes of righteousness, with joy put on,
  And feel within their hearts new life begin. . . ."

Hopkins the son was never blind to the sins of the Rich ; yet for him too, at all times, those Christian fundamentals, holiness and piety, easily maintained their primacy over every purely materialistic concept—even over the new humanistic ideal of economic and social security for all.

It was not until 1871 that Hopkins wrote his now famous ' Communist ' letter, and from this remarkable confession we shall in due course quote. But before 1871 the writer of those stinging comments had been subjected to many other influences, both cultural and religious, and it is best to see the various phases of his development in their right perspective.

After 1850 the national outlook seemed to be improving. The new middle-class plutocracy of trade and commerce, to which Manley Hopkins was professionally attached, assumed the rôle of a new aristocracy, and there was a widespread faith in an ultimate El Dorado of material prosperity. As a freshman of Balliol in 1863, Gerard was bent on acquiring sound scholarship, on preparing himself for a career in which the predominant factor, Art or Religion, was still undecided. More important to him, at that time, than the political or economic *future* were the various manifestations of a great revival of interest in the *past*—in the pagan splendours of Classical antiquity, in the romantic, monastic and even feudal virtues of the Christian Middle Ages.

Of the austere classicism of Matthew Arnold and the nostalgic colourful medievalism of Tennyson and the Pre-Raphaelites we shall say more when we come to relate them to those important intellectual movements of the century—Culture and Aestheticism. If the new medievalism owed much to Keats, the new classicism was mainly indebted to Goethe, whose influence, as Hopkins saw it, was pervasive but not altogether salutary. Writing, in 1864, some notes for a college essay on *Some Aspects of Modern Medievalism*, he ponders :

> " Goethe, whose balanced mind must not be considered as the ideal of the century, representing the most desired union of the classical and the medieval." [1]

Those words may be taken to mean that he saw in the great German a breadth and balance which few of his successors even tried to emulate.

It was German Liberalism and the new science of aesthetics, the new cults of Humanism and Beauty of the school of Lessing and Goethe, which paved the way for those two powerful monitors of the first half of the century—Carlyle and Ruskin. Like Goethe himself, they had antagonized Hopkins by their rejection of Christian dogma ; but despite his adverse criticism of both prophets, there can be no doubt that he had been duly impressed by their handling of language and by some of their tenets. Carlyle's belief in " the silent charm of rhythmic human companionship " ; Ruskin's equally authoritarian faith in " the beneficency of the strict military order in society "—these ultimately Platonic concepts were not alien to the temperament of a Jesuit Platonist. More balanced than Carlyle the " master ", Ruskin combined art with ethics in a manner which, for Hopkins, partly excused the great critic's indifference to the visible Church. Ruskin anticipated Matthew Arnold's attack on the middle-class Philistines—the men who put Wealth before Life. He bitterly denounced a society which allowed ugliness and poverty to exist amid ample economic resources, and in so doing he profoundly influenced two young poets—William Morris and Gerard Hopkins. Separated by an interval of ten years, these two men went up to Oxford with almost identical aims and interests ; but each took the road that the other might have

---

[1] *Note-books*, p. 21. But cf. *Letters*, vol. i. p. 25 (Feb. 27, 1879) : " . . . that sort of ascendancy Goethe had or even Burns, scoundrel as the first was, not to say the second. . . ."

taken but did not.   Morris, putting the stress on economics,
turned left into secular art and materialistic Socialism ; Hopkins,
basing all upon ethics, turned right into Christian supernaturalism
and a qualified faith in British Imperialism.

With Ruskin we associate also the doctrine of ' work for all ',
the joy of craftsmanship and the dignity of manual labour.
This was the inspiration of Ford Madox Brown's famous picture
called *Work*,[1] and also indirectly of two of Hopkins's poems,
Tom's Garland and *Harry Ploughman*.   An interesting link between
Ruskin and Hopkins is the sonnet which Madox Brown wrote
as a pendant to his painting.   In 1865 Hopkins copied the poem
into the anthology already mentioned, and as it is probably the
seed from which *Tom's Garland* grew, we quote it in full :

" Work ! which beads the brow and tans the flesh [2]
Of lusty manhood, casting out its devils ;
By whose weird art transmuting poor men's evils
Their bed seems down, their one dish ever fresh ;
Ah me, for want of it what ills in leash
Hold us ; its want the pale mechanic levels
To workhouse depths, while master spendthrift revels :
For want of work the fiends him soon enmesh.

Ah, beauteous tripping dame with bell-like skirts,
Intent on thy small scarlet-coated hound,
Are ragged wayside babes not lovesome too ?
Untrained their state reflects on thy deserts,
Or they grow noisome beggars to abound
Or dreaded midnight robbers breaking through."

Altogether, in spite of Lord Shaftesbury and the great writers
who constantly attacked the abuses of their time, the years 1840
to 1880 present a grim contrast between the strict sabbatarian
piety of the well-to-do classes and the misery of the depressed
poor.   Though Hopkins's poetic muse was seldom directly
motivated by it, this " woe, world-sorrow " was actually implicit,
subliminal, in all his mature work.

Advanced social reformers have frequently denounced the
salvific ministrations of the Christian Church as being irrelevant,
ineffectual, if not positively anti-progressive.   That was the
view of Carlyle and Ruskin, of Marx and Morris ; with such a
view Hopkins, of course, profoundly disagreed.   He, like Patmore
and Francis Thompson, was virtually a ' child ' of the Oxford

---

[1] Tate Gallery.   [2] The ' sprung ' opening of this sonnet is noteworthy.

Movement : hence a brief account of the origin and development of this upheaval in the Established Church is necessary to a complete understanding of his background.

II

Though the Free Churches were strong, the Establishment, from 1820 onwards, was in serious decline. " The Church as it now stands," said Dr. Arnold in 1832, " no human power can save." Worldliness and apathy within the Church and the growth of utilitarian doctrine without had, indeed, sapped the faith of many ; but the fact that sacramental Christianity could still command allegiance was proved by the enduring popularity of John Keble's poetical calendar, *The Christian Year* (1827), the ninety-fifth edition of which coincided in 1866 with Hopkins's conversion to Roman Catholicism.

The Oxford Movement began in 1833, when Keble of Oriel College, in a sermon on " National Apostasy ", raised the question of ' authority '. Whence, he asked, did the English Church derive its authority ? His answer was that it came from the Apostolic Succession of the Holy Catholic Church—a concept in which his disciples, the Tractarians, discovered " a neglected wellspring of holiness ". Besides this refurbishing of High Church opinions (and the traditions of the Hopkins family were moderately ' High Church ' and ' Jacobite '), the inspiration of the Oxford Movement

> " was in a felt and experienced personal relationship to our Lord. . . . It was the inspiration of the monastic revivals of the Middle Ages." [1]

A spiritual revival which was both pietistic and moralistic, a striving towards the ideal of " Be ye perfect ", was followed by the restoration of Roman ritual and vestments. Newman's comment on his fellow-Tractarian, R. H. Froude, illustrates that asceticism which later seemed so necessary to Hopkins : " He slept on the floor and fasted on certain days until night—an awful reality of devotion."

As principal contributor to *Tracts for the Times*, Newman eventually realized the anomaly of his position. It was the storm of criticism aroused by his Tract XC which led to his secession in 1845 and incidentally ended the first phase of the

[1] *The Oxford Movement and After* (1932), by C. P. S. Clarke.

Movement. Newman had felt the need, as Hopkins did later, of that doctrinal certainty and unity of practice which only an absolute central authority can bestow.

Others, though relatively few, followed Newman into the Church of Rome. At Oxford, even in Hopkins's time, there was a steady trickle of ' verts ', as they were called (they were ' converts ' to some, ' perverts ' to most). Yet the Anglican *Via Media* still had its impressive champions : Pusey and Liddon, though they had adopted ' Catholicism ', were determined never to bow to the authority of Rome.

After 1845 the more extreme followers of the Tractarians suffered opprobrium under the name of Ritualists ; and when in 1850 the Papal Proclamation reinstated the Roman Catholic hierarchy in England and Wales, popular feeling against Rome and the ' Romanizers ' ran exceedingly high. *Punch*, for instance, claiming to be the mouthpiece of John Bull, denounced the " viperine expectorations " of Catholic apologists, attacked the " Scarlet Lady " (the Papacy), Cardinal Wiseman, and the Pope himself in almost every issue, ridiculed the Ritualists in lampoons and cartoons often of the coarsest type, and commended Jowett, Bishop Colenso, and everyone else who had the boldness to oppose established authority, whether Anglican or Roman. Bishop Tait's threat against the Ritualists, "who brought their toys to church ", was heartily applauded ; the Confessional was called " a dangerous and disgusting practice ". Such was the trend of national opinion when, in 1864, Hopkins paid two visits to St. Alban's, Holborn, a church well known for its ritual, and at Oxford made his first ' confession ' to Canon Liddon.

Pusey had joined the Tractarians with the object of stemming the rising tide of German Liberalism or Rationalism, and Oxford in the 1860's was the scene of an intense struggle between the Broad and the High Churchmen. Liberalism, according to Newman, was " false liberty of thought ", the claim to determine on purely rational grounds " the truth and value of propositions which rest for their reception on the external authority of the Divine Word ". In 1855, Benjamin Jowett, Regius Professor of Greek and Fellow of Balliol, published an edition of St. Paul's Epistles in the notes to which certain basic Christian dogmas were questioned. This work Hopkins knew ; and in his reading list of February–March 1865 [1] we notice the significant juxtaposition of *Tracts for the Times* and *Essays and Reviews*. The latter work

[1] *Note-books*, p. 40.

(1860) was the chief manifesto of the Rationalists, and contained theological essays by such men as Mark Pattison and the two scholars who were later Hopkins's tutors—Jowett and Rowland Williams. In Oxford, the home of orthodoxy, the new theology (or ' neology ') aroused such antagonism that Jowett was deprived of his professorial emoluments for ten years. This persecution only increased his influence over the younger men ; and one who revered him tells us that even Hopkins, though a Ritualist, admired the " purity " of Jowett's character.[1]

The mind of Hopkins was not altogether obsessed by the religious controversy. His letters to Baillie at this time are full of playful humour, passages in which matters grave and gay are whimsically blended. In March 1864 he turns abruptly from St. Alban's, Holborn, to an amusing mock-essay by " Francis Lo. Verulam, Viscount St. Alban ", which begins :

> " It was a good saying of *Petronius Gallus* when *Augustus Caesar* would have him to sign the Thirty-nine Articles, that he would do that very willingly, for that oft times the food of a Fool must be a Wise Man's physick." [2]

The above-mentioned reading list indicates the range (considerable but not extraordinary) of his miscellaneous browsing. " Bacon's Essays " and " Browning's Paracelsus " are followed by six of Shakespeare's plays and " Wordsworth ". Next to " Matthew Arnold's Essays " comes " life of Lacordaire " ; and the coupling of these two great educationists—the English humanist who relinquished Anglicanism, and the French ' liberal ' who returned to the Roman fold—is piquant. Art is represented by two books on church architecture and by Ruskin's *Modern Painters*[3] ; and while the latter work reminds us of that intensive cultivation of Beauty which was carried to such a pitch of exclusiveness in the ' aestheticism ' of Walter Pater,[4] the appearance on the same list of Malory's verse prototype, *Le Morte Arthur*, shows the fascination of the more naïve romantic medievalism. William Morris's *Defence of Guenevere and Other Poems* and the first of Tennyson's *Idylls* had been published in 1858 and 1859 respectively ; and in 1868 Hopkins was trying to obtain a

---

[1] *A Son of Belial* (1882), by Nitram Tradleg (E. M. Geldart), pp. 155–6.
[2] *Further Letters*, p. 61.　　　　　　　　　[3] See below, pp. 36–8.
[4] See vol. i. chap. 1, of the present work. Hopkins's intimacy with Pater is revealed in a letter of 1867 : " Pater is going to ask me down to Sidmouth " ; and in another of 1889 : " When I was at Oxford Pater was one of the men I saw most of." (*Further Letters*, pp. 25 and 99.)

copy of Morris's latest poem, *The Earthly Paradise*, in order to write an essay on that work and the entire medieval school of poets.[1] That task, like so many others, was probably never begun. Yet from a letter of 1864 we learn that his literary and artistic ambitions had been stimulated by an introduction, " at the Gurneys ", to Christina Rossetti, Holman Hunt, and George Macdonald ; for on the same page he says : " I have now a more rational hope than before of doing something—in poetry and painting." [2]

With an almost calculated normality Hopkins turned with obvious delight from his more academic reading to novels, and especially to those of Dickens, Thackeray, Charlotte Brontë and George Eliot. *Romola*, read in 1865, he pronounced " a great book, though not at all so great as *Shirley*." [3] But having made himself happily wretched over the fall of Savonarola, he followed up the subject by reading Villari's *Life and Times* of the great reformer. " I must tell you," he writes to Urquhart,

> " he is the only person in history (except perhaps Origen) [4] about whom I have a real feeling, and I feel such an enthusiasm about Savonarola that I can conceive what it must have been to have been one of his followers." [5]

Indeed, we can easily imagine him in such a rôle. He had read also the account of that powerful personality given by Rio in *De l'art chrétien*, and for Hopkins the conjunction of art and ascetic religion was irresistible. He calls Savonarola " the prophet of Christian art " and speaks of " the poetical and picturesque character of his mind " ; but he does not dwell on that quality in the reformer which some critics would attribute, as a weakness, to Hopkins himself—an almost excessive intensity of moral fervour, a passion for depth and consistency at the expense of breadth and variety in human endeavour.

Hopkins points a contrast between the fates of two reformers : Savonarola, martyred in the Church ; Luther, successful and admired as the author of world-wide heresy in schism. As early

---

[1] *Further Letters*, p. 39.   [2] *Ibid.* p. 67.

[3] *Ibid.* p. 77. For a poetic ' echo ' from Charlotte Brontë's *Shirley*, see below, chap. v. p. 279.

[4] Origen (*c.* 186–*c.* 254), the most famous and influential Christian writer of his century. Even in his own day he was suspected of heresy.

[5] *Further Letters*, p. 7. " George Eliot," he adds, " from being a pagan, clever as she is, does not understand him." See also *Note-books*, pp. 11 and 40.

as July 1863, moreover, Hopkins had begun to show an interest in another Catholic martyr, Sir Thomas More ; and the first version of *Heaven-Haven* (written a year later) suggests that he was considering the sanctity of More as a model for his own life.[1] Indeed, between 1864 and 1866 Hopkins was seriously considering his position as a member of the Anglican Protestant Church. He was honestly trying, as Dr. Pick says, to *vindicate* that position. He copied from Mark Pattison (that vigorous opponent of the Oxford Movement) a citation from Locke on the mere fortuitousness of the Roman Catholic conception of salvation [2] ; in a reading-list of 1864 we find William Gresley's *Short Treatise on the English Church.* On the other hand we can hardly exaggerate the influence exerted during these critical years by the example and published works of Dr. Newman. The great man's one effort at fiction, *Loss and Gain*, was appropriately the story of a convert. There were his *Lectures on Certain Difficulties felt by Anglicans in Submitting to the Catholic Church* (1850), to which Hopkins refers in a letter written in 1868 to convince his clerical friend Urquhart of the terrible consequences of remaining outside the Roman communion.[3] In 1864 Newman published his great *Apologia*, which his young admirer could only have ignored by being out of the fashion ; and when a year later *The Dream of Gerontius* appeared, the religious poet in Hopkins must have been struck by the contrast between the courageous orthodoxy, the frankly medieval tone of Newman's dramatic poem, and the equally bold ' neology ' of a Pattison or a Jowett.

In 1865 Hopkins was associated with a nation-wide Anglo-Catholic movement, the object of which was to bring about some form of workable union between a disestablished Church of England and the Church of Rome. At the same time he belonged to an undergraduate Anglo-Catholic society, in the organ of which, *The Union Review*, he published *Barnfloor and Winepress.*[4]

Though almost silent, the original poet in Hopkins was not asleep. This fallow period was not without importance for his art. There is strong presumptive evidence that he had read Newman's *Idea of a University* (1852) ; but the celebrated portrait

---

[1] See *Further Letters*, p. 52 ; also below, chap. i., p. 73.

[2] " Or shall a poor countryman be eternally happy for having the chance to be born in Italy ? etc." (*Essay*, bk. iv. chap. xix. 3.).

[3] *Further Letters*, p. 37.

[4] For thsee facts I am indebted to Mr. Humphry House.

of a ' gentleman ' could not have impressed him more deeply than the following passage :

> " Literature is the personal use or exercise of language. . . . Language itself in its very origin would seem to be traceable to individuals. Their peculiarities have given it its character. . . . And while the many use language as they find it, the man of genius uses it indeed, *but subjects it withal to his own purposes and moulds it according to his own peculiarities.*" [1]

The italics are ours ; but how those words must have pleased Hopkins ! In 1873 he described Newman as " our greatest living master of style " and " widest mind " ; yet in 1887 he accused the master himself (and Patmore too) of not knowing what prose really *is*, because his style did not show enough " brilliancy ", " *belonging* technic ", " own proper eloquence "— that is to say, personal and peculiar moulding of the medium.[2]

From boyhood onwards, Hopkins's own empirical attitude to language had been encouraged by the new and fashionable science of Philology, which had been created by the researches of Bopp, the brothers Grimm and others. Like R. C. Trench, enthusiasts now studied words with delight as ' fossil history ' and ' fossil poetry '.[3] Hopkins never lost his zest for derivation-hunting. As late as 1887-8 he wrote twice to the overworked Skeat about the etymology of ' scope ', ' kieve ', and many other words.[4] Dialects always fascinated him, so he inquired about an Anglo-Irish dictionary. He was, in short, one of the few English poets of genius who have been sufficiently interested in the raw materials and tools of their art to explore their utmost possibilities, to convert the seeming pedantries of the philologist and prosodian into the living accents of inspired song.

Returning to Newman and the religious controversy, we find that in 1864 Hopkins read Matthew Arnold's *Cornhill* essay on *The literary influence of Academies* ; and the lessons of moderation therein made him painfully aware of the " pettiness, vulgarity, injustice, ignorance and cant " of many who contributed letters to *The Church Times* and *The Dublin Review*. He cites Newman as the ideal controversialist : though " the extremest of the extreme ", Newman was yet " a MODERATE MAN ". [5]

---

[1] " Essay on Literature ", ed. of 1919, p. 275. For Hopkins's cogitations on the nature of a ' gentleman ', see *Letters*, vol. i. pp. 174-6.

[2] *Further Letters*, pp. 43 and 231-2.

[3] See Bishop Trench's well-known lectures *On the St·dy of Words* (1851).

[4] *Further Letters*, p. 282.   [5] *Ibid.* pp. 73-4

It might be urged that if Hopkins had lived within the period and aura of Wesley he would have become an ardent Evangelical. The degree of probability, however, may perhaps be gauged by his opinion of the Evangelicals, who at that time constituted the great majority of English Christians. In a letter of 1865 he mentions an exhortatory circular which certain Evangelical zealots had left in the ' high ' church that he attended :

> " An honest and manly opposition must at least inspire respect, but I cannot tell you the plaintive twaddle of this thing, which makes one feel what is the intellectual position of such a man's school." [1]

The intellectual weakness of that school is now generally admitted ; but in compensation the Evangelicals left no mean monument in their records of personal devotion and good works.

In the same letter Hopkins asks : " Why does not Colenso's trial go on ? " This was an allusion to the sensational trial for heresy of John William Colenso, the Anglican Bishop of Natal, whose critical examination of the Pentateuch and the Book of Joshua (1862–79) brought home to an alarmed public the trend of modern Biblical criticism. The new rationalism had already produced, in the works of Strauss and Renan, a frankly Socinian interpretation of the life and works of Christ ; and now the new evolutionism (an old theory made suddenly credible and vital by Darwin) had inspired Colenso's inquiry into the historical authenticity of the early books in the Old Testament.

Hopkins was not unaware of the Evolutionists. After the publication of *The Origin of Species* in 1859, T. H. Huxley had set about the task of exterminating for ever the claim of Biblical supernaturalism to rest upon rational thinking. The situation as Hopkins saw it in 1865 is recorded in a letter which aims at wooing Baillie over to the Catholic faith :

> " I am amused to find how far the advance of thought or science is from being on every side an encroachment on Christianity. I think I see them retiring from old positions before it in important parts." [2]

Such a remark would have astonished Huxley and provoked the cry, " Instance, sir ! " It illustrates the fact, however, that the ' Puseyites ', not being so rigidly tied to the actual word of Scripture as the Evangelicals, were better able to assimilate and weather the new mode of attack.

[1] *Further Letters*, p. 8.   [2] *Ibid.*, p. 80.

Hopkins's later allusions to Darwinism show that he was not infected with the general fears for the future of Christianity. His confidence might have been strengthened by Newman's lectures on " Christianity and Physical Science " and " Christianity and Scientific Investigation," in which the Cartesian view was put forward that Science and Theology were independent modes of inquiry and that only by an irrational breach of frontiers could they clash.[1] In 1883 it seemed to Hopkins that Darwinists could blunder egregiously : a theory of music based on ' sexual selection ' is described as mere " poison " ; and the notion that we enjoy music

> " because our apish ancestors serenaded their Juliet-apes . . . that sexual business will, in short, be found by roking [scraping] the pot "

elicits an impatient " Would that I had my materials ready to talk sense ! "[2]   A year before his death he argues with Bridges that the phrase " everything is Darwinism ", though largely true, does not prove a mere mechanical necessity in the development of variations and of ideal forms, such as the cells of the honeycomb.[3]   Yet it was a new miraculous dogma of evolutionary ' mechanism ' that Huxley was then raising over what he took to be the ruins of Christian supernaturalism. For Hopkins, the situation had not changed. The personal God (so improbable for Matthew Arnold), the All-Powerful (so incredible to Thomas Hardy), the All-Wise and All-Loving (so inconceivable to the ' tooth-and-claw ' school of Evolutionists)—in short, the God of St. Paul and St. Augustine still stood, for Hopkins, unshakably behind all phenomena.

In a letter to Patmore in which he is deprecating a sneer at Disraeli's Jewish origin, Hopkins adds :

> " His Christianity was a shadowy thing, I know, but so is that of thousands."[4]

Never could it be said of Hopkins himself that his religion was shadowy : it was most solidly orthodox in every article of ' faith and morals '. One whole sermon and many passages in the letters prove that he accepted the Biblical account of the Fall of Man.[5]   In his commentary on the *Spiritual Exercises* he does

---

[1] *The Idea of a University*. In recent years this view has been expressed by Prof. J. A. Thomson, Sir A. Eddington, and other scientists.
[2] *Letters*, vol. i. pp. 171–2.   [3] *Ibid.*, p. 281.   [4] *Further Letters*, p. 195.
[5] E.g. *ibid.*, p. 194, and *Note-books*, pp. 277–84.

indeed speak of the serpent as " a symbol of the Devil " ; and this may suggest a purely symbolic reading of the whole story.[1] But there can be no doubt that, in spite of Darwin, the *Book of Genesis* retained for him (as it still does for Roman Catholics) its absolute theological value as the embodiment of abiding metaphysical truth.

In the autobiography of E. M. Geldart we have a picture of Hopkins at Balliol.[2] " My ritualistic friend, Gerontius Manley," was convinced of " the shallowness of Protestant orthodoxy " and believed that the right of private judgment would inevitably lead to rationalism. In the religious discussions then frequent among the undergraduates " gush " was often more conspicuous than logic ; and " Gerontius gushed too, but then he meant it." That admission of his sincerity, written in 1882, goes far towards explaining the rare poetic intensity which flushes *The Wreck of the Deutschland* and all the works it released.

Hopkins's real moderation was shown in his comments on the exaggerated medievalism of Digby Mackworth Dolben, the young poet and religious enthusiast whose sudden death in 1867 affected him so deeply. According to Hopkins, Dolben had been " living on excitement ", and just after *Punch* had pilloried the Norwich " Histrio Anglicanus " and his troop of mimic monks, Dolben in Birmingham

> " went in his habit without sandals, barefoot. I do not know whether it is more funny or affecting to think of." [3]

Hopkins himself might have lived on excitement had not Newman persuaded him to stick to his studies and make a good class. Like Newman, he did not succumb to religious emotionalism. For a whole year he resisted the " silent conviction " that he was to become a Catholic. He was not unduly attracted by the mere externals of Roman Catholic practice : " to see or hear ' Romanising ' things wd. throw me back on the English Church as a rule." [4] Early in 1866 he wrote *Nondum*, a cry for Divine guidance which recalls the hymn Newman composed in similar circumstances—" Lead, kindly Light ".

The mystical elements in Hopkins's conversion are either incommunicable or else they are implicit in his early poems.

[1] *Note-books*, p. 347.   [2] *A Son of Belial*, pp. 155–6, 167–8.
[3] *Letters*, vol. i. p. 7. See the *Memoir* by Robert Bridges, prefixed to his edition of Dolben's poems.   [4] *Further Letters*, p. 17.

The philosophic *Anschauung* which confirmed him in his decision
to embrace the oldest and most completely uncompromising form
of Christianity is clearly indicated in his letters and unpublished
academic essays.   His thoughts on religion were seldom entirely
divorced from his aesthetic sensibility, and during his Oxford
days the influence of Pater would partly account for this.   In an
essay *On the Origin of Moral Ideas* he says that in art we strive to
realize not only unity but also difference, variety, contrast ;
whereas in morality the highest *consistency* is the highest excellence.   In an essay written for Pater he discredits the Utilitarian
view of morality ;   elsewhere he speaks of those who are " quite
grimed with the concrete, like the lesser Positivists."[1]   He reacted
against the growing tendency of his age to make humanism and
the sociological approach to life the very tap-root of the religious
attitude.   Yet for him too the secular argument existed, but as
a strong side-root feeding the stem of faith :

> " You will no doubt understand what I mean by saying that
> the *sordidness* of things, which one is compelled perpetually to
> feel, is perhaps, taking ἐν ἀνθ' ἑνός, the most unmixedly painful
> thing one knows of ;   and this is (objectively) intensified and
> (subjectively) destroyed by Catholicism.   If people could all
> know this, to take no other ground, no other inducement would
> to very many minds be needed to lead them to Catholicism and
> no opposite inducement could dissuade them from it." [2]

By this challenging assertion Hopkins meant that Catholicism
gave mankind a spiritual criterion whereby the inadequacy of
the materialistic Progress-myth could be exposed ; it offered
man a personal remedy for the ills of contingent being—
an escape from the ' prison-house ' in which he works the
remorseless treadmill of the daily round.   Hopkins elucidates
this point in a letter to E. H. Coleridge, who was loth to
believe that the " issues of eternity " could depend upon anything so trivial and inadequate as this life.   " It is incredible,"
Hopkins writes,

> " and intolerable if there is nothing which is the reverse of trivial
> and will correct and reverse the triviality of this life.   To myself
> all this trivialness is one of the strongest reasons for the opposite
> belief and is always in action more or less." [3]

---

[1] MSS. at Campion Hall, Oxford.
[2] Letter to Baillie, of 1865 (*Further Letters*, pp. 79–80. Gk.=" one thing compared
with another ").
[3] *Ibid.*, pp. 8–9.

He then goes on to reveal the depth of his belief in the Incarnation ; for by this Divine act, he says, the difficulty presented by the trivialness of life is utterly destroyed.

We see these paradoxes " in action " in such a poem as *God's Grandeur*,[1] where the objective intensification and the subjective destruction of the " sordidness " are balanced and complete. On the other hand, in a sonnet written twelve years later, " The shepherd's brow, fronting forked lightning ", [2] the sordidness is intensified but the doctrinal corrective is in abeyance.

III

On leaving Balliol, Hopkins was for two terms on the staff at the Oratory School, Birmingham ; there, under the guidance of Newman, he could get used to Catholic ways and consider his probable vocation for the priesthood. In a letter of February 1868 he says that philosophy is now the only interest he feels quite free to indulge in. Like so many Oxford men who had taken ' Greats ', he retained a profound respect for Plato's *Republic*, with its concept of " law, order, and unity flowing in on the citizens from every association of life " [3] ; and the publication of a book by Ruskin evokes the comment that Ruskin, for all his follies, is one of ' the true men ', with whom he feels more and more sympathetic as against the " Sophistik " elements— the men who in one way or another were vigorously criticizing and revising conventional morality. Rather than support the " Philistine, Doctrinaire, Utilitarian, Positive, and on the whole Negative ", causes, he prefers to " err with Plato " ; and this reminds him to say that Aristotle, as far as he knows him or knows about him, seems worthy to be called " the end-all and be-all of philosophy ".[4]

The passage in question shows some confusion of ideas, for Philistine and Doctrinaire sit uneasily together ; but the letter is significant for its clear suggestion of the influence of Hopkins's great predecessor at Balliol, Matthew Arnold. The latter became Professor of Poetry at Oxford in 1857, and though there is no clear evidence that Hopkins attended any of his lectures,[5] there is

---

[1] *Poems*, No. 7.   [2] *Ibid.*, No. 69.
[3] From an unpublished essay ; see above, p. 22, Note 1.
[4] *Further Letters*, p. 84.
[5] But in his yet unpublished Journal of 1866 G. M. H. records (May 26) : " Matthew Arnold lectured on the Celtic element in English poetry."

enough to show that he was aware of what the critic stood for—Classicism in literature, moderation in politics, and "right reason" (which meant Liberalism) in religion. In May 1867 Arnold had delivered his concluding lecture from the Chair of Poetry : its title was "Culture and its Enemies", and it was soon published as the first of a series of six articles in the *Cornhill Magazine*, of which Hopkins was a fairly regular reader.[1] These urbane and searching essays were in 1869 incorporated in *Culture and Anarchy* ; and the picture given in this book of the social, political and religious background of the 1860's, with a valuation by the touchstones of "true culture", "sweetness and light", and other Hellenistic concepts, was undoubtedly very close to Hopkins's own estimate of the same scene and period.

The two men, despite their divergence in matters of religion, had much in common. Refined sensibility and a strong ethical bias enabled both to diagnose the many strains of vulgarity and egoism in literature and religion, to expose the spiritual anarchy underlying the prevalent optimism. In their likes and dislikes they were both actuated by a deep sentiment for Oxford : Hopkins's three sonnets on that subject may be set beside well-known passages in Arnold's two finest poems, *The Scholar Gipsy* and *Thyrsis*.[2] In days when the qualities of repose, stability, and harmonious perfection were being rudely eclipsed in a welter of discord and innovation, that "sweet city with its dreaming spires" was for both men the embodiment of a tradition which could not be ignored without grievous loss to the spirit.

Hence as late as 1883 Hopkins reproved Bridges for belittling Arnold, a critic (he adds) who is not to be "damfooled" without a narrowing of the mind :

> "I do not like your calling Matthew Arnold Mr. Kidglove Cocksure. I have more reason than you for disagreeing with him and thinking him very wrong, but nevertheless I am sure he is a rare genius and a great critic." [3]

This "very wrong"-ness in Arnold probably refers to his complete severance from Christian orthodoxy after the publication of his *Literature and Dogma* in 1873.[4] As a critic he had impressed Hopkins, as he impresses us to-day, by his balanced, cosmopolitan

---

[1] See *Further Letters*, pp. 74 and 77.   [2] See below, Chap. i.
[3] *Letters*, vol.. i. p. 172.   [4] *Further Letters*, p. 43.

view, his understanding of the European as opposed to the merely insular or sectarian mind. Though he criticized the beliefs and practices of the Roman Church, he was sometimes its defender, praising its dignified ritual, its marriage code, its very catholicity. It was this breadth of sympathy which allowed him to do justice to Eugénie de Guérin, " one of the rarest and most beautiful souls "—the Catholic woman whose devout unrest was so like that of Hopkins. It was a culture deep and broad which enabled both men to appreciate the sound philosophy and durable beauty in Wordsworth, and to look with the strictest caution on the " specious Liberal stuff " which, despite much genuine feeling and vision, frequently mars the poetry of Shelley and Swinburne.

The mission of Ruskin and Arnold as social critics was to hold a mirror up to British complacency. And in like manner Hopkins, as a member of the universal Church, was often able to stand apart from his own countrymen and see them as others saw them. On one occasion he retorted to Bridges that if indigent Italian monks were dirty so were Cambridge undergraduates who (to quote Bridges himself) kept their rooms " dirty, yea filthy " ; and they were *not* poor :

> " And in general we cannot call ours a cleanly or a clean people : they are not at all the dirtiest and they know what cleanliness means, as they know the moral virtues, but they do not always practise it. We deceive ourselves if we think otherwise. And our whole civilization is dirty, yea filthy, and especially in the north ; for is it not dirty, yea filthy, to pollute the air as Blackburn and Widnes and St. Helens are polluted . . .? The ancients with their immense public baths would have thought even our cleanest towns dirty." [1]

Arnold did battle against blatant demagogues, arrogant middle-class philistines, and intellectually effete aristocrats. Hopkins, as a priest, served all classes ; but it redounds to his honour that as a young man of twenty-six he too could point an accusing finger at rottenness in the state, and even envisage a remedy in terms which were, for a Jesuit, unusually bold. To Bridges he wrote, in 1871 :

> " I must tell you I am always thinking of the Communist future. The too intelligent artisan is master of the situation I believe."

[1] *Letters*, vol. i. p. 299.

After this Shavian beginning he goes on to say that he is afraid some great revolution is not far off :

> " Horrible to say, in a manner I am a Communist.   Their ideal bating some things is nobler than that professed by any secular statesman I know of (I must own I live in bat-light and shoot at a venture),   Besides it is just.—I do not mean the means of getting to it are.   But it is a dreadful thing for the greatest and most necessary part of a very rich nation to live a hard life without dignity, knowledge, comforts, delight, or hopes in the midst of plenty—which plenty they make.   They profess that they do not care what they wreck and burn, the old civilization and order must be destroyed.   This is a dreadful look out but what has the old civilization done for them ?   As it at present stands in England it is itself in great measure founded on wrecking. But they got none of the spoils, they came in for nothing but harm from it then and thereafter." [1]

In this letter, which anticipated by nine years the disturbing thesis of Henry George's *Progress and Poverty*, there is nothing which (as Hopkins later protested) might not fairly be said by an English patriot and orthodox Catholic.

He was at that time a Jesuit ' scholastic ' taking his course in Philosophy at St. Mary's Hall, Stonyhurst.[2]   The Jesuits have frequently been called the enemies of progress, and it is true that their attitude to new ideas has always been marked by the caution of those whose mission it is to preserve the integrity of the Catholic Faith.   But when we remember that in the seventeenth century the Society founded and successfully conducted in Paraguay a Christian-communistic state which was described by Voltaire as " a triumph of humanity ", Hopkins's reading of the portents does not seem so startling.   In the sequel he insists, as Ruskin and Morris did, that the economic condition of the people ultimately determines their attitude towards art and all the graces of civilized life.

Ten years later, William Cobbett (that sturdy champion of the peasantry) is called " an honest thinker " but not an honest Anglican ;   because having shown that the Reformation impoverished the main body of the people in England and Ireland, Cobbett had not logically returned to the Catholic fold.   Hopkins adds that he would have liked to follow up Cobbett's theory of

---

[1] *Letters*, vol. i. pp. 27–8.   Cf. the thought in *Summa* (*Poems*, 3rd edn., No. 98).

[2] In this three-year course he would study the modern systems of Descartes and Kant, mainly for the purpose of defining their limitations and refuting their ' inconvenient ' propositions.

the origin of pauperism, for parish and mission work in Liverpool
and Glasgow had laid upon his own mind

> " a truly crushing conviction of the misery of town life to the
> poor and more than to the poor, of the slavery of the poor in
> general, of the degradation even of our race, of the hollowness
> of this century's civilization : it made even life a burden to me
> to have daily thrust upon me the things I saw." [1]

If the Laureate Tennyson, planting and pruning in the lotus-air
of his garden at Farringford, had been as deeply disturbed by
this social degradation, his poetical flowers might have grown
from thorny stems, more pungent and much hardier. We may
regret, too, that Hopkins did not work the rich vein discovered
in the social theme of *Tom's Garland*, delving with insight and
sympathy into the lives of the common people. Had he lived
longer he might have done so. But the later modification of his
always diffident Radical tendencies was due to the pressure of
circumstance : the daily task ; intercourse with men of strong
Tory principles—Bridges, Baillie, and especially Patmore ; the
ferocity of the Communist campaign against religion,[2] and the
enforced wariness of the Church—all these together with the
growing problem of his own physical and spiritual adjustment to
the life he had chosen.

Hopkins agreed with Arnold that all who bore the burden of
riches required an " extraordinary grace " to avoid the evils
of self-indulgence. He urged the socially secure Bridges to give
alms " to the point of sensible inconvenience " ; and later,
when his friend had retired from the medical profession, he
exhorted him not to lead a self-centred existence in his manor
house at Yattendon :

> " I should be sorry to think you did nothing down there but
> literary work : could you not be a magistrate ? This would be
> honourable and valuable public duty. Consider it." [3]

Obviously Hopkins's whole conception of the arts was diametrically opposed to that of the extreme aesthetes—Whistler, the

---

[1] *Letters*, vol. ii. pp. 96–7. See Cobbett's *A History of the Protestant Reformation in
England and Ireland, etc.* (1824–7), Letters, IX and XVI. Hopkins preferred London
to any other large town : "Very much may be said for life in London ; though my
dream is a farm in the Western counties, glowworms, new milk . . ." (*Further
Letters*, pp. 145–6.)

[2] " I have little reason to be red : it was the red Commune that murdered five
of our Fathers lately." (*Letters*, vol. i. p. 29.)

[3] *Letters*, vol. i. pp. 60–1 and 152.

Stinging Butterfly, and Oscar Wilde, the "utterly utter" as
Hopkins (who loved Gilbert and Sullivan) had called him. For
these men Art and the artistic Ego were all in all : no other
obligation, moral, social or political, existed. Hopkins's priestly
vocation enabled him without priggishness to transfix, in one
quiet sentence, the dangerous delusion that poetry (or any art)
is sufficient to engross a man's whole spiritual allegiance : " if
we care for fine verses how much more for a noble life ! " [1]
Seven years later, while reminding Bridges of his "patriotic
duty" to write more poetry and win fame, he gives the same
thought a specifically Christian turn :

> " Art and its fame do not really matter, spiritually they are
> nothing, virtue is the only good ; but it is only by bringing in
> the infinite that to a just judgment they can be made to look
> infinitesimal or small or less than vastly great." [2]

Although (as Freudians would say) the Super-ego in Hopkins
had successfully controlled the selfish ambitions of the Id, it
came as a surprise to many when in poems and letters he
apparently identified himself with the prevailing national egoism,
the Jingoist fervour of the years after 1880. In this period he
wrote *The Soldier* (the *patria* of which is Heaven) and his recruiting
song, " What shall I do for the land that bred me ? " [3] Yet the
letters show that he was actually very far from chauvinism :
" What marked excellence," he asks Baillie, " has England to
show to make her civilization attractive ? " [4] His love of
England, for all her faults, was deep and genuine. It weighed
with him that England, though stoutly Protestant, was more
hospitable to Jesuits than some Catholic countries. Though he
felt, and implied, the need for authority and control—as did
also Carlyle, Marx, Ruskin and Arnold—he retained a strong
regard for the democratic liberties :

> " ' Freedom ' : it is perfectly true that British freedom is the
> best, the only successful freedom, but that is because, with
> whatever drawbacks, those who have developed that freedom
> have done so with the aid of law and obedience to law."

Like Arnold, however, he blamed Englishmen for desiring
Freedom *only*—the right to do as one likes. The British Empire

---

[1] *Letters*, vol. i. p. 61.   [2] *Ibid.*, p. 231.

[3] *Poems*, Nos. 39 and 59 (both of 1885).

[4] *Further Letters*, p. 219. Again : " It is good to be in Ireland to hear how enemies,
and those rhetoricians, can treat the things that are unquestioned at home " (*loc. cit.*).

was politically good : it was a step towards world unity ; but its " civilization " was defective :

> " It shd. have been Catholic truth. That is the great end of Empires before God, to be Catholic and draw nations into their Catholicism. But our Empire is less and less Catholic as it grows." [1]

Yet he trusted in the Salvific Will. The mother country had foundered on the shoals of heresy, and Hopkins's two poems of shipwreck are both rounded off with a prayer for the conversion of England.[2]

This typically Jesuitic optimism would account for his bitter condemnation of Gladstone over the question of Home Rule for Ireland. Hopkins did not favour separation because he was loth to see a portion of the precious Catholic leaven withdrawn from the heavy, unkneaded dough of the Empire. As Professor of Classics at University College, Dublin, he felt the unfriendly atmosphere of that city and in 1887 gave Newman an " appalling " account of the situation ; but the cardinal's comment was not immediately helpful : " If I were an Irishman, I should be (in heart) a rebel." [3] Three months later Hopkins reminded Bridges that in the past the Irish had been robbed and oppressed, and implored his friend to assist in bringing home to his apathetic countrymen the true state of affairs in Ireland. After more vilification of Gladstone, as the " Grand Old Mischief-maker . . . like the Devil . . . meddling and marring all the fiercer for his hurry ", he paradoxically concedes that Home Rule, now likely to come,

> " may perhaps in itself be a measure of a sort of equity and, considering that worse might be, of a kind of prudence." [4]

Stylistically, many passages in the *Letters* suggest an almost conscious imitation of Matthew Arnold ; but the witty animus and lack of moderation in Hopkins's diatribes against Gladstone remind us rather of Carlyle. Yet by Carlyle himself he was at once attracted and repelled :

> " I do not like his pampered and affected style, I hate his principles, I burn most that he worships and worship most that he burns . . . but the force of his genius seems to me gigantic. He seems to me to have more humour than any writer of ours except Shakespeare." [5]

---

[1] *Further Letters*, p. 219. [2] *Poems*, Nos. 4 and 17. [3] *Further Letters*, pp. 265–6.
[4] *Letters*, vol. i. p. 257. Cf. *Further Letters*, p. 146. [5] *Letters*, vol. ii. p. 59.

That tribute to the Touchstonian brilliance of *Sartor Resartus* is perfectly justified. But Carlyle, he said, was not consistent, showed an " incapacity for general truths," lacked the " high seriousness " of Ruskin and Arnold :

> " always to be affected, always to be fooling, never to be in earnest . . . is not to fight fair in the field of fame."

As Arnold had called Carlyle a moral desperado, so Hopkins agreed with Dixon that he was " morally an impostor, worst of all impostors a false prophet." [1]

Hopkins saw that genius does not *ipso facto* work for good ends ; and we must concur in his verdict on Carlyle as a false prophet. But he was surely wrong in denying to Carlyle all sincerity in matter and style. Carlyle was extravagantly in earnest ; too voluble-passionate, headstrong-sure ; that was his weakness ; he did not sit back calmly and think out the full implications of his words.[2] Moreover, his mature style was as much a part of the man, an attribute of genius, as Hopkins's own manner ; and wittingly or not, the poet had himself been influenced by the syntactical and lexical audacities, the eclectic idiosyncrasy and studied barbarism of Carlyle's ' Gothic ' style. Without those German constructions, stenographic devices and compound epithets, Teufelsdröckh's peculiar verve and vividness would not have appeared ; and the same reservation will hold good, in another literary mode, for Hopkins. It was not mere dislike that made him parody Carlyle so often.[3]

In actual fact Carlyle, no less than Ruskin and Arnold, had been appalled by the spectacle which the nineteenth century presented of so much physical, intellectual and even spiritual energy running to waste for want of a rational plan—some authoritarian system whereby the highest and best forces could be given free play and the general tone of the masses would be raised by the new effluence from above, by the irresistible emanations of Manners, Beauty, and Culture. To Ruskin's profound influence on the arts we shall return later. In Arnold's poetry (*Empedocles on Etna*, *The Scholar Gipsy*, *Dover Beach*) we find the best epitome of that spiritual uncertainty and unrest which, according to Hopkins, was " a dreadful feature of our days " and drove many to suicide.[4] Hopkins's answer to the threat of pessimistic nihilism was the positive faith of the Catholic Church.

---

[1] *Letters*, vol. ii. p. 75.
[2] Cf. Carlyle and the recent history of Nazism.
[3] See *Further Letters*, p. 84.
[4] *Ibid.*, p. 107.

Arnold's challenge to the forces of disintegration was his doctrine of Culture.

Arnold's definition of true culture included the claims of religion ; but in its final assumption it was, perhaps, unrealistic. Organized religion, he said, indoctrinates the masses,

> " but culture works differently. It does not try to teach down to the level of inferior classes. . . . It seeks to do away with classes ; to make the best that has been thought and known in the world current everywhere, to make men live in an atmosphere of sweetness and light." [1]

That, Hopkins would have agreed, was a noble aim ; but he would have rebutted the suggestion that inculcating Christian faith was in any derogatory sense teaching *down* to the level of the lowest. Christianity had in one sense already eliminated the classes, and he would have said that in the scale of Christian moral values the privileged, enlightened people were not conspicuously higher than the orders called " inferior " ; that the aim of the Church was to raise all men—including priests, poets and social critics—nearer to the level of Christ.

Arnold's own rationalism, together with the unavoidable suggestion of ' caste ' in his doctrine of Culture, encouraged in many that very individualism tending to caprice of which he was himself the sternest critic. From social pride or pure conceit was struck that debased intellectual coinage which Hopkins alluded to, in 1881, as " cultshah " and " the modern nonsense ".[2] This affectation in taste and manners had become closely associated with the exotic cult of Aestheticism—a movement which, though it owed something to Ruskin and Rossetti, was mainly imported from the French school of Baudelaire by Swinburne and Whistler.[3]

At its best, in Whistler's painting and Pater's prose, this new enthusiasm for Beauty and a pure or neutral art was perhaps a necessary reaction against the puritanical drabness and sentimentality of Victorian middle-class culture. In its milder, weaker form it produced nothing worse than those fatuously

---

[1] *Culture and Anarchy* (ed. J. Dover Wilson, 1932), p. 70.
[2] The wife of Rae, the painter, showed " a real enthusiasm for art and understanding of it and had nothing whatever of the ' cultshah ' manner." (*Letters*, vol. i. p. 130.)
[3] The excesses of Pater, Arnold, Ruskin, Jowett, Swinburne, Huxley, etc., were all exposed in W. H. Mallock's little masterpiece, *The New Republic* (1877). See *Letters*, vol. i. p. 72.

' intense ' people who were ridiculed in *Punch* and *Patience* [1] ;
but at its dangerous nadir it resulted in the amoral perversions
which overthrew Simeon Solomon, Oscar Wilde and other men
of fine talent.

Hopkins himself was not unaffected by the aesthetic creed as
it was concerned with the principles of pure design and ' exclusiveness ' : some of the more wilful contortions and involutions
in his thought and syntax indicate a touch (but only a touch) of
that contempt for ' nature ' (in the form of popular taste) which
inspired the sartorial and verbal eccentricities of Wilde. In the
main, however, Hopkins stood for all that was good and militated
strongly against all that was dubious or bad in the secular aims
of Culture and Aestheticism. The words ' cultivated ' and
' Philistine ' were frequently on the lips of the most irresponsible
aesthetes. Culture, indeed, works differently from organized
religion ; but without organized religion Culture frequently
does not work at all.[2]

The balanced union of Hebraism and Hellenism which
Arnold desiderated is not irrelevant to the study of Hopkins.
Hebraism was defined as " the paramount sense of the obligation
of duty, self-control, and work ", whereas Hellenism implies
" the idea of perfection at all points, the encouraging in ourselves
spontaneity of consciousness, the letting a free play of thought
flow around all our activity." [3] By modern secular standards
Hopkins appears almost fanatical in his Hebraic *strictness of conscience* ; yet in spite of the limitations imposed on his intellectual
activity by dogma, vows, and personal qualms, his letters show
a considerable range of thought, and in some directions his
outlook is more liberal than that of Bridges or Patmore. Besides,
spontaneity of consciousness is, broadly speaking, the one quality in
his poetry which his non-Catholic readers unanimously admire.
Arnold said very shrewdly that Hellenism, by bringing new life
and movement into that side of us with which alone Hebraism
concerns itself, " may thus actually serve to further the designs
of Hebraism." It had already done so in its philosophic contribution to the Scholasticism of Aquinas and Scotus, upon which
the poetry of Hopkins was firmly based.

[1] Produced in 1881. Bunthorne, the " utterly utter ", was an innocuous
caricature of Wilde.

[2] " One remembers Wilde's comment that had his father allowed him to be a
Catholic when he went up to Oxford the catastrophe of his later life would not
have occurred." (B. Ifor Evans in *Later Nineteenth Century Poetry*, 1933 ; p. 306.)

[3] See *Culture and Anarchy*, chaps. iv. and v.

Hopkins was in no sense a ' broad-minded ' pagan Hellenist like Swinburne, Pater, or Housman : he considered Christianity a great advance on Greek thought.   Nevertheless Hellenism, working on his artistic sensibility, furthered the designs of his deeply moral nature—in a way, too, that Arnold could not have foreseen and would probably not have approved.   In Chapter II we shall see how Hopkins made one important aspect of Greek culture " bring new life and movement " into English poetry ; at the same time he awakened (to quote once more the prophetic Arnold) "a healthier and less mechanical activity" in the reader.[1]

Any historical reference to the poetic Hellenism of Hopkins would be uncritical unless tribute were paid to the creative activities of his predecessors in that fruitful field.   Yet when we remember that the classical tradition was for centuries supreme in English education, we may perhaps wonder at the fewness of those works of English poetry which make a bold attempt to incorporate or adapt the richer Greek forms :   pre-eminent among them are the odes of Dryden, Cowley, and Gray, the classic dramas of Milton, Shelley, and Swinburne.   As a modern appreciator of Swinburne says :

> " We may continue to debate whether *Atalanta on Calydon* is more or less Greek than *Prometheus Unbound*, or whether either of them is Greek at all.   But if we are asked by one who knows only English what we may read in our great literature to get the best idea of the work of the Attic dramatists, we shall reply either *Samson Agonistes* or *Erechtheus*." [2]

In this Greek invasion of English waters Milton is the solid vessel, Shelley the sail, and Swinburne the flying spray.   We must add, however, that no English verse, in its diction and movement, conveys the ' feel ' of Greek melic poetry so well as that of Hopkins.   The writer just quoted has confessed that the poetry of Swinburne was to him the most potent inducement to learn Greek.   We contend, however, that the English reader who turns for the first time from a translation of a Pindaric ode or Sophoclean chorus to the original Greek will probably be reminded of Hopkins rather than Swinburne.

As Greek lyric poetry was inseparable from music (for music then was a regular part of a liberal education), so Hopkins's interest in Greek metric was closely allied to his love of the sister art.   Hence, before we complete our picture of his literary

[1] *Culture and Anarchy, ed. cit.*, p. 158.
[2] *Swinburne, A Nineteenth Century Hellene*, by W. R. Rutland (1931), pp. 4–5.

and artistic background, it will be expedient to say something about his musical studies and ambitions.

His lifelong preoccupation with music is important, firstly because music undoubtedly influenced his prosodic theory and practice, and secondly because the grand scale of his later efforts at composition indicates a confidence in his own natural powers which, in one so untrained, was phenomenal. That he possessed an exquisite natural ' ear ' is proved by the quality of his air for Dixon's *Fallen Rain* [1] : this tune, when suitably harmonized, carries a delightful suggestion of a mode beyond time and fashion, like Peter Warlock's. More and more Hopkins found in music a welcome relief from his intense concern for moral values. Music, like architecture, was a pure or neutral art, free from that bleak dichotomy of " black, white ; right, wrong " which gives such a painful poignancy to his later poems. Music was also, as he said, more " professional " than the poetic art. Fumbling fingers and the lack of regular opportunity prevented him from attaining any proficiency on the piano ; and violin lessons, begun at the Oratory in 1868, were never mentioned again. Still, he had seen possibilities in Greek enharmonic music, had a loving familiarity with Gregorian chant, and knew enough elementary theory to set down many of the tunes which came to him with a Schubert-like readiness as he read the song-lyrics of Bridges, Dixon, and Patmore.

In this art, as in poetry, he was always striving towards something new and distinctive. Feeling the need for a harmony " bolder " than the straightforward accompaniments provided by his sister Grace, he began, at the age of thirty-six, to work through Stainer's *Primer of Harmony* ; to this study he later added a book on Counterpoint by J. F. Bridge. To follow Hopkins on this new voyage of discovery, in which after a time the Rules of Composition appeared like rocks to be sedulously avoided (and in which the Rules of Counterpoint, not the learner's frail barque, were eventually in smithereens !), is really a task for the musical expert ; but a general summary called ' Hopkins and Music ' has been attempted in Appendix A.

IV

The main movements of the nineteenth century which complete the relevant background to the poetry of Hopkins comprise

[1] *Letters*, vol. ii. p. 169 ; reproduced below, opp. p. 389.

the chief poetic schools and tendencies, the development of 'chromatic' prose, and the powerful influence exerted by Ruskin in bringing about a closer connexion between the graphic arts and literature. Of the contemporary poetic schools the most significant for Hopkins were the Wordsworthian, the Neo-Romantic or Pre-Raphaelite, the Neo-Classical, and the Neo-Metaphysical one-man school of Patmore.

The deep and permanent quality of Wordsworth's poetry was germinative throughout the century. This great poet's later adoption of orthodox Anglicanism was not altogether surprising; neither was it a formal recanting of his 'natural' religion. Rather it was an illustration of a principle first enunciated apropos of Baudelaire : " Once a Christian, it is impossible to dispossess oneself of the spirit of Christianity "; for Christianity is deep and wide enough to include *Tintern Abbey* and most of the *Prelude*. Wordsworth's greatest poetry is full of Christian morality and theistic implications, and the revised version of the *Ode to Duty* (his turning-point) might well have been renamed " Hymn to the Holy Ghost ". A similar intellectual humility was present beneath the surface complacency of Wordsworth's disciple, Matthew Arnold ; for having rejected dogmatic theology and fallen back on that one phrase, " the necessity of righteousness ", he could still say : " the profession of righteousness, except as Jesus Christ interpreted righteousness, is vain." [1]

Patmore and Hopkins were both in the direct line of that Christian tradition from which Wordsworth, though true to the kindred points of Heaven and the Lake district, had formally divagated. In the simple domesticities of *The Angel in the House* Patmore developed one strain of the homely Wordsworth ; while the Dorset poet, William Barnes (whom Patmore and Hopkins both warmly praised) multiplied with equal fluency the corresponding rusticities. [2] In his *Unknown Eros* odes Patmore advanced to a subtle Platonic mysticism, in which Christian connubial love became the supreme unifying experience ; whereas Hopkins, rating this new metaphysical poetry at its true value but wisely avoiding all imitation, developed in his own intensely Catholic way the Wordsworthian nature-mysticism. Both poets were in direct opposition to the main trend of their age, which was veering from the 'creedless Christianity' of Tennyson and Browning to the pagan, pantheistic, or frankly agnostic poetry of Swinburne, Meredith, Clough, and Arnold. At a still further

---

[1] *Literature and Dogma*, XII.   [2] See below, chap. iv.

remove were the atheistic 'pessimists', James Thomson and Thomas Hardy, the sub-title of whose work was Nature's Indifference.

Despite the animosity or sadness stirred in such men as de Vigny, Thomson, and Hardy by the cold inscrutability of the universe, there was throughout the century a keen awareness of natural beauty, a heightened personal intimacy with nature as a whole. In England this was largely due to Wordsworth, to the great landscape painters, and to the aesthetic prose of Ruskin.

Partly because of this confluence of Wordsworth and Ruskin, the poetic potential of unrhymed, unmetrical language had been enormously raised—a fact which helped to make the more limber, variable poetry of Whitman and Hopkins possible. Lamb and Carlyle had revealed the full chromatic and diatonic possibilities of the prose medium, and it was due mainly to them and to Ruskin that Hopkins could observe with truth, in 1887 :

> " Wordpainting is, in the verbal arts, the great success of our day." [1]

It was in modern novels, he said, that wordpainting most abounded. He admired Charles Reade and Blackmore ; but it was for the epic brilliance of Hardy and the continuous poetic precision of Stevenson (whom he ranked above Scott) that he reserved his highest praise.[2] In poetry, no doubt, the great Romantics had taught the Victorians much of their skill in painting vignettes direct from nature. Yet whenever we find (as in the verse of Meredith, Hopkins and Bridges) those individual and vivid delineations of sky, cloud, and water, we think at once of the first volume of *Modern Painters* (1843), with its amply written but poetically felt sections on *Truth of Skies*, *Truth of Clouds*, *Truth of Earth*, *Truth of Water*, etc. Moreover, since these precise and suggestive observations of Ruskin were in the first place evoked by the landscape painting of Turner, it is true to say that the great painter profoundly influenced the development of English poetry and prose. In the firmament of the century's nature-cult, Wordsworth and Turner shone like twin stars, for Ruskin himself regarded the great voice of Rydal as the soundest oracle in such matters. Having advised young painters to go to nature in its wild, unspoiled condition, " trustingly, rejecting

---

[1] *Letters*, vol. i. p. 267.   [2] *Ibid.*, pp. 239, 251, 262.

nothing, selecting nothing " ; having said that what the artist follows must be " the pure wild volition and energy ", Ruskin quotes the assurance of Wordsworth that " Nature never did betray/The heart that loved her ".

Ruskin, like Wordsworth, endowed nature with personality. He spoke of the " character " and " state of mind " of clouds, and generally by his sensitive explorations gave later verbal artists a clue to the possibilities of hyperaesthesia—that heightened sense of the kinship between man and external nature which produced diverse results in the work of Hardy and Meredith, Whitman and Hopkins. All these writers represent an important phase in the evolution of man's psychic relationship to his environment ; but of these Hopkins alone, in our judgment, preserves the balance of Creation and the dignity of man by uniting the new nature-mysticism and the old concept of ' man made in the image of God '.

Ruskin was one of ' the true men ' because he was not a two-dimensional materialist but a three-dimensional metaphysical aesthete and social reformer. Hopkins must have admired the pervasive didacticism of his critical method, his religious insistence upon the artist's obligation to design and execute every subject to the glory of God. Thus the concluding words of the first volume of *Modern Painters* remind us of Hopkins's own aspiration as a poetic artist :

> " Let each exertion of [Turner's] mighty hand be both a hymn and a prophecy ; adoration to the Deity, revelation to mankind."

In 1848 a group of young artists, encouraged by Ruskin to forsake the Old Masters for the Old Mistress, Nature, crystallized their views and confirmed their revolutionary practice by forming the Pre-Raphaelite Brotherhood. The best Pre-Raphaelite paintings of Millais, Holman Hunt, and Rossetti are close in spirit, in their feeling for colour and in the exquisite finish of their workmanship, to the finest early lyrics of Tennyson ; and all these artists, verbal and graphic, together with the Pre-Raphaelite poetry of the Rossettis, early Morris, early Swinburne, Thomas Woolner, and R. W. Dixon constituted the major contemporary influence in the artistic development of Hopkins during his formative years from 1855 to 1865. In his note-books he lovingly copied out D. G. Rossetti's *The Blessed Damozel, Lost Days*, and three other poems, Christina's *Hope*, and some extracts

from Woolner's *My Beautiful Lady*. In his first letter to Baillie
(July 10, 1863) he says :

> " Those three pictures by Millais in this year's Academy have
> opened my eyes. I see that he is the greatest English painter,
> one of the greatest of the world."

He goes on to say of the Pre-Raphaelites :

> " . . . that school, represented in the greatest perfection by him,
> passing through stage after stage, is at last arriving at Nature's
> self, which is of no school—inasmuch as different schools represent
> Nature in their own more or less truthful ways, Nature meanwhile
> having only one way." [1]

Yet Millais is *not* one of the world's greatest painters ; and in
later comments Hopkins puts his finger on Millais's great weakness,
his deficiency in the highest imaginative quality of design.
Writing in his *Journal* (1874) of that painter's *Scotch Firs*, Hopkins
remarks : " instress absent, firtrunks ungrouped . . . quite
casual install of woodland." Again, in *Winter Fuel* he observes
an " aimless mess or minglemangle of cut underwood in under-
your-nose foreground ; aimlessly posed truthful child on shaft of
cart ".[2] There speaks the critic who is himself quietly developing
into a creative artist : he sees the difference between truth to
nature and truth to art ; but he also recognizes the double
truth when it appears :

> " but then (he continues) most masterly Turner-like outline of
> craggy hill, silver-streaked with birch-trees, which fielded in an
> equally masterly *rust-coloured young oak, with strong curl and seizure
> in the dead leaves*." [3]

The words we have italicized bring to the mind's eye an exact
and vivid image of this painter's best individual manner.

Against such precise and Ruskinesque censure and praise we
may set Hopkins's opinion of Whistler, from a letter of 1886 :

> " I agree to Whistler's striking genius—feeling for what I call
> *inscape* (the very soul of art) ; but then his execution is so negligent,
> unpardonably so sometimes (that was, I suppose, what Ruskin
> particularly meant by ' throwing a pot of paint in the face of
> the public ') : *his* genius certainly has not come to puberty." [4]

---

[1] *Further Letters*, p. 54.
[2] Cf. *Letters*, vol. i. p. 132. " [Millais] has, I have always seen, no feeling for
beauty in abstract design, and he never designs ; but he has a deep feeling, it is plain,
for concrete beauty, wild or natural beauty, much as Keats had " (16 June 1881)
[3] *Note-books*, p. 192. Cf. p. 194.   [4] *Letters*, vol. ii. p. 135.

By one of Time's curious revenges Hopkins himself was later accused of tearing pages out of a dictionary and hurling their contents with dissonant violence at ears accustomed to the gentle impact of Tennysonian poetry ; and Hopkins too has by some critics been denied ' maturity of genius '. The truth is that Whistler and Hopkins are both fully developed artists, and despite the enormous divergence in their characters, they hold collateral status in their respective arts. But for most Victorians (including Hopkins) the strain of aesthetic transvaluation from Pre-Raphaelitism to Impressionism was as great as that experienced by those later critics and reviewers who turned for the first time from the traditional Georgian verse of De la Mare and Rupert Brooke to the naïve and learned audacities of Hopkins. Throughout his life, however, the latter preserved the true critic's nice discrimination between *form* and *execution* ; it is significant too that in the heyday of Mallarmé, Verlaine, and *La Décadence*, he could write to the relatively conventional Bridges in the following strain :

> " ' The first touch of decadence destroys all merit whatever ' : this is a hard saying. What, all technical merit—as chiaroscuro, anatomical knowledge, expression, feeling, colouring, drama ? It is plainly not true. And, come to that, the age of Raphael and Michelangelo was in a decadence and its excellence is technical. Everything after Giotto is decadent in form, though advancing in execution. Go to." [1]

The word " Everything " here exaggerates and somewhat distorts a profound truth, which would require a whole treatise for its elucidation.

Hopkins's own taste in Victorian painting is fixed by his extremely generous praise of Frederick Walker, whom he compared to Keats : " The sense of beauty was so exquisite ; it was to other painters' work as poetry is to prose ; his loss was irretrievable." This preference leads him to stress again the importance of " masterly execution " in every art : it is, he adds, " a kind of male gift and especially marks off men from women".[2] Now while it is true that few women have approached the mastery of the greatest male artists, we detect in Hopkins's estimate of such women writers as George Eliot, ' Michael Field ', and Katharine Tynan a note of extra-literary disapproval : this is due to the Victorian opinion (expressed particularly by Patmore, but shared incidentally by such earlier authorities as

---

[1] *Letters*, vol. i. p. 300. (Feb. 23, 1889.) [2] *Ibid.*, vol. ii. pp. 133–4.

Pericles and Addison) that the proper sphere of feminine activity is not poetry, fiction, or politics, but the domestic virtues.

The foregoing remarks on the literary background will be supplemented in Chapter IV, where we record Hopkins's appreciation or criticism of the poets who attracted or repelled him. On the whole, he reacted against the general prolixity and growing worldliness of the contemporary poetry. The fleshly and " sophistik " Swinburne revolted him. The slickness of Browning and the restraint of Arnold (with a prosaic something in each) left him unmoved. Yet by the real poetic power and technical skill of all three he was quite definitely influenced. For Tennyson and the Pre-Raphaelites he retained a warm though qualified affection, for these men had brought the corrective and balm of innocuous beauty to a generation which was becoming more and more " seared with trade ; bleared, smeared with toil " ; they had impressed upon his boyhood the great truth that all art should create beauty, should provide a spiritual and cultural orientation.

V

It will be fitting to conclude this Introduction with a brief account of that part of Hopkins's background which for twenty years was really the *foreground* of his daily existence—the Society of Jesus. Our approach to a religious poet with definite beliefs and inhibitions is eminently susceptible to warping and stultifying prejudices ; and it may safely be said that no institution has been more widely misunderstood and misrepresented than that to which Hopkins, by deliberate choice, dedicated his life. Professor Abbott, for instance, has told us that Bridges entertained, " and rightly ", a profound distrust of the Society of Jesus [1] ; and that stigma will continue to widen the gap between Hopkins and many of his non-Catholic readers.

In 1877, about the time when Hopkins was ordained priest, Bridges said something in his honest brusque manner which elicited the reply : " You say you don't like Jesuits. Did you ever see one ? " And that query should be pondered by every student of Hopkins's poems and letters. In the 1870's, when the feeling against ' Popery ' and the ' Romanists ' ran high, it was perhaps natural that a conception of Jesuitry nourished by Kingsley's *Westward Ho !* should prevail in the minds of those who had made no serious attempt to understand the aims and

[1] *Letters*, vol. i., Introduction, p. xlv.

activities of the Society since its foundation by St. Ignatius
Loyola in 1538. In the minds of most Englishmen, then as now,
the Jesuits were associated with the Counter-Reformation, with
the machinations, allegedly treasonous, of Father Persons and
his followers ; with the acrobatic and Jacobitical antics of
Thackeray's Father Holt ;[1] with certain anti-British and ' anti-
progressive ' schemes and with nothing more. Granted, the
Jesuits have frequently been ejected from even Catholic countries
by political parties who resented their attempts to intervene in
politics (a thing for which the Church is constantly blamed for
doing and not doing). Moreover, those Jesuits who defied the
rigorous penal laws of Elizabeth by coming to England (trained
martyrs such as Campion, Walpole, and the poet Southwell)
certainly did so with the express purpose of winning the whole
country back to the Church of Rome : " Our King back, oh,
upon English souls ! " exclaimed Hopkins in *The Deutschland* ;
and readers of this poet need have no doubt that he too, in
defiance of Keats, has " palpable designs upon them ". It is
not generally known, however, that the charges of treason on
which Campion and Southwell were hanged, drawn, and
quartered were never satisfactorily proved and were almost
certainly false. The heroic single-mindedness of these saintly and
talented men stirred in Hopkins the desire to celebrate in verse
and emulate in his life that virtue which he prized above all
others—self-sacrifice in the cause of Christ.

Hopkins himself seems to justify his friend's distrust of his
Order when he writes to Bridges : " The Puseyites are up to
some very dirty jesuitical tricks." [2] This frankly concedes that
in the past some Jesuits, through excess of zeal, have sought to
achieve spiritual ends by worldly means. But the withers of
Hopkins were unwrung : he knew that the Jesuits had never
inculcated the immoral doctrine that it is defensible deliberately
to do evil that good may come. Besides which, he had no
inordinate respect for " Christian antiquity " [3] : the principles
of his Church and Order were plain for all to see, and he was
not least among his contemporaries in putting them into practice.

Since the principles and discipline of the Society of Jesus and
its text-book, *The Spiritual Exercises*, were so deeply involved in
the making of Hopkins's poems, a few facts about Jesuit history

---

[1] In *Esmond*. [2] *Letters*, vol. i. p. 58.
[3] *Further Letters*, p. 39. Among his books in 1867 was Manning's *The Last Glories
of the Holy See Greater Than the First* (1861).

may lead to a less biased assessment of the poet himself. An open-minded inquiry reveals something more than a mere record of human weakness and error : it reveals the record of self-dedication, constructive genius, and unsurpassed effort for the maintenance and furtherance of man's spiritual welfare. The student of Hopkins should at least know of the initiative and heroism of St. Francis Xavier, the 'Apostle of the Indies', whose Latin hymn Hopkins translated into English and Welsh ; of the remarkable Jesuit *conquista espiritual* in South America ; of the Jesuit aloofness from, and even disapproval of, the Inquisition ; of its direct opposition to the doctrines of predestination and 'the divine right of kings', neither of which is to-day widely regarded with favour. He should know that the Jesuits have always been the advocates of free will : " I can find God at all times whenever I wish to ", wrote St. Ignatius, and he urged his followers " to lead man to his highest goal with the aid of his natural aspirations and senses ". Even the Jesuit system of casuistry, so wittily attacked by Pascal, was a proof of their love of humanity, their essential and even excessive humanism. The business of the early Jesuits was to keep worldings in the Church, to inure them to a higher and more spiritual life, to keep all men within sight of hope.

Hopkins himself had the same purpose. He urged righteousness, deprecated quarrelling, sought to make converts. So unworldly was he that he refused to allow Canon Dixon to publish *The Loss of the Eurydice*, pleading that its writer's character might be injured by the imputation of secular ambition, and that Dixon himself, as an Anglican clergyman, could not in good conscience sponsor a Catholic poem.[1] Hopkins, by his humility, patience under ill-health and disappointment, and steady determination to carry out the appointed task whatever the cost, was being quite simply a good Jesuit and not the unique and pitiable exception to a rule of life and type of humanity fit only to be regarded with " profound mistrust ". [2]

The Jesuits, pioneers in scientific education, have always studied the individuality of their pupils. It has always been the policy of the Society to find for each of its members the work for which he is peculiarly fitted, and usually they succeed. For

---

[1] *Letters*, vol. ii. pp. 30–1 and 93.

[2] Cf. Luxmoore's words, in 1890 : " To his lasting honour be it said he was too good for them. . . ." (*Further Letters*, p. 249). For the most poignant private statement of G. M. H.'s suffering, see below, chap. vii. pp. 343–4, 363–4.

reasons which are not perfectly clear (though his indifferent health and practical exigencies are no doubt among them) Hopkins was subject to frequent uprootings ; and with some temperaments this uncertainty and bag-packing militates against the continuity of intellectual and imaginative endeavour. It was as a teacher that he was able to employ most fully and professionally his varied gifts—his knowledge and thoroughness, vividness and originality in exposition, his intense sympathy with the young. After his ordination in 1877 he spent most of his time at one or other of the Jesuit colleges—Manresa House, then Stonyhurst, and lastly at University College, Dublin, where he resided from 1884 till his death. Lecturing in this establishment ought to have been congenial work ; but according to opinions still current at the college he was too simple-minded, eccentric, and unpractical to hold the attention of his classes. Such oral tradition, however, is seldom quite reliable. No doubt Hopkins's ' human material ', like his own health, was frequently below par ; his best work as a teacher was probably inspirational rather than strictly practical ; but we refuse to believe that the man who wrote, at Roehampton in 1874, the conscientious and brilliant Lecture Notes on Rhetoric, etc., was quite the simpleton that the anecdotists present to us :

> " From a quixotic sense of justice toward members who failed to attend, he refused to allow his examination questions to refer to his lectures, consequently students only came to find out what would not be set."

This, from Eleanor Ruggles's recently published " Life " of the poet (p. 192), strikes us as being " strictly funny " in the true Hopkinsian sense of that term.

Apart from his lectures the concomitant duty of setting and marking papers in Classics for six examinations yearly at the Royal University, of which he had been elected Fellow—this was an unconscionable burden, and for imposing it on a man who was plainly unfit to bear it his superiors, it would seem, were to blame. It must be remembered, however, that Hopkins was a fussy, over-scrupulous marker of scripts, and the College records show that he was given more ' rests ' and short holidays than most Jesuits.[1]

[1] " . . . there came up last year 750 candidates. . . . I am not at all strong, not strong enough for the requirements, and do not see at all how I am to become so " (March, 1884).

" . . . 331 accounts of the First Punic War with trimmings have sweated me down to nearer my lees and usual alluvial low water mudflats, yearnings, groans, and despair " (Oct. 1886). [*Letters*, vol. i. pp. 190 and 236.]

In this soul-deadening task he should obviously have been given adequate assistance ; then perhaps much of the weariness, despair and sterility of his last years would have been obviated.

The Jesuit rule of obedience to superiors, though binding in all but a few exceptional circumstances, must at times have proved irksome ; yet it was not alien to his nature :

> " When a man has given himself to God's service, when he has denied himself and followed Christ, he has fitted himself to receive and does receive from God a special guidance, a more particular providence. This guidance is conveyed partly by the action of other men, as his appointed superiors, and partly by direct lights and inspirations." [1]

One who knew him intimately at Dublin said that he would scarcely take a cup of tea without permission. But though the discipline of the Society was strict, even to the extent of making the private correspondence of its members subject to censorship (a prerogative seldom exercised except during the Novitiate and the last probation, or Tertianship), these Jesuits, in their austere but well appointed houses, were by no means unduly ascetic. Renunciations beyond the ordinary, of course, all Jesuits must make, from the vow of celibacy to the general sacrifice of their liberty ; but asceticism in the sense of deliberate self-privation of the bare necessaries and comforts of life was not then, and is not now, the rule. Any mortifications practised by Hopkins subject to the approval of his confessor would be regarded as a personal and private matter, provided they did not impair his efficiency as a Jesuit ; and in his later years Hopkins was abstemious in this form of spiritual nourishment.

He is reported to have said that he could get on quite happily with no other book than his Breviary [2] ; yet the statement seems at variance with his own complex personality. Threatened with the fate of Alexander Selkirk, he would have snatched up his Breviary before any other book ; but as the *Letters* clearly prove, Hopkins needed for his continued happiness the stimulus of creative effort in the field of Art. He felt that he *ought* to be satisfied with spiritual aspirations, and at times the wish became a fact. But the very earnestness of his resolution to leave his valuable poems in manuscript and to resign their ultimate fate, as he believed, to the will of Christ (" best of critics ") shows that he knew the value of what he was renouncing ; he knew also the moral value of his renunciation, though this knowledge

[1] *Letters*, vol. ii. p. 93.   [2] *Life* (Lahey), p. 145.

did not mitigate the keenness of his sense of loss. He tells us that in pursuing " outward occupations ", which were sometimes necessary, he found that worldly interests freshened and worldly ambitions revived. At times he must have felt that perhaps after all it was God's will that he, like Coventry Patmore, should receive the poet's reward of praise and encouragement, and wondered with agony of spirit whether he was not culpably burying his talent [1]; but then his faith would conquer all doubts, as when he declared to Dixon :

> " Now if you value what I write, if I do myself, much more does our Lord. And if he chooses to avail himself of what I leave at his disposal he can do so with a felicity and a success which I could never command." [2]

That was written in 1881. In 1886 he commiserates Dixon in words which tell us much about himself : Christ, he says, would have wished to succeed by success, for that is prudence ; but he was doomed to succeed by failure :

> " However much he understood all this he found it an intolerable grief to submit to it. He left the example : it is very strengthening, but except in that sense it is not consoling." [3]

Though Hopkins did not ' hit it off ' with Father Parkinson during his parish work at Oxford, his relations with his family and the people about him testify to the beauty of his character. Patmore's respect for him was such that when he expressed a moral disapproval of the older poet's eroto-mystical prose work, *Sponsa Dei*, Patmore incontinently burnt the manuscript.[4] Hopkins's intimate friends in the Society of Jesus have invariably paid tribute to his priestly spirit, which showed itself not only in the reverential way he performed his sacred duties but in his whole conduct and conversation [5] ; but they were equally explicit about his " stamp of originality ", his reserve, eccentricity, abstraction, and (saving grace !) his keen sense of humour.[6] Not that a sense of humour is anything exceptional in a body of

---

[1] *Letters*, vol. ii. p. 76.   [2] *Ibid.*, p. 93.   [3] *Ibid.*, pp. 137–8.
[4] Cf. *Robert Bridges*, by Edward Thompson (1944), p. 95 : " Bridges too read it in manuscript and discussed it with Hopkins. They both thought it worthless and in bad taste. . . . Hopkins did not want to hurt Patmore's feelings, so all he said was, ' That's telling secrets.' "
[5] *Life* (Lahey), *loc. cit.*
[6] See below, chap. iv. ; also two facetious letters to Miss Kate Hopkins (*Further Letters*, pp. 40 and 46).

Jesuit Fathers, but in the critical raillery and occasional witty playfulness of Hopkins, as revealed in the *Letters*, there is more than a dash of Charles Lamb.

In one important sense he was, as a Jesuit, " counter " and " strange "—to cite his own *Pied Beauty* ; and the reason why he appears so was given by himself unconsciously when he was accounting to Dixon for the comparatively small number of Jesuits who had achieved any fame in the arts. St. Ignatius looked on individual fame as the " most dangerous and dazzling of all attractions ". Having mentioned such men as Campion, Bourdaloue, Suarez, and Molina, Hopkins adds :

> " I quote these cases to prove that show and brilliancy do not suit us, that we cultivate the commonplace outwardly and wish the beauty of the king's daughter the soul to be all from within. " [1]

When, in a Farm Street sermon, he compared the grace-dispensing visible Church to a milch cow wandering through the pastures of the world and offering its full udders (the Sacraments) to all who sought them, he was cultivating the commonplace in the manner of a seventeenth-century poet or a Welsh country minister but not in a manner which would please a conventional Victorian upper-class congregation.

Hopkins, for all his artistic idiosyncrasy, respected rule, convention ; he even regarded ' prejudice ' as a necessary guardian of the virtues. Hence he wrote his brilliant poetry and dreamed of his almost entirely unwritten music with something resembling a sense of guilt. Yet as a poet he had before him the example of Blessed Robert Southwell, S.J., who, before being martyred at Tyburn in 1595, had written *The Burning Babe* and a score of other poems, all distinguished by a noble piety and a felicity of trope and ' conceit ' which drew from Hopkins himself the qualified praise—" a minor poet, but still a poet ".

" Our Society," Hopkins wrote to Dixon, " values and has contributed to literature, to culture ; but only as a means to an end." [2] The traditional attitude of Jesuits towards poetry was for over two hundred years framed by a treatise called *Poeticae Institutiones*, which was the *ars poetica* of Jacobus Pontanus, a Bohemian Jesuit and Professor of Humanities, who died in 1626.

---

[1] *Letters*, vol. ii. pp. 93–6.

[2] *Letters*, vol. ii. *loc. cit.* For the opinion of an expert touching the Jesuitic influence on the development of music in Germany, see Appendix A.

According to Pontanus, poetry, like music, painting, and artistic beauty in general, must not be regarded as an end in itself. The pleasure it gives must not be cultivated or enjoyed for its own sake but only in so far as it is made to serve the cause of virtue, to lead *ad majorem Dei gloriam*. Horace had said :

Aut prodesse volunt, aut delectare poetae [1] ;

and if the Renaissance stressed " delectare ", the Counter-Reformation put all the accent on " prodesse ". Pontanus defines poetry as an art which represents the actions of men, and sets them forth in verse, for the better ordering of man's life. What we must consider is not the story or the characters but " quam ob rem, qua mente, quibus rationibus " (to what end, in what mind, for what reasons). The poet, says Pontanus, should borrow freely from the great masters of morals, so that the source and fountain of good writing may be wisdom : passion and the self are to be rigorously suppressed. To the question, " Why then should poetry exist at all ? " the answer is that some concession must be made to the fallen condition of human nature, which is not strong enough to endure the nakedness and severity of eternal truth.

Three hundred years before Hopkins, Robert Southwell had taken these injunctions to heart, and in the preface to *St. Peter's Complaint* had stated his purpose as a poet :

" Poets, by abusing their talents, and making the follies and failures of love the customary object of their base endeavours, have so discredited this faculty, that a poet, a lover, and a liar are by some reckoned but three words of one signification. . . . For in lieu of solemn and devout matter, to which in duty they owe their abilities, they now busy themselves in expressing such passions as only serve for testimonies to what unworthy affections they have wedded their wills. And because the best course to let them see the error of their works is to weave a new web in their own loom, I have here layed a few coarse threads together, to invite some skilfuller wits to go forward in the same, or to begin some finer piece ; wherein it may be seen how well verse and virtue suit together."

That invitation to " go forward " was heeded by Donne, Quarles, Herbert, Crashaw, and Vaughan.

Obviously, a too general acceptance of the limitations imposed by Pontanus would have exercised a cramping effect upon the whole art of poetry ; but as a warning and corrective his precepts

[1] ' Poets wish either to *improve* or to *delight* their readers ' (*De Arte Poetica*, i. 333).

were, and still are, beneficent.[1] Southwell turned the Gongorism
and Marinism of his age to the glory of God, transmuting the
overworked carnal affections of the lesser Elizabethans into the
rarer spiritual ardours of *New Prince, New Pomp,* and *Our Ladie's
Salutation* ; in a similar manner Hopkins gave " back to Christ "
his *rifacimento* of the English language, of poetic rhythm and the
sonnet, at the same time reacting powerfully against the popular
sophistic and neo-pagan elements of his time.

Speaking of his own poetry in 1884, Hopkins said : " Our
society cannot be blamed for not valuing what it never knew of." [2]
Yet there will always be critics who will accuse the Jesuits of
neglect and even of cruelty for not publishing the poems in the
poet's lifetime. It must be allowed, however, that a lack of
literary percipience in the few Jesuits who saw the poems was far
more excusable than the same defect in professional writers such
as Hall Caine and his " critic of utmost eminence " [3], both of
whom rejected three of Hopkins's plainer but still characteristic
sonnets. Moreover, a drastic modification of the traditional
Jesuit attitude towards highly personal and sensuous poetry was
evident in the words written by Fr. Joseph Keating, S.J., as
early as 1909 :

> " It would seem that the time has now come for Father
> Hopkins's poems to appear in a collected form as a distinct and
> valuable addition to the literary heritage of the Catholic Church."

If, after this, the Jesuits were content to wait another nine years,
they can hardly be blamed (except by other Catholics) for
deferring to the judgment of Robert Bridges.

We shall now resume our inquiry into the manner in which
Hopkins, following the lead of Southwell but adopting a more
arduous method of trial and error, laid his own bright threads
on the old loom to produce a new web of an even more startling,
stimulating, and satisfying beauty.

[1] *Jacobi Pontani Societatis Jesus Poeticarum Institutionum,* Libri III. (1594). See also
Robert Southwell (1935), by Pierre Janelle, pp. 118 *et seqq.*
[2] *Letters,* vol. i. p. 196.   [3] Possibly M. Arnold ; see *Letters,* vol. i. p. 134.

PART I

TRADITION AND INNOVATION

PART I

TRADITION AND INNOVATION

EARLY POEMS AND FRAGMENTS [1]

" . . . the examples of the great masters are the
soul of education. . . ."
        (G. M. H., *Letters*, vol. i. pp. 181–2.)

HOPKINS began his poetic career at Highgate School with more
energy and thoroughness than one would expect to find in a
man whose later life was so pathetically milestoned with fragments, abortive efforts, and frustrated hopes. We have already
given a general account of his early artistic proclivities ; in the
present chapter we shall deal with individual poems mainly in
chronological order, noting the traditional influences in each and
showing how Hopkins, in feeling towards the best expression of
his own personality, frequently sloughed off a borrowed skin or
abandoned a too imitative effort : indeed, many of these early
verses are deficient in those first desiderata of poetic form—
completeness and finality.

These poems and fragments were all written between 1860 and
1875, though the last of those that can be dated with certainty
belong to 1866. During his first three years at Oxford, Hopkins
worked intermittently at two verse plays and at least two long
narrative poems ; and the two note-book diaries in which these
things are entered in pencil contain also a considerable number
of shorter poems, some apparently complete, others fragmentary ;
but not even the more finished pieces can be held positively to
represent the poet's final intention. Some of these note-book
drafts were later developed or revised and sent to friends, and all
such versions which have not been lost are now included in the
Third Edition of the *Poems*.

[1] In this chapter, all references to poems from G. M. H.'s early diaries give the
page-numbers of the poems as they were first printed in *Note-books and Papers* (1937).
The corresponding references to these verses in *Poems of G. M. H.*, Third Edition
(1948) are given in Appendix F (p. 401).

It has always been assumed that all the poems written between January 9, 1866 and September 1868 were burnt when Hopkins entered the Jesuit Novitiate—with the exception of *Summa*, *Nondum*, *Easter*, and the later versions of *Heaven-Haven* and *St. Dorothea*. It is probable, however, that after his conversion, and as his final examination approached, Hopkins restricted his verse-writing and finally abandoned it altogether for intensive study ; hence it is not likely that the verses destroyed were either numerous or important. Moreover, since 1938, when Mr. Humphry House published, in *Note-books, Etc.*, a catalogue of all the extant early MSS., a number of autograph English and Latin poems (mainly translations) have been discovered at Farm Street, together with the poet's Journal for the years 1866–68. One of the Latin poems undoubtedly belongs to 1865, and the rest of these verses were almost certainly written before Hopkins became a Jesuit.

It has been said that the more ambitious of the diary poems " were chiefly schemes in which to experiment, and in which isolated lines and fragments might later be incorporated." [1] Yet it would be wrong to assume that these early poems were all written primarily as experiments,—that is, with all the emphasis on the manner as opposed to the matter ; for almost every one bears the mark of emotional and intellectual sincerity. The poet had something to say, though its purport was sometimes slight : in the projected plays, for instance, he had obviously no complete imaginative experience to communicate. In each poem or fragment the manner was, in the main, an involuntary adaptation of contemporary forms, or else an approximation to poetic modes which, up to that time, had impressed Hopkins most deeply. Everywhere, however, amid so much that is incomplete, we find touches of strength and originality which sustain the promise that was not to be fulfilled until the beginning of 1876.

The two earliest poems of known date are *The Escorial* (1860) and *A Vision of the Mermaids* (1862). [2] The former, being a school Prize Poem, was of course consciously fashioned on a prescribed subject, and is therefore to be regarded mainly as an exercise in poetic technique. In fourteen Spenserian stanzas, Hopkins describes the building of the Escorial by Philip II, its plan, style, decoration, and use, and finally its spoliation and decay. The

---

[1] *Note-books*, p. xxi.
[2] *Poems*, Nos. 76 and 77 (2nd edn.). (For the corresponding numbers in the Third Edition, see Appendix F.)

epigraph from Theocritus (" and I compete like a frog against
the cicadas ") may perhaps be taken as a precocious recognition
of the fact that important poetry seldom emerges from a competition. Nevertheless, the young poet prepared himself thoroughly
for the task before him, as his own historical and archaeological
notes to the poem clearly show. The passion for explanation,
to which he afterwards confessed, is here mildly adumbrated.
His enthusiasm for the visual arts is revealed in his allusions to
Velasquez, Raphael, Titian, Rubens, Claude,—to three styles
of architecture and to the Belvedere Apollo. Something of the
sureness and delicacy of his touch when describing architecture in
the Journal is anticipated here, with the added charm of metre :

> " No finish'd proof was this of Gothic grace
>   With flowery tracery engemming rays
>   Of colour in high casements face to face ;
>   And foliag'd crownals (pointing how the ways
>   Of art best follow nature) in a maze
>   Of finished diapers, that fills the eye
>   And scarcely traces where one beauty strays
>   And melts amidst another ; ciel'd on high
> With blazon'd groins, and crowned with hues of majesty.

> " This was no classic temple order'd round
>   With massy pillars of the Doric mood
>   Broad-fluted, nor with shafts acanthus-crown'd,
>   Pourtray'd along the frieze with Titan's brood
>   That battled Gods for heaven ; brilliant-hued,[1]
>   With golden fillets and rich blazonry,
>   Wherein beneath the cornice, horsemen rode [2]
>   With form divine, a fiery chivalry—
> Triumph of airy grace and perfect harmony."

Here the influence of Keats and the Pre-Raphaelites is more
immediate than that of Spenser. As in *The Eve of Saint Agnes*,
there is a colourful sensuousness, a tendency to linger on the high
lights. Keats is again indicated in the rich compounds : *zeal-
rampant*, *acanthus-crown'd* ; even so early, the surprisingly apt
epithet appears : " *laver'd* founts ", " *postured* stone ". Elsewhere
we find touches of Byronic vigour :

> " For that staunch saint still prais'd his Master's name
>   While his crack'd flesh lay hissing on the grate ;
>   Then fail'd the tongue ; the poor collapsing frame
>   Hung like a wreck that flames not billows beat."

[1] The Parthenon, etc., were magnificently coloured and gilded. (Author's note.)
[2] The horsemen of the Panathenaic processions. (Author's note.)

That last simile, and the bold image of " fiery constancy " at the
end of the stanza, are remarkable for a schoolboy.

There are, moreover, lines which echo Milton, Gray, and
Tennyson :

> " A faithful guard of inner darkness fix'd."
> " The skill of dreamy Claude, and Titian's mellow gloom."
> " Adown the clattering gullies swept the rain."

As a whole, the poem is lacking in form : it has no vital development or climax.   There is an awkward hiatus where the ninth
stanza is missing, so that altogether the composition reads like
part of a discarded canto of *Childe Harold*.   It is, incidentally, the
only poem in which Hopkins expresses a distaste for asceticism :

> " the proudest home
> Of those who strove God's gospel to confound
> With barren rigour and a frigid gloom——"

The second poem, *A Vision of the Mermaids* (Christmas 1862) [1]
marks a great advance—in form, metre, diction, and imagery.
Its formal prototype is the rhyming couplet with free enjambe-
ment as used by Keats in *Endymion*, and like that poem it harks
back to the sensuous abandon of Marlowe's *Hero and Leander*.
The influence of Dryden, through Keats and *Lamia*, is also dis-
cernible in one bracketed triplet and occasional alexandrines.

The boy Hopkins equals the twenty-two-year-old Keats in the
luscious quality of his Romantic imagery.   In *Endymion* we read :

> " Although, before the crystal heavens darken,
> I watch and dote upon the silver lakes
> Pictured in western cloudiness, that takes
> The semblance of gold rocks and bright gold sands,
> Islands and creeks and amber-fretted strands
> With horses prancing o'er them, palaces
> And towers of amethyst. . . ." [2]

and in Hopkins :

> " Plum-purple was the west [3] ; but spikes of light
> Spear'd open lustrous gashes, crimson-white ;
>
> And through their parting lids there came and went
> Keen glimpses of the inner firmament :
> Fair beds they seem'd of water-lily flakes
> Clustering entrancingly in beryl lakes. . . ."

---

[1] Long held by family tradition to be another school prize poem ; but as Mr.
House has discovered, there is no documentary evidence to support this belief,
which is further discredited by the very *subject* of the poem.

[2] Book I, ll. 739–45.   [3] Cf. " dappled-with-damson west " in *The Deutschland*, 5.

The manner of Keats is imitated to excess in the copious images drawn from the precious and semi-precious stones : in a poem of one hundred and forty-three lines, we find pearl, ruby, sapphire, garnet, beryl, turquoise, onyx, jacinth, coral, and lapis lazuli[1]; and there is a similar profusion of Keatsian classical allusions. Much of the imagery is, however, as Keats would have it—" sweet and strong ", and is not without subtlety :—" rosy-budded fire " ; " the drenched hair of slabby weeds " ; " A piteous Siren sweetness on the sea " ; " A stealthy wind crept round, seeking to blow ". The extreme of emotional sensitiveness is betrayed in the recurrent pathetic fallacy of a blushing, sighing, trembling, languishing, throbbing, and shivering Nature.

Hopkins uses as lavish a palette as a Pre-Raphaelite painter. At times his description is too lush, and drops into the sentimentally trite, as in a passage near the beginning, where we find " rose of air ", " rosy-lipp'd ", " rosy-budded ", and " isle of roses "—all within seven lines. Epithets of colour pass before the eye with such frequency that the impression we receive is of unstable reds and blues which have " run " ;—*purple, crimson, scarlet, carmine, pansy-dark, violet, blood-vivid, crimson-golden*. Yet we can hardly condemn an excess which is integral to the total effect.

The poetry is at its best when the luxury of a Keats is whipped into movement by something like a Shelley's dynamism :

> " Soon—as when Summer of his sister Spring
> Crushes and tears the rare enjewelling,
> And boasting ' I have fairer things than these '
> Plashes amidst the billowy apple-trees
> His lusty hands, in gusts of scented wind
> Swirling out bloom till all the air is blind
> With rosy foam and pelting blossom and mists
> Of driving vermeil rain. . . ."

The simile is elaborated successfully throughout eighteen lines.

This imaginative affinity with Shelley was destined to outlive the affinity with Keats ; for both Shelley and Hopkins were interested in the flux of nature, though not entirely for the same

[1] Cf. the poem called *Mabel* in Manley Hopkins's *Spicilegium* :
> " Ye elves who deep in glist'ning caves
> Concoct each pure and priceless gem,
> Who mould beneath the emerald waves
> Pearls to grace queenly diadem ;
> Say how ye fix in rainbow light
> Opal and sunny chrysolite."

reasons. To Shelley, the chief analogical significance of the flux was the necessity of change and regeneration in all the processes of life, including the life of the political and social body : to Hopkins, its significance lay first in the sheer beauty of " sliding " inscape,[1] and then, through that, in the numinous emotion, the mystical apprehension of the immutable One behind the changing Many. It is true that Shelley also speaks of the One and the Many,[2] that the finest lyrical Chorus he ever wrote was like a great Christian hymn[3] ; but premature death prevented him from reducing his doctrinaire atheism and Platonic idealism to anything like a clear and logical system.

In *A Vision of the Mermaids* we find the first exuberant expression of Hopkins's genius for analysing the varied effects of light and wind upon vapour and water, for fixing in shining images the colours and patterns of a " damasqued " and " fretted " creation. The poetic myth is flimsy material, and much of the diction is archaic and precious : *withouten, argent, languent, satin-purfled*—an affectation which was later completely renounced. Structurally, however, the poem is satisfying. Working up to a strong climax in the lusty water-gambols of the mermaids, it then sinks to a dying fall, and concludes on a note of " sweet sadness ". The end harks back to the bare rock and gurgling tide of the beginning, and the last line emphasizes the dream-like quality of the whole vision.

Of two other poems which are known to belong to the school-days—*Spring and Death* and *Winter with the Gulf Stream*,[4] the former (undated) is interesting as a slight Romantic treatment of the poignant theme of the later *Spring and Fall* (1880). It is another dream-poem, in which Death appears in Spring as

> " a dismal mirky stamp
> On the flowers that were seen
> His charnelhouse-grate ribs between. . . ."

From a Chaucerian beginning we pass through echoes of Keats, Coleridge, Blake, and Shelley to the conclusion :

> " It seem'd so hard and dismal thing,
>   Death, to mark them in the Spring."

---

[1] See *Note-books*, pp. 148–9.
[2] In *Adonais*, stanza 52. Cf. also Spenser's *Mutabilitie*.
[3] In *Hellas* : " Worlds on worlds are rolling ever
            From creation to decay. . . ."
[4] *Poems*, Nos. 75 and 83.

The crudely allegorical figure of Death, and the strained fancifulness of the whole idea, suggest that the above-mentioned influences have here been transmitted through the medium of *The Philosopher's Stone*, for Manley Hopkins could not resist a " dismal mirky " apparition. The other poem, *Winter with the Gulf Stream*, was, in its original version, Hopkins's first published work.[1] Several allusions in the *Letters* [2] show that he regarded the poem with some affection, and as late as 1871 he wrote out the revised and considerably improved version which appears in the *Poems* (No. 83). Even in the earlier draft, we find a number of influences strongly knit up in a style which is on the verge of becoming truly individual, and the later alterations are clear signs of increasing energy and precision. The boy of eighteen had written :

> " Frost-fringed our ivies are, and rough
>
> With spikèd rime the brambles show,
> The hoarse leaves crawl on hissing ground,
> What time the sighing wind is low."

The man of twenty-six preferred :

> " Frost-*furred* our ivies are and rough
>
> With *bills of rime* the brambles shew.
> The hoarse leaves crawl on hissing ground
> *Because* the wind is sighing low."

Similarly " reefs of violets " and " brindled wharves " are more distinctive than " beds of violets " and " tawny-golden shore " ; the removal of these archaisms and poetic clichés was a decisive gesture.

In this poem the observation is frequently direct and Wordsworthian, as in

> " A simple passage of weak notes
> Is all the winter bird dare try "—

but there is also an ethereal touch of Shelley, and a suggestion of Tennysonian artistry :

> " So like a berg of hyaline,
> And pencilled blue so daintily. . . ."

The sunset-piece at the end of the poem is vivid and dramatic, in the manner of Coleridge.

---

[1] In *Once a Week*, Feb. 14, 1863. It is reprinted in *Further Letters*, p. 285.
[2] See *Letters*, vol. i. pp. 83 and 142 ; and *Further Letters*, p. 6.

On the subject of the poems and fragments hidden away in the two Oxford note-books and elsewhere, Hopkins elected to maintain (as we now think) an unnecessarily discreet silence. But when someone expressed the desire to copy the early verses preserved in MS. " A ", Hopkins replied, to Bridges : " Your friend may do as she likes, but I disavow those things. I believe I should not disavow but retouch ' Elected silence ' and St. Dorothy." [1] Such disavowals are frequent and natural with artists whose mature work has opened up new paths ; and it must be admitted that although these early verses contain much good poetry, their interest now is mainly biographical and psychological : they are signposts which enable us to follow the poet's progress in striking out a path of his own parallel to, but aloof from, the broad highroad of tradition. Yet in spite of sporadic indications, we cannot trace, in these early poems, any continuous and steady development towards the later style. The final change, when it came with *The Wreck of the Deutschland*, was sudden and unexpected.

One of the verse-exercises of the Highgate or undergraduate years was a blank verse translation of two short passages from the *Prometheus Desmotes*.[2] The opening lines are vigorous and commendably literal :

> " Divinity of air, fleet-feather'd gales,
>   Ye river-heads, thou billowy deep that laugh'st
>   A countless laughter, Earth Mother of all,
>   Thou sun, allseeing eyeball of the day,
>   Witness to me ! " [3]

" A countless laughter " and " allseeing eyeball " are direct and Shakespearian ; we note also, in line 3, a hint of that natural stressing which was later to be rationalized as " sprung rhythm ". But the translation as a whole barely suggests that unique and magnificent rendering of Aeschylus which the mature Hopkins, with his combined scholarship, diction, and rhythm, might conceivably have made.[4]

---

[1] *Letters*, vol. i. p. 198.   [2] *Note-books*, p. 4.   The date given is 1862–3 (?).
[3] *Prom. Des.*, ll. 88–91 :

$$\tilde{\omega} \ \delta\hat{\iota}os \ a\hat{\iota}\theta\acute{\eta}\rho, \ \kappa a\grave{\iota} \ \tau a\chi\acute{\upsilon}\pi\tau\epsilon\rho o\iota \ \pi\nu o a\acute{\iota},$$
$$\pi o\tau a\mu\hat{\omega}\nu \ \tau\epsilon \ \pi\eta\gamma a\acute{\iota}, \ \pi o\nu\tau\acute{\iota}\omega\nu \ \tau\epsilon \ \kappa\upsilon\mu\acute{a}\tau\omega\nu$$
$$\grave{a}\nu\acute{\eta}\rho\iota\theta\mu o\nu \ \gamma\acute{\epsilon}\lambda a\sigma\mu a, \ \pi a\mu\mu\hat{\eta}\tau\acute{o}\rho \ \tau\epsilon \ \gamma\hat{\eta}$$
$$\kappa a\grave{\iota} \ \tau\grave{o}\nu \ \pi a\nu\acute{o}\pi\tau\eta\nu \ \kappa\acute{\upsilon}\kappa\lambda o\nu \ \grave{\eta}\lambda\acute{\iota}o\upsilon \ \kappa a\lambda\hat{\omega}\cdot$$

[4] Cf. " I do not like verse-renderings of verse (according to the saying *Traduttore traditore*)." (*Letters*, vol. i. p. 88.)

The above specimen of Hopkins's blank verse, together with a fragment of 1864 beginning " I am a slip of comet ", shows clearly that he possessed considerable skill in the handling of this medium. The following lines (believed to be part of an abandoned play called *Floris in Italy*) hold the promise of greater intensity and subtlety than are to be found in the vast bulk of Victorian blank verse [1] :

> " I am like a slip of comet
> Scarce worth discovery, in some corner seen
> Bridging the slender difference of two stars,
> Come out of space, or suddenly engender'd
> By heady elements, for no man knows ;
> But when she sights the sun she grows and sizes
> And spins her skirts out, while her central star
> Shapes its cocooning mists ; and so she comes
> To fields of light ; millions of travelling rays
> Pierce her ; she hangs upon the flame-cased sun,
> And sucks the light as full as Gideon's fleece :
> But then her tether calls her ; she falls off,
> And as she dwindles shreds her smock of gold
> Between the sistering planets, till she comes
> To single Saturn, last and solitary ;
> And then she goes out into the cavernous dark.
> So I go out : my little sweet is done :
> I have drawn heat from this contagious sun :
> To not ungentle death now forth I run." [2]

Again the poet is looking to Shakespeare for a model : " heady elements ", " sistering planets ", " my little sweet is done ". There are touches also of Vaughan, or Crashaw,—" a slip of comet ", " the slender difference of two stars " ; and the ethereal image is reminiscent of the Shelley who, as Thompson said, " dabbled his fingers in the stars ". Considered as dramatic style, the poetry is in some danger of forgetting its objective purpose in the very fluency of its contemplative lyricism. Yet when the dramatic instinct is as strong as the poetic, much can be achieved in this manner, as in Shakespeare's *Richard II*. In the few scraps of plays left by Hopkins there is no very positive evidence that he possessed the essential gift of dramatic invention : there is evidence, however, that he could write a speech of real dramatic intensity.[3]

---

[1] Cf. " Just think the blank verse these people have exuded, such as *Paracelsus*, *Aurora Leigh* . . . *Festus*, and so on." (*Letters*, vol. i. p. 111.)

[2] *Note-books*, p. 30.

[3] E.g. the impassioned speech by Caradoc in *St. Winefred's Well* (*Poems*, No. 58.)

There is a certain Aeschylean and Biblical magnificence in another fragment belonging to the same year (1864) :

> " No, they are come ; their horn is lifted up ;
> They stand, they shine in the sun ; Fame has foregone
> All quests save the recital of their greatness ;
> Their clarions from all corners of the field
> With potent lips call down cemented towers ;
> Their harness beams like scythes in morning grass ;
> Like flame they gather on our cliffs at evening,
> At morn they come upon our lands like rains ;
> They plough our vales ; you see the unsteady flush
> Heave through their flaring columns. . . ." [1]

The urgency of all this whets our curiosity ; but at this point the poet breaks into a number of variant readings, and from now onwards he reveals a fastidiousness which is not easily distinguished from a failure of creative power. But this failure was also partly due to misdirected effort, for nothing could be less dramatic than the speech from *Floris in Italy* which begins :

> " Beauty it may be is the meet of lines,
> Or careful-spacèd sequences of sound,"

The work was originally conceived as a narrative, and to narrative the following Donne-like image is, perhaps, more suited :

> " Allow at least it has one term and part
> Beyond, and one within the looker's eye ;
> And I must have the centre in my heart
> To spread the compass on the all-starr'd sky."

The fragment is interesting as an earnest of that vein of purely secular poetry which Hopkins, in other circumstances, might have developed ; the theme here is love, and the swift rhetoric, in one part, again points to Shakespeare :

> " No, love prescriptive, love with place assign'd,
> Love by monition, heritage, or lot,
> Love by prenatal serfdom still confined,
> Even to the tillage of the sweetest spot,—
> It is a regimen on the imperfect wind,
> Piecing the elements out by plan and plot." [2]

It is finely expressed ; but the difficulty of the last two lines would be a bar to dramatic immediacy. Few poets have had Shakespeare's gift of being intellectually difficult and dramatically lucid at the same time.

[1] *Note-books*, p. 31.   [2] *Note-books*, p. 50.   (Sept. 28, 1865.)

Another probable reason for Hopkins's failure to complete the projected narrative poems and plays of this period is the critical attitude which he had by now taken up towards poetic diction and style. He divides the language of verse into three kinds : the first, and highest, is the language of inspiration [1] ; the second is Parnassian, the language that genius " speaks " but does not " sing in its flights " [2] ; the third and lowest kind is the language of poetasters. Much of *Paradise Lost* and *Paradise Regained* is Parnassian, and " nearly all the *Faery Queen* ".[3] Shakespeare does not pall, because he wrote so little Parnassian ; but no author palls so much as Wordsworth, who was guilty of an " intolerable deal " of Parnassian.

As a " good instance " of this poetry written without inspiration, Hopkins quotes nine lines of Tennyson's *Enoch Arden*[4] ; two of these lines—

> " The lustre of the long convolvuluses
>   That coil'd around the stately stems. . . ."

call forth an illuminating remark : " I think the picture of the convolvuluses does touch ; but only the picture : the words are Parnassian." In a fine piece of inspiration, he says, " every beauty takes you as it were by surprise . . . it could not in any way be predicted or accounted for by what one has already read." That is the great difference between *Hamlet* and *Enoch Arden*. Hopkins could imagine himself, *qua* Tennyson, writing

> " The glows
> And glories of the broad belt of the world,"

—than which nothing could be " more idiomatically Parnassian " ; but, he adds, one can*not* conceive oneself as Shakespeare writing *Hamlet*. To Hopkins, Tennyson's words, in *Enoch Arden*, were transparent, like a slightly magnifying lens held in front of some beautiful aspect of nature. The resultant poetic beauty is that of a true but essentially conventional representation of nature ; it is not a distinctive, original view forced upon the reader by the poet's masterly handling of words. To be distinctive, the words must be solid, opaque, like pigment ; the poet must *work* them to the utmost to produce a double beauty— that of the concept, and that of the medium.

---

[1] Hopkins adds : " The word inspiration need cause no difficulty. I mean by it a mood of great, abnormal in fact, mental acuteness, either energetic or receptive, according as the thoughts which arise in it seem generated by a stress and action of the brain, or to strike into it unasked." (Letter to Baillie, Sept. 10, 1864 ; *Further Letters*, p. 69.)

[2] *Further Letters*, loc. cit.   [3] *Note-books*, p. 29.   [4] Ll. 572-80.

Such an ideal of poetic style, with its nice distinction between the objective words and the subjective picture, was bound, in a young man of twenty, to restrict the usual output by applying frequent cold douches of conscience to the generous ardours of natural feeling.　Indeed, Hopkins seems to have had an early premonition that he would never be among the voluminous poets.　In that same year (1864), he had written in his diary :

> " It is a happy thing that there is no royal road to poetry. The world should know by this time that one cannot reach Parnassus except by flying thither.　Yet from time to time more men go up and either perish in its gullies fluttering *excelsior* flags or else come down again with full folios and blank countenances. . . . Every age has its false alarms." [1]

Hopkins had no wish to inherit the blank countenance, to be another false alarm.　His own father's muse was rather a warning than a stimulus.　He wanted his poetry always to sing in its flights ; he was not content, as most people are through long stretches of their work, merely to speak.　Many of his early poems and fragments contain much Parnassian, imitative, second-rate poetry : his finished mature poems contain remarkably little, the most obvious specimen of a " speaking " Hopkins being some of the dialogue of *St. Winefred's Well*.

The failure of creative enthusiasm during the Oxford undergraduate period was due to many natural causes, such as preoccupation with study, religion, and technical experiment ; it was due also, in part, to a dissatisfaction akin to that felt by Keats with regard to the style of the first *Hyperion*, a poem which (as Hopkins would have said) contained too much Miltonic Parnassian.　Moreover, with Hopkins the diffidence, the failure of inspiration, was probably the *cause*, and not (as Mr. House suggests) the result, of his undertaking so many different poems at the same time : when a writer is confident in his powers and the direction they are taking, he goes on with a work and finishes it because he must ; without this confidence he is apt to turn from one thing to another in the hope of striking a richer vein, and to console himself by enumerating, to a friend, his many projects, as though time and opportunity alone were necessary for their completion.　With one unfinished poem,[2] indeed, Hopkins declared himself to be " in the fatal condition of

---

[1] *Note-books*, p. 9.　(The note is headed : " Poetry at Oxford.")

[2] *A Voice from the World* (June '64–January '65).　See the letter to Baillie dated July 20 August 14, 1864 ; quoted in *Note-books*, p. xviii.

satisfaction " ; but implicit in this very confession is a deeper, scarcely realized dissatisfaction, which is equally apparent in the final comment : " So, though I finish nothing, I am not idle ".[1]

The first three pieces of continuous verse in the *Note-books* are all fragments of religious poems belonging to the period 1864–5. First come the stanzas of *Pilate*,[2] of which only six (Nos. 2–7) are indubitably in their correct order. It is clear, however, that the poem is intended to be a monologue by the spirit of the dead Pontius Pilate on the theme of retribution and salvation. Hopkins may have taken a hint from one of Crashaw's *Divine Epigrams*,[3] but a more likely source is the punishment of the High Priest Caiaphas in the *Inferno*.[4]

Pilate is conceived as a kind of unheroic and penitent Prometheus or Loki, separated " from God and man " and banished to a barren mountain where impenitent winds

> " swathe and lace the shroud-plaits o'er my face." [5]

He has lost all sensation except thought—the realization that he had slain the Son of God and that only by contrition and pur-gatorial suffering could he be saved. He re-enacts the trial of Christ ; but when he asks for water to wash his hands a Dantesque nightmare ensues !

> " Vespillo my centurion hacks out
>> Some ice that locks the glacier to the rocks
>> And in a bason brings the blocks.
>
>> I choose one ; but when I desire
>> To wash before the multitude
> The vital fire does suddenly retire
>> From hands now clammy with strange blood.
> My frenzied working is not understood.
> Now I grow numb. My tongue strikes on the gum
> And cleaves, I struggle and am dumb."

He hears the multitude tramp by ; and then Christ whispers comfort :

>> " If thou have warmth at heart
> Take courage : this shall need no further art." [6]

---

[1] *Note-books, loc. cit.*   [2] *Note-books*, p. 12.   [3] *To Pontius washing his Hands.*
[4] xxiii. 115.   [5] Stanza 5.
[6] Cf. *Purgatorio*, xix. 91 92 :
>> " Spirto, in cui pianger matura
> Quel, senza il quale a Dio tornar non puossi."

Pilate knows that he must expiate his crime by a condign sacrifice :
he will find " a flint, a fang of ice ", make a cross out of a tree,
and crucify himself

> " With hope, with shut eyes, fixedly ; " [1]

The whole fragment is little more than a first rough draft,
and its chief interest lies in its occasional vigorous diction and
Dantesque images :

> " The clouds come like ill-balanced crags,
>   Shouldering.   Down valleys smokes the gloom.
> The thunder brags.   In joints of sparkling jags
>   The lightnings leap. . . ." [2]

The subject and treatment of this poem required judicious
handling, the symbolism tending to be both artificial and melo-
dramatic [3] ; it is not surprising therefore that Hopkins abandoned
the effort, as he abandoned also the idea of another similar poem
on Judas.   There was less reason, however, for his apparent
failure to complete his next work, *A Voice from the World* ; it is,
indeed, more than probable that what we now have under that
title is merely the first draft of the missing poem called *Beyond
the Cloister.*[4]

Christina Rossetti's *The Convent Threshold*,[5] to which Hopkins's
fragment is an " answer ", appeared first in *Goblin Market and*

---

[1] This retribution, and the tramping multitude, recall Caiaphas in the *Inferno*
(*loc. cit.*) :

> " Quel confitto, che tu miri . . .
> Attraversato e nudo è nella via,
>   come tu vedi, ed è mestier ch' e' senta
>   qualunque passa com' ei pesa pria ; "

[2] Cf. *Purgatorio*, xvi. 1–6 :

> " Buio d'inferno, e di notte privata
>   d'ogni pianeta sotto pover cielo
>   quant' esser può di nuvol tenebrata,
> non fece al viso mio sì grosso velo
>   come quel fumo ch' ivi ci coperse,
>   nè a sentir di così aspro pelo : "

With this last line cf. the first in *Poems of G. M. H.* (No. 45) :

> " I wake and feel the fell of dark, not day."

[3] Cf. Hopkins's own criticism of the *Inferno* and *Faust* in *Letters*, vol. i. p. 225.
(See below, chap. iv. pp. 184, 186–7.)

[4] *Note-books*, pp. 16–21. In January 1867 G. M. H. says that part of *Beyond the
Cloister* was written in the summer of 1864, and that the finished poem was sent
" first to Macmillan's, which is always having things of Miss Rossetti." (*Further
Letters*, pp. 22–23.)

[5] Reprinted in *Note-books*, Appendix IV and at the end of *Poems*, Third Edition
(1948).

Other Poems (1862). It is a longish poem in octosyllabic lines, the stanzas being of irregular length, the rhymes capricious and flowing—a measure admirably suited to the passionate out-pourings of a woman who is about to take the veil, having renounced her lover on the grounds that

> " There's blood between us, love, my love,
>   There's father's blood, there's brother's blood ;
>   And blood's a bar I cannot pass."

She pleads with her lover to repent ; she cannot face the prospect of heaven without him, for the outcome of her conflicting emotions is the realization that

> " all is small
> Save love, for love is all in all."

It is a true poem, an intense experience of idealized love and romanticized devotion tinged with mysticism. It has a more " Catholic " character, more colour and *élan* than the majority of English religious poems ; and that perhaps is why Hopkins was attracted to it.

His own poem consists of seven fragments of uncertain con-tinuity and arrangement. That printed first was the only one which was here revised ; yet from this we gather that his inten-tion was to imitate fairly closely the form, metre and style of his original, while trying to express the emotions of the lover, about whom the woman had said :

> " Your eyes look earthward, mine look up."

In this respect the fragment is interesting as a sort of parable on the subject of Hopkins's own internal conflict between poetic sensualism and religious asceticism, a theme implicit in other poems of the years 1864-6 (*Rest* and *The Habit of Perfection*) and again later in *The Windhover*.

There can be no doubt that the poetry of Christina Rossetti exerted a strong influence on the Hopkins of these early poems. She could be richly sensuous, as in *Goblin Market*, yet in her religious poems natural scenery and images drawn from nature are used with a sure sense of their necessary subordination to the higher spiritual theme ; they are not pushed into the foreground as being important for their own sakes. It is this restraint, this sense of proportion, which gives a characteristic lightness and almost angelic delicacy to her religious poetry.

4

The difference of temperament in Hopkins quickly forces itself into view despite the self-imposed restraints of imitation. Nature at once usurps the foreground. The rejected lover compares his now cloistered lady to a bird piping alone on a winter's day ; but the image grows and seems to burgeon beautifully in its own right :

> " Now like the bird that shapes alone
> A turn of seven notes or five,
> When skies are hard as any stone,
> The fall is o'er, told off the leaves,
> 'Tis marvel she is yet alive."

(Hopkins stands in a similar relation to Christina Rossetti as Francis Thompson stood to the more sober Patmore and Alice Meynell ; and the next four lines anticipate Thompson as clearly as they anticipate the later Hopkins !

> " Once it was scarce perceivèd Lent
> For orience of the daffodil ;
> Once, jostling thick, the bluebell sheaves [1]
> The peacock'd copse were known to fill ; ")

The sound of the woman's voice in the springtime of their love is rendered in a charming touch of Wordsworthian bird-lore :

> " Late in the green weeks of April
> Cuckoo calls cuckoo up the wood,
> Five notes or seven, late and few ; "

The man has been ravished by love and the beauty of

> " Fruit-cloistering hyacinth-warding woods " ;

yet the attitude fostered throughout the poem is one of sincere but painful renunciation !

> " Your comfort is as sharp as swords ;
> And I cry out for wounded love. . . .
>
> You should have been with me as near
> As halves of sweet-pea-blossom are ; "

He who had formerly been the expert teacher in matters of

[1] Cf. the
> " juicy and jostling shock
> Of bluebells sheaved in May "
>   (*Poems*, No. 63).

love and beauty is now the backward learner of humility and penitence :

> " How turn my passion-pastured thought
> To gentle manna and simple bread ? "

Much of this fragment is wordy and vague ; but where the thought is clearly enunciated it is " flush " with a stronger, more heady poetry than that of Christina Rossetti.   Once only there is a touch of the more extravagant Crashaw :

> " My cry is like a bleat ; a few
> Intolerable tears I bleed."

But in the following lines there is real passion, and something like the later stark manner of W. B. Yeats :

> " This ice, this lead, this steel, this stone,
> This heart is warm to you alone ;
> Make it to God.   I am not spent
> So far but I have yet within
> The penetrative element
> That shall unglue the crust of sin.
> Steel may be melted and rock rent.
> Penance shall clothe me to the bone
> Teach me the way : I will repent."

To judge by the extant fragment, and by the poet's own comments on the finished version [1] (if *Beyond the Cloister* is the same poem), the latter was probably one of the early works which were burnt in 1868. The change of title was not an improvement, and the final draft may have suffered, as the fragment does, because Hopkins had attempted a too rigid parallelism ; he tried to fabricate dreams and visions to match those of the nun, a process which forced his vein ; and Hopkins's authentic individual vein was of the kind that will not be forced.

After two poems dealing with penitence and retribution, he turns, in his next fragment, to the theme of rebelliousness.   Of the *Soliloquy of one of the Spies left in the Wilderness* [2] Mr. House

---

[1] " I have ceased to care for *Beyond the Cloister* being put into a magazine.   Too many licences are taken for a beginner, but the objection is on the score of morality rather than of art, and as the licences in themselves I still think justifiable I need not alter what I cannot publish.   Part of it was written two and a half years ago and though that does not sound much one changes very fast at my age, and I should write better now, I hope." (*Further Letters*, p. 23 ; January 16, 1867.).

It is interesting to note that here, as in later years, G. M. H. admits a certain fault (" too many licences ") and then immediately nullifies the admission.

[2] *Note-books*, p. 23.   For the Biblical source, see *Numbers*, xiii–xiv.   The poem contains also allusions to *Exodus*, xii–xxvii.

says : " It is more unified than the other fragmentary poems of
the time ; it is more direct, vigorous, and self-explanatory ; and
also has more remarkable anticipations of later poems." [1] This
last clause, however, might lead one to expect greater resemblances to the mature style than the poem actually presents.

The idea of reconstructing a great historical event or episode
from the point of view of one anonymous or unimportant character may have been derived from the historical novel, or
possibly from Browning's poetical studies of interesting non-
entities ; or again, Hopkins may have taken a hint from the old
mystery plays, in which Noah's wife and the Bethlehem shepherds
are given a fictitious individuality. Browning's *Men and Women*
had appeared in 1855, *Dramatis Personae* in 1864 (the year of the
Soliloquy) ; and in the latter volume we find, in *A Death in the
Desert*, something like a parallel to Hopkins's poem.

The *Soliloquy* is also remarkable as a foreshadowing of the
method employed by Mr. T. S. Eliot in his *Journey of the Magi*.[2]
In each poem the historical event is merely a background to the
details of personal experience, yet that experience derives all its
importance from the historical event.   Hopkins's spy says :

> " Your hands have borne the tent-poles : on you plod :
>   The trumpet waxes loud : tired are your feet.
>   Come by the flesh-pots. . . .
>
> " Sicken'd and thicken'd by the glare of sand
>   Who would drink water from a stony rock ? "

And Mr. Eliot's magus complains of

> " the camels galled, sore-footed, refractory
>   Lying down in the melting snow."

Hopkins's desert-worn Israelite dreams of the comparative
comfort and even luxury of bondage in Egypt :

> " In beds, in gardens, in thick plots I stand,
>   Handle the fig, suck the full-sapp'd vine-shoot " ;

and in like manner Mr. Eliot's Magi regret

> " The summer palaces on slopes, the terraces,
>   And the silken girls bringing sherbet."

In their conclusions, the two poems express the obverse and
reverse of the same theological motive.   Hopkins's spy is the

[1] *Note-books*, p. xx.   [2] *Collected Poems* (1936), p. 107.

type of man who seeks physical and mental ease even at the price
of spiritual degradation : Mr. Eliot's magus, on the contrary, is
the man who obeys the divine injunction, pursues the spiritual
good, in spite of the physical inconveniences. Both poems are
ostensibly objective ; yet each is the oblique projection of its
author's own spiritual problem. The spy presents the sort of
man Hopkins himself might have become without grace and
self-discipline ; and Mr. Eliot's similar though not identical
conflict is poignantly expressed in *Ash-Wednesday*.

Technically, the *Soliloquy* marks an advance in the control of
stanza-form. The rhythm is graceful yet sinewy, like that of
Herbert ; there is also a Miltonic delight in proper names :

> " Rise : match your strength with monstrous Talmai
>   At Kirjath-Arba : go.—"

The later Hopkins appears in a sudden burst of feeling :

> " Egypt, the valley of our pleasance, there ! "

Or in a rush of syllables :

> " Are you sándblind ? [1]   Slábs of water many a mile
>   Blaze on him all this while."

Yet the phrasing and diction of one passage, though streaked
with vigorous Hopkins, can still suggest Tennyson's *Lotos Eaters* :

> " Give us the tale of bricks as heretofore ;
>   To knead with cool feet the clay juicy soil.
>   Who tread the grapes are splay'd with stripes of gore,
>   And they who crush the oil [2]
>   Are spatter'd. We desire the yoke we bore,
>   The easy burden of yore."

It was not until September of this year (1864) that Hopkins
began to " doubt Tennyson " ; [3] and the influence of Keats as
refracted through Tennyson, D. G. Rossetti, and R. W. Dixon is

---

[1] Cf. *The Candle Indoors* (*Poems*, No. 26) :
> " Are you beam-blind, yet to a fault
>   In a neighbour deft-handed ? "

[2] Cf. *God's Grandeur* (No. 7) :
> " It grows to a greatness, like the ooze of oil
>   Crushed. . . ."

[3] *Further Letters*, p. 68.   (To Baillie, Sept. 10, 1864.)

still apparent in the two almost complete stanzas on Autumn.[1]
The first begins :

> " Now I am minded to take pipe in hand
>   And yield a song to the decaying year ;
>   Now while the full-leaved hursts unalter'd stand,
>   And scarcely does appear
>   The Autumn yellow feather in the boughs. . . ."

The last line is either an echo of Dixon or an unusual coincidence ;
for in 1864 Dixon published *Historical Odes*,[2] which contains the
song so much admired by Hopkins :

> " The feathers of the willow
>   Are half of them grown yellow. . . ."

In the same volume appeared Dixon's ode *To Summer*, which
Bridges tried to defend against the objection that it was too
much like Keats.[3]   Hopkins's fragment, though not so good,
has the same diluted Hippocrene—
Dixon :

> " Thou who dost set the prop to crooked arms
>   Of apple-trees that labour with their store. . . ."

Hopkins :

> " The fruit against the wall
>   Loose on the stem has done its summering. . . ."

As Dixon shows, it is possible to produce a fine poem in the
manner of Keats ; but the challenge to Keats is usually detrimental to the challenger.   Hopkins may have felt this when
writing his poem on Autumn.

Only once more do we hear distinct echoes of Keats, and
these are in the four fragments of *Richard*, a modern pastoral set,
like Matthew Arnold's *Scholar Gipsy*, in the country round
Cumnor, near Oxford.   Hopkins's intention seems to have been
to reverse the fable of Arnold's poem,[4] for whereas in that work
an Oxford student forsakes his studies to join a band of gipsies, in

---

[1] *Note-books*, p. 31.

[2] See *ibid.* p. 53 (1866) : " Revd. R. W. Dixon. . . . He has written also
Historical Odes."

[3] *Selected Poems of R. W. Dixon* (O.U.P.), p. 195.   For Hopkins's opinions of
Dixon's poems, see below, chap. iv. pp. 215-8.

[4] For this suggestion (too valuable to be omitted) I am indebted to Mr. Humphry
House.

Hopkins's pastoral " a shepherd of the Arcadian mood " undergoes a change which elicits four questions—all, alas, unanswered :

> " But what drew shepherd Richard from his downs,
> And bred acquaintance of unusèd towns ?
> What put taught graces on his country lip,
> And brought the sense of gentle fellowship,
> That many centres found in many hearts ?
> What taught the humanities and the round of arts ?
> And for the tinklings on the falls and swells
> Gave the much music of our Oxford bells ? "

The fragments contain two allusions to Wordsworth ; and it
would appear that the nostalgic and symbolic beauty of Arnold's
Scholar Gipsy and *Thyrsis* (impregnated as they are with the cult
of Nature and the nature of Culture) had stirred in Hopkins the
spirit of emulation. Some of his vignettes are delicately painted :

> " There was no bleat of ewe, no chime of wether,
> Only the bellèd foxgloves lisp'd together.
> Yet there came one who sent his flock before him ;
> Alone upon the hill-top, heaven o'er him,
> And where the brow in first descending bow'd
> He sat and wrought his outline on a cloud."

There is nice observation and deft phrasing in the description of
the sheep : " Their changing feet *in flicker* all the time " ; and
of the rainbow, which was seen to fill

> " From one frail horn that crumbled to the plain
> His steady wheel quite to the full again."

These fragments were written between October 1864 and July
1865, and the last of them (selected for inclusion in *Note-books*) is
sufficient to show that the young Hopkins chronologically and
specifically bridges the gap between the Keats of " I stood tip-
toe " and the Rupert Brooke of *Grantchester* and *The Great Lover* :

> " There was a meadow level almost : you traced
> The river wound about it as a waist.
> Beyond, the banks were steep ; a brush of trees
> Rounded it, thinning skywards by degrees,
> With parallel shafts,—as upward-parted ashes,—
> Their highest sprays were drawn as fine as lashes. . . .
> Great butter-burr leaves floor'd the slope corpse ground
> Beyond the river. . . ." [1]

[1] *Note-books*, p. 48.

There is a modern ring in the words—

> " a spiritual grace
> Which Wordsworth would have dwelt on, about the place ",

but the immediate sequel slips right back into Keats :

> " Led Richard with a sweet undoing pain
> To trace some traceless loss of thought again." [1]

It was hardly an accident that Richard's friend, Sylvester, reclined in a very Pre-Raphaelite landscape

> " reading Keats'
> Epistles, while the running pastoral bleats
> Of sheep from the high fields and other wild
> Sounds reach'd him."

As pendents to the three religious poems examined above, and belonging to the summer of the same year (1864), there are four more devotional fragments, the most interesting of which is *Rest*,[2] the first and longer version of *Heaven-Haven*. The two revised stanzas (*Poems*, No. 2) are perfect in their kind, and all the improvements on the first draft are masterly. For instance,

> " To fields where flies not the unbridled hail "

is conventional when compared with

> " To fields where flies no sharp and sided hail ".

" Sided " is a typically precise and forceful epithet : the poet feels the facets and edges of the hailstone as though he were about to draw the object in his minute Pre-Raphaelite manner. Similarly, the revised last line :

> " And out of the swing of the sea "

has a liquid swell in its anapæsts which shows that already Hopkins was feeling out towards a freer metric.

Appended to *Rest* are two other stanzas which, although obviously belonging to the same emotional idea, were judiciously omitted in the revised version. The sub-title of *Heaven-Haven* is *A nun takes the veil*, and the additional stanzas were apparently intended to symbolize the dangers and hardships of the religious

---

[1] Cf. Keats's " A little noiseless noise among the leaves ".

[2] *Note-books*, p. 27.

vocation. The imagery is expressive of what Hopkins called later " my winter world " : [1]

> " I must hunt down the prize
> Where my heart lists.
> Must see the eagle's bulk, render'd in mists,
> Hang of a treble size.
>
> Must see the waters roll
> Where the seas set
> Towards wastes where round the ice-blocks tilt and fret,
> Not so far from the pole." [2]

The earlier *Winter with the Gulf Stream* is already a setting for that arctic " night of the soul " which informs many of the poet's last sonnets. The above stanzas anticipate, mildly,

> " what sights you, heart, saw, ways you went ! " [3]

and the second one is a sterner, more masculine variation of Shakespeare's

> " Chanting faint hymns to the cold fruitless moon." [4]

Hopkins may have felt, however, that these images of rigorous manly adventure were hardly congruous with the quiet tenour of a nun's life, no matter how severe her trials and desolations ; and rejected the stanzas for that reason. To " restore " them to *Heaven-Haven*, as someone has suggested, would be to flout the better judgment of both Hopkins and Bridges.

It is at this time that we are first able to trace the influence of George Herbert, one of Hopkins's most admired poets.[5] Herbert's frank avowal of Christ ; his passionate yet restrained colloquies

---

[1] *Poems*, No. 51, line 13.

[2] In the first of these two stanzas there is an obvious echo from Manley Hopkins's poem called *Clouds* (1843), in which the setting sun " *hangs* mid air and wave " and at last "sinks, but gathers *treble size* " (our italics). But as Mr. R. G. Howarth of Sydney has pointed out, *Rest* and its pendent stanzas may owe their conception to the last lines of that address to Fortune which (according to Roper) Sir Thomas More composed while awaiting execution :

> " Trust shall I God, to enter in a while,
> His haven of heaven sure and uniforme.
> Ever after thy calm, looke I for a storme."

The ultimate original of both More's verses and *Rest* was probably the ' storm-calm-haven ' passage in *Psalm* cvii. (29–30).

[3] *Poems*, No. 45.   [4] *M. N. D.*, I. i. 73.

[5] See Vol. I. of the present work, chap. v. pp. 170–2. Also below, chap. iv. p. 196.

4*

with God ; his vigorous and subtle exposition of doctrine ; his significant quaintness and happy conceits,—all these elements are found, in duly modified form, in the later Hopkins. But the most patently Herbertian of all his verse is a poem of 1864 with the characteristic title *New Readings*.[1]   It begins :

> " Although God's word has said
> On thistles that men look not grapes to gather,
>   I read the story rather
> How soldiers plaited thistles round His head
> Where fruit of precious wine was shortly sped." [2]

The poem is another plea for asceticism, and expresses the deep conviction that Christ's suffering was an example of sacrifice to be followed and not merely a perfection to be distantly admired. The last stanza foreshadows the attitude of *The Windhover*, the final decision of *St. Alphonsus Rodriguez* :

> " Hard ways, rough wanderings
> Made Him not fruitless ; in the thorns he shed
>   Grains from his drooping head,
> And would not have that Legion of wing'd things
> Bear him to heaven upon easeful wings."

Moreover, this theme of sacrifice, treated here in a vein of tender lyricism, was to emerge with greater poignancy and dramatic force eleven years later in *The Wreck of the Deutschland*.

If *New Readings* hints at desolations to come, the next poem (which seems complete) is a joyous confession of faith. The motive and much of the imagery and diction are Biblical :

> " He hath abolished the old drouth,
>   And rivers run where all was dry. . . . [3]
> He hath put a new song in my mouth,
>   The words are old, the purport new. . . ." [4]

In the mouth of an ardent Christian reading the Classics, the " purport new " resembles the rout of the pagan pantheon as in

---

[1] *Note-books*, p. 26.   A later draft, from MS. " A ", is reproduced in *Poems*, Third Edition.

[2] Cf. Herbert :
> " Then on My head a crown of thorns I wear ;
>   For these are all the grapes Sion doth bear,
>   Though I My vine planted and watered there :
>   Was ever grief like mine ? "
>
>   (*The Sacrifice*).

Cf. also Herbert's *The Bunch of Grapes*.

[3] Cf. *Isaiah*, xxxv. 6.   [4] Cf. *Psalm* xcviii.

Milton's *Nativity Ode*. The poem is addressed to a friend, and was probably one of those sent to Baillie, whom Hopkins no doubt desired to wean from his stoical indifference to the question of survival :

> " . . . I shall live, I shall not die,
>> But I shall when the shocks are stored
>> See the salvation of the Lord. . . .
>> We shall be sheavèd with one band
>> In harvest and in garnering,[1]
>> When heavenly vales so thick shall stand
>> With corn that they shall laugh and sing." [2]

This early assimilation of wheat-sheaves and the saints in heaven needs only the addition of an isolated quatrain of 1866 to complete the materials for the sestet of *The Starlight Night* (1877). Here is the quatrain :

> " The stars were packed so close that night
>> They seemed to press and *stare*
>> And gather in *like hurdles bright*
>> The liberties of air." [3]

From ancient to latter-day paganism was an easy step for a mind so critical, as this poet's always was, of lapses from an absolute sincerity in so-called Christians. In another fragment— nine lines of a Blake-like intensity [4]—he satirizes the pompous and un-Christian lugubriousness of the Victorian funeral—the black-plumed horses, the crêpe, the expensive paraphernalia of Despair:

> " Why should their foolish bands, their hopeless hearses
>> Blot the perpetual festival of day ?
>> Ravens, for prosperously-boded curses
>> Returning thanks, might offer such array."

Hopkins deplores the deliberate exclusion from these gloomy obsequies of any sincere allusion to Christ's promise :

> " Heaven comfort sends, but harry it away,
>> Gather the sooty plumage from Death's wings
>> And the poor corse impale with it and fray
>> Far from its head an angel's hoverings.
>> And count the rosy cross with bann'd disastrous things."

---

[1] Cf. *Matt.* xiii. 19. [2] Cf. *Job* xxxviii. 7.
[3] *Note-books*, p. 53. Cf. with the italicized words the " elves-eyes " and the " piece-bright paling " of *The Starlight Night* (*Poems*, No. 8). See vol. i. of the present work, chap. v. p. 166, and below, pp. 235-6. [4] *Ibid.* p. 27.

Six additional lines seem intended to develop the theme of day's
" perpetual festival " : if Despair is the right note, nature, too,
should be decadent :

> " And in grey bands the sun should still be born . . .
> And, swarter still, the rolling pines should cast
> Their heads together in a stormy blot."

The above Spenserian stanza affords yet another example of
the impression made upon the young Gerard by his father's poems
of 1843.   Manley Hopkins's title poem, *The Philosopher's Stone*,
mentions a " raven grey ", the sign " of the Rosie Crosse " (i.e.,
Rosicrucian), and an Alchymist's mammonistic indifference to
the deaths of his nearest of kin.   In another poem, *In a Time of
Mortality*, we read :

> " The streets are full of mourning ; train meets train
> With plumes and all Death's dark festivities."

But Hopkins *père* attacks not the festivities but the sinful onlookers,
who refuse to be admonished by Death's " black car."

The ' funeral ' poem is the first of a number of epigrammatic
obiter dicta (all of 1864) which illustrate further the range of
Hopkins's interests and experiments.[1]   At Maentwrog he writes
a poetic note on the difficulty of reconciling the Berkeleyan theory
of vision with common-sense deductions :

> " The rainbow shines but only in the thought
> Of him that looks.   Yet not in that alone,
> For who makes rainbows by invention ? "

With more subtlety than Dr. Johnson, he opines that

> " The sun on falling waters writes‧the text
> Which yet is in the eye or in the thought." [2]

But he concludes, as he began, by admitting that " it was a hard
thing to undo this knot."   Again, while " in the van between
Ffestiniog and Bala ", he jots down an interesting confession :

> " Of virtues I most warmly bless,
> Most rarely seen, Unselfishness.
> And to put graver sins aside,
> I own a preference for Pride."

---

[1] *Note-books*, pp. 28–29.
[2] Cf. *Floris in Italy* (p. 50) :
> " Beauty . . . has one term and part
> Beyond, and one within the looker's eye."

His predilection for economy in expression draws him into imitations of the satirical epigram as cultivated by Herrick, Prior, and Blake :

> " You ask why can't Clarissa hold her tongue.
> Because she fears her fingers will be stung."

His fondness for a play on words helps him to pillory the man who borrowed " his sermons " ; and two more epigrams, one on " Modern Poets " and the other " On a poetess ", are interesting mainly as early indications of a dissatisfaction which he felt all his life both with the popular poets of the age and with the artistic efforts of women in general.

In one more epigram he sums up his attitude towards economy and fastidiousness in art, and at the same time faintly adumbrates his own mature style :

> " Boughs being pruned, birds preenèd, show more fair ;
>   To grace them spires are shaped with corner squinches ;
> Enrichèd posts are chamfer'd ; everywhere
>   He heightens worth who guardedly diminishes ;
> Diamonds are better cut ; who pare, repair ;
>   Is statuary rated by its inches ?
> Thus we shall profit, while gold coinage still
> Is worth and current with a lessen'd mill." [1]

The accuracy of line 2 is as doubtful as the rhyming of *squinches* and *diminishes* ; but the felicity of *pare, repair* looks forward to the rich phonal patterning of *Spelt from Sibyl's Leaves* (1885).

The epigram was at least a whetstone for sharpening the mind which later produced the witty turns and pointed images of *Spring and Fall* and *The Blessed Virgin*.[2] But apart from theology and Jesuit discipline, Hopkins was at no period tied to a system, not even to one of his own making ; hence it is not surprising to find him practising simultaneously the epigram and the art-ballad—or rather, closely imitating the old ballad, with its peculiar combination of dramatic terseness and repetitive conventional syntax.

In writing *The Queen's Crowning* (1864),[3] Hopkins probably had no other motive than the desire to master an excellent traditional form. Certainly at that time the ballad, like the *ballade* a few years later, was " in the air " ; but the ballads produced between 1850 and 1865 by the Rossettis, Morris, Swinburne and others were all frankly art-ballads, sincere and

---

[1] *Note-books*, p. 39.   [2] *Poems*, Nos. 31 and 37.   [3] *Note-books*, p. 34.

sometimes successful attempts to adapt the old form to personal
and modern uses, as in *The White Ship* and *A Ballad of Boding*.[1]
Hopkins's close imitation of the stylistic mannerisms and
historical " keepings " of the genuine old ballad leaves no doubt
about the purely experimental character of his poem.

It is the kind of story which, with a little more precision in
the telling, would have been pathetic in its day and would seem
so still to a child.   A king's son marries a lady of low degree,
leaves her to go abroad, succeeds to the throne, and on his
return is murdered by his three envious brothers.   The brothers
seek out the widowed queen, and two of them claim to be her
husband.   She rejects them, and at night is visited by the spirit
of her true lord, whom she recognizes by the emblem of Paradise
he carries—the lily and the rose.   On his giving her three kisses
" cold as ice " she falls to the ground ;   he then takes her to
Paradise, and " There shall her crowning be."

In the best medieval manner, Hopkins wastes no time on
preliminaries :

> " They were wedded at midnight
>   By shine of candles three,
>   And they were bedded till daylight
>   Before he went to sea."

The climax, too, shows a skilful use of contrast and compression :

> " The more she asked, the more he spoke,
>   The fairer waxèd he.
>   The more he told, the less she spoke,
>   The wanner wanèd she." [2]

The concluding motive was probably derived from the old
ballad of *Sweet William's Ghost*,[3] though Hopkins may have seen
Bürger's unequalled *Lenore*, or Scott's translation of it.   Moreover,
those sacred symbols, the lily and the rose, which are also found
in several old ballads, seem to have had the same significance for
Hopkins as for the early poets, for he uses them again, with much
greater originality, in *The Wreck of the Deutschland*.   Similarly, the
charmed number ' three ', conditioned in the ballad by continuous rhyme, is matched in the greater poem by a ' five ' which
seems equally fortuitous until we realize that for Hopkins this
number bore a profound theological significance.[4]

---

[1] By D. G. and Christina Rossetti respectively.   [2] Stanza 36.
[3] Child's collection, No. 77.   [4] Stanzas 21, 22 and 23.

Such an exercise in the control of lyrical narrative and in the more freely stressed ballad-metre was not wasted on the poet of *The Eurydice*. All experience in the control of stanza-forms is valuable to the poet who has the potential genius to " do otherwise " ; and that, perhaps, is the only justification of a two-stanza poem called *The Summer Malison* [1]—a neatly turned piece of playful cynicism which expresses a mood common to all people at certain times.

We come now to a group of " more directly personal poems ", which have far more intrinsic merit. The most important of these are nine sonnets (all written between April and October 1865), in which Hopkins steps without strain into a considerable mastery of the traditional sonnet-form. The rhyme-scheme is always that of the first Italian mode, though, in six of the nine he prefers, like Milton, to run the octave into the sestet ; and he never observes the rule of quatrain and tercet pauses. Milton is, on the whole, cleverly blended with Wordsworth ; but in spite of the form, diction and symbol are frequently Shakespearian, as in—

> " See how Spring opens with disabling cold." [2]

The first sonnet [3] is an intensely earnest address to some " friend " who cannot be clearly identified. Written in April 1865, it coincides, as Mr. House says, with a crisis in the poet's spiritual development. In February he had met Digby Dolben for the first and only time ; on March 12 he records " A great day of the mercy of God " [4] ; and from now on his conversion and religious vocation must have seemed ever greater possibilities. It may be true, as Mr. House suggests,[5] that Dolben was connected with this crisis ; but his connexion with the sonnet is not certain, despite the fact that in the diary (C. II) there are a number of contiguous but cryptic allusions to this particular acquaintance. The opening lines—

> " Where art thou friend, whom I shall never see,
>   Conceiving whom I must conceive amiss ? "

are not easily reconciled with the fact that Hopkins had already seen Dolben and looked forward to seeing him again.[6]   We

---

[1] *Note-books*, p. 41.   [2] *Ibid.* p. 47.   [3] *Ibid.* p. 42.
[4] *Ibid.* p. 41.   [5] *Ibid.* p. xxi.
[6] Cf. *Letters*, vol. i., August 30, 1867 :

> " I looked forward to meeting Dolben and his being a Catholic more than to anything."

know, however, from statements made after Dolben's death, that
Hopkins, while admiring the beauty of his charaeter, found his
enthusiasm " wholly and unhappily irrational ",[1] and hoped that
he would eventually become a Catholic ; in the light of which
the last six lines of the sonnet may well express the wish that
Dolben, like Hopkins himself, would see " where the only
consistent position wd. lie " : [2]

> " —if. the sound
> " Of God's dear pleadings have as yet not moved thee,—
> And for those virtues I in thee have found,
> Who say that had I known I had approved thee,—
> For these, make all the virtues to abound,—
> No, but for Christ who hath foreknown and loved thee." [3]

In the absence of positive evidence, however, a totally
different reading is at least possible.   In the wording of the
sonnet there is nothing incompatible with the theory that
it was addressed to an actual unknown, some " fascinating
stranger ",[4] male or female—the woman, for instance, whom
Hopkins, but for " God's dear pleadings ", might have loved
and married.   It is feasible that in 1865 he was already contemplating the priesthood and celibacy, and for a poet who
always held strong views on the desirability of marriage,[5] the
sentiment, in such a private confession as this sonnet appears
to be, would be quite natural.   Moreover, his solicitude for
the spiritual welfare of a stranger can be matched in many
later poems.[6]

The next two sonnets, though only " rough copies " of more
polished versions which were sent to Addis, are graceful and
sincere effusions in praise of Oxford.   We give the first and
better one in full, as an example of his more conventional

---

[1] *Loc. cit.*

[2] Hopkins's first letter to Newman, August 28, 1866.

[3] Further evidence that Hopkins thought much about Dolben is in a Journal
entry of 1873 :

> " Aug. 30—Sept. 8—Retreat. . . . I received as I think a great mercy
> about Dolben."

This may tacitly refer to the misconception mentioned in the sonnet (line 2).

[4] See *Letters*, vol. i. p. 8.

[5] Cf. " The reason of course why I like men to marry is that a single life is a
difficult, not altogether a natural life. . . ." (*Letters*, vol. i. p. 194.   See also *ibid.*
pp. 39 and 198.)

[6] E.g. *Poems*, 2nd edn., Nos. 10, 16, 17, 23 and 26.

handling of a form which he afterwards moulded freely to his own purposes :

> " New-dated from the terms that reappear,
> More sweet-familiar grows my love to thee,
> And still thou bind'st me to fresh fealty
> With long-superfluous ties, for nothing here
> Nor elsewhere can thy sweetness unendear.
> This is my park, my pleasaunce ; this to me
> As public is my greater privacy,
> All mine, yet common to my every peer.
>
> Those charms accepted of my inmost thought,
> The towers musical, quiet-walled grove,
> The window-circles, these may all be sought
> By other eyes, and other suitors move,
> And all like me may boast, impeachèd not,
> Their special-general title to thy love." [1]

Another sonnet, *Easter Communion*,[2] is a moving piece of devotion, though its full appeal will be limited to those who, sharing the poet's faith, are able to respond also to the similar sacerdotal fervour of *The Bugler's First Communion* (1879). Although Hopkins was not yet a priest, he writes here as though he were regarding the communicants (both ' gownsmen ' and ' townsmen ') from beyond the altar-rail. This poem may well be that " discipline wrapped up in a sonnet " which he did *not* propose to send to Pater with his best love. Certainly lines 2-5, though they may be read figuratively, are a plain allusion to the practice of ascetic flagellation, which was not uncommon among extreme Anglo-Catholics at that time :

> " You striped in secret with breath-taking whips,
> Those crooked rough-scored chequers may be pieced
> To crosses meant for Jesus ; "

and the hair-shirts worn by Dr. Pusey and other ' Puseyites ' are glanced at favourably in the sestet. Throughout the sonnet the phrasing is strong and distinctive, and lifts the poem well above the ruck of Victorian sonneteering : " thin and pursuant cold " ; " You serged fellowships, You vigil-keepers with low flames decreased " ; " Give myrrhy-threaded golden folds of ease ".

In an earlier sonnet of 1865, " Myself unholy, from myself unholy "[3], Hopkins had plaintively voiced that moral self-disapproval which is prosaically explained in the excessive scrupulosity of his Oxford spiritual diary, and which was later intensified

---

[1] *Note-books*, p. 46.   [2] *Ibid.* p. 47.   [3] *Poems*, Third Edition, No. 11.

in the bitter self-loathing of " I wake and feel the fell of dark "
(1885).   A second, more comprehensive self-audit, " See how
Spring opens " (June, '65),[1] records under the images of "long-
dying snow " and late-opening buds the poet's regret for his
own spiritual sluggishness ; we hear also for the first time that
note of self-denunciation so frequent in the *Letters* :

> " Chilling remembrance of my days of old
> Afflicts no less, what yet I hope may blow,
> That seed which the good sower once did sow,
> So loading with obstruction that threshold
> Which should ere now have led my feet to the field."

The diction grows more and more Miltonic ; and comparing
this sonnet with the one Milton wrote in his twenty-third year,
we perceive beneath the obvious resemblance a striking difference : Milton concludes on a note of resolute optimism which
promises full achievement, whereas in Hopkins there is an
ominous note of frustration :

> " It is the waste done in unreticent youth
> Which makes so small the promise of that yield
> That I may win with late-learnt skill uncouth. . . ."

Two other short poems of this year are equally prophetic of
desolations to come.   One begins :

> " My prayers must meet a brazen heaven
>   And fail or scatter all away."

and ends :

> " A warfare of my lips in truth,
>   Battling with God, is now my prayer."

" Unclean and seeming unforgiven ", he feels, even at twenty-
one, " the long success of sin ".[2] The second fragment anticipates
the pathetic conditions of sterility described in *Poems*, No. 50 :

> " Trees by their yield
> Are known ; but I—
> My sap is sealed,
> My root is dry."[3]

Father Lahey pronounced these early confessions "too personal
and introspective to appeal " ; but they are surely contributory to
a full understanding of the mature poems : they show that the
desolations of 1885–9 cannot be attributed solely (as some critics

---

[1] *Loc. cit.*   [2] *Note-books*, p. 49. Cf. *Poems*, Nos. 32 and 40.
[3] *Ibid.* p. 51.

have virtually maintained they can) to his life as a Jesuit. Here, as in the later poems, the poet's faith is undiminished. In this very fragment he says ' although self-sentenced, still I keep my trust '. Moreover, the last two poems in the *Note-books*[1] treat the subject of divine love with the ardour of Herbert or Christina Rossetti. The first of these, which is also the last of the early sonnets, has a real charm and delicacy, and indicates clearly that the path he had chosen, however rugged and steep, commanded some fair prospects :

" Let me be to Thee as the circling bird,
　Or bat with tender and air-crisping wings
　That shapes in half-light his departing rings,
　From both of whom a changeless note is heard.
　I have found my music in a common word,
　Trying each pleasurable throat that sings
　And every praisèd sequence of sweet strings,
　And know infallibly which I preferred.

" The authentic cadence was discovered late
　Which ends those only strains that I approve,
　And other science all gone out of date
　And minor sweetness scarce made mention of :
　I have found the dominant of my range and state—
　Love, O my God, to call Thee Love and Love."

The images from music are, perhaps, too cleverly sustained ; but the last line, which can be paralleled in several of Christina Rossetti's later sonnets,[2] illustrates also that remark by Geldart, Oxford friend of the poet : " Gerontius (Hopkins) gushed as well, but then he meant it."[3]

The next piece, *The Half-Way House*, is the most obscure of all the early poems ; it is, nevertheless, of great biographical interest. The second stanza embodies his growing dissatisfaction with the *Via Media* :

" My national old Egyptian reed gave way ;
　I took of vine a cross-barred rod or rood.
　Then next I hungered : Love when here, they say,
　Or once or never took Love's proper food ;
　But I must yield the chase, or rest and eat.—
　Peace and food cheered me where four rough ways meet."

The first line must mean that the Church of England, as a national Establishment, had already failed him ; moreover

[1] Pp. 52 and 53.
[2] E.g. " I, Love, am Thine ; Thou, Lord my God, art mine."
　　　" Give me thy love—So be it, my God, my God."
[3] *Further Letters*, p. 108. See above, *Introduction*, p. 21.

" Egyptian reed " (with its hint of ' papyrus ' and ' Moses ')
suggests that the traditional English belief in the *literal* truth of
the Old Testament had been shaken by the new Biblical criticism.
Line 2 supports this theory by stating, under the symbols of
Christ (" vine " and " rood "), that Hopkins, like the Roman
Catholics, had deliberately turned from Old Testament to New
Testament aspects of Christian truth (e.g. " This is my blood of
the new testament, which is shed for many"). Line 4 refers to the
Last Supper : " Take, eat ; this is my body." The insistence on
"food" seems to indicate the Host, or Communion in one species.
The image of "four rough ways" is puzzling : to us it implies that
the poet, having reached the ' crossroads' on his spiritual journey,
found himself at the centre of the Cross—the Sacred Heart—Love.
That he had found comfort in the Eucharist received as the Real
Presence is stated in the third stanza, first as a paradox :

> " Love, when all is given,
> To see thee I must [see] thee, to love, love ; "

then more explicitly :

> " You have your wish ; enter these walls, one said :
> He is with you in the breaking of the bread."

Barely nine months after writing this poem Hopkins entered in
his journal (July 17, 1866) : " It was this night I believe but
possibly the next that I saw clearly the impossibility of staying in
the Church of England. . . ."

No doubt the ' essential Hopkins ' of 1865 is to be found in
these poems written under the influence of Herbert and Miss
Rossetti. Yet as though to correct the balance, another side of
his nature is revealed in the sequence of three sonnets which bears
the title *The Beginning of the End*. The theme is secular : the poet
confesses to a loved one that his love " is lessened and must soon
be past ", his passion is exhausted. The only direct evidence that
the love is sexual is in the last line of the fragment of another
sonnet, which immediately follows :

> " O worshipful the man that she sets higher."

The subject of this fragment is, however, quite different : it is the
consuming " shame " of the rejected lover.

The first and third sonnets of the sequence were eventually
revised and sent to Bridges, who subscribed, in MS. " A ", the
cryptic note : " These two sonnets must *never* be printed."
Because this injunction has dubious implications, we deem it
advisable to examine the relevant biographical data.

The spiritual diary of 1865 contains many confessional notes to the effect that Hopkins regarded himself as prone to the sins of gluttony, sloth, envy, pride, etc. ; and one of the lesser sins may be fairly described as an ' inordinate attachment ' to the physical beauty of choristers and certain of his fellow alumni. The suggestion of something vicious must be exorcised at once, for anyone who reads these notes without prejudice will feel that the scrupulosity of the man is at times almost comic. It certainly aggravated his nervous disease and fostered his spiritual anhedonia, though its final outcome was the perfect fusion of poetry and ethic in his mature verse. Already " mortal beauty " was " dangerous " ; but in our opinion there is nothing in these diaries to suggest, let alone prove, that Hopkins was tainted with any serious homosexual abnormality. (The question would not be raised here had it not been raised elsewhere by certain uninformed or misguided critics.) There is, on the contrary, one short, self-contained entry of 1865 (deleted, like all the rest of these confessional notes) in which Hopkins, with that unusual Christian candour which points to ultimate sanctity, records the sin of looking a little too long and admiringly at a certain married woman. Although he somewhat pedantically, but no doubt accurately, describes this sin as " adultery of the heart ", the really significant aspect of this unique entry is that it establishes Hopkins's physical normality as surely as it testifies to his spiritual earnestness.

At the same time there is no evidence that his erotic instincts were either deeply or lastingly stirred by any known woman. He could enjoy female company, as when he wrote :

> " We have four Miss Storys staying in the house, girls from Reading. This is a great advantage, but not to reading." [1]

Yet his attitude towards the sex was always one of calm or even severe critical detachment, as we see in his satirical verses on " Miss Story's character ", written in 1864 :

> " Miss Story has a moderate power of will,
> But having that believes it greater still,
> And hide it though she does one may divine
> She only nourishes a wish to shine.
> Is very capable of strong affection,
> Though apt to throw it in a strange direction ;
> Is fond of flattery as any she
> But has not learnt to take it gracefully. . . ." [2]

---

[1] *Further Letters*, p. 66.　　　[2] Hitherto unpublished.

The whole 32-line poem shows that Hopkins could deal with the foibles of women with something like the waspishness of Pope.

That Hopkins the undergraduate toyed imaginatively with erotic themes is proved by scraps of Catullan Latin verse and by a fragment in note-book C.I called " *A Lover's Stars* (a trifle in something like Coventry Patmore's style) ", which belongs to July 1864. In these verses, astrology is relieved by such lines as—

> " He meets her stintless of her smile
>   Her choice in roses knows by heart
>   Has danced with her : and all the while
>   They are Antipodes apart
>
> " His sick stars falter. More he may
>   Not win, if this be not enough
>   He meets upon Midsummer day
>   The stabbing coolness of rebuff.
>
> .   .   .   .   .   .
>
> " The other leaves the West behind
>   Or it may be the prodigal South,
>   Passes the seas and comes to find
>   Acceptance round his mistress' mouth " [1]

If we add to that last line one of his Latin couplets :

> " Quo rubeant dulcesve rosae vel pomifer aestas
>   Est rubor in teneris virginis ille genis ",[1]

we shall conclude that Hopkins at twenty was not entirely insensitive to the feminine graces.

To return to *The Beginning of the End* and the note by Bridges, we see no reason why the note should bear any derogatory interpretation. We cannot believe that Hopkins could be so devoted to any *man* as to write :

> " I cease the mourning and the abject fast,
>   And rise and go about my work again. . . ."

In this first sonnet the unreality of the passion is betrayed by a marked inconsistency of tone : the first seven lines imply that the person addressed will be grieved by the poet's defection ; the last seven lines do more than suggest that the recipient had been " unpassioned " from the beginning.

The evidence, both internal and external, leaves us free to suppose that the poems are not based upon an actual experience ; the emotional stimulus to " young man's fancy " (they were

[1] Hitherto unpublished.   Punctuation as in MS.

written in May 1865), was rather Elizabethan than experiential, for the second sonnet, with its astrological imagery, is an entirely factitious attempt to revive an archaic mode. The first, however, is interesting for the resemblance it bears to Drayton's " Since there's no help, come, let us kiss and part ". Hopkins too says " I have ceased to love you, yet— " ; and the *volte face* is almost Shakespearian in diction :

> " But ah ! if you could understand how then
> That *less* is heaver 3 higher even yet
> Than treble-fervent *more* of other men,
> Even your unpassioned eyelids might be wet."

The third sonnet and the fragment suggest another comparison —with George Meredith's sequence of sixteen-line ' sonnets ', *Modern Love* (1862). The psychological insight and wealth of detail presented in this gloomy domestic tragedy was certainly known to Hopkins, as we gather from a penitential note in the diary. In Hopkins's poem, the basis of actuality is lacking ; yet the following would not seem out of place in Meredith's sequence :

> " Else, I am well assured I should offend
> With fiercer weepings of these desperate eyes
> For love's poor failure than his hopeless rise.
> But now I am so tired I soon shall send
> Barely a sigh to thought of hopes forgone.
> Is this made plain ? "

The young poet's effort to make this plainer is a charming betrayal of immaturity :

> " What have I come across
> That here will serve me for comparison ?
> The sceptic disappointment and the loss
> A boy feels when the poet he pores upon
> Grows less and less sweet to him, and knows no cause." [1]

The similitude has truth ; but one feels that Hopkins was more concerned with Tennyson's diminished sweetness than with his own lost love.

To complete our account of the early secular poems we have to consider a lyrical monologue and then a lyrical ballad. *The Alchemist in the City* [2] (1865) is both direct and oblique. The alchemist, confined by a barren labour, yearns for a freer life unencumbered by worldly ambition. A recluse, he longs for an

---

[1] *Note-books*, p. 44, and *Poems*, Third Edition, No. 9.   [2] *Note-books*, p. 44.

easy familiarity with his fellow men ; but what he desires most
is a breath of wild nature :

> " the wilderness
> " Or weeded landslips of the shore."

The weeds and the wilderness were to reappear in *Inversnaid*
(1881) ; and as in the sonnet quoted above, winged creatures
are symbolic of that freedom and peace towards which the
spirit of man aspires :

> " I see the city pigeons veer,
> I mark the lower swallows run

> " Between the tower-top and the ground
> Below me in the bearing air ;
> Then find in the horizon-round
> One spot and hunger to be there."

This alchemist is an early projection of that personality " in
hiding " which was deeply moved by the behaviour of the
windhover ; and all his life Hopkins was possessed by this
symbol of the wild free bird.[1]   In the alchemist's craving for
" silence and a gulf of air " there is a universal emotion, something akin to Wordsworth's revulsion from an industrial world
which is too much with us.   The poem ends with a stanza which
might have been written by W. H. Davies :

> " There on a long and squarèd height
> After the sunset I would lie,
> And pierce the yellow waxen light
> With free long looking ere I die."

The Nightingale (1866) is Hopkins's nearest approach to the
Wordsworth of the *Lyrical Ballads*.   Its theme is the pathos of
love and death, and as in Wordsworth's *Ruth* and Dixon's *Love's
Consolation*, the effect is heightened by " influences of nature ".
The speaker, Frances, recalls her reactions to the singing of a
nightingale in the early dawn, when her sailor-lover, unheard
because of the " warbling bird ", is on his way to sea—and

---

[1] With the wildness is closely associated the idea of the homing pigeon, as in
The Deutschland (3), *Peace*, and *The Handsome Heart*. But in 1881 Hopkins tells Dixon
of a " noble passage " in Christina Rossetti :

> " As an Eagle, half strength and half grace
> Most potent to face
> Unwinking the splendour of light. . . ."

>   (*Letters*, vol. ii. p. 77 and Note H.)

death. The conclusion is something like one of Thomas Hardy's little ironies :

> " While he was washing from on deck
> She pillowing low her lily neck
> Timed her sad visions with his wreck."

The description of the nightingale's singing is simple and vigorous Wordsworth, with just that touch of mystery and macabre which R. W. Dixon sometimes affected :

> " ' For he began at once and shook
> My head to hear. He might have strung
> A row of ripples in the brook,
>   So forcibly he sung. . . .

> " ' I thought the air must cut and strain
> The windpipe when he sucked his breath
> And when he turned it back again
>   The music must be death.
> With not a thing to make me fear,
> A singing bird in morning clear
> To me was terrible to hear.' " [1]

Yet how much finer—more spacious and ' greater-Words-worthian '—are the seven stanzas of an untitled fragment of January 5, 1866 ! The opening is impressively mystical :

> " The earth and heaven, so little known,
> Are measured outwards from my breast.
> I am the midst of every zone
> And justify the East and West ;

> " The unchanging register of change
> My all-accepting fixèd eye,
> While all things else may stir and range
> All else may whirl or dive or fly."

Though this is, apparently, Hopkins speaking in his own person, it suggests a larger concept—that God, the κινῶν οὐ κινούμενος, is speaking through the person of Hopkins.

In the remaining stanzas the poet limns epigrammatic word-pictures of motion and change in bird, cloud, and stream :

> " In motion is no weight or pain,
> Nor permanence in the solid world "

—as Shelley might have sung. We feel the poet's intense participation in what his " fixèd eye " perceives ; we share the

[1] *Poems*, No. 79.

centrifugal urge of his spirit ; so that the Shelleyan unrest of the unrevised close is almost expected :

> " the streams are full
> And millbrook-slips with pretty pace
> Gallop along the meadow grass.—
> O lovely ease in change of place !
> I have desired, desired to pass . . ." [1]

The finished poems of 1866 are remarkably smooth and facile in rhythm and diction. Those which remain to be examined (all ' devotional ') fall into two groups. First there are poems like *Barnfloor and Winepress*, *Nondum*, and *Easter*, in which doctrinal matter, Biblical imagery, and relatively conventional meditation are welded, with fastidious talent rather than genius, into a polished formalism—a style which constitutes, for the poet, a technical *impasse*. As devotion, they are as nearly perfect as works of this kind can be ; but as poetry they are deficient. To this class belong also the anapaestic *Rosa Mystica* and the Swinburnean *Ad Mariam*, a poem which is by some critics rejected as uncanonical. The second group comprises a few poems of more marked individuality : *The Habit of Perfection* we have already cited ; [2] and something of the same personal quality—a sharpness of image and flexibility of rhythm—is to be found in the two published versions of *St. Dorothea*.

Barnfloor and Winepress [3] (begun in 1864) was printed in 1865, and we know from allusions to it in the *Letters* that Hopkins once thought highly of it. Motivated by the words of Jehoram, king of Israel, to his starving subject (" If the Lord do not help thee, whence shall I help thee ? Out of the barnfloor, or out of the winepress ? "), [4] the poem develops, with verve and symmetry, an elaborate figuration of the Passion and Blessed Eucharist :

> " Sheaved in cruel bands, bruised sore,
>   Scourged upon the threshing-floor ;
>   Where the upper mill-stone roof'd His Head,
>   At morn we found the heavenly Bread,
>   And on a thousand Altars laid,
>   Christ our Sacrifice is made."

---

[1] *Poems*, Third Edition, No. 97.
[2] See Vol. I. of the present work, chap. i. p. 15.
[3] In the *Union Review*, vol. iii. p. 579. See *Poems*, No. 78.
[4] 2 *Kings* vi. 27.

The divine conceits are as sincerely felt as second-hand imagery can be ; but the very neatness of the scheme and the tripping fluency of the metre make us wish for something of Herbert's intimacy or Crashaw's fine abandon, qualities that proceed from imagination rather than intellection. *Easter*[1] suffers, as poetry, from the same facility. Its images are either conventional—

> " Break the box and shed the nard. . . .
> Hither bring pearl, opal, sard. . . ."

or unconsciously borrowed :

> " Flowers do ope their heavenward eyes ".

Though a true Christian hymn of praise, it lacks the tender personal quality and rhythmic variety of Herbert's two Easter poems.[2]

In *Nondum*[3] (with its epigraph—" Verily Thou art a God that hidest Thyself.") we have further evidence that Hopkins's Catholicism was no facile emotional surrender. His religious experience before his conversion resembled that of Newman, whose *Lead, kindly Light* (also written just before the momentous step was taken) Hopkins had copied into his Journal in 1865.[4] The two poems are alike in the steady faith in God which underlies, and finally resolves, the doubts of a mind groping for " that sense beyond ". Newman cries, " One step enough for me " ; and Hopkins :

> " Speak ! whisper to my watching heart
> One word—as when a mother speaks
> Soft, when she sees her infant start,
> Till dimpled joy steals o'er its cheeks.
> Then, to behold Thee as Thou art,
> I'll wait till morn eternal breaks."

In its restrained earnestness, *Nondum* is the heart-cry of the sensitive, cultured, but quite ordinary Christian ; it provides an extraordinary contrast to the poems of ten years later—to the passion of *The Deutschland*, the rapture of *The Starlight Night*. In those ten years Hopkins had reached maturity not only in the creative mind but also in the spirit.

Turning to the two posthumous undated pieces, *Ad Mariam* and *Rosa Mystica*,[5] we find that the frankly conventional rhythmic

---

[1] *Poems*, No. 81. [2] *Easter* and *Easter Wings* (*The Temple*).
[3] *Poems*, No. 80. [4] *Note-books*, p. 52. [5] *Poems*, Nos. 84 and 85.

formalism of the 1866 poems has here reached its limit. *Ad Mariam* is rightly described by Bridges as " direct and competent imitation of Swinburne " ; so competent, indeed, is the imitation of a poet whom Hopkins always criticized with contemptuous severity that many critics refuse to believe that Hopkins would at any time have condescended to ape him.[1] We know, however, that between his entry into the Society of Jesus and 1875, Hopkins wrote " one or two little presentation pieces which occasion called for ", and also that it was the custom every May, at Stonyhurst, to write polyglot poems in honour of the Virgin Mary. *Ad Mariam* was printed in 1894 in the *Stonyhurst Magazine*, having been sent by a person who believed the poem to have been written in 1884.[2] But in that year Hopkins was already in Dublin,[3] and in the previous May he had written a very different poem for the " Month of Mary ".[4] It is far more likely that the correspondent was mistaken, and that *Ad Mariam* was composed during Hopkins's first stay at Stonyhurst (1870–3) ; for, as Bridges admits, it bears some resemblance to the " light lilting manner " of *Rosa Mystica*.

The autograph manuscript of *Rosa Mystica*,[5] with its careful emendations, testifies to the pious zeal with which Hopkins wrote it. In the handling of conventional sacred symbols, as in general method and style, it is akin to *Barnfloor and Winepress* ; there are, however, two interesting passages describing the Rose and its petals which anticipate images in stanza 22 of *The Deutschland*. The first is :

> " But what a wild flush on the flakes of it stood,
> When the Rose ran in crimsonings down the Cross-wood."

And the second :

> " How many leaves had it ? Five they were then,
> Five like the senses, and members of men ;
> Five is the number by nature. . . ."

This combination of lilting anapaests and serried alliteration

---

[1] E.g. Professor C. C. Abbott, the editor of the *Letters*, who says : " Only the discovery of a manuscript copy in his handwriting will begin to shake my unbelief." (*Letters*, vol. i. p. xvii. Note 2.)

[2] See *Poems*, p. 155, Note 84.

[3] From 1884 until his death in 1889, he was Professor of Classics in University College, Dublin. His first letter from Dublin is dated March 7, 1884.

[4] *The Blessed Virgin Compared to the Air We Breathe.*

[5] Preserved at Campion Hall, Oxford.

shows that Hopkins, like everyone else in the 'sixties and 'seventies, had felt the fascination of Swinburne's manner,—though Hopkins, more critical than most, fully realized its dangers and limitations. But granted the temporary fascination, we have no difficulty in believing that he wrote *Ad Mariam*, if only in the spirit which made General Booth ask, " Why should the Devil have all the good tunes ? " One can dislike a poet's ethic, despise his matter, and still admire his metre, or at least think it suitable for certain impersonal purposes. In writing a Marian poem for the Stony-hurst festal occasion, Hopkins's main desire would be to *please* : indeed, he made that very admission in relation to *The Blessed Virgin*.[1] That chorus in Swinburne's *Atalanta* which begins " When the hounds of spring are on winter's traces " was, metrically, well worth imitating [2] ; and if Hopkins did not write

" When a sister, born for each strong month-brother,
    Spring's one daughter, the sweet child May,
  Lies in the breast of the young year-mother
    With light on her face like the waves at play. . . ."

we should like to know what other Jesuit poet of the time had the sheer talent to do it. Such a man could not have remained entirely unknown in the Society.

In spite of the " positive objections of verbal criticism " (which Bridges, however, did not state in detail) [3] there is positive internal evidence that Hopkins did write *Ad Mariam*. First there is the line

" O thou, proud mother and much proud maiden— "

It would be difficult to find another Catholic poet or versifier who, in an age of Tennyson and syntactical decorum, would have written " much proud " ; yet in 1877 Hopkins wrote " much-thick and marsh air ".[4] Also there are characteristic phrases, like " wandering wondering breath ", " ruinous reigns ",[5] ' deep-groved Aidenn " (in his early poems, Hopkins frequently affected exotic proper names—Thecla, Pactolus, Libanus).

---

[1] *Letters*, vol. i. p. 179 :
    " It is partly a compromise with popular taste, and it is too true that the highest subjects are not those on which it is easy to reach one's highest."
[2] The same metre is used in *The Triumph of Time*.
[3] *Poems*, p. 102.
[4] *Poems*, No. 10. Cf. also *Richard* : " the *much* music of our Oxford bells."
[5] Cf. Swinburne in the *Atalanta* chorus :
    " For winter's rains and ruins are over . . .." (line 25).

Again, the following lines indicate the point at which Swinburne and the poet of *The Deutschland* meet, though for a moment only, before they part company :

> ' Wherefore we love thee, wherefore we sing to thee,
>   We, all we, through the length of our days,
> The praise of the lips and the hearts of us bring to thee,
>   Thee, oh maiden, most worthy of praise. . . ."

The prepositional genitives in line 3 are like

> " Let him easter in us, be a dayspring to the dimness of us "

in *The Deutschland*. Finally, this poet who thinks of Mary as " dew to grass and tree " may well be identical with the one who compares her to " the air we breathe ".

The truth is, surely, that the rhythm of *The Deutschland* owes much to Swinburne ; it might even be held, with reason, that a poet who had not started with some mastery of Swinburne's logaoedic metre could not have attained, at one leap, the more canorous rhythms in *The Deutschland*.

Tentative steps in the direction of a new and freer rhythm were taken in the later version of *Lines for a Picture of St. Dorothea*. The earlier *St. Dorothea* (1866 ?), which stands first in the Early Poems printed in the original and second editions, has daintiness and a Pre-Raphaelite charm of colour and image, together with something of that cunning simplicity (or naïve subtlety) which is common in Crashaw and is found also in such a poem as Marvell' *The Nymph complaining for the Death of her Fawn*. In order to make the present study complete we must borrow, with due acknowledgment, from Miss E. E. Phare,[1] who has already shown the affinity between Hopkins and Crashaw by placing together the last stanza of the shorter *St. Dorothea*, which describes the ' assumption ' of the virgin martyr, and the opening lines of Crashaw' *In the Glorious Assumption of Our Blessed Lady* :

Hopkins

> " Had she a quince in hand ?   Yet gaze :
>   Rather it is the sizing moon.
> Lo, linkèd heavens with milky ways !
>   That was her larkspur row.—So soon ?
> Spherèd so fast, sweet soul ?—We see
>   Nor fruit, nor flowers, nor Dorothy."

[1] *The Poetry of Gerard Manley Hopkins* (1933), p. 8.

CRASHAW

" Hark ! she is call'd, the parting hour is come ;
Take thy farewell, poor World, Heaven must go home.
A piece of heavenly earth, purer and brighter
Than the chaste stars whose choice lamps come to light her,
While through the crystal orbs clearer than they
She climbs, and makes a far more Milky Way.

.   .   .   .

Rise up, my fair, my spotless one !
The Winter's past, the rain is gone :
The Spring is come, the flowers appear,
No sweets, but thou, are wanting here."

Miss Phare has shown also how both versions of Hopkins's
St. Dorothea contain reminiscences of Massinger's play, *The Virgin
Martyr* ; for example :

" See my lilies : lilies none,
    None in Caesar's garden blow."
                            Hopkins (No. 82, st. 2).

" What flowers are these ?
In Dioclesian's gardens the most beauteous
Compared with these, are weeds ; is it not February
The second day she died ? "
                            (*The Virgin Martyr*, V. ii.)

The same critic accurately notes that " Massinger's metrical
effects and style . . . at once colloquial and involved " might
well have made him a writer who was congenial to Hopkins.[1]

In *Lines for a Picture of St. Dorothea* Hopkins made his first
serious attempt at a stress-metre, though the experiment hardly
justifies the name or forestalls the triumphs of the full-fledged
" Sprung Rhythm ". Lines here are marred by a clumsy and
artificial allocation of beats, as in

" Which is it, star, or dew ? "
" Served by messenger ? "

Yet in this poem we see the beginnings of his strong and individual use of alliteration, and there is promise of greater
directness and urgency in diction and image—the quality of the

[1] *Op. cit.* p. 68–9.

Journal jottings : as Theophilus gazes into " tufts of evening sky ",
he thinks—

> " It waned into the world of light,
> Yet made its market here as well :
> My eyes hold yet the rinds and bright
> Remainder of a miracle.
> O this is bringing ! Tears may swarm
> Indeed while such a wonder's warm."

Poetry of such force and vividness is little inferior to his mature
style : it may, indeed, be a fairly late revision.

Since the above study of the early verse was written, other
Hopkins manuscripts have come to light ; but the only English
verse which marks any development in poetic style is the almost
complete translation of Horace's *Odi profanum volgus et arceo*,[1]
which was made at Edgbaston between '67 and March '68. The
rhythm is still " standard ", but the diction is vigorous and
individual from the start :

> " Tread back—and back, the lewd and lay !—
> Grace guard your tongues !—what never ear
> Heard yet, the Muses' man, to-day
> I bid the boys and maidens hear."

Hopkins tackles his poet like a lion-tamer : there is nothing of
the well-bred parrot in this :

> " Kings herd it on their subject droves
> But Jove's the herd that keeps the kings—
> Jove of the Giants : simple Jove's
> Mere eyebrow rocks this round of things."

With an anvil-ding, he forges Horace into current English idiom
—suitably heightened :

> " Who stops his asking mood at par [2]
> The burly sea may quite forget
> Nor fear the violent calendar
> At Haedus-rise, Arcturus-set. . . ."

He can charm us with an unpardonable obscurity :

> " Fish feel their waters drawing to
> With our abutments : there we see
> The lades discharged and laded new
> And Italy flies from Italy."

Without the original, who would associate that with the building
of a Roman seaside villa ?

[1] *Odes*, III. i.   [2] " desiderantem quod satis est. . . ."

There may be a significance in the fact that at the very time when he was hopefully awaiting " a vocation to the priesthood ", Hopkins translated two Horatian odes [1] which praise the simple life.

We have watched the 'prentice hand, and followed the uneasy twistings and turnings of an ardent spirit and versatile mind, both bent on finding their true form of poetic expression. So far there has been much conscious and unconscious imitation. We have reviewed a number of passages and a few completed poems which have a high poetic value ; but apart from one poem, *The Habit of Perfection*, nothing that is supremely individual. Many of the note-book fragments contain interesting ' field-work ' —first impressions and rough sketches for later occasions on which the poet's full powers and resources could be utilized. We have to remember also that better poems or more worthy versions of existing fragments may have been burnt in 1867 or otherwise lost. With Hopkins, however, there was to be a second and more auspicious beginning—a thing which rarely happens to an artist after his thirtieth year. To the stylistic origins and prototypes of that new beginning we shall now turn.

[1] The other was *Persicos odi, puer, apparatus* (*Odes*, I. xxxviii.). See *Poems*, Third Edition, Nos. 128–9.

N.B. Three more early verse-fragments by G. M. H. have come to light since the proofs of this volume were passed. For the sake of completeness, a Postscript covering this new material has been added at the end of the Appendices (p. 404).

CHAPTER II

THE NEW RHYTHM—I

IN tracing the lineage of Hopkins's poetic rhythms, we shall remember that to him ' rhythm ', in practice if not always in theory, included something more than the principles which govern the pitch, force, and duration of spoken syllables : it was, in short, something more than mere prosody or metric. As we have seen in our examination of *The Wreck of the Deutschland*,[1] the quality and incidence of vowels and consonants—what we have called tone-values, and the subtle relations between sound, sense, and feeling, all go to build up a poetic instrument of great variety and expressiveness, a forceful yet flexible " rhetoric of poetry ". The isolation of purely prosodic elements is valuable and, indeed, necessary up to a point ; but when we are estimating the total effect of all the rhythmic elements, not only in Hopkins but also in his traditional prototypes, we find that the relations between prosody and such devices as alliteration, assonance, rhyme and the repetition of word and phrase must be constantly emphasized.

In the following pages we shall give special prominence to those poetic forms and modes which, from the Greek poets onwards, must have exerted a direct influence upon Hopkins. As far as possible, we shall use his own words to point an illustration or corroborate an inference. At the same time, we shall indicate less direct influences, and adduce parallels from certain poets and schools with which Hopkins, so far as we know, was either not familiar at all or only partially familiar. It is sometimes difficult to say just at what point ' influence ' ends and ' coincidence ' begins ; yet the element of coincidence is often much smaller than would appear from the known evidence ; for at any given time certain ideas may be ' in the air ' without being specifically recorded, and may be spread by some opportune allusion or by the general contagion of cultured intercourse. In any case, our purpose is to consider Hopkins's contribution to poetic tradition historically and, as it were, *sub specie aeternitatis* ; to show that any reader of 1889 (when Hopkins died), provided

[1] See Volume I. chapter ii.

he possessed both the necessary knowledge of the European poetic tradition and the ability to make the required synthesis, could have recognized Hopkins's ' new rhythm ' as a bold, original and sincere reforging of universal modes and experiences.

We begin with the direct influence of Greek poetry, with which Hopkins, as student, teacher and professor, was at all times deeply conversant.

It was not until he was Professor of Greek at Dublin (1884–9) that he began in earnest his researches on the origin and nature of the Dorian and Aeolian rhythms ; and the " great and solid discovery " which he then made and upon which he hoped to complete a " sizeable book ", introducing mathematics, meta-physics, and " stiff reading ", was that

> " The Dorian rhythm, the most used of the lyric rhythms, arises from the Dorian measure or bar. The Dorian bar is originally *a march step in three-time executed in four steps to the bar*." [1]

Whatever was written of this work has unfortunately not survived. The " great discovery ", moreover, is now numbered with the many discredited theories. We have, in the *Letters*,[2] an example of this musical principle applied to Greek lyric in the setting of Sappho's *Ode to Aphrodite* " barred as for Dorian Rhythm " ; there is also among the unpublished papers a musical scansion, made at Dublin, of certain lines from one of Pindar's odes. It is important because it shows that Hopkins read Greek lyric verse with a somewhat arbitrary system of stressing :

$$\text{'}\epsilon\kappa \ \sigma\epsilon\theta\epsilon\nu\cdot \ \zeta\dot\omega \ | \ \epsilon\iota \ \delta\epsilon \ \mu\acute\alpha\sigma\sigma\omega\nu \ | \ \text{``}o\lambda\beta os \ \text{'}o\pi\iota \ | \ \zeta o\mu\acute\epsilon\nu\omega\nu \ \pi\lambda\alpha\gamma\acute\iota \ \|$$

$$\text{Γ Γ} \ \alpha\iota s \ | \ \delta\grave\epsilon \ \phi\rho\acute\epsilon\nu\epsilon\sigma\sigma\iota\nu \ \| \ (= \text{-}\alpha\iota s \ \delta\grave\epsilon \ \phi\rho\acute\epsilon\nu\epsilon\sigma\sigma\iota\nu).[3]$$

In spite of our ignorance of the rules governing stress in Greek verse, the obvious resemblances between Hopkins's rhythms and Greek lyric metres can be explained only by taking into account the natural ictus or oratorical stress with which the latter have usually been read by Englishmen. In his Preface to the *Poems*, Hopkins declared that Greek and Látin lyric verse " are in sprung rhythm " ; so that any inferences we may draw from a reading

---

[1] *Letters*, vol. i. p. 233 ; cf. *Further Letters*, p. 231 (May 1887).

[2] *Ibid.* p. 239.

[3] MS. Note-book at Campion Hall, Oxford. It is line 7 of *Isthmia* iii. ; lines 15–16 are similarly scanned.

of Greek metres which assumes a rhythmic beat on certain (usually long) syllables will at least be in keeping with Hopkins's own theory and practice.

It has been suggested that Hopkins, when conceiving his " new rhythm ", may have been influenced by Dr. J. H. H. Schmidt's *Griechische Metrik* (1872).[1] He mentions Schmidt in 1886, and uses his system in describing his own theory of Dorian rhythm ; [2] but since the American translation of this work was not published until 1878 (and there is no evidence that Hopkins knew the work, either directly or indirectly, before that date), it cannot be assumed that the elaborate rationalizations of Schmidt had any share in moulding Hopkins's ideas on rhythm before 1875. Nevertheless, as Professor Tierney of Dublin has already pointed out, there is a striking resemblance between Hopkins's theory of sprung rhythm and Schmidt's " determined effort at fitting Greek quantitative metres into accentual rhythmic phrases ".[3] Schmidt's representation, for instance, of a whole foot by one prolonged syllable, as in the " syncopated trochee $(\boxed{})$ " or the " syncopated spondee $(|\underline{}|)$ ", is equivalent to Hopkins's statement of 1879, that one of his monosyllabic feet has, in a sense, absorbed the slack syllables that normally accompany the stress.[4] Sprung rhythm is, in effect, a syncopated rhythm, and stands in the same relation to the regular syllabic metres as the prevalent syncopation of modern dance music stands to the regular musical rhythm.

Professor Tierney seems to be near the truth when he says :

" Whether or not Hopkins was influenced by Schmidt's work in the ultimate formulation of his theory, there seems every likelihood that his practice was influenced by his own profound acquaintance with the poetry of which Schmidt's work was a particular metrical interpretation." [5]

The subtle rhythmic effects in Greek lyric, as noted and described by such recent investigators as Headlam and Thomson, were

[1] See *Times Lit. Supplnt.*, Correspondence, Feb. 16, 1933, and next three issues. Schmidt's system has been made familiar, since the 'eighties, in Jebb's editions of Sophocles.

[2] *Letters*, vol. i. p. 233.   In MS. " A " there is a translation by Hopkins into Greek Dorian rhythm of the song " Orpheus with his lute made trees ", together with a metrical scheme which is headed : " Dorian rhythm, syncopated, and with triplets in resolution."   The metrical notation used is that of Schmidt.   See below, Appendix B, p. 393, and *Poems*, Third Edition, No. 141 (vii) and Note.

[3] *Times Lit. Supplnt.*, Feb. 16, 1933.

[4] See Vol. I. of the present work, p. 45 ; also *Letters*, vol. i. pp. 233-4.

[5] *Times Lit. Supplnt.*, Correspondence, March 9, 1933.

at least practically known to Hopkins through the ear ; and when it is a question of rhythm, the ear of a true poet needs no theoretical bush.

Hopkins's " new rhythm " was largely intuitive in origin. Nevertheless, Professor Tierney is right when he demurs to Mr. Herbert Read's further claim that " the virtue of Hopkins's theory of sprung rhythm is that it justifies every departure from *regularity* of rhythm ; it justifies, in fact, free rhythm." [1]   As Professor Tierney says, sprung rhythm has its own laws, and " an analysis would show a remarkable similarity between Hopkins's metres and those of a Greek ode." [2]

Greek lyric poetry was closely allied to music ; and nothing is more natural (as Thomson says) than that the poets, who were also musicians, should have revealed in their poetry a musical technique.   But Hopkins too was a lover of music and an amateur composer ; he was also, like his contemporary Sidney Lanier in America,[3] a poet deeply interested in " the science of versification ", and his prosodic theories, especially in later life, were always closely bound up with his musical theories.[4]   Unfortunately, these musical theories were never very clearly enunciated ; but the first quality that strikes the reader of *The Wreck of the Deutschland* and *The Leaden Echo and the Golden Echo* is their affinity with music.   As the poet himself said of the latter, " I never did anything more musical " ; and as we have already noted, one critic has gone so far as to say that with Hopkins, as with Verlaine, it was always " la musique avant toute chose ".[5]

Much of this musical effect was due to the influence of the complex or accumulated rhythm ($\mu\acute{\epsilon}\tau\rho\text{o}\nu$ $\acute{\epsilon}\pi\iota\sigma\acute{\nu}\nu\theta\epsilon\tau\text{o}\nu$) of Greek melic poetry.   Hopkins himself calls them " individual metres " :

> " that is / invented for the occasion, one ode, as in Pindar, or even one ' system ', as in the dramatists and not repeated even by the inventor, much less others : "

[1] See Mr. Herbert Read's letter, *Times Lit. Supplnt.*, Feb. 23, 1933.

[2] *Loc. cit.*

[3] For a brief account of Lanier in relation to Hopkins, see Appendix C.

[4] E.g. " I wish I could pursue music ; for I have invented a new style, something standing to ordinary music as sprung rhythm to common rhythm : it employs quarter tones.   I am trying to set an air in it to the sonnet ' Summer ends now '." (*Letters*, vol. i. p. 103.)   See Appendix A.

" There is room . . . for a freer musical time and a stricter verse-prosody " (*ibid.* p. 120).

[5] J. Middleton Murry, in *The Athenaeum*, June 6, 1919 ; reprinted in *Aspects of Literature* (1920).

He then links them up with his reading of Scotus :

> " these are called εἴδη ; they are *in specie infima* and in fact *in specie individua*." [1]

His constant preoccupation with these metres is revealed in a confession of 1882 ; he has just been praising Aeschylus, and adds :

> " But what I pay most attention to is the art of the choric parts, for this was one of the subjects on which I had proposed to write, the art of the Greek lyric poets, including of course the lyric parts of the dramatic poets." [2]

The work which Hopkins failed to complete has been carried out, in part at least, in such a book as Thomson's *Greek Lyric Metre*,[3] an exposition which explains admirably many of those aspects of the Greek " individual metres " which bear the most striking resemblance to the rhythms of Hopkins. In dealing with the relative freedom of Greek lyric measures, Thomson says :

> " The modern composer invents his phrases as he goes along. Bound by no convention, he gives free rein to his fancy, and the only authority to which he owes obedience is his ear. So to some extent with the Greek poet ; he too is at liberty to invent phrases of his own if he pleases." [4]

At the same time the Greek poet possessed, in common with his audience, a large stock of metrical phrases which had become stereotyped by constant usage. The phrase was the true rhythmic unit—a combination of two or more of the seven basic types of quantitative feet ; [5] and the variety of rhythmical design allowed by the numerous permutations and combinations of these feet afforded the Greek choric poet a much greater freedom, in both tempo and diction, than any English poet before Hopkins had ever enjoyed. We must set against this advantage, however, a fact to which Thomson does not give sufficient weight when he is discussing the " characteristic ", " imitative ", or expressional rhythms of Greek lyric—the fact that the poet was obliged by

---

[1] MS. Note-books G1 and 1(a), at Campion Hall, Oxford ; from Notes on Bergk's *Poetae Lyrici Graeci*, made at Dublin.
[2] *Letters*, vol. i. p. 150.
[3] Cambridge University Press, 1929.
[4] *Greek Lyric Metre*, p. 6.
[5] See *Rhythm and Other Structural Parts of Verse* (*Note-books*, pp. 227-31).

convention to make the metre of the *strophe* agree with that of the *antistrophe* ; for this reason, many of the effects which Thomson attributes to deliberate intention will be thought by some scholars to be merely happy accidents.

The four main types of rhythmical phrase—the Dorian, the Ionian, the Aeolian, and the Paeonic—were skilfully used by Pindar and the dramatists to express certain specific moods, actions, and reflections. These modes of " significant rhythm " were introduced like the *leitmotif* of Wagnerian opera. Dorian prosodiacs and epitrites, for instance, with their strong rhythm of dactyls and trochees, typified the manly Dorian virtues, 'the exploits of the Greeks, Zeus and the other austere gods. The Ionian phrases, with their initial short syllables, induced a feeling of something softer, more exotic, sentimental and feminine. A slightly modified form of the Dorian dactylo-epitritic is the Aeolian couplet which, together with the Aeolian tripody, was traditionally associated with love or marriage : it was also used to suggest sensuous beauty or exalted reflection, as in the first line of Pindar's first Olympian ode :

Ἄριστον μὲν ὕδωρ, ὁ δὲ χρυσὸς αἰθόμενον πῦρ

In the next verse, a " quick " dochmiac (with second syllable resolved) contrives an easy transition to the more plangent Dorian :

ἅτε διαπρέπει νυκτὶ μεγάνορος ἔξοχα πλούτου· [1]

In Greek, says Hopkins,

" scanning is by time and rhythmic beat, that is beat belonging only to the rhythm-words, not to the sense-words." [2]

In the same passage from the lecture notes on Rhetoric (written before *The Deutschland*), Hopkins expresses his belief that the word-accent, which was probably tonic, disappeared in chanting ; that " emphatic accent " was weak and disappeared also unless, as often happened, it agreed with the beat of the verse. In later life, his adherence to the bar-theory would often lead him to

---

[1] Thomson : *op. cit.* chap. vi. Translation : " Best of all is water ; and gold, as blazing fire at night, shines out, beyond compare the brightest treasure of lordly wealth." (See also *Rhythms and their Characters* in *Note-books*, p. 230.)

[2] *Note-books*, p. 237.

stress short syllables more freely than a modern metrist like
Thomson would ; but although we cannot say *precisely* what the
above verses meant either to a Greek of 472 B.C. or to Hopkins
in 1874, there is enough evidence to show that just as Swinburne,
in his vigorous mixture of accentual trochees and dactyls, owed
much to these variable choric metres, so Hopkins too found in
them the prototype of his own more complex sprung and
" logaœdic " rhythms.

The full flavour of sprung rhythm is found chiefly in the
Paeonic phrases of Pindar's ode, with their undulating (or
" rocking ") bachii and cretics and their quick, strenuous,
polysyllabic paeons—phrases which are so suitable for excited,
agitated and dithyrambic utterance :

μηδ' Ὀλυμπίας ἀγῶνα φέρτερον αὐδάσομεν·
ὅθεν ὁ πολύφατος ὕμνος ἀμφιβάλλεται
σοφῶν μητίεσσι κελαδεῖν.
Κρόνου παῖδ' ἐς ἀφνεὰν ἱκομένους
μάκαιραν Ἱέρωνος ἑστίαν.[1]

This passage from the first strophe gives out a rhythmic
theme which is taken up and intensified in the corresponding
part of the antistrophe, where the speed of Hiero's racehorse is
suitably characterized by the many short syllables—

ὅτε παρ' Ἀλφεῷ σύτο δέμας
ἀκέντητον ἐν δρόμοισι παρέχων,
κράτει δὲ προσέμιξε δεσπόταν . . .

(. . . when by the Alpheüs he ran, giving his body ·ngoaded in
the course, and brought victory to his master.—ll. 20–22.)

Thomson shows with what skill and apparently conscious
purpose Pindar could shift the metre from a falling to a rising
rhythm and back again, in accordance with corresponding shifts
in the sense and feeling of the words : " These delicate transitions

---

[1] *Olympia*, I. ll. 7–11. The stressing, which may seem arbitrary, is based upon
Thomson's system.   He gives the "quick" dochmiac as ◡ ◡ ◡ _́ ◡ _́ or
◡ _́ ◡ ◡ ◡ _́ (*op. cit.*).   Translation : " Neither shall we proclaim any games
mightier than the Olympian ; whence comes it that the glorious hymn enters the
minds of minstrels, so that they celebrate the son of Kronos, when to the rich and
happy hearth of Hiero they are come."

of rhythm are to my mind the most beautiful features of the poem." [1] He then quotes :

Aeolian couplet : δαμέντα φρένας ἱμέρῳ χρυσέαισιν ἀν ἵπποις
Love

Dorian : ὕπατον εὐρυτίμου ποτὶ δῶμα Διὸς μεταβᾶσαι,
Olympus

Aeolian : ἔνθα δευτέρῳ χρόνῳ⎫
trochaic   ⎬Festivity [2]
pherecratic : ἦλθε καὶ Γανυμήδης⎭

—and so on to the Paeonic μαχαίρᾳ τάμον κατὰ μέλη.

A similar passage is to be found in the fourth strophe, where the Love—Valour—Festivity motives are followed by the hurrying tribrachs of Πέλοπος, ἵνα ταχυτὰς ποδῶν ἐρίζεται. [3] Pindar's bold dithyrambics seemed to Horace what Hopkins's verses seemed to Mr. Read—the work of an impetuous genius :

numerisque fertur | lege solutis. [4]

Yet Jebb says of Pindar's odes what Hopkins, in effect, frequently said of his own poems : " Each is a work of the most elaborate and complex art, calculated and refined to the smallest detail." [5]

On reading The Echoes, Bridges accused Hopkins of being unduly influenced by the free rhythms of Walt Whitman. At considerable length, Hopkins repudiates the suggestion of imitation : Whitman's long lines, like his own, are in irregular rhythms, but " there the likeness ends ". He maintains with truth, and with a misquotation tries to demonstrate, that the dozen poems of Whitman he has read are in " an irregular rhythmic prose ". What the Echoes are really like, he adds,

[1] Op. cit. p. 80. Cf. Jebb : " But the comparison between the Pindaric ode and the oratorio . . . turns on those rapid transitions from one tone of feeling to another, from storm to calm, from splendid energy to tranquillity, from triumphant joy to reflection or even sadness, which in Pindar are so frequent and so rapid that they are reconciled with art only by the massive harmonies of rhythm and language which hold them together. . . . Pindar himself could hardly have made them in any modern tongue." (Greek Lyric Poetry, 1893, p. 159.)

[2] Ll. 41–44. (" . . . his heart vanquished by love, [he bore thee] in his golden chariot to the house of august Zeus, whither in after time came Ganymede.")

[3] " [courses] of Pelops, where there is rivalry in swiftness of foot."

[4] Odes IV. ii. ll. 11–12 (" and he sweeps along in rhythms freed from law ").

[5] Op. cit. p. 161.

5*

" is the rhythm of Greek tragic choruses or of Pindar ; which is
pure sprung rhythm. And that has the same changes of cadence
from point to point as this piece. If you want to try it, read one
till you have settled the true places of stress, mark these, then
read it aloud, and you will see. Without this these choruses are
prose bewitched ; with it they are sprung rhythm, like that
piece of mine." [1]

In actual fact, the rhythm of the *Echoes* is something entirely
new : it has not the exact strophic form of the Greek, yet it is
further removed than Whitman's from the rhythm of prose—
even ' numerous ' prose. As Hopkins says, " Extremes meet, and
the savagery of Whitman's art comes near the last elaboration of
mine " ; but the *Echoes*, he claims, are " very highly wrought
. . . everything in them is weighed and timed ".[2] The difference
in rhythm, moreover, is emphasized by further distinctions in
diction, syntax, and phonal ' texture '.

    The Leaden Echo begins on a marked " trochaic " base : in
the first four lines, for instance, twenty-eight out of the forty-
two feet are accentual trochees ; of the remainder, five are
paeons, and four of these, by the concession of a secondary
stress to the third syllable, may be considered prosodically as
double-trochees :

" How to keep—is there any any, is there none such, nowhere
        known some, bow or brooch or braid or brace, lace, latch
        or catch or key to keep
    Back beauty, keep it, beauty, beauty, beauty, . . . from
        vanishing away ?
    Ó is there no frowning of these wrinkles, rankèd wrinkles deep,
    Down ? no waving off of these most mournful messengers, still
        messengers, sad and stealing messengers of grey ? " [3]

In MS. " A ", certain syllables are made to carry a stronger
ictus (marked ″) ; but although both *Echoes* range freely through

---

[1] *Letters*, vol. i. pp. 154–57.   [2] *Ibid.*, vol. i. p. 157.
[3] In the following scansion of these lines, 1–4, the oratorical ictus (˅) and the
musical pause on " lace " are taken from MS " A " :

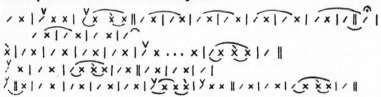

the whole gamut of monosyllabic, dactylic, and paeonic variations (the sense-groups falling frequently into both "rising" and
"rocking" rhythm), they hark back continually to the original
trochaic base :

> ". . . loose locks, | long locks, | lovelocks, | gaygear, | going-
> gallant, | girl grace— | "

It is this feeling of a fixed base or centre, however wide the
incidental departures from it, which gives to Hopkins's irregular
poems (*Binsey Poplars*, *The Echoes*, *Epithalamion*) a more pronounced *poetic* rhythm than is to be found in the majority of
Whitman's. As Saintsbury said in a review which Hopkins
mentions, Whitman's rhythm is " many-centred ; it takes fresh
departures as it goes on." [1] Hopkins admits that Whitman's
" savage " style has advantages ; but he insists also on the
sacrifice :

> " You cannot eat your cake and keep it : he eats his off-hand,
> I keep mine. It makes a very great difference."

He does not deny all resemblance : he notices in *Spirit that
Form'd this Scene*, Whitman's preference for the alexandrine : " I
have the same preference : I came to it by degrees, I did not
take it from him." [2] Again, we observe that Whitman is constantly breaking out into lyrical passages which are *rhythmically*
as much like a Greek tragic chorus as anything in Hopkins :

> " Come, lovely and soothing Death,
> Undulate round the world serenely arriving, arriving,
> In the day, in the night, to all, to each,
> Sooner or later, delicate Death." [3]

He has short bursts of Hopkinsian alliteration, exclamation,
diction : " Life immense in passion, power, and pulse " ; " Far
breath'd land ! Arctic braced ! Mexican breez'd ! " [4] Moreover, in the second passage quoted above from *The Golden Echo*,
as elsewhere in the same poem, we have something like the
Whitmanesque " prose-recitative ", the extended catalogue of
names, places, attributes, etc. In Hopkins, however, the catalogue
is not a prosaic suspension of the lyrical rhythm : it is essentially
part of that rhythm.

---

[1] *Letters*, vol. i. Note P, p. 315.   [2] *Loc. cit.* p. 157.
[3] *Death-Carol* from *President Lincoln's Burial Hymn* ; see Saintsbury, *loc. cit.*
[4] *One's-self I sing* and *Starting from Paumanok* (*Leaves of Grass*).

Both poets were clearly influenced by the rhythms of the Bible in English ; but whereas in Hopkins the similarity to Biblical style is mainly in imagery and parallelism, in the grouping and presentation of ideas, in Whitman the division into versicle and the general march of the rhythm indicates a much more palpable derivation. Hopkins was right in giving Greek choric metre priority as the prototype of *The Echoes* ; but there was also much probability in the suggestion made by Bridges, that the immediate stimulus provided by Whitman's original contribution to English rhythm was greater than Hopkins himself had suspected. Saintsbury's important review of *Leaves of Grass* appeared in *The Academy* in October 1874, an intensely formative year (as we shall see) in the development of Hopkins's theories on poetic rhythm and diction. Speaking, in 1882, of the little he had read of Whitman, he says :

> "This, though very little, is quite enough to give a strong impression of his marked and original manner and way of thought and in particular of his rhythm. It might be even enough, shall not deny, to originate or, much more, influence another's style." [1]

According to Thomson, the reading of a Greek chorus is mainly a test of one's feeling for semantic rhythm ; the method is the same, apparently, as in reading Whitman :

> "If we may assume that the rhythm of the music followed the rhythm of the words, then the surest way of discovering the metre of Greek lyric is to read it according to the sense. Recite it aloud, marking the natural pauses and word groupings, the climaxes and the cadences, which the sense of the words dictate to the understanding, and the ear will grasp the rhythm. . . ."
> "The dominant factor in the rhythm of Greek lyric is *the natural rhythm dictated by the sense of the words*." [3]

In dealing with Greek metres Hopkins did not assume so much as Thomson does as regards the conformity of the musical rhythm to the semantic rhythm ; [4] yet Thomson's ruling for the reading of Greek lyric is fundamentally the same as that required for the best reading of Hopkins's Counterpointed, Mixed, and Sprung Rhythms ; it brings out that rhythmic quality which is lacking in Whitman and in all " free verse "—the subtle interplay and conflict between the metrical pattern and the natural speech

---

[1] *Letters*, vol. i. p. 154. [2] *Op. cit.* p. 4.
[3] *Ibid.* p. 26. [4] See above, pp. 102-5.

mphasis. It is this quality which builds up the most complex
nd satisfying poetic rhythms.

In Greek lyric, the words may be so grouped " as to break
cross the outlines of the metrical pattern, thus creating a
hythmical undercurrent, as it were, of their own ".[1] When this
endency of spontaneous utterance is controlled by the poet we
et the rhythmical devices called *Echo*, *Overlap*, and *Concurrence*.
The following examples are interesting anticipations of Hopkins's
ontrolled variations in counterpointed and sprung rhythm.

Echo is heard in :

πέφανται δ' ἐκτίνουσ'

ἀτολμήτων ἀρὴ

πνεόντων μεῖζον ἢ δικαίως

φλεόντων δωμάτων ὑπέρφευ

ὑπὲρ τὸ βέλτιστον. ἔστω δ'ἀπή-

μαντον, ὥστ' ἀπαρκεῖν

εὖ πραπίδων λαχόντα

The trochaic movement is first heard as an undercurrent beneath
he undulating rhythm of the bachii and cretics, and then
beneath the rising rhythm of the dochmiacs ; but presently it
emerges as an independent phrase, and so affords an easy transi-
ion to the falling rhythm of the final pherecratic.[2] Hopkins,
of course, does not produce his effects with regular syllabic
quantities and conventional phrases ; his aim was to produce
something *like* the Greek subtlety and flexibility by using all the
resources of popular English rhythms. We may compare with
the above the constant re-emergence of the trochaic beat in *The
Echoes* and *Spelt from Sibyl's Leaves*. In the latter poem especially
the final predominance of the " trochee " is a masterpiece of
rhythmic virtuosity.[3]

Overlap is a device for effecting a transition from one metre to
another, and rises when certain syllables are simultaneously
heard as the conclusion of one phrase and the beginning of
another in a different mode. *Overlap*, however, reaches its highest
point of development

> " in a continuous contrapuntal effect, in which two different
> rhythms are made to run side by side for the duration of several
> phrases. This may be called *concurrent* rhythm." [4]

[1] Thomson, *ibid.* p. 26.
[2] *Agamemnon*, ll. 385–91, or Loeb edn. ll. 374–80. (See Thomson, *op. cit.* pp. 27–8.)
[3] See Vol. I. of the present work, pp. 104–5.
[4] Thomson, *op. cit.* p. 30.

In the following example from the *Prometheus Vinctus* [1] it will be noticed how the Anacreontic phrase breaks across the Iambo-choriambic colometry :

Iambo-choriambic

μηδὲν   φοβηθῇς   φιλία

Ana-

Iambo-choriambic

γὰρ ἤδε τάξις   πτερύγων

creontic   *Ana-*

Iambo-choriambic

θοαῖς ἁμίλλαις   προσέβα

creontic

Pherecratic

τόνδε   πάγον,   πατρῴας

Iambo-choriambic

μόγις παρειποῦσα φρένας.

Two lines further on, the Iambo-choriambic and Anacreontic counterpoint begins again :

κτύπου γὰρ ἀχὼ χάλυβος
διῆξεν ἄντρων μυχὸν, ἐκ δ'ἔπληξέ μου.

Both phrases are indispensable to the design—the Iambo-choriambic because it forms the basis of the metrical pattern, the Anacreontic because the natural grouping of the words demands it :

φιλία γὰρ ἤδε τάξις
πτερύγων θοαῖς ἁμίλλαις . . .

Moreover, in the whole strophe the pherecratic cadence, twice in its simple and twice in its extended form, is skilfully worked in for variety, e.g.—

. . . μυχόν, ἐκ δ'ἔπληξέ μου
τὰν θεμερῶπιν αἰδῶ·
σύθην δ'ἀπέδιλος ὄχῳ πτερωτῷ.

[1] Lines 128–32, or Loeb edn. ll. 127–31. Translation : " Be not alarmed ! For this our band hath come in winged rivalry of speed unto this crag in love to thee, having won our sire's consent as best we might."

The distinctive feature of the passage as a whole, says Thomson, is its lack of phrase-pauses :

> " Before we approach the end of one phrase we are carried on by the beginning of the next. The effect is undulating. Could Aeschylus have devised a happier rhythmical accompaniment to the flight of his Ocean Nymphs as they ride through the air on their winged sea-horses ? " [1]

Nothing so precise and elaborate as this is possible in English poetry, which has no traditional rhythmic phrases ; but a form of *Concurrence* is to be heard in that passage already quoted from *The Deutschland* :

> " Ah, touched in your bower of bone
>
>   Are you ! turned for an exquisite smart,
>
> Have you ! . . ."

The metrical pattern is rising or " anapaestic " ; the natural grouping of the words, the semantic or speech rhythm, is falling or " dactylic :

> " . . . touched in your bower of bone are you !
>
>   turned for an exquisite smart have you ! " [2]

This contrast and tension between the basic metre and the speech rhythm is, of course, to be found in all good English poetry ; but outside the freer yet strictly controlled rhythms of Hopkins, we rarely find anything approaching the " beautiful variety " and " infinite flexibility " of the Greek lyric forms.

Thomson analyses with subtlety that chorus in the *Agamemnon* which is in some ways a parallel to the storm and stress of *The Deutschland* and *The Eurydice* : it is the passage which tells how bad weather delayed the Greek ships at Aulis, and how the seer pronounced the cruel remedy.[3] The trochaic opening of the antistrophe is followed by a second subject—

εὖτ᾽ ἀπλοία κεναγγεῖ βαρύνοντ᾽ Ἀχαιϊκὸς λεώς

---

[1] *Op. cit.* p. 31. Cf. also *Electra* (ll. 1058–62). In the *Ajax* (ll. 695–701) Sophocles compounds Anacreontic with Glyconic.

[2] Cf. stanza 31, in lines 1 and 3 of which *Concurrence* is set up by the reverse process of " borrowing " syllables from lines 2 and 4.

[3] *Agamemnon*, ll. 194 *et seqq.* See Thomson, *op. cit.* p. 107. Translation (Loeb edn., ll. 187–92) : " . . . what time the Achaean folk, on the shore over against Chalcis in the region where Aulis' tides surge to and fro, were sore distressed by opposing winds and failing stores ; and the blasts that blew from the Strymon, bringing them grievous leisure and hunger, keeping their ships at anchor. . . ."

in which a suggestion of bacchii and iambics is made to run counter to the cretic and trochaic figures :

εὖτ' ἀπλοία κεναγγεῖ βαρύ-   — ◡ — | — ◡ — | — ◡ —
νοντ' Ἀχαϊκὸς λεώς   — ◡ — | ◡ — ◡ —

" The effect is not merely to retard the rhythm ; we have here a direct anticipation of the rising rhythm in the next strophe ", a dochmiac movement for which the ear has been prepared by scattered dochmiacs in earlier sections.   Here again the words break across the phrasing with peculiar felicity :

dochmiac	dochmiac
πνοαὶ δ'ἀπὸ | Στρυμόνος | μολοῦσαι	
κακόσχολοι, νήστιδες, δύσορμοι	

The rhythm is expressional or " imitative ".   Thomson asks :

> " Does not this straining effect, this tense struggle between dochmiac and trochaic, suggest as clearly as rhythm can the straining of the ropes as the fleet lies at anchor, pitching and rolling in the storm ? "

Not all prosodists will agree with Thomson's method of aesthetic criticism, especially when he speaks of " slow-moving, ominous trochees " and " barbarous spondees " ; but Hopkins, we believe, would have assented to the above examples and conclusions, since they illustrate a conception of poetic rhythm which was substantially his own.

Abraham Cowley, who (to Dr. Johnson's disgust) " sometimes attempted an improved and scientific versification ", hoped to achieve in English something like the flexible, " characteristic " rhythms of Pindar and the Greek dramatists.   Having written the line—

> " Some from the rocks cast themselves down headlong,"

he adds, in a note :

> " The thing is that the disposition of the words and numbers should be such, as that, out of the order and sound of them, the things themselves may be represented." [1]

The line, as we see, is pure sprung rhythm.   Similarly, in his own way, Dryden attempted, in *Alexander's Feast*, an approximation

[1] See Johnson's *Life of Cowley* (*World's Classics*, vol. i. p. 52.)   Yet, as the sequel shows, Cowley was ostensibly imitating Virgil, not the Greek poets.

to the variety and flexibility of the Greek ode ; yet neither he
nor his most notable successors—Gray (in *The Bard* and *The
Progress of Poesy*) and Wordsworth (in the *Immortality Ode*) made
any drastic break with conventional metre. Dryden, Gray, and
Campbell were all admired by Hopkins for their individual
handling of rhythm ; but it was Milton whom he called
" master ". Although " the Pindarique way " had been
practised by Ben Jonson and Cowley, Hopkins regarded the
calculated irregularities of Milton's verse as the first significant
attempt to achieve the rhythmic felicity of Greek and Latin
verse.[1]

Robert Bridges, in his searching study of Milton's prosody,
says that Milton's admiration of Dante's rich rhythms was the
main cause of his own. To prove this, Bridges cites the universal
synaloepha (or vowel elision) and the frequent inversion of the
accent in the *Commedia* ; inversion in the second foot, for example :

> " Són le léggi d'Abísso cósi rótte ? "
> " Dónna scése del ciel, &c." [2]

Similar inversions of the relatively sensitive second and fourth
feet are fairly common in the Miltonic epics.

Hopkins, however, links up Milton with the earlier Latin
poets. At least thirteen years before Bridges's first essay " On
the Elements of Milton's Blank Verse (1887), Hopkins, in his
lecture notes on Rhetoric, had traced the development in Latin
from accentual to quantitative verse, and had remarked that
" Latin accent was probably both tonic and emphatic. It plays
an important unacknowledged part in Latin verse . . . by way
of counterpoint." [3] Later, in his fourth rule for avoiding " the
monotony of bare rhythm ", he says :

> " In Latin, accent was marked and was made use of by the
> poets, especially the great masters of metre, as Horace and
> Ovid, to give a counterpoint beat by which they produced
> forms, as especially the Latin pentameter and Sapphic, though
> less flexible more organic than the corresponding Greek ones or
> any others perhaps."

[1] Cf. " I have paid a good deal of attention to Milton's versification and collected
his later rhythms. . . . I found his most advanced effects in the *Paradise Regained*
and, lyrically, in the *Agonistes* " (*Letters*, vol, ii. pp. 13–4).

[2] *Milton's Prosody* (1921), pp. 115–16. But Hopkins had already quoted Dante and
Tasso for the same purpose in *Note-books* (Lecture Notes), p. 237.

[3] *Note-books*, p. 237.

He then discusses a difficulty about the " working of the word-accent and the verse-accent together ", and from this conflict he deduces counterpoint :

> " The counterpoint of the pentameter is commonly this—
>
>   ·/   ·/ ·/ ·/ ·/ ·/
>
> Cum mala per longas convaluere moras

This divergence between the metrical and the speech rhythms he illustrates with a diagram :

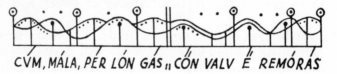

After further illustrations, including a Sapphic verse :

> " In English Milton made experiments in accentual counterpoint, as—
>
>   /   /   /   /   /
>
> ' Home to His mother's house private returned.' " [1]

In the *Samson Agonistes* choruses, this principle becomes an elaborate system of " imitative " rhythm. Milton's basic rhythm is the conventional syllabic metre with the accentual iamb ($\times$ ‑) as the standard foot : free variation of line length, and the frequent fiction of dactylic movement, do not disguise the essentially " iambic " basis of the verse. Yet the opening of the first chorus is as near to the Greek lyric rhythm as non-quantitative English verse could be :

> " This, this is he ; softly awhile,
> Let us not break in upon him.
> O change beyond report, thought or belief !
>
> See how he lies at random, carelessly diffused,
> With languish't head unpropt. . . ." [2]

The choriambic or " rocking " rhythm of the first line is followed by a perfect four-foot line in falling rhythm. Then comes a

[1] *Note-books*, pp. 239–41. See Vol. I of the present work, p. 230, Note 2.

[2] Bridges shows how, in the first seventeen lines (" as an example "), the rhythm of each line exactly imitates or describes the content : e.g. line 4 : " describing great Samson stretched on the bank, it describes itself ". (*Op. cit.* pp. 62–3.)

change to the standard rising rhythm, broken by the choriambic inversion in line 3 and the suggestion of dactyl and paeon in line 4 :

" Sée how he lies at random, carelessly diffused.

This " mounting " of a second rhythm upon a clearly stated basic metre is what Hopkins called Counterpointed Rhythm.   In the *Samson* choruses, however, the reversed feet occur most thickly at the beginning of a passage ; hence Hopkins complains that Milton

> " does not let the reader clearly know what the ground rhythm is meant to be and so the choruses have struck most readers as merely irregular." [1]

Again, he says :

> " The choruses of *Samson Agonistes* are intermediate between counterpointed and sprung rhythm.   In reality they are sprung, but Milton keeps up the fiction of counterpointing the heard rhythm (which is the same as the mounted rhythm) upon the standard rhythm which is never heard but only counted and therefore does not really exist." [2]

It is difficult to agree with Hopkins ; for out of nearly five hundred lines of choric utterance, there are not more than *forty* which show unusual or complete substitution of falling rhythm for the standard rising rhythm, the rhythm of all the other seventeen hundred lines in the play.   Hence, in spite of occasional lines which move, like Dalila, " with doubtful feet and wavering resolution ", the ground rhythm is clearly retained in the mind. Although Hopkins was the first to discover the rhythmic principle of these choruses, it is Bridges who, in the final analysis, is the surer guide.[3]

An examination of Hopkins's theory and practice of Counterpointed Rhythm has already been made in Volume I of the present work.[4]   The task in hand is to indicate those elements of

---

[1] *Poems* (2nd edn.).   Author's Preface, p. 3.

[2] *Letters*, vol. i. pp. 45-6.

[3] The question as to how far, if at all, Milton was influenced, or stimulated, by the stress-rhythm of Old and Middle English alliterative verse can only be a matter of unprofitable speculation.   That he knew the substance of *Caedmon* through the Junius MS. is certain ; but that he was able to read Old English is not certain.

[4] Chapter iii.

rhythm which Hopkins could have assimilated directly from Greek and Latin poetry.

This brings us to the consideration of *quantity* as a positive and controlled factor in English poetic rhythm :

> " But for the εὖ εἶναι of the new rhythm great attention to quantity is necessary. And since English quantity is very different from Greek or Latin, a sort of prosody ought to be drawn up for it, which would be of wider service than for sprung rhythm only." [1]

We have already seen how " the strength (or gravity) and length " of syllables affects the rhythmic beat in *The Deutschland* ; in this same letter Hopkins makes some elementary comments on the relative lengths of *bidst*, *bids*, and *bid*, on the value of voiced and voiceless consonants, as in *bid* and *bit* : indeed, the data for the " prosody " he desiderates is to be found in any good primer of English phonetics.   But when he says :

> " You will find that Milton pays much attention to consonant-quality or gravity of sound in his line endings ; indeed, every good ear does it naturally more or less / in composing," [2]

he seems to admit that prosody-making of the kind suggested is not a poet's concern and may perhaps be a superfluity.

He discusses quantity with as much academic seriousness as Bridges wrote classical hexameters to test the theories of William Johnson Stone :

> " My quantity is not like ' Fĭftў-twō Bĕdfŏrd Squāre ', where *fĭftў* might pass but *Bĕdfŏrd* I should never admit. Not only so but Swinburne's dactyls and anapaests are halting to my ear : I never allow e.g. *I* or *my* (that is diphthongs, for *I* = a + i . . .) in the short or weak syllables of those feet, excepting before vowels, semi-vowels, or *r*, and rarely then, or when the measure becomes amphibrachic—thus : ◡ – ◡ | ◡ – ◡ | ◡ – ◡ |, for then the first short is almost long." [3]

The censure of Swinburne is not justified by the critic's own impeccability, for in *The Deutschland* we find :

> " Carrier-witted, I am bold to boast," (stanza 3)

Now according to the poet's prosody of stress and quantity, the

[1] *Letters*, vol. ii. p. 41. See also *Note-books*, pp. 225-6.   [2] *Ibid.*
[3] *Letters*, vol. i. p. 44. (For " amphibrachic " Hopkins wrote " molossic ".)

second foot is to be condemned as a *heavy* paeon. Similarly, in a line by Bridges :

" My hedges of rose and woodbine, with walks between ",[1]

Hopkins finds " woodbine, with " a " heavy dactyl ". The truth is that both lines are satisfying rhythmically ; for in each case the comma introduces a new sense-group with a natural and pleasing change to rising rhythm.[2] Strict Sprung Rhythm, says Hopkins, does not properly allow of counterpoint, " because its great variety amounts to a counterpointing ". There we have it : both the above lines " amount to a counterpointing ", and the quantities are justified by the strictly oratorical rhythm.

When Hopkins declares to Bridges :

" In fact all English verse, except Milton's, almost, offends me as *licentious* ",[3]

we must take this apparent smugness rather as a gesture of irritated idiosyncrasy than as an important criticism. In his mature poems, Hopkins observed syllabic quantity with as much aural precision as a good poet, working on an accentual basis, can be expected to ; his guiding principle was not an elaborate prosody but the " auditory imagination " assisted by the scholar's respect for classical rule and the experience of other poets. It is this instinctive feeling for syllabic quality which enabled Cowley to say :

" Brass was his helmet, his boots brass, and o'er
His breast a thick plate of strong brass he wore." [4]

Or Coleridge :

" On the other side it seems to me
Of the huge broad-breasted old oak tree." [5]

And Hopkins :

" Furred snows, charged tuft above tuft, tower. . . ." [6]

Hopkins was no slavish imitator of Greek metric ; but we may fittingly conclude this section by noticing how frequently

---

[1] *The Voice of Nature (Letters*, vol. ii. p. 81).

[2] Bridges's line may, indeed, be scanned as rising rhythm :

Cf. " Bridges in the preface to his last issue says . . . that all sorts of feet may follow one another, an anapaest a dactyl, for instance . . . : so they may. . . ." (*Letters*, vol. ii. p. 40).

[3] *Letters*, vol. i. p. 45.   [4] Quoted by Johnson (*Life of Cowley*).

[5] *Christabel*.   *Penmaen Pool* (*Poems*, No. 5).

his Sprung Rhythm echoes some of the standard rhythmic phrases of Greek lyric.   That he was aware of this resemblance is proved by a remark in a letter to Dixon :

> " It is the virtue of sprung rhythm that it allows of ' dochmiac ' or ' antispastic ' effects or cadences." [1]

The antispast is heard in such forceful phrases as " the heart's cheering ", " with sighs soaring " ; the dochmiac in " Of pied and peeled May ", " of thoughts sour as blood ", or again, varied, in describing the ash-bough combs that creep " Apart wide and new-nestle at heaven most high." [2]

The odes of Pindar employed chiefly the Dorian and Aeolian modes ; similarly *The Wreck of the Deutschland*, which was to some extent modelled on Pindar, has a basic rhythm which resembles a blending of these two modes, with the Paeonic mode worked in for certain effects.   The dactylic tripody or prosodiac is fairly common :

> " Read the unshapeable shock night " (29)
>
> " Ears, and the call of the tall nun " (19)

Aeolian rhythms—Glyconic, pherecratic cadence, and the tripody—are frequent in the four- and three-stress lines :

> " Fells or flanks of the voel, a vein " (4)
>
> " Though : felt before, though in high flood yet—" (7)

The following also, heard as Glyconic rhythms, illustrate the principle of Equivalence—a point on which Hopkins felt very strongly : [3]

> " Starlight, wafting him out of it ; and " (5)
>
> " Do, deal, lord it with living and dead " (28)

[1] *Letters*, vol. ii. p. 40.   Cf. *Note-books*, pp. 231 and 233.

[2] See *Poems*, Nos. 4 (stanza 26), 36, 58 (p. 78), and 56.   Since there is no fixed scale of quantities in English verse, the quantities marked here, and below, are approximate and relative.

[3] " I cannot but hope that in your metrical Paper [later to become *Milton's Prosody*] you will somewhere distinctly state the principle of Equivalence and that it was quite unrecognized in Milton's time and still more in Shakespeare's time. All, but especially young students, need to be made clearly to understand what metrical Equivalence is, that it is in use in English now, and that it was not then— and that it was Milton's artifices, as you explain them, that helped to introduce it." (*Letters*, vol. i. p. 259).   (Bridges treats Equivalence in *op. cit.* p. 16.)

The pherecratic is heard in

> "Mark, the mark is of man's make" (22)
> "From life's dawn it is drawn down," (20)

and the Aeolian tripody in

> "Dead to the Kentish Knock;" (14)

or in a beautiful antispastic variation:

> "And storms bugle his fame." (11)
> "O world wide of its good!" (20)

The same figure repeated makes two effective alexandrines in *St. Winefred's Well*:

"My heart, where have we been? | What have we seen, my mind?"
"What have we seen? | Her head, sheared from her shoulders, fall,"

Hopkins was particularly fond of the cretic foot:

"Trenched with tears, carved with cares," (No. 4, stanza 15)
"What is sound? Nature's round" (No. 6)
"Day and night I deplore" (No. 17)

Further, the quantitative εὖ εἶναι of Sprung Rhythm is assisted by the molossus:

> "Unchrist, all rolled in ruin—" (No. 17)
> "Too late; lost; gone with the gale." (No. 17)

—by the bacchius:

> "As sheer down the ship goes." (No. 17)

—by the rising and falling Ionic, the choriambus, and the so-called reizianum:[1]

"Of the Yore-flood, of the year's fall;" (No. 4, stanza 32)
"More bright(e)ning her, rare-dear Britain, as his reign rolls,
"Pride, rose, prince, hero of us, high-priest," (4, 35)
"Burden, in wind's burly and beat of endragoned seas." (do. 27)

[1] I.e., — | — ◡ ◡ — | ⏑. It is heard in:
Glow, glory in thunder (No. 4, stanza 5).

Hopkins has himself made an interesting comment on this kind of rhythm in Greek lyric :

> " Pindar and all the poets continually pass from heavier feet, like $-\smile$ — — or $\smile\smile$ — —, to lighter, — $\smile\smile$ —, where by the stress falling sometimes on a long or crotchet, sometimes on a short or quaver, a beautiful variety is given, and the variety is further enhanced by making an imperfect Ionic follow a chori-ambus, thus : — $\smile\smile$ — | $\smile\smile$ —, by which a dactylic cadence is given but with the stress falling on different syllables of the dactyls. With all this the rhythm came to have an infinite flexibility, of which the Greeks seem never to have tired." [1]

As we have already stated, we are attributing a wider mean-ing to the term ' poetic rhythm ' than is customary with the prosodists. Hopkins was profoundly influenced by the *metres* of both Greek and Welsh classical poetry ; he was influenced hardly less by the *syntax* of both schools.[2] This is no mere coin-cidence, for in the more complex expressional rhythms there is a subtle relationship between the *auditory* rhythm and the *semantic* rhythm (the internal rhythm of thought).

The Greek and Latin poet enjoyed an enviable freedom in being able to place his words just where rhythm, emphasis, and tone-pattern required them. The Welsh and English poets, lacking the advantage of full inflexions, had greater difficulty in securing the emotional intensity of poetry without violating too drastically the grammatical conventions of prose.

The view of poetic language expressed by a recent critic is highly relevant to the practice of Hopkins :

> " Prose progresses gradually and cumulatively through a continuous series of propositions. . . . Poetry, however, over-riding the intermediate connexions of grammar, tends to fuse its separate and scattered statements into a complicated and instantaneous whole. It is ' esemplastic ', to use Coleridge's word. The parts of a poem must be read against a background of awareness of the whole." [3]

The merit of Gray's famous inversions, apart from the fact that they may evince a psychological or dramatic *logic*, lies in the necessity they enforce of seeing the part in relation to the whole. They are not due to mere metrical convenience ; and the smoother early poems of Hopkins make it clear that the tortuous turns of

[1] *Letters*, vol. i. p. 234.
[2] For the Welsh influence, see the next chapter, pp. 143–58.
[3] F. W. Bateson in *English Poetry and the English Language*, p. 18.

his later syntax have nothing to do with this trivial motive.   Both poets, like Milton before them, were trying to rejuvenate English poetic language with an infusion of Greek and Latin flexibility.

Imagination, the esemplastic power, as Coleridge calls it, manifests itself in Greek and Latin poetry (especially the former) through an esemplastic syntax—a syntax that shapes the whole thought or concept into a unified mode of utterance, welding beginning, middle and end so that each receives light and heat from the other two simultaneously.

The elastic freedom of the Greek intellect, says Jebb, is reflected in the " flexibility and plastic power " of the Greek language ; [1] and just as Latin writers like Catullus, Horace, and Tacitus adopted Greek grammatical modes to secure greater terseness, variety, or even mere novelty,[2] so a deep knowledge and love of Greek undoubtedly helped to shape Hopkins's genius for subtle and idiosyncratic expression.[3]

That " spontaneity of consciousness " which Matthew Arnold found in all Hellenism ; [4] the rapid and excitable nature of Greek verse, together with that instinct " pervading and archi-tectonic " which ensures restraint and repose—these are qualities which are equally characteristic of Hopkins.   Combined with what Bridges calls " the magic of melodious expression ", Hopkins has also the Greek instinct for emphatic condensation.   Yet Greek economy and intensity were not conspicuous qualities in English verse of the later nineteenth century.   It is significant that three lines of the *Agamemnon* :

> κρίνω δ'ἄφθονον ὄλβον
> μήτ' εἴην πτολιπόρθης
> μήτ' οὖν αὐτὸς ἁλοὺς ὑπ' ἄλλων βίον κατίδοιμι [5]

had to be rendered by Lewis Campbell (1897) in a passage three times as long :

> " Mine be the moderate lot
> That envy blasteth not !
> I would not run the royal conqueror's course
> Nor yet would I be conquered, and behold
> The life I shared of old
> Subdued to strangers, and my country's folk
> Writhing beneath an alien yoke."

---

[1] *Growth and Influence of Classical Greek Poetry*, pp. 266–7.

[2] E.g. Catullus, iv. i. 2 ; Horace, *Odes*, ii. 9 17, and iii. 27, 73.

[3] Cf. Bridges : " He was flattered when I called him περιττότατος, and saw the humour of it " (*Poems of G. M. H.*, p. 99).

[4] *Culture and Anarchy* (Cambridge, 1932), p. 132.   [5] Lines 471–3.

That such verbosity was typical of the age has been clearly proved
by Mr. F. W. Bateson.[1]

Hopkins was not the first English scholar-poet to be influenced
by Greek syntax. Milton's exotic constructions were more often
of Latin origin, but he imitated the terse and adaptable participial
form in Greek :

" To thee first, reverend Manoah, and to these
My countrymen, whom here I knew remaining. . . ." [2]

Similarly a phrase like Pindar's

θεὸς ὁ πάντα τεύχων βροτοῖς.
Literally : " God, the all-things-creating for men "

almost certainly inspired the original opening of *The Deutschland* :

" Gód mastering mé
Gíver of bréath and bréad ; "

and no less the more clearly 'instressed' final version :

" Thóu mastering mé
God ! gíver of bréath and bréad ; " [3]

Of the two borrowings, Milton's is the more obscure. That of
Hopkins is more organic, for it combines with alliteration and
stress to determine the force and direction of the total complex—
the new rhythm. A reader familiar with the Greek construction
(and even one who is not) has little difficulty in appreciating the
peculiar felicity of Hopkins's departure from normal English
idiom.

Hopkins appears to have been impressed by an aspect of
Greek syntax which was also noted by Schmidt. Having said
that Greek, on account of its many short syllables, could be
pronounced with great rapidity and ease, Schmidt adds :

" This is also seen in the fact that the pause between the
single words was very short and that consequently an entire
sentence sounded, in comparison with an English sentence,
almost like a single word."

Much of this is dogmatic, but this " single word " immediacy is

[1] *Op. cit.* pp. 123-4. Mr. Bateson contrasts Cory's diffuse *Heraclitus* with Mackail's
concise version of the same Greek poem.
[2] *Samson Agonistes*, l. 1549.   [3] The alteration occurs in MS. " A ".
[4] *Griechische Metrik*, trans. J. W. White, Boston, 1878 : p. 8, § 4.

a Greek quality which Hopkins strove to achieve more assiduously than any other English poet. A sentence like :

$$\mu\acute{\alpha}\nu\tau\iota\varsigma \ \ \check{\epsilon}\kappa\lambda\alpha\gamma\zeta\epsilon\nu \ \pi\rho o\phi\acute{\epsilon}\rho\omega\nu \ \ \ \H{A}\rho\tau\epsilon\mu\iota\nu \ \ \H{\omega}\sigma\tau\epsilon \ \ \chi\theta\acute{o}\nu\alpha \ \beta\acute{\alpha}\kappa-$$
$$\underline{\tau\rho o\iota\varsigma \ \ \epsilon\pi\iota\kappa\rho o\acute{u}\sigma\alpha\nu\tau\alpha\varsigma \ \ \underline{{}^{\prime}A\tau\rho\epsilon\acute{\iota}\delta\alpha\varsigma}} \ \ \delta\acute{\alpha}\kappa\rho\upsilon \ \mu\grave{\eta} \ \epsilon\pi\alpha\sigma\kappa\epsilon\hat{\iota}\nu,[1]$$

in which a whole phrase is the equivalent of a single word, may have suggested to Hopkins the strangeness and intensity of " the wimpled-water-dimpled, not-by-morning-matchèd face " and of

> " are you that liar
> And, cast by conscience out, spendsavour salt ? " [2]

In one of Pindar's odes we read :

$$\dot{o}\rho\theta\grave{\alpha}\varsigma \ \delta^{\prime}\alpha\ddot{\upsilon}\lambda\alpha\kappa\alpha\varsigma \ \dot{\epsilon}\nu\tau\alpha\nu\acute{\upsilon}\sigma\alpha\iota\varsigma$$
$$\H{\eta}\lambda\alpha\upsilon\nu^{\prime}, \ \dot{\alpha}\nu\grave{\alpha} \ \beta\omega\lambda\alpha\kappa\acute{\iota}\alpha\varsigma \ \delta^{\prime} \ \dot{o}\rho\acute{o}\gamma\upsilon\iota\alpha\nu \ \sigma\chi\acute{\iota}\zeta\epsilon \ \nu\hat{\omega}\tau o\nu$$
$$\gamma\hat{\alpha}\varsigma.$$

" Straight and the furrows (he) stretching
drove, up- (of clodded) and a fathom's length -ripped a ridge
of earth." [3]

A barbarous literal translation such as this, which plunges like a ploughshare through the conventional concords and juxtapositions of English, produces on ear and mind an effect not unlike that of Hopkins's bold individuating or 'inscaping' of rhythms and images in a passage on the same theme :
> " See his wind- lilylocks -laced ;
Churlsgrace, too, child of Amansstrength, how it hangs or hurls
Them—broad in bluff hide his frowning feet lashed ! raced
With, along them, cragiron under and cold furls—
> With-a-fountain's shining-shot furls." [4]

The tmesis in the first line (with its rapid flutter of l's), the artfully jumbled words which, on analysis, reveal a tendency to conglomeration on the one hand (to express the co-ordination of muscular effort) and to disintegration on the other (to suggest $\dot{\alpha}\nu\grave{\alpha} \ \beta\omega\lambda\alpha\kappa\acute{\iota}\alpha\varsigma \ \sigma\chi\acute{\iota}\zeta\epsilon \ \nu\hat{\omega}\tau o\nu \ \gamma\hat{\alpha}\varsigma$), the strangeness of a compound like " with-a-fountain's " (a kind of fusion of Greek dative and genitive cases)—all these make such a passage caviare to the plain reader ; it should, however, stand a good chance of

---

[1] *Agamemnon*, ll. 201–2. Translation : " the seer proclaimed, urging Artemis (as cause), so that the *earth-with-their-staves-smiting-sons-of-Atreus* stifled not their tears ".
[2] *Poems*, Nos. 36 and 26.   [3] *Pythia*, iv. ll. 227–8.
[4] *Harry Ploughman* (*Poems*, No. 43).

acceptance by the sensitive reader of Greek lyric, for the syntactical problem is one that he has already faced :

> " Most of the difficulties of Pindar's *Odes* arise from his rapidity and fulness of thought, which often seem to have made him sacrifice the formal expression of the connexion of his ideas. Their vividness of presentment and rapidity of sequence interfered with the precise indication of their mutual relations. On the other hand, whenever poetic instinct aims at exhibiting concisely and gracefully the subtle connexions of ideas, a different class of difficulties arises comprising in the main mixtures of construction, and complicated, involved sentences." [1]

When we turn from the syntax and semantic rhythm of Greek poetry to its *texture* we find again certain characteristics which are, in varying degrees, reproduced in Hopkins as in no other English poet. By texture we mean those phonal devices like alliteration, assonance, consonantal patterns and vocalic scales, by means of which subsidiary rhythms are set up within the larger metrical structure and the semantic rhythm is often considerably strengthened. These textural qualities contribute to Dryden's " third happiness of the poet's imagination—*elocution*, the art of clothing and adorning thought in apt, significant and sounding words." [2] Hopkins uses the word *rhetoric* in a similar manner :

> " The universal fault of our literature is its weakness in rhetoric. The strictly poetical insight and inspiration of our poetry seem to me to be of the very finest, finer perhaps than the Greek ; but its rhetoric is inadequate—seldom first rate, mostly only just sufficient, sometimes even below par. By rhetoric I mean all the common and teachable element in literature, what grammar is to speech." [3]

In his *Lecture Notes on Rhythm and Other Structural Parts of Rhetoric—Verse*,[4] Hopkins defines and partially illustrates these phonal devices under the title " Lettering of Syllables ", thereby clearly implying that these are among the " teachable " elements of poetry. It is also obvious that he is not using the term " rhetoric " in the sense in which it is commonly applied to such works as Addison's *Cato*, or, at a higher level, to much of Byron. This explanation of " rhetoric " as a teachable element is perhaps misleading : it may be argued that ultimately the ability to express poetic insight in apt, significant and sounding

[1] C. A. M. Fennell : *Pindar's Olympian and Pythian Odes* (1893), Intro. p. xxi.
[2] Preface to *Annus Mirabilis*.
[3] *Letters*, vol. ii. p. 141.   [4] *Note-books*, pp. 221-48.

words depends upon the "auditory imagination", and in its authentic manifestation is as much a gift of nature as insight or vision. Yet Hopkins was right in implying, by his own practice and precept, that English poetry could learn much from poetic languages of richer texture, like the Greek, the Latin, and the Welsh.

Marsh was voicing a commonplace of the schools when he said that in Greek and Latin poetry, owing to the large amount of assonance and rhyme forced upon the poet by inflections, repetition of sound was, whenever possible, "sedulously avoided". Yet when we look closely at Greek poetry, we find that the poet often plays with rare effect on phonal repetitions :

> Σύν μοι πῖνε, συνήβα, συνέρα, συστεφανηφόρει,
> Σύν μοι μαινομένῳ μαίνεο, σὺν σώφρονι σωφρόνει.[1]

That, as a specimen of 'popular' verse, is as compact and resonant as a piece of Hopkins. Even in Pindar alliteration and the juxtaposition of identical syllables are admitted for effect : πολὺν ὗσε χρυσόν; δίδοι τέ Ϝοι αἰδοίαν; λαχοῖσαι, αἵτε ναίετε; ἕλε βελλεροφόντας; οὔ τί που οὗτος.[2] Similarly the terseness and charged quality of dramatic dialogue is frequently enhanced by an assonance partly enforced, partly modulated and artfully exploited by the poet. Ismene asks :

> ἦ γὰρ νοεῖς θάπτειν σφ', ἀπόρρητον πόλει;
> (What, wouldst thou bury him—a thing forbidden to the city ?)

to which Antigone replies :

> τὸν γοῦν ἐμὸν κοὐ τὸν σόν, ἢν σὺ μὴ θέλῃς
> ἀδελφόν.[3]
> (Yes, *my* brother and not *thine*, unless thou wish it.)

The latter speech is a compact improvisation on two sounds, ον and η; and in the first speech ει is not "sedulously avoided". In effect it is similar to Shakespeare's

> "If it were done when 'tis done then 'twere well
> It were done quickly."

and

> "What we would do
> We should do when we would." [4]

---

[1] An anonymous scholion, cited by Athanaeus, XV. 695, D.
[2] *Odes* : Olym. 7, 7, 14, 13 ; Pyth. 4.   [3] *Antigone*, ll. 44–6.
[4] *Macbeth* I. vii. 1 ; *Hamlet* IV. vii. 118. Of the former passage Hopkins says : "How fine it is everybody sees and nobody disputes." (*Letters*, vol. i. p. 50.)

In the following we hear a distinct progressive harmony of consonants, vowels, and diphthongs, an effect which Hopkins calls " vowelling on " and " vowelling off ", and of which, he says, Euripides was a master :

> Ζεῦ Ζεῦ τέλειε, τὰς ἐμὰς εὐχὰς τέλει·
> μέλοι δέ τοί σοι τῶνπερ ἂν μελλῇς τελεῖν.[1]

In his lecture notes, Hopkins observes that alliteration was used " very thickly in Latin verse, more sparingly in Greek " ; but he must have noticed the frequency of both assonance and alliteration in Sophocles : the rhetorical verve of lines like

> Ποίαντι πατρὶ πρὸς πάτρας Οἴτης πλάκα.
> ἃ δ' ἂν λάβῃς σὺ σκῦλα τοῦδε τοῦ στρατοῦ[2]

played some part in the subsequent fashioning of

> " I caught this morning morning's minion, king-
> dom of daylight's dauphin, dapple-dawn-drawn falcon. . . ."

How frequently too does Hopkins contrive a striking correspondence between the tone-values and the meaning of a passage, as Sophocles does in the words of the disillusioned Oedipus :

> οἷον ἄρά με
> κάλλος κακῶν ὕπουλον ἐξεθρέψατε.
> νῦν γὰρ κακός τ' ὢν κἀκ κακῶν εὑρίσκομαι[3]

The repetition of κα emphasizes the antithesis of κάλλος κακῶν, and expresses the king's disgust and self-loathing : its continuation in κἀκ κακῶν certainly seems deliberate.

An extract from the *Antigone* will serve to recapitulate what we have said about the Greek threefold influence on Hopkins— imitative rhythm, esemplastic syntax and significant tone-values :

> ὅμοιον ὥστε ποντίαις
> οἶδμα δυσπνόοις ὅταν
> Θρῄσσαισιν ἔρεβος ὕφαλον ἐπιδράμῃ πνοαῖς,
> κυλίνδει βυσσόθεν κελαινὰν
> θῖνα, καὶ δυσάνεμοι
> στόνῳ βρέμουσιν ἀντιπλῆγες ἀκταί.[4]

Agamemnon, ll. 973-4.   [2] *Philoctetes*, ll. 1430-1.
[3] *Oedipus Tyrannus*, 1394-6. Translation : " How seeming fair was I your nursling, and what ills were festering beneath ! Now as an evil thing, stemming from evil, I stand revealed." Cf. in Hopkins, *Poems*, Nos. 29 (ll. 13-14) ; 34 (ll. 3-4) ; 36 (*passim*) ; 43 (sestet) ; 45 (ll. 9-11).
[4] Lines 586-92. Translation : " Like as, when the surge before the fierce Thracian blasts courses over the darkness of the deep, and rolls up from the depth the black sand, and the wind-vexed cliffs, repelling the shock, resound with a groan."

Citing this passage, a correspondent in the *Times Literary Supplement* has said :

> " The actual wording of Hopkins's poetry greatly resembles that of the Greek choruses, and particularly those of Sophocles. Sophocles gets his effects very largely by a heaping together of words whose syntactical connexion is comparatively unimportant." [1]

We may note besides how the separation of πνοαῖς and its three epithets (which are also associated with οἶδμα) binds the whole fervid description into a single " poetic word ", and at the same time produces the effect of confusion, the rough and tumble of waves.[2] Metrically, there are the rapid short syllables in line 3 (which Phillimore, most Hopkinsian of translators, renders :

> " Blasts of Thrace rude-blowing urge,
> Runs over the unilluminable abysses creaming : ") [3]

The speed and unity of the Greek is emphasized by the almost complete absence of punctuation : the mind must sweep on, like a sea-surge, to overtake the meaning. There is a constant suspense and suspension in thought ; the gathering emotion is buoyed up and driven forward as on a wave. Such is the effect of esemplastic syntax.

The texture is enriched by vocalic and consonantal repetitions. There is the assonance or " vowelling on " of οι in lines 1 and 2 ; αι occurs six times in as many lines. There is deliberate repetition, with " vowelling off ", in δυσπνόοις—πνοαῖς-δυσάνεμοι ; [4] and an ominous muffled echo of the pejora-

---

[1] R. S. Stanier in *T.L.S.*, February 23, 1933.

[2] Cf. the binding function of τί and πλέον in ll. 39–40 :

> τί δ', ὦ ταλαίφρον, εἰ τάδ' ἐν τούτοις, ἐγὼ
> λύουσ' ἂν ἢ 'φάπτουσα προσθείμην πλέον ;

[3] *Sophocles* (1902), p. 161. Phillimore's introductory essay is full of suggestive material. As a translator he was probably influenced by the excitable, exclamatory style of Browning ; e.g. :

> " Then with a levelled flame He felled him
> Just at the finish—aloft now !—leaping
> To upraise an *Hurrah* ! victorious ! " (*Antig.* 131–3.)

For other ' Hopkinsian ' renderings, see *op. cit.* pp. 8, 122, 152.

[4] Cf. *Note-books*, p. 243 : " Although pure assonance is, so far as I know, only used regularly in Spanish and Portuguese verse it plays a wide part as an unessential grace and finish in prose and verse elsewhere and gives a very subtle beauty to it or this is given by *vowelling*, which is either *vowelling on* (assonance) or *vowelling off* or changing of vowel down some scale or strain or keeping. Euripides is a great master of this vowelling."

tive δυσ- is heard in βυσσόθεν. This is psychologically apt in a simile which drives home the force of the earlier lines :

> οἷς γὰρ ἂν σεισθῇ θέοθεν δόμος, ἄτας
> οὐδὲν ἐλλείπει γενεᾶς ἐπὶ πλῆθος ἕρπον·[1]

Turning to the consonants, we find μ, ν, σ, π, and τ repeated in the first two lines with the addition of one other consonant, δ :

What seems a more intentional vowelling off and consonancy gives a marked rocking rhythm to line 4 :

This resembles the " consonant chime " or *cynghanedd* which Hopkins admired in Welsh poetry and freely imitated in *The Wreck of the Deutschland*.[2]

We have found similar " lettering " in Aeschylus :

> τιθέμενος ἄγναμπτον νόον
> δάμναται οὐράνιαν
> γένναν· οὐδὲ λήξει, πρὶν ἂν ἢ κορέσῃ κέαρ, ἢ παλάμᾳ τινὶ
> τὰν δυσάλωτον ἕλῃ τις ἀρχάν.[3]

A consonantal analysis reveals what Hopkins would call figures of repetition, " *oftening, over-and-overing, aftering* of the inscape "[4] :

The ripples of " qualitative " phonal rhythm and the rhetorical astringency given by these intermittent correspondences will be more obvious when we consider the vowelling also, by placing together ἄγναμπτον and δάμναται ; οὐράνιαν, γένναν, and πρὶν ἂν ; κορέσῃ and κέαρ ; παλάμα, δυσάλωτον, and ἕλη τις.

---

[1] Lines 583-4 : " For them, whose house has been shaken from heaven, no curse faileth, creeping on over the multitude of their generation." The texture of ll. 593 *et seqq.* is also noteworthy.

[2] See below, pp. 148-53.   [3] *Prometheus Vinctus*, ll. 169-72.   [4] *Note-books*, p. 249.

Finally, two characteristic examples from the " great master ",
Euripides :

αὖρα, ποντιὰς αὖρα
ἅτε ποντοπόρους κομίζεις
θοὰς ἀκάτους ἐπ' οἶδμα λίμνας,
ποῖ με τὰν μελέαν πορεύσεις;

.   .   .   .

ἢ Παλλάδος ἐν πόλει
τᾶς καλλιδίφρου τ' Ἀθαναίας ἐν κροκέῳ πεπλῳ
ζεύξομαι ἅρματι πώλους,
ἐν δαιδαλέαισι ποικίλλουσ' ἀνθοκρόκοισι πήναις
ἢ Τιτάνων γενεὰν . . . [1]

The melody or " scaping " of this verse is exquisite—the consonancy and vowelling-off in ποντιὰς αὖρα—ποντοπόρους—πορεύσεις; ἐπ' οἶδμα λίμνας, ποῖ με τὰν μελέαν; Παλλάδος—πόλει τᾶς
—καλλιδίφ-. There is the paronomasia of κροκέῳ—ἀνθοκρόκοισι
and the harmonious interweaving of inflectional vowels and
diphthongs in πώλους δαιδαλέαισι ποικίλλουσ', etc.

Such effects are too frequent to be dismissed as accidental ; [2]
and whether they are accidental or deliberate is beside the point :
they are unmistakable, and Hopkins both admired and imitated
them :

" Flower of beauty, fleece of beauty, too too apt to, ah ! to fleet,"

> " dark heaven's baffling ban
Bars or hell's spell thwarts. This to hoard unheard,
Heard unheeded, leaves me a lonely began." [3]

Two other characteristics of Greek choral poetry are found
in Hopkins : one is the repetition of *motif*-words, the other is
the piling up of epithets—the cumulative phrase. The first is
heard in ὕπν' ὀδύνας, ἀδαής, ὕπνε δ' ἀλγέων, and in " When, when,
Peace, will you, Peace ? " [4]

The second is frequent in Aeschylus !

μίμνει γὰρ φοβερὰ παλίνορτος
οἰκονόμος δολία μνάμων μῆνις τεκνόποινος. . . [5]

---

[1] *Hecuba*, ll. 444–7 ; 462–6.
[2] Cf. *ibid.* 155–62 ; 1063–7 ; 1092–7.
[3] *Poems*, Nos. 36 and 44. See also No. 19, ll. 7–9.
[4] *Philoct.* 827 ; *Poems*, No. 22.
[5] *Agamemnon*, ll. 154–5. Note again the repetition of μν (νμ) and o in this passage.
Translation (literal) : " For there remains terrible, a treacherous warder of the
home, ever-mindful, *wrath*—child-avenging."

6

Six adjectives to one substantive may be found elsewhere in English poetry, as in Shakespeare's

> " Bloody, bawdy villain,
> Remorseless, treacherous, lecherous, kindless villain " ; [1]

but the practice becomes truly Aeschylean only in Hopkins, where we feel it to be a natural outcome of exuberance, an integral part of the complex pattern of rhythm and style :

> " Earnest, earthless, equal, attuneable, | vaulty, voluminous, . . . stupendous
> Evening. . . ." [2]

Accumulations of epithets, nouns, and verbs are used by Hopkins in the building up of a powerful *cumulative rhythm*, a form of poetic rhythm of which he is, undoubtedly, the greatest master in English, perhaps in any language. Of this cumulative rhythm *Spelt from Sibyl's Leaves* is, probably, the most splendid example.

There is in Hopkins one other device, ancillary to rhythm, which must be traced ultimately to Greek lyric, and that is the synapheia of

> " her dápple is at an énd, as-
> tray or aswarm. . . ." [3]

In the texts of the dramatists (e.g. above, p. 109) synapheia frequently depends upon the editor ; but in a Sapphic stanza it is unavoidable :

> πύκνα δινεῦντες πτέρ' ἀπ' ὠράνω αἴθε-
> ρος διὰ μέσσω.

The device is met with in serious poetry of the early seventeenth century—in Jonson, Campion, and Lord Herbert of Cherbury,[4] but thereafter only in light or comic verse. Hopkins revives it successfully, partly to help the over-reaving of his lines, to give architectonic compactness to the sonnet-strain, and partly for rhythmic μίμησις or onomatopoeia : " from swarm- | ed Rome " (38) ; " No ling- | ering ! " (41) ; " I wear- | y of idle a being " (44). His practice in this matter is closely bound up

---

[1] *Hamlet* II. ii. 616.   [2] *Poems*, No. 32.   [3] *Ibid.*
[4] E.g. in Jonson's *Pindaric Ode* (Ep. 3) and Lord Herbert's *To Her Mind.* Cf. G. M. H.'s use of this device in his Latin poem *O prædestinata bis* (*Poems*, Third Edition, No. 139).

with his theory and practice of Rhyme, a subject to which we shall return when dealing with the Welsh influence.

We have seen how, for Hopkins, Greek lyric poetry provided a definite criterion of perfection in matters of rhythm and texture, form and rhetoric—aspects of poetry in the fusion of which are united the *inwardness* of thought and emotion and the *outwardness* of movement and expression. As regards Latin poetry, Hopkins himself has told us how the Sapphics and Elegiacs of Horace and Ovid provided him with models of Counterpoint in strictly measured forms of verse ; [1] how, in the history of stress-rhythms, the early Latin Saturnian verse, which (following Ritschl) he assumed to be wholly accentual,[2] was linked up with the alliterative stress-rhythm of *Piers Plowman* and the sprung rhythm of popular rhymes.[3] There are other ways, however, in which Hopkins was influenced by the great tradition of Latin poetry from Ennius to the medieval Christian hymn-writers.

The success of Horace would intensify his desire to achieve *multum in parvo* and the utmost precision in phrasing ; a distinctly Horatian turn is given when his syntax borrows the freedom of an inflected language :

> " Their magnifying of each its kind
>   With delight calls to mind
>   How she did in her stored
>   Magnify the Lord." [4]

That tmesis of Ennius, an attempt to achieve Greek flexibility— *saxo cere- comminuit -brum* [5]—was an isolated " desperate deed " which was to have repercussions not only in Hopkins but in a good deal of twentieth-century " modernist " poetry ; [6] but most of Hopkins's probably unconscious adaptations of Latin modes were less sensational. When he gave a peculiar twist to his syntax it was always to bring about some precise rhythmical or rhetorical effect to integrate object, experience, and language in the individually distinctive beauty of *inscape*.

---

[1] *Note-books*, pp. 239–41.
[2] He quotes :

> Quod re suá diffidens | aspere afflicta
> Parens timens hic vovit | voto hoc soluto . . . (*ibid.* p. 234).

[3] *Note-books*, pp. 234–5.
[4] *Poems*, No. 18, stanza 8.
[5] See *Poems*, p. 116, note on *Harry Ploughman*.
[6] E.g. that of E. E. Cummings. See Vol. I. of the present work, chap. vii.

Such a line as Ovid's

labitur ex oculis nunc quoque gutta meis [1]

would seem at first sufficiently remote from English idiom :

" flows from-eyes even now the tear from-mine ".

Such a separation of noun and possessive adjective is impracticable without inflections. Yet to produce an effect of passionate, almost impatient entreaty tinged with protest, Hopkins cries :

" Mine, O thou Lord of Life, send my roots rain." [2]

The separation is achieved : there is, after " Mine ", just that element of suspense which gives the classical syntax its esemplastic quality. We feel that Hopkins would have preferred

" Mine, O thou Lord of Life, send roots rain."

But the necessity of repeating (with a difference) the personal pronoun becomes a virtue ; for besides the additional emphasis, it supplies a clinching assonance which is equivalent to the Latin ocul*is* . . . me*is*.

Professor Mackail has said that poetry is " the art of making patterns or designs in words ".[3] Hopkins, too, stresses the formal side when he says :

" Some matter and meaning is essential to poetry, but only as an element necessary to support and employ the shape which is contemplated for its own sake. (Poetry is in fact speech only employed to carry the inscape of speech for the inscape's sake— and therefore the inscape must be dwelt on . . .") [4]

Such definitions do account for certain rhythmic and musical qualities to be found in Latin poetry, as in Greek, though the difference of idiom gives rise to corresponding differences of pattern or inscape.

From Ennius onwards we find frequent exploitation of all forms of " lettering "—alliteration, assonance, internal rhyme, half-rhyme, and paronomasia or what Mr. E. E. Sykes calls " verbal juxtaposition" or "verbal plays" [5]. From an overworked alliteration like that of Accius—

Major mihi moles, majus miscendumst malum—

---

[1] *Tr.* i. 3.   [2] *Poems*, No. 50.
[3] *Lectures on Poetry*, p. 12.   [4] *Poetry and Verse* (*Note-books*, p. 249).
[5] See *Roman Poetry* (1923), pp. 256–71 ; and also *Allitteratio Latina* (1921), by W. J. Evans.

we pass to the subtle vowelling-off and verbal plays of a line from Ennius :

> mater optuma, tu multo mulier melior mulierum.

Here are those delicate harmonies which are so fascinating in Hopkins's *Echoes* : *tu mult-* is a musical variant of *-tuma* ; *-to mul-* of *tu mul-* ; *melior* of *mulier* ; while *mulierum* makes a perfect recapitulation and cadence. The total effect is a kind of crooning tenderness.

Similar means are employed to fuse the auditory and semantic rhythms in a line like Ovid's

> verbera cum verbis mixta fuere meis

The bold image is strengthened as much by the pun as by the hissing ablatives.

Latin poetry frequently flaunts a peculiar kind of assonance and repetition in which one word seems to blossom out of the preceding one :

Ovid :
> Non potes avelli : simul ah, simul ibimus, inquit.
> te sequar : et coniunx exulis exul ero.

Catullus :
> mutuis animis amant, amantur.

Laberius :
> viri excellentis mente clemente edita. . . .

These are typical examples of that untranslatable verbal inscape which can make even commonplace matter poetry : wedded to original ideas the device is highly effective and memorable, and Hopkins seems to be the only English poet who has adapted it to his needs as a regular poetic mode : " where gold, where quickgold lies " (8) ; " Our make and making break, are breaking down " (11) ; " earliest stars, earl-stars " (32) ; "Resign them, sign them " (36) ; " in a wind lifted, windlaced " (43).

The rich ornamentation of the Graeco-Roman period left its mark on Virgil and accounts for many of his finest effects. Juxtapositions like *anxius angit, flentem flens, lacus lacunae* are common, and he could not resist the lure of alliteration and assonance of all shades of intensity. Usually they are muted and interwoven, as in the ever-fresh

> tendebantque manus ripae ulterioris amore ;

but at times they are obtrusive and plangent :

> se causam clamat crimenque caputque malorum . . .
>
> hoc metuens, molemque et montes insuper altos
> imposuit. . . .
>
> clamorque virum clangorque tubarum. . . .

—lines which Hopkins would certainly not find " deficient in rhetoric ".[1]

This tradition of subtle inscape was continued through the Silver Age and so-called decadence.   There is an exquisite felicity and concentration in this, from Ausonius :

> Dum dubitat Natura, marem faceretne puellam
>   Factus es, O pulcher, paene puella puer.[2]

Again, the close-knit organic rhythm and Hopkinsian manner (but not matter !) of this, from Petronius :

> sed sic sic sine fine feriati
> et tecum jaceamus osculantes.
> Hic nullus labor est ruborque nullus :
> hoc juvit, juvat et diu juvabit ;
> hoc non deficit, incipitque semper.

In a letter to Baillie, Hopkins praised the *Pervigilium Veneris* : " as beautiful as or more beautiful than anything of the same length in Latin ".[3]   In the famous line :

> cras amet qui nunquam amavit, quique amavit cras amet,

the " figure of grammaı "[4] is no mere rhetorical repetition ; it has a real bearing on poetic form, and the same principle re-emerges in Hopkins's

> " The thunder-purple seabeach plumèd purple-of-thunder ".[5]

The phonal similarity sets off a likeness with a difference : the mental eye swings up from the cloud-shadowed waves to the wave-shadowing clouds—and then down again to the plumes of the " stormfowl " !

The history of the European poetic tradition seems to show that as the *matter* of poetry becomes more conventional, dogmatic, or circumscribed by authority, so the *manner* tends frequently (though not always) to redress the balance by putting on more finery, more external ornament.   This preoccupation with what

---

[1] See Sykes, *Roman Poetry*, *loc. cit.*   G. M. H. employs ' verbal plays ', etc. in his own Latin verses (See *Poems*, Third Edition, Nos. 127 and 141, Note.).

[2] Sykes, *loc. cit.*   [3] *Further Letters*, pp. 85–6.

[4] Cf. *Note-books*, p. 249.   [5] *Poems*, No. 21.

Hopkins calls " graces " may be artificial and mechanical—like the preciosity of *Euphues* (which is quasi-poetical) and much of the alliteration in Middle English verse and even in Swinburne. On the other hand, it may manifest itself in a genuine sensibility which, released from the burden of creative thinking, and challenged by the perfection of an earlier " Augustan " form, spontaneously chooses a newer mode, a more brilliant *décor*, which will recapture the reader's or hearer's attention and direct his mind once more to neglected or forgotten matters. Of this kind, perhaps, is the delicate artifice of Hadrian's

> Animula vagula blandula,
> hospes comesque corporis. . . .

and to this class belong some of the best medieval Latin hymns and sequences, with their rich " lettering " and stanzaic variety. The *Trinitas* of Pierre de Corbeil, Atchbishop of Sens (d. 1222) has a textural pattern and a canorous cumulative rhythm which Hopkins would have admired :

> . . . Sol lumen et numen, cacumen, semita,
> Lapis, mons, creator, amator, redemptor, salvator
> luxque perpetua,
> Tu tutor, et decor, tu candor, tu splendor, et odor quo
> vivunt mortua.
> Tu vertex et apex, regum rex, legum lex et vindex, tu
> lux angelica,
> Quem clamant, adorant, quem laucant, quem cantant, quem
> amant agmina coelica.
> Tu theos et heros, dives flos, vivens ros, rege nos,
> salva nos, perduc nos ad thronos superos et
> vera gaudia.
> Tu decus et virtus, tu justus et verus, tu sanctus et
> bonus, tu rectus et summus Dominus, tibi
> sit gloria.[1]

[1] *Carmina e Poetis Christianis Excerpta, etc.*, ed. Félix Clément, Paris, 1884, p. 518. Clément comments : " Cette composition originale se distingue surtout par la trinité perpetuelle de ses sons et des syllabes, et par sa division en groupes ternaires. Chantée sous les voutes de nos admirables cathédrales du moyen âge, elle produisit *des effets vraiment populaires et saisissants.*"

G. P. Marsh (*Lectures on the English Language*, 1863, p. 399) quotes the following from a hymn by " a Christian writer belonging to the school of the later Orphic poets " :

> χαῖρε κόρη χαρίεσσα, χαρητόκε, χάρμα τοκήων,
> παρθέν' ἐφημερίοις οὐρανίοις τε φίλη.
> χαῖρε κόρη πάντων μέγα χάρματι χάρμα λαβοῦσα,
> χάρμα μεγασθενέων χάρμα τ'ἀφαυροτέρων.
> χαῖρε πόνων τε λύτειρα δόμων ῥύτειρα τ'ἀνάκτων.

For Marsh, see below, p. 138.

This piece has nothing of the poetic subtlety of Hopkins's *Pied Beauty* and *Echoes* ; yet to these poems and to the packed " dithyrambic " lines of the conclusion of *The Deutschland* it bears a certain generic likeness.   It has those rhythmic elements which Hopkins hoped would make his own work " popular ". There is the sudden change from an amphibrachic to a cretic movement in

Tu vértex et ápex, régum réx, légum léx

and the same in the last line but one—a bold effect of varying tempo that Hopkins loved.   There is again, as Clément says, " une accumulation d'épithètes, de qualifications majestueuses et sonores " ; as in that last stanza of *The Deutschland*, an ardent religious sensibility, joined to a gift for impassioned rhetoric, expresses itself in a breathless rush of symbolic attributes.   We may conclude therefore that Hopkins's complex expressional rhythm is the result of a remarkable tension and compromise—a fusing of the perfervid religious enthusiasm of a Corbeil, the spontaneous vigour of the anonymous folk-poet, and the more controlled, aesthetic rhythm and rhetoric of the great classical poets—Pindar, Aeschylus, Sophocles, Virgil, Horace, Ovid, and Milton.

In the sequel-chapter we continue our survey of the evolution of the " new rhythm " by enumerating those influences and analogies which postdate and lie outside the classical tradition,— which belong, in fact, to the Romance, Teutonic, and Celtic schools of poetry.

CHAPTER III

THE NEW RHYTHM—II

In spite of the attempt once made to reduce alliteration and assonance in Latin verse to a fixed rule,[1] it has usually been held that in Latin practice, as in Greek, these tonal devices were sporadic and inspirational rather than structural. It was not until quantity had finally given way to accent as the means of marking rhythm that end-rhyme and internal rhyme became regular and fashionable ; and this attempt to replace the roll and rise of the old quantitative metres by an ordered " lettering of syllables " brought medieval Latin verse into closer relationship with the old Teutonic and Celtic poetry, in both of which alliteration was needed to give structural definition to an otherwise loose and colourless stress-rhythm.

By 1874, when the *Lecture Notes* were written, Hopkins had decided that a form of stress-rhythm was preferable to the conventional syllabic or " counted " metres (to be called later Standard or Common Rhythm); and as we know, his first extant experiment with stresses (the " A " MS. version of *St. Dorothea*)[2] had been shown to Bridges at least as early as 1868. We may safely assume, however, that Hopkins, like ourselves, found this early form of Sprung Rhythm indeterminate and unsatisfying ; something was needed to make up for the loss of regularity—that ease and grace which syllabic metre imparts. Despite the resemblance to " popular rhymes and jingles " achieved by the doubtful method of stressing normally weak syllables (" by ", " -ger ", " with ", " it ", etc.), the revised *St. Dorothea*, though not without some alliteration, lacks that coherence and strength in its movement which *The Deutschland* and later poems have forced us to expect.

Although Chaucer, with his Romance affiliations, despised the " rum, ram, ruf " of alliteration, many great poets since his time have found that the regular flow of syllabic metre does not

---

[1] By W. J. Evans, *op. cit.*

[2] Unpublished ; though an excerpt is given in *Letters*, vol. i. p. 24, Note 3. The version from the MS. now at Campian Hall, Oxford (*Poems*, No. 82), is certainly of a later date : the stress-rhythm is more forthright.

allow of the highest rhetorical verve unless the natural resources of a language " overstocked with consonants " (as Johnson said) are aptly and artfully exploited : it was probably the example of Spenser, Shakespeare (in the Sonnets), Dryden, and Byron which induced Hopkins to say, of alliteration : " One may indeed doubt whether a good ear is satisfied with our verse without it." [1] There is of course much good English poetry in which alliteration has been either largely avoided or subtly disguised (Milton's and Tennyson's, for instance) ; in Swinburne, on the other hand, exuberance is more usual than nervous selection—that astringent, tense relation between sound and meaning which Hopkins produced in such phrases (at once unexpected and inevitable) as " fastened me flesh ", " a melting, a madrigal start " (4), " crisps of curl " (11), " limber liquid youth " (23), " flesh filled, blood brimmed the curse " (45). Hopkins's method was partly the adoption and partly the corrective of Swinburne's richness of lettering.[2]

It is probable, however, that Hopkins's strong natural tendency to improve the " inscape " of his new stress-rhythm by means of assonance, internal rhyme and half-rhyme received a considerable impetus from his early reading of G. P. Marsh's *Lectures on the English Language* ; [3] the following, for instance, is a perspicacious argument for eclectic originality :

> " The interest which the study of native English, old and new, and of the sister dialects, now so generally excites, prompts the inquiry whether it be not possible to revive some of the forgotten characteristics of English poetry, and thus aid the efforts of our literature to throw off or lighten the conventional shackles which classical and Romance authority has imposed upon it. I propose to illustrate, by specimens original and imitative, the leading peculiarities of Anglo-Saxon and Old-Northern verse, as well as of one or two Romance metrical forms hitherto little if at all attempted in English, and to suggest experiment upon the introduction of some of them into English poetry." [4]

Although he must have known, through Marsh, that stress and alliteration were structurally important in Old English poetry, Hopkins had not, in 1874, any direct knowledge of that

---

[1] *Note-books*, p. 243.

[2] Cf. Charles Williams's Introduction to *Poems*, 2nd edn. (pp. xi.-xii.).

[3] Marsh (1801–82), was an American philologist ; wrote also *Grammar of the Icelandic Language* and *The Origin and History of the English Language.*

[4] Edition of 1863, chap. xxv. p. 387.

poetry.   He quotes " Piers Ploughman " in the *Lecture Notes* ; [1]
yet he did not begin a serious reading of that work until 1882,
when, speaking of Sprung Rhythm, he says :

> " So far as I know—I am inquiring and presently I shall be
> able to speak more decidedly—it existed in full force in Anglo-
> Saxon verse and in great beauty ; in a degraded and doggere l
> shape in Piers Ploughman (I am reading that famous poem and
> am coming to the conclusion that it is not worth reading) " [2]

The formal relationship between Old English verse and Sprung
Rhythm will be dealt with more fittingly in a later section ; at
present we must pass on to consider those of Marsh's illustrations
which directly influenced the surface rhythms, texture, or
rhythmic inscape of Hopkins's mature poems.

There is first what Hopkins calls " a beautifully rich combination " of alliteration, assonance, internal rhyme and final
half-rhyme or ' shothending ' in a specimen of Icelandic verse :

> " Hilmir hjálma skúrir
> herðir sverði roðnu,
> hrjóta hvítir askar,
> hrynja brynja spángir ;
> hnykkja Hlakkar eldar
> harða svarðar landi,
> remma rimmu gloðir
> randa grand of jarli." [3]

In the initial and final consonant rhyme of pairs like *hrjóta—*
hvítir and *remma—rimmu*, Hopkins notes that the effect is " not
that the vowels go for nothing but that they seem to be sided or
intentionally changed, vowelled off." [4]

---

[1] *Note-books*, p. 235 : " The beat varies for the most part between anapaestic
and iambic or dactylic and trochaic but it is so loose that not only the syllables are
not counted but not even the number of beats in a line, which is commonly two in
each half-line but sometimes three or four :

[And this féire féld fúl of fólk | féire I schåll ow schéwe]

It almost seems as if rhythm were disappearing and repetition of figure given only
by alliteration."

Not all of the *Vision* is as loose and " degraded " as the piece Hopkins quotes
(the opening of Part II. *The Vision of Holy Church*).

[2] *Letters*, vol. i. p. 156.   On p. 163 he writes : " In fact I am learning Anglo-
saxon. . . ."

[3] *Note-books*, p. 247 (See Note, p. 410).

[4] Marsh explains (*op. cit.* p. 402) that the use of half-rhymes in Scandinavian
verse is " neither an accident nor the arbitrary adoption of a purely conventional
form of poetical ornament, but it is the natural result of the Old-Northern system of
inflexions."   Strong inflexions were prevalent in all classes of words which admit of
declension or conjugation.

In order to encourage English poets to experiment on these lines, Marsh improvises in the following strain :

> " *So*ftly now are *si*fting
> *S*nows on landscape *fro*zen.
> Thic*kly* *f*all the *f*la*ke*lets,
> *Feather*y light to*gether*. . . ."

It is surely significant that Hopkins echoes some of these lines in *The Deutschland* :

> " I am *soft sift*
> In an hourglass. . . ." (Stanza 4)

> " She to the black-about air, to the breaker, *the thickly*
> *Falling flakes*. . . ." (Stanza 24.)

—and " feathery delicacy " appears in Stanza 31.

Other peculiarities of Marsh's verse—a kind of rhyme which " is not employed to mark off lines or bars or clauses ", together with alliteration that almost systematically " reaves " or joins one line to the next—these are characteristic features of Hopkins's verse from 1875 to 1877. A suggestion that vocalic *quality*, instead of the classical *quantity*, might be used as a means of marking rhythm is found in Marsh. Having said that the inflexional vowel-change in the Icelandic language rendered the ear more acutely sensible to vowel sounds, he continues :

> " Hence the vowels might readily become metrical constituents of a character not less important than that which they possessed in the classic metres, and occupy as conspicuous a place in the prosody as in the grammar of the language." [1]

Hopkins comes near to such a prosody without sacrificing the organic and variable nature of his rhythm. Yet although he himself stopped short of mechanical repetition, he could appreciate the sheer decorative preciosity of two " beautiful specimens " from Italian poetry, both quoted by Marsh ; the first is the twenty-third stanza of Pulci's *Morgante Maggiore*, which continues as it begins :

> " La casa cosa parea bretta e brutta,
> Vinta dal vento ; e la natta e la notte
> Stilla le stelle ch' a tetto era tutta. . . ."

The second is a sonnet in the Pisan dialect :

> " Similimente · gente · criatura·
> La portatura · pura · ed avenente·
> Faite plagente · mente per natura·
> Sicchen altura · cura · vola gente· . . ." [2]

---

[1] *Loc. cit.*   [2] *Note-books*, pp. 410–11.

Such novelties, facilitated by the profusion of rhymes in
Italian, are delightful to a foreign ear, and especially to the ear
of a poet so much in love with pattern for pattern's sake as
Hopkins was. But Hopkins evinced an equally strong passion
for freedom and *mimesis*. Retaining the possibility of such
regular mosaic as a basis for subtle variation, he modelled his
inscape upon the sound indigenous example of poets like Shakespeare and Sir Philip Sidney. The latter has passages which,
like the Italian excerpts, are " with some art curiously written " :

> " Yet while I languish him that bosom clips
> That lap doth lap, nay lets, in spite of spite
> This sour-breath'd mute taste of those sugar'd lips."

> " Some do I hear of Poet's fury tell
> But (God wot) wot not what they mean by it." [1]

This is largely bravura work ; but how significant are the effects
of alliteration and assonance in the following :

> " if the assassination
> Could trammel up the consequence and catch
> With his surcease success " ! [2]

Guilt, strain, and growing resolution uttered between the teeth are
heard in the sibilants and hard c's; *assassination*, *trammel*, and *catch*
are linked by grammar and assonance ; and in the consonancy of
surcease success two distinct ideas are deliberately made to coincide.

Rare even in Shakespeare, such effects, original, mimetic and
most often musical, are frequent in Hopkins. Macbeth's identification of *surcease* and *success* is paralleled by the fate of the
Deutschland :

> " The *goal* was a *shoal*. . . ." [3]

and again of a rural scene :

> " even where we mean
> To *mend* her we *end* her." [4]

More elaborate is the effect in stanza 8 of *The Deutschland*,
where a forceful image is powerfully " instressed, stressed " by
the lettering of the syllables :

> " We lásh with the bést or wórst
> Word lást ! How a lúsh-kept plúsh-capped slóe
> Will, móuthed to flésh-búrst,
> Gúsh !—flúsh the man, the béing with it. . . ."

[1] Sonnets lix. and lxxiv. in *Astrophel and Stella*.
[2] *Macbeth, loc. cit.* (See above, p. 125.)
[3] Stanza 12.   [4] *Binsey Poplars* (*Poems*, No. 19).

The sharpness of the sensation, the astringency of the total experience, is conveyed by the packed phonal correspondences. In thirteen feet, nine arses and two theses are connected by lettering with the first two arses, *lash* and *best* :

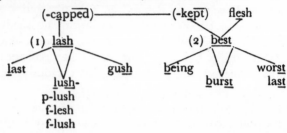

Moreover, the repetition of -sh and -st is not capricious. The four words connected by -st (*best, worst, last, burst*) all express the idea of extremity. Again, monosyllabic native words (and many others besides) which end with the consonant -sh (∫) are usually informed with the ideas of fullness and richness or speed and violence ; hence *lash Gush*, and (in line 6) *flash* suggest the speed and violence of the sensation, while *lush-, plush-, flesh-,* and *flush* accentuate the richness and fullness of the fruit, the flavour and value of the whole spiritual experience.[1]

From his early youth Hopkins seems to have made a close if unsystematic study of the relationship between sound and meaning in the growth of the English vocabulary. In the *Note-books* we find lists of words, like " Grind, gride, gird, grit, groat, grate, greet, κρούειν, crush, crash, κροτεῖν, etc.", followed by the inference that " the onomatopoetic theory has not had a fair chance ".[2]

This neglect was certainly repaired in the poems, for besides expressive groups like " pour and pelt ", " spill and spend " (11), " heaven's baffling ban / Bars " (44), we sometimes find alliterative consonants and chiming vowels running like threads through the woof of the poem with a continuous onomatopoeic suggestion. Throughout *Harry Ploughman*, for instance, br- (or b . . . r . . .) and l are used like *motifs* to signalize the two chief characteristics of Harry's physique and action—strength and grace. The keywords of the first *motif* are *broth* (cf. the Irish " broth of a boy "),

[1] Cf. *Spring* (" all in a rush / With richness "), and *The Sea and the Skylark*, where the songster's volubility is " rash-fresh ". For a further note on -sh and the ' onomatopoetic theory ' see Appendix D, p. 397.

[2] Page 6. Mr. House compares Frederic Farrar's *Essay on the Origin of Language* (1860), chap. iv. of which argues for the ' onomatopoetic origin of many words and roots '. (*Note-books*, p. 356.)

barrelled, barrowy, brawn, beechbole, broad, and bluff (*hide*). At the beginning of the sestet, the two *motifs* are delicately interlaced (with the addition of a second liquid, w), the alliteration being disguised partly by medial and final position and partly by the lack of heavy stress :

> " He leans to it, Harry bends, look. Back, elbow, and
>   liquid waist
> In him, all quail to the wallowing o' the plough : etc."

The voiced b of *bends* seems, under the influence of the liquids, to be gradually softened down to the voiceless p of *plough* ; and how cunningly is the smoothness of the l's and w's relieved by the hard q's of *liquid* and *quail* ! The whole poem comes as near to " the condition of music " as language may.

A similar blending of strength and beauty, power and grace, is expressed through the b's and l's of *The Windhover* (*rebuffed, big, Brute beauty, Buckle* !, *billion, level, lovelier, chevalier, sillion*). It would, however, be a mistake to seek a systematic, Wagnerian application of these alliterative *motifs* throughout the rest of the poems. Often, as in *The Starlight Night*, b's are used partly for *mimesis* (" Wind-beat whitebeam ") but mostly for sheer rhetorical verve (" bright boroughs ", " Buy then ! bid then ! ").

This mastery of subtle, varied, and vigorous musical consonancy was not achieved at one stroke. It was due in some measure to a sensitive appreciation of similar effects in Sophocles and Virgil, in Shakespeare and other English poets, among whom must be numbered the famous contemporary so deeply admired by the younger Hopkins : in *Enid and Geraint* Tennyson had written :

> " Broad-faced with under-fringe of russet beard
>   Bound on a foray, rolling eyes of prey."

The consonancy in this passage might have been suggested by Tennyson's reading of the Welsh *cynfardd*, ' Llywarch Hen '.[1] But it was mainly Hopkins's own excursus into the Welsh language (undertaken originally to glean

> " some ears for Christ in this wild field of Wales ")[2]

---

[1] See *Tennyson and Wales*, by Herbert Wright, in *Essays and Studies* (Eng. Assocn.), vol. xiv. p. 81.
[2] *Sir John Oldcastle* (Tennyson). See *Note-books*, pp. 210, 217.

that determined the immediate direction of his experiments in metrical tone-pattern. In the consonantal and vocalic effects of Welsh poetry he found a system at once more strict and more concise, and therefore as it seemed more valuable, than the flowing, decorative schemes of Swinburne.

In August, 1874, Hopkins went to St. Beuno's, North Wales, to read Theology. By his professorial writings of the same year, we know that he was at that time engrossed with the idea of poetry as intricate pattern, figure, inscape. When the rhythmic figure, he says, is repeated intermittently, as in alliteration and rhyme (ABCDABEFABGH), the result is more " brilliancy, starriness, quain, margaretting " [1] (The *N.E.D.* gives us little help with the last two attributes ; but " quain " is from " quaint " in the sense of " artificially elegant ", while " margaretting " may have been suggested by the delicate grain on mother-of-pearl—Greek μαργαρίτης) ; and it is just this rich distinctiveness of texture that makes the earlier mature verse of Hopkins look and sound more like the verse of Cynddelw or Tudur Aled than that of any traditional English poet.

In the whole corpus of Hopkins's literary remains, both published and unpublished, there is no mention by name of any Welsh poet. As we have stated, however, in the note to the poem No. 135 in the recently published Third Edition of Hopkins's *Poems*, there is to be found among his loose papers in MS. " H " a long newspaper cutting of 1875 which contains the complete Welsh text, with an English translation, of the well known *Cywydd i Wenfrewi Santes* by the early sixteenth-century bard Tudur Aled. By good fortune, too, MS. " H " contains the autograph of a Welsh poem, a *cywydd*, by Hopkins himself.[2] This has now been included, with a commentary, in *Poems* (Third Edition), together with what seems to be a translation by Hopkins into Welsh " free " verse of the Latin hymn, *O Deus, ego emo te*.[3]

We know from the *Journal* (Feb. 7, 1875) that Hopkins received Welsh lessons from a Miss Susannah Jones (who probably lived in St. Asaph), and the evidence in his two Welsh poems goes to prove that he had a good working knowledge of the language and a very considerable knowledge of classical

---

[1] *Note-books*, p. 251.

[2] See below, Appendix E.

[3] As the MS. of this poem (No. 134) is in another hand, the attribution to G. M. H. is based only upon internal evidence of subject and style.

Welsh metrics. True, the *cynghanedd* in his *cywydd* is very faulty, but his adaptation of this system in the English verse of *The Wreck of the Deutschland* proves that he knew all the rules.

About his Welsh studies Hopkins was unusually diffident :

> " I have learnt Welsh. . . . I can read easy prose and can speak stumblingly, but at present I find the greatest difficulty, amounting mostly to total failure, in understanding it when spoken and the poetry, which is quite as hard as the choruses in a Gk. play—and consider what those would be with none but a small and bad dictionary at command—I can make little way with." [1]

As Dr. Idris Bell says, however, the magically melodious quality of much of the classical poetry can be appreciated by any reader acquainted with the pronunciation of Welsh.

To Hopkins, Welsh poetry was " very rich in sound and imagery ", and the following allusion to its rhythm is significant :

> " Such rhythms as French and Welsh poetry has is sprung, counterpointed upon a counted rhythm, but it differs from Milton's in being little calculated . . . it is in fact the native rhythm of the words bodily imported into verse." [2]

This generalization does not apply to all Welsh poetry, but only to that written in the *Mesurau Caethion* or Strict Measures. The other kind of verse, the *Mesurau Rhyddion* or Free Measure, is identical in form with regular English syllabic metre, and is " free " only in the sense that its rhythm is not determined by *cynghanedd*—that strict and intricate set of rules governing internal rhyme and alliteration which characterized the bulk of Welsh poetry from the fourteenth to the eighteenth centuries and which is still widely used to-day.

In the Strict Measures (of which there are twenty-four in all) [3] rhythm is dependent not upon count of beats, as in Free Measure, but upon the number of syllables in the line, together with the number and disposition of the rhyming and alliterative elements. These elements are partly controlled by the word-accent (which, in the line, may be " rising " or " falling "), and the great variety of *cynghanedd* does not permit of regular rhythm. Mr. Thomas Taig has already pointed out that the metres of the

---

[1] *Further Letters*, Jan. 6, 1877 : cf. *Letters*, vol. i. pp. 31, 38, etc.
[2] *Letters*, vol. i. p. 46.
[3] The standard work on them is *Cerdd Dafod*, by Sir J. Morris Jones (Clarendon Press, 1925).

penillion singers were almost as free in the outline of their stress-rhythm as the Old English verses ; the following lines illustrate the *cywydd* stanza, which has a special relevance to our inquiry :

> " Lleddf, lleddf yr awron yw'r llŷn,
>   Ádeg ei ósteg éstyn
>   Drósto rhyw hwyrol drístwch
>   Lle rhwyfai dáu, gýnnau gẃch." [1]

The rules of *cynghanedd* were evolved gradually, and the system was not fully established until the fourteenth century, at which time Dafydd ap Gwilym first popularized the *cywydd*. This stanza consists of two seven-syllabled lines which rhyme in a manner peculiar to Welsh poetry : one of the lines (it is immaterial which) must end with rising accent and the other with falling accent, which means that an accented syllable rhymes with an unaccented one (llŷn—éstyn ; drístwch—gẃch). A complete *cywydd* may run to any number of stanzas, but each line must contain one of the four types of *cynghanedd* (see below).

In what appears to be his only attempt to write Welsh verse, Hopkins uses this form with perfect mastery as regards metre but with no strictness as regards *cynghanedd*. This is not surprising, for the effort of conveying his meaning with sincerity throughout eighteen lines of the *cywydd* metre must have taxed his resources. Even the Welsh poets themselves may, at times, have welcomed the metrical easement afforded by such devices as *tor ymadrodd* and *gair llanw* (see below) ; and in the stricter forms the sense was occasionally obscured if not distorted.[2] The rules of *cynghanedd*, however, are not difficult to understand or memorize, and the fact that Hopkins knew them (even though he did not apply them rigidly) will scarcely be doubted when we come to examine his imitation of *cynghanedd* in the English poems.

---

[1] *Rhythm and Metre*, p. 46 (University of Wales Press). According to Dr. Bell, the earliest scansion " was probably by stress-accent ; but this is now obscured owing to the fact that by the tenth or eleventh century a shifting of accent from the final to the penultimate syllable had occurred in Welsh. This rendered the earlier poems unrhythmical ; "—hence arose the method of scanning by number of syllables, aided by rhyme and *cynghanedd*. (*The Development of Welsh Poetry*, p. 34.)

[2] Cf. Hopkins in *Letters*, vol. i. p. 163. Speaking of the first draft of *The Sea and the Skylark* (1877), he says : " It was written in my Welsh days, in my salad days . . . and as in Welsh *englyns*, ' the sense ', as one of themselves said, ' gets the worst of it '. . . ." (The *englyn* is a ' strict ' epigrammatic, four-line stanza.)

Hopkins's *cywydd*, like *The Silver Jubilee* and one of the Latin poems,[1] is addressed to the first Bishop of Shrewsbury, and like the English tribute is dated 1876. Our present concern being mainly with the development of rhythm, we may note with what skill Hopkins achieves a musical consonancy, even though it is defective as *cynghanedd*. The poem begins :

> " Y *m*ae'*n* *ll*ewyn yma'*n* *ll*on
> Â *ff*rydan llawer *ff*ynon,
> *Gw*eddill *gw*yn *g*adwyd i ni
> *Gan* *F*euno a *Gwen*frewi."

> (Our focal point here is bright and glad
> With the streamlet of many a fountain,
> A holy remnant kept for us
> By Beuno and Winefred.)

The Hopkinsian texture is at once apparent ; but the full significance of this exercise in relation to the poet's development will be more easily appreciated after some account has been given of the rules of *cynghanedd* and the way he adapted them to the needs of his English verse.

We cannot say to what extent Hopkins was familiar with the Welsh poetry written before the *cynghaneddion* had been fully elaborated ; in much of it, however, there is an orotund, dithyrambic quality which recalls the medieval Latin canticle of Pierre de Corbeil [2] and anticipates the rich texture of Hopkins. In the following, from Dafydd Benfras's ode to Llewelyn, the impetuosity and vigour of the " sprung " rhythm is emphasized by repetition, internal rhyme, assonance, and alliteration :

> " Oedd breisg weisg ei fyddin,
> Oedd brwysg rwysg rhac y godorin,
> Oedd balch gwalch golchiad ei lain,
> Oedd beilch gweilch gweled ei werin,
> Oedd clywed cleddyfau finfin,
> Oedd clybod clwyf ym mhob elin. . . ." [3]

Here the effect is somewhat mechanical, as in the Italian specimens ; but nothing could be more " richly lettered " or

---

[1] *Ad Episcopum Salopiensem*, Third Edition, No. 136.

[2] See above, chap. ii. pp. 135–6.

[3] Quoted by Dr. Bell in *The Development of Welsh Poetry*, p. 54. Dr. Bell translates : " Great and nimble was his host, strong their onset before the tumult of battle, proud was the hawk of war for the laving of his blade, proud were the hawks to see his host. There were swords to hear, edge to edge, there were wounds to feel in every joint. . . ."

show more delicate vowel-gradations than the poem written by Cynddelw on his death-bed.   With a devotion worthy of Hopkins himself, the Welsh poet makes his submission to God :

> " Cyfarchaf-i Dduw, cyfarchwel ddawn,
>   I foli fy Rhi rhwydd rhadlawn.
> *Un Mab Mair a bair pyrnhawn a bore*
>   Ac aberoedd ffrwythlawn,
> A wnaeth *coed a maes a mesur* iawn,
> A ffrwythau a doniau Duw ryddigawn,
> A wnaeth gwellt a gwydd, a grug ym mynydd,
>   A wnaeth dedwydd yr dedfryd iawn,
> *Ac arall ar wall, ar wellig* ddawn,
>   Yn eissiwedig ag yn ddigllawn. . . ." [1]

With musical phrases like those italicized above one could find many parallels in Hopkins (" earliest stars, earl-stars ", " care-coiled, care-killed ", etc.).   This manner, moreover, was not a mere sporadic peculiarity of one poet ; it even appears in a proverb : *Nid ar redig y mae aredig* (He who ploughs does not run). Such deliberate interweaving and stringing together of vowels and consonants, either in ringing rows or in subtly modulated scales, is the rule rather than the exception in early Welsh poetry : " An*war* don *lavar levawr* wrthi " (A wild wave talking, crying beside it) ; " gorne gwawr fore ar fôr diffaith " (bright as the dawn of morning on a desert sea).

In *cynghanedd*, the rules of alliteration are much stricter than in English.   Words of more than one syllable alliterate when *all* their consonants, except the final ones, are the same and in the same order.   Thus *moonlight* requires a word like *manly* (m—nl—). Again, the accent must fall on corresponding syllables in both words ; thus *búllock* : *béllow* (but not *belów*).   The alliteration is further varied (and to an English ear partially obscured) by the fact that *w* and *h* need not count in the alliterative scheme, so that *gŵr hyfwyn* (g—r— f—) is matched by *grefydd* (gr— f—), although the former has one more syllable than the latter.

The simplest type of *cynghanedd* is that called *lusg* (' drag '),

---

[1] Dr. Bell translates : " I salute God, giver of refuge, that I may praise my King, the gracious giver ; *the only Son of Mary, who fashions evening and morning* and fruitful rivers, who made *wood and field and righteous rule*, and fruits and all gifts of God's giving, who made grass and trees, and the heather on the mountains, whose just judgement made one man blessed *and another in want, needy* of gifts, impoverished and sad."   (*Ibid.* p. 53.)

in which the accented penultimate syllable in the verse rhymes
with a preceding syllable :

"Tra fu'r *măb* ar ĭ *áb*erth [1]

Hopkins imitates this in

" Tongue true, *vaunt-* and *taunt*less " (23, st. 4) ;

but like the Welsh poets, he probably regarded *cynghanedd lusg* as
not sufficiently rich and complex for extensive use.

In the next type, *cynghanedd draws* (' traverse '), the first part
of the line alliterates with the last part, there being a portion in
the middle which is ' traversed ' or passed over :

A *Chará*dog (ni) *chré*dai,   (' falling accent ')
  1 2 3   1 2 3

Min ĭ *gl*édd (dryw) ĭ *m*wnwgl ái,[2] (' rising accent ')
 1 2   3   1   2   3

The third type, *cynghanedd groes* (' cross '), is on the same principle,
but the whole of the first half alliterates with the second half,
there being no middle part ' traversed ' :

" Y *ferch* wén, *fu*'r ychwáneg . . .
    1 2 3   4   5 | 1 2   3 4 5

   *Gwen*fréwi *d*ég, un *fr*yd oédd.[3]
    1   234   5 |1   2 34 5

Hopkins introduces variations of these two types into *The
Wreck of the Deutschland.* Like the Welsh poets, he tries to " lock
sense in beauty ", but he allows himself plenty of latitude ; he
does not indulge in " filling-in phrases ", or distort his matter
to suit a preordained form. We find a close approximation to
draws in

" To *b*áthe in his *f*áll-gold (mércies,) to *br*éathe in his
    1 2   3 4 5 6   1   2

                              *a*ll-*f*ire *gl*ánces." [4]
                               4   3   56

The transposition of *f* and *ll* in the second half was an inspired
licence ; moreover, the admission of non-alliterative consonants

---

[1] *Cywydd i Wenfrewi* (Tudur Aled), l. 27.   [2] *Ibid.* ll. 9–10.
[3] Tudur Aled, *loc. cit.* ll. 1 and 4. See Appendix E, p. 400 for another reference
to these lines.   [4] Stanza 23.

does not prevent the general effect from being similar to that of the regular Welsh *cynghanedd* :

" Wárm-laid gráve (of a) wómb-life gréy," [1]

" How a lúsh-kept, (p)lúsh-capped slóe " [2]

" Is it lóve in her of the béing | as her lóver had béen ? " [3]

Indeed, as Gweneth Lilly has shown in an excellent recent article on this subject,[4] this kind of imperfect *cynghanedd draws* is also to be found in the medieval Welsh poets ; for example :

" A *ll*u o *Bryd*ain | a *ll*wrw hy*bryd*edd "

where there is nothing in the first half of the line to correspond with the *r* of " llwrw ".

In Hopkins's poems we have found no absolutely perfect example of the *groes* form ; but again we are indebted to Gweneth Lilly for pointing out that he frequently uses a legitimate Welsh variation of *groes* and *draws* called *cynghanedd bengoll* (i.e. ' with the head or end missing ') :

" *N*ow *burn*, / *n*ew *born* to the world " [5]

" The *cross to h*er (she calls) *Christ to h*er, christens her
                                                    wild-worst Best." [6]

In both lines the last three or four words are outside the alliterative scheme. Again, the peculiar chime of the more strict *cynghanedd* is freely imitated in the following passages from *The Deutschland* and *The Woodlark* :

" The swóon of a héart that the swéep and the húrl of thee tród " [7]

" Of the Yore-flood, of the year's fall ; " [8]

" The blood-gush blade-gash . . .
And lace-leaved lovely
Foam-tuft fumitory "

" Through the velvety wind V-winged " [9]

The richest form of *cynghanedd* is that called *sain* (' tone '), which combines internal rhyme and alliteration. Here the line is divided into three parts ; the end of the first part rhymes with the end of the second part, while the second and third parts are

---

[1] Stanza 7.   [2] Stanza 8.   [3] Stanza 25.
[4] *The Modern Language Review*, July 1943 ; pp. 192–205.
[5] Stanza 34.   [6] Stanza 24.   [7] Stanza 2.
[8] Stanza 32.   [9] *Poems*, No. 64.

bound together by alliteration. The phonal beauty of which this device is capable is heard to perfection in a well-known couplet of Dafydd ap Gwilym's *cywydd* on the ladies of Llanbadarn :

> Na mor*wyn* / *fwyn* / of*y*naig,
> Na merch b*ach*, / na *gwrach*, / na *gwraig*.[1]
>
> (Not a virgin-maid, gentle in hope,
> Or a young girl, or a hag, or a wife.)

Hopkins himself has an excellent example of *sain* in his own Welsh poem :

> " Gwan ddwfr a *ddwg*, nis *dwg* dŷn,
>
> (Weak water brings, man brings it not)

The consonantal change from *dd* (pronounced like ' th ' in ' there ') to *d* corresponds with the sharp contrast in meaning.

In the *Poems* Hopkins does not keep strictly to the correct accentuation of *cynghanedd sain*. He does so in the line

> "In grim*y* / vast*y* / vault " (No. 37) ;

but as his lines are usually longer than those of the Welsh *cywydd* (and since his habit was to " admire and do otherwise ") he adopted a freer handling which suited his purpose better :

> " Time's *tasking*, it is fathers that *asking* for ease " (No. 4, 27).

More frequently he uses *sain* in lines which are further enriched, either by ' free ' alliteration or internal rhyme, or even by other forms of *cynghanedd*.

> " The *down-dugged ground-hugged* grey " [2]

This is a rich combination of *sain* and *groes* (n-d-g-d-gr / nd-g-d-gr) ; but in

> " *Banned* by the *land* of their birth ",[3]

the *sain* pattern has been deliberately varied. In the highest degree musical, elaborate and original is the first line of *The*

---

[1] See Dr. Bell, *op. cit.* p. 65.   [2] *Poems*, No. 4, stanza 26.   [3] No. 4, stanza 21.

Leaden Echo, with its double (almost treble) *cynghanedd sain*, its delicate but emphatic gradations of tone :

" . . . *bow* or *brooch* or braid or *brace*, *lâce*, latch or

catch or key to keep

Back beauty. . . .".

How deeply the Welsh device influenced the rhythmic **pattern** of the mature poems can be seen in the following :

" . . . *He* in *three* of the thunder-throne ! "   (No. 4, st. **34**)

" . . . . diamond *delves* ! the *elves'*-eyes ! "   (No. 8)

" Left *hand* off *land* I hear the lark. . . ."   (No. 11)

" . . . our sor*did* tur*bid* time," [1]   (*ibid.*)

" *Fall*, *gall* themselves, and gash. . . ."   (No. 12)

" *Forms* and *warms* the life within ; "   (No. 18)

" All things *rising*, all things *sizing*

Mary sees,"   (*ibid.*)

" . . . *skeined stained vêined* variety . ."   (No. 32)

" . . . that *toil*, that *coil*, since (seems) I kissed. . . ."
   (No. 40)

" . . . rare *gold*, *bold* steel bare. . . ."   (No. 42)

" . . . *bears cares* and combs. . . ." [2]   (No. 51)

" . . . dear*est* veri*est* vein. . . ."

" . . . land*mark*, sea*mark*, or soul's star ? " } (No. 54)

It is interesting to examine Hopkins's variations and **development**s of *cynghanedd*. One line contains a combination of *draws* and *sain* in a kind of metrical tmesis :

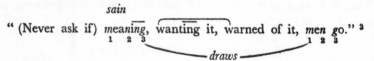

sain

" (Never ask if) mean*ing*, wanting it, warned of it, *men* go." [3]

     1   2   3   1   2   3

               —— *draws* ——

---

[1] In *cynghanedd*, two words rhyme when their final syllables do so, even though, as here, they are unaccented.

[2] Bridges changed ' combs ' to ' moulds ', because he could make no sense of ' combs '. The original word has been restored in the Third Edition.

[3] *The Wreck of the Deutschland*, stanza 8.

He is fond of variants which may be termed *reversal* and *resolution* :

" Night *r*oared, with the *heart-b*reak *h*earing a *h*eart-*b*roke *r*a*bb*le." [1]

In each of the following lines, the first alliterative group is resolved into its elements ; first regularly (fr > f + r) :

(*a*) " And *f*rightful a nightfall | *f*olded *r*ueful a day ; " [2]

then with reversal (dr > r + d) :

(*b*) " But we *dr*eam we are *r*ooted to earth—*D*ust ! " [3]

A consonant may be repeated for reinforcement (br > r + b + r):

(*c*) " The *br*eakers *r*olled on her *b*eam with *r*uinous shock ; " [4]

The process is akin to music : a theme is given out, then varied and modified.   Each time the effect is " characteristic " : in (*a*) the ideas of *alternation* and concentrated horror are emphasized by the lettering ; in (*b*) the reversed consonants support the ironic contrast ; in (*c*) we are made to feel the " buck and flood of the wave ".   In all these examples the initial alliteration is thoroughly English ; but the deliberate patterning is an offshoot of *cynghanedd*.

There is one more metrical device which, very rare in Welsh poetry before the nineteenth century, seems to have been used for the first time in English by Hopkins : this is ' linked rhyme ', the trick of making the initial consonant of one line the last consonant in the rhyme-word of the previous line, e.g. :

> Ar ael y fron araul *fry*
> Saif yr hoenlon syw frein*lys*. [5]

---

[1] *The Wreck of the Deutschland*, stanza 17.   [2] *Ibid.* stanza 15.
[3] *Ibid.* stanza 11.   [4] *Ibid.* stanza 14.
[5] From the *awdl* ' Gwledd Belsassar ', by Ieuan Geirionydd (Early nineteenth century. See *Cyfres y Fil*, p. 40). Mr. T. Parry of University College, Bangor (who kindly supplied this example) writes : " The linked rhyme is a late thing. As Morris Jones states in *Cerdd Dafod* (§ 438), the older poets were always aware of a definite break at the end of a line, even in the *cywydd* couplet, where the two lines form one concise whole. Morris Jones quotes one example from the eighteenth century, but it is only a stray instance, apparently written as a joke. It was in the last century that it became common, and there are, no doubt, scores of examples, if only one took time to read a few of the *awdlau*." Hopkins, presumably, had read some of these odes.

The purpose of such a device (in Hopkins certainly) can only be to emphasize the close ' over-reaving ' of the lines :

> " She drove in the dark to *leeward,*
>   She struck—not a reef or a rock
> But the combs of a smother of sand :   night *drew her*
>   Dead to the Kentish Knock ; " [1]

Again, in the rapid, excited stanza 31 of the same poem we find the phrase " rést of them " rhyming with " bréast of the / Maiden ", and again " *Próvidence* " rhyming with the unexpected but (at the correct speed) phonetically tolerable " ring óf it, and / Startle. . . ." The remaining three examples are all in the sister poem, *The Loss of the Eurydice.*[2]

Between Hopkins and the Welsh poets there are other points of resemblance which, though strictly belonging to the subject of an earlier chapter, are not unconnected with rhythm in its larger sense and may conveniently be treated here.

Despite the sensitiveness of the early Welsh poets to the music of words, their style, like that of Hopkins, was " exclamatory rather than predicative ; such minor but useful parts of speech as articles, prepositions, pronouns and the copula are freely dispensed with ".[3] Their delight in a terse verbal felicity is shown in a free use of compound words (both nouns and adjectives) many of which can be translated only by a complete clause. A number of these compounds are made for purposes of metre ; for instance

> o'r iselgrom risialgraig
> (from the lowbeetling crystalrock)

---

[1] *The Deutschland*, stanza 14.   Cf. stanza 35, ll. 1–2.

[2] Lines 23–24 ; 67–68 ; 91–92. It is interesting to note that the recently discovered French poet, Aragon, has introduced into his live and passionate verse a number of startling linguistic and metrical innovations, among which are *internal* and *linked* rhymes, like those of Hopkins. For example :

> " O revenants bleus de Vimy vingt ans après
>   Morts à demi Je suis le chemin d'aube h*élice*
>   Qui tourne autour de l'obélisque et je me *risque*
>   Où vous errez Malendormis Malenterrés."
>   La Nuit de Mai (*Les Yeux d'Elsa*, 1942).

Cf. *Ourcq*—vau*tour*/Camion, and others in " J'Attends Sa Lettre Au Crépuscule " (*Le Crève-Cœur*). Very ' Hopkinsian ' too is his remark : " Il m'était apparu que non seulement l'art des vers est l'alchimie qui transforme en beautés les faiblesses dans le langage, mais aussi dans la métrique. Presque tous les poètes ont fait des vers admirables en transgressant les règles, parce qu'ils les transgressaient " (Préface, *Les Yeux d'Elsa*).   [3] Dr. Bell, *op. cit.* pp. 42–43.

is a re-ordering, as *cynghanedd groes*, of

> o'r graig o risial, isel a chrom
> (from the rock of crystal, low and beetling).

The necessity of conforming to a strict metrical system forced the poet to be more resourceful than usual in fashioning new compounds ; and the same is true of Hopkins. As a Welsh critic has pointed out, Hopkinsian words like *swiftproud*, *clearrain*, *hellregion* are very common in Dafydd ap Gwilym and his contemporaries.[1]

The syntactical freedom claimed by the Welsh poets is well illustrated by a striking couplet from Cynddelw. This poet has been compared to Pindar, and a literal translation of the following lines (like that made above, in Chapter II, from the Greek poet's fourth Pythian ode) reminds us of the " queer " Hopkins :

> Lliw goleu tonneu taenverw gwenic
> Llanw ebyr ar llyr lle ny mawrdric.

Dr. Bell says :

> " Rendered quite literally, without the insertion of the particles and prepositions which are indispensable in English but can be omitted in Welsh, this reads :
>
> ' Colour light waves spread-boiling billows
> Flood-tide river-mouths on sea where not long-abides.'
>
> What is the uninitiated reader to make of this ? "[2]

We recall the appeals for paraphrases sent to Hopkins by Bridges and Dixon.

But a much more remarkable resemblance to Welsh poetry (and one which can hardly be a coincidence) is in Hopkins's frank use of devices known as *trawsfynediad* (' going across '), *tor ymadrodd* (' break in the sense '), and *gair llanw* (' filling-in phrase '), and especially of the former two. *Trawsfynediad* is a device which gives the poet something of that syntactical freedom which is the rule in inflected languages : words which are logically required in juxtaposition are separated, so that the meaning ' goes across '

[1] Mr. Glyn Jones in *Life and Letters To-day*, June, 1939, p. 53. See also Dr. Bell, *op. cit.* pp. 65 and 67 : *riain feinael* (*fine-eyebrow* maid, i.e. daintybrowed ; *Ynghoed tywylldew* (Inwood *thickdark*, i.e. in the close darkness of the wood ; *gweddeiddblu* gwŷdd (*comelyplumage* of trees).

[2] *Op. cit.* pp. 42–43. It seems to be a dramatic, cumulative sequence of genitives up to *ebyr* : " Colour of light of waves, etc." The momentary flash is from the meeting of river-flood and sea.

some intervening word, phrase, or clause, as when Tudur Aled
writes :

> *Gwin* a rout im *gwyn* o'r tau
> (*Wine* thou gavest me *white* of thine)

which is, of course, " White wine of thine thou gavest me ".
In *tor ymadrodd*, a kind of syntactical tmesis is produced by the
abrupt breaking of one train of thought by another :

> A bydd, *dywaid na byddaf,*
> Fwynas coeth, *fyw onis caf.*

> (And be, *say that I shall not be,*
> A refined kind servant, *living if I do not get her.*) [1]

A good but less difficult example of this device is found in
Hopkins's own *cywydd* :

> Gwan ddwfr a ddwg, *nis dwg dyn,*
> Dyst ffyddlon am ein dyffryn ;

> (Weak water brings, *man brings it not,*
> Faithful witness to our vale ;)

In *gair llanw* the relation between syntactically unconnected
trains of thought is sometimes so hard to seize that, as the name
implies, it was considered to be mere expletive ; in the following
the meaning is fairly clear :

> Fal petwn, *frwydr dalgrwn frad,*
> Ynghenol geol gaead.

> (As if I were, *battle complete betrayal,*
> In the midst of an enclosed gaol.) [2]

When we turn to Hopkins's English poetry, we find that he
adapts the above devices in passages which " read strangely
similar to the literal translation of a *cywydd* from the hand of a
Welsh poet " : [3]

> " O is there no *frowning* of these wrinkles, ranked wrinkles deep,
>   Down ? "   (No. 36 ; *i.e.* ' no frowning down of these wrinkles.')

> " . . . *gold* go garlanded
>   With, *perilous,* O no . . ." (No. 42 ; *i.e.* ' perilous gold ')

[1] Dafydd ap Gwilym ; the meaning is : " Have the kindness to tell her with
all courtesy that I shall die if she will not be mine."

[2] Dafydd ap Gwilym ; the *gair llanw* means : " after the lost battle ".

[3] From an essay on Dafydd ap Gwilym, by Mr. David Bell, under the title " The
Problem of Translation ", in *Dafydd ap Gwilym : Fifty Poems*, by H. Idris Bell and
David Bell (*Y Cymmrodor*, vol. xlviii, 1942).

Turning from *trawsfynediad* to the more drastic ' rupture ' of *tor ymadrodd*, we find :

> " Be adored among men,
> God, three-numberèd form ;
> Wring thy rebel, *dogged in den*,
> Man's *malice*, with wrecking and storm.
> Beyond saying sweet, past telling of tongue,
> Thou art lightning and love, *I found it*, a winter and warm. . . ."
> (No. 4. 9)

> " Angels fall, *they are towers*, from heaven—— " (No. 69).

The strong natural tendency in Hopkins towards all kinds of syntactical freedom might well have been strengthened as much by his reading of the *cywyddwyr* as by his more intimate knowledge of Greek and Latin poetical precedents. The figure tmesis itself, which Hopkins used so boldly in " brim, in a flash, full " and " wind- lilylocks -laced ",[1] has been used with equal boldness in Welsh. Mr. T. Parry writes :

> " Mr. D. Gwenallt Jones, in his *Blodeugerdd o'r Ddeunawfed Ganrif*,[2] p. 115, in dealing with the figure called Tmesis, mentions the fact that G. M. Hopkins uses it in English. . . . Here is one from Wm. Llŷn :
>
> > Dywed *fardd*, da yw dy fodd,
> > *Teulu* pwy a'th atalodd ? [3]
>
> Strictly speaking, perhaps it should not be called a tmesis, as the words do not really form a compound, but it is more than the usual parenthesis or *tor ymadrodd*. There are a few instances of the real thing, such as
>
> > *Ysgafar-*, yn âr y nos,
> > -*Nogod* sydd yma'n agos,[4]
>
> for *ysgyfarnogod*, 'hares.' "

We may sum up by saying that if the " echo of a new rhythm " which had been haunting Hopkins's ear before 1875 was primarily an echo of English nursery rhymes and Greek melic poetry, it was the greater precision of the Welsh system of ' strict ' metres which gave form and clear definition to the English poet's theory and practice.

[1] See *The Deutschland*, 8, and *Harry Ploughman*.
[2] Anthology of the Eighteenth Century.
[3] " Say *bard* (good is thy mode) *of the household*, who has hindered thee ? "
[4] " Hares, in the ploughed land at night, are in this place near ". Morris Jones gives other examples in *Cerdd Dafod*, § 126.

All these abrupt, condensed, parenthetic, spontaneous modes
of expression produce a peculiar semantic rhythm which rein-
forces, and is itself reinforced by, the natural sprung rhythm of
passionate speech. Of the poets before Hopkins, only Shakespeare
and Donne are comparable masters of this complex internal and
external rhythm, and of the two, Donne is perhaps the nearer to
Hopkins and the Welsh poets. Donne too was fond of assonance,
a subtle chiming of vowels which echoed the correspondences of
thought with thought, image with image ; [1] but when the phonal
correspondences are controlled and artfully patterned as in
cynghanedd or in the Hopkinsian variations of that system, the
result is a poetic instrument capable of great variety and sweetness. In the making and use of such an instrument Hopkins
alone, among English poets, bears a striking resemblance to the
masters of the Welsh strict measures.

We embark now upon the last stage of our historical and
roughly chronological survey of those various elements of metre
and texture which make up the rich and complex music of
Hopkins's " new rhythm " : this, of course, is the purely English
tradition, ranging from Old English poetry to the work of those
of Hopkins's contemporaries who either influenced him directly
or struck out poetic rhythms similar to his own.

Hopkins claimed to have invented not *sprung rhythms* but only
sprung rhythm ; yet as we have seen, he admitted in 1882 that
sprung rhythm or something very like it " existed in full force in
Anglo-Saxon verse and in great beauty ".[2] The " great beauty "
of Old English verse has not always been so generously acclaimed ;
but we must now see how far the early Teutonic poets, and not
Hopkins, were the real inventors of English (as distinct from
Classical) sprung rhythm.

The middle decades of the last century saw a great awakening
of interest in Old English verse. Scholars like Guest and Marsh
had described its advantages and possibilities as a metrical
system, and later, at about the same time that Hopkins was
composing *The Deutschland*, Sidney Lanier in America was
demonstrating the rhythmical beauty of some of the Old English
poems.[3] But for our present purpose, the most pertinent and
authoritative statement on this subject came from Coventry

---

[1] E.g. the first eight lines of the third Holy Sonnet, The *Second Anniversary*, ll. 23–26,
and *passim.* See also below, pp. 172–4.

[2] *Letters*, vol. i. p. 156.   [3] See Appendix C.

Patmore, whose essay on *English Metrical Critics* had appeared in 1857.[1]

Hopkins probably never saw this essay until it was reissued with *Amelia and Other Poems* in 1879 ;[2] yet many passages in it were an unconscious breaking of the ground for the new alliterative sprung rhythm :

> " Like rhyme, alliteration is no mere ' ornament ' of versification : it is a real and powerful adjunct when properly employed. If rhyme . . . is the great means in modern languages of marking essential metrical pauses, alliteration is a very effective mode of conferring emphasis on the accent, which is the primary foundation of metre."[3]

After a brief account of Old English verse, Patmore adds :

> " This law is most admirably adapted to fulfil the conditions of a truly accentual metre, which, totally abandoning the element of natural syllabic quantity, takes the isochronous bar as the metrical integer and uses the same kind of liberty as is claimed by the musical composer in filling up that space."[4]

Without " totally abandoning " the element of syllabic length and strength, this, in effect, is what Hopkins succeeded in doing.

Patmore realized the " vast variety " allowed, in alliterative verse, for the position of the accents—a variety, he remarks, not possible where the accents are not *artificially indicated*. Finally, after quoting some verses from *Piers Plowman*, he " ventures " to say :

> " No good ear, when once accustomed to it, can fail to perceive in this law a fountain of pure and beautiful metrical character, or at least to absolve it from the charge of any essential quaintness or oddity."

It is strange, therefore, that he could not absolve Hopkins's verse also from this very charge.

The Old English or ' Anglo-Saxon ' alliterative metre (of

---

[1] *North British Review*, vol. liii. p. 127–61.

[2] Now entitled *Prefatory Study on English Metrical Law*. For Hopkins's comments on the reprint, see *Further Letters*, pp. 176–86.

[3] *Amelia and Other Poems* (1878), pp. 52–63.

[4] On " isochronous intervals " he says (p. 38) : " Not only may metrical intervals differ thus from their nominal equality without destroying measure, but the marking of the measure by the recurrent ictus may be occasionally remitted, the position of the ictus altered, or its place supplied by a pause."

which the metre of *Piers Plowman*, *Patience*, and other Middle
English poems is in many ways a corrupt form) is a rhythm of
' variable base '. The elaborate system underlying the apparently
capricious fluctuations of the metre was first explained by Sievers.
For purposes of comparison with Hopkins, the barest résumé of
that system will suffice here.

Each line must contain four stressed syllables (*arses*), though
the number of unstressed syllables may vary *ad libitum*. The line
is divided into two parts by a strongly marked caesura ; and the
half-line, with its two stresses, constitutes the unit of scansion.
The two half-lines, which may vary considerably in structure, are
linked by alliteration, the rule being that one or both of the
arses in the first half-line must alliterate with the first *arsis*, and
that only, in the second half-line. Therefore, in terms of sprung
rhythm we may say that the feet range from the single stressed
monosyllable to the foot with *increased thesis*—that is, with from
two to four or even five slack syllables before or after the stress.
In no case, however, can the *thesis* be increased at the *end* of the
half-line or line.

By changing the respective positions of *arsis* and *thesis*, in the
half-line, we obtain the three simplest metrical types :

Type A.	⁄ × . . ⁄ ×
Type B.	× . . . ⁄ × . . . ⁄
Type C.	× . . . ⁄ ⁄ ×

Type A is sometimes varied by the prefixing of an *Auftakt*
or anacrusis : (× . .) ⁄ × . . . . ⁄ ×. Two more types arise
when a *secondary arsis* ⸀ compensates for the loss of one *thesis* :

Type D₁ ⁄ | ⁄ ⸀ × ;	D₂ ⁄ | ⁄ × ⸀
Type E₁ ⁄ ⸀ × | ⁄ ;	E₂ ⁄ × ⸀ | ⁄

Patmore seems not to have realized that the Old English poet
paid more attention to syllabic length than do most modern
poets. The *arsis* was regularly a syllable which was long by
nature or by position (i.e. followed by two consonants), and the
secondary arsis was invariably long. A short syllable immediately
preceded by an *arsis* could itself bear a full stress, and resolution
of the *arsis* was common. But as in Hopkins's rhythm, long
syllables were not excluded from the *thesis*.

Since the predominant metrical type was A, the rhythm was
mainly ' falling ' or ' trochaic ' ; but the variations described
above introduce a rich ' counterpoint ', a constant alternation of

what Hopkins (defining sprung rhythm) called ' falling ', ' rising ', and ' rocking ' feet : [1]

	Falling		Rocking	
Types A and C.	clyppe ond cysse	•	ond on cnéo lecge	
	Falling		Rising	
,, A and B.	honda ond héafod,	•	swā hē hwilum ǣr	
	Rocking		Falling	
,, C and E₁.	in géardagum	•	giefstólas bréac.	
	Rising		Falling	
,, B and A.	Đonne onwaecneð eft	•	winelēas gúma.	
	Rising		Falling	
,, B and A.	Gesihð him biforan	•	fealwe wēgas,	
	Falling		Falling	
,, A and A.	baðian brimfuglas	•	brǣdan feðra. . . .	

The rhythm of this passage from *The Wanderer* is truly ' sprung ', since it allows of paeonic and monosyllabic feet whenever the poet feels one or the other to be the most natural, forceful, or convenient mode of expression. The lines, moreover, can be freely " over-rove ", although a full pause never breaks the half-line.

With regard to the caesural pause, Patmore says that certain types of modern verse, like the alexandrine, require that this pause should be clearly marked : " it is very questionable ", he adds, " whether English verse has gained by the entire disuse of the caesural dot ". Hopkins revived the caesural mark (|) in five poems where he employs the sprung alexandrine ; [2] but in early English the caesural pause never falls in the middle of a word, as it frequently does in Hopkins :

Drowned. " O pity and indig|nation ! Manshape, that shóne "
(No. 48)

The sprung alexandrine, though partly derived from the classical hexameter, is also partly a Teutonic throwback. There

[1] *Poems of G. M. Hopkins*, Author's Preface, p. 1.
[2] *Poems*, Nos. 32, 38 and 48 ; also in a MS. " H " version of No. 39 (*The Soldier*), and in the MS. " A " version of No. 58 (see Third Edition, No. 105).

is one Old English poem, the *Later Genesis* (or *Genesis B*), which, being almost certainly based on an Old Saxon original, has longer lines than any other poem of the period.[1] Dramatic in quality, flexible in rhythm, its lines vary in length from the usual four-stress

> sē ðe helle forð · healdan sceolde (l. 348)

to longer ones which, if they are not actually six-stress lines, certainly invite two extra secondary stresses and are therefore more easily read as alexandrines : they do, in fact, strongly resemble the alexandrines of Hopkins's *Deutschland* and *St. Winefred's Well* fragment, e.g. :

1. Ācwaeð hine þā fram his hyldo · ond hine on helle wearp
2. on þā dēopan dala · þær hē to dēofle wearð.
3. Se fēond mid his gefērum eallum · fēollon þā ufon of heofnum
4. þurh swā longe · swā þrēo niht ond dagas (ll. 304–7).

The disposition of the syllables and stresses in line 3 makes it almost identical in rhythm with one in the *Deutschland* :

" The treasure never eyesight got, nor was ever guessed what for
    the hearing " ; [2]

while line 4 is not unlike

    " Tarpeian-fast, but a blown beacon of light ", [3]
or
    " The sour scythe cringe, and the blear share come." [4]

We have seen how, in Hopkins, sprung rhythm begets a kind of ' sprung ' syntax. So in Anglo-Saxon poetry the highly inflected language made possible those inversions and far-stepping syntactical relationships which are occasionally so puzzling in Hopkins. In *The Wanderer* we read :

> flēotendra ferð · nō þær fela bringeð
>
> cūðra cwidegiedda. (lines 54–5)

This means : the mind (*ferð*) brings not back there many of the familiar sayings (*fela cūðra cwidegiedda*) of the floaters of the air (*flēotendra*, i.e. ' revenants ').

Though excellent for narrative or elegy, the Old English

---

[1] See Wyatt's *Anglo-Saxon Reader* (1922), pp. 275–6.
[2] Stanza 26.   [3] Stanza 29.   [4] Stanza 11.

sprung rhythm, with its regular lineal alliteration, suffers like most ' continuous ' verse from a certain monotony ; it is not suited to swift, subtle or passionate lyrical utterance. Hopkins gave the old stress-metre a new lease of life by wedding it to the more varied rhymed verse-forms of Romance origin. Such a bold fusion, together with a more imaginative use of alliteration, preserved the best and avoided what was effete in the older Teutonic and Romance modes and rhythms.

Turning to English poets of the modern period (from 1500 onwards), we find that sprung rhythms are occasionally introduced as effective variants of the standard metres ; but nowhere is sprung rhythm adopted as a universal principle. Hopkins gives a blunt explanation :

> " *if they could have done it they would* : sprung rhythm, once you hear it, is so eminently natural a thing and so effective a thing that if they had known of it they would have used it. Many people, as we say, have been ' burning ', but they all missed it ; they took it up and mislaid it again." [1]

Putting aside Milton's case, which he calls " altogether singular ", he affirms that Robert Greene (1560–92) was " the last who employed sprung rhythm at all consciously and he never continuously ".[2] But there is no evidence that Greene used these rhythms more consciously, or even more frequently, than many of the later poets quoted below. Hopkins was probably thinking of certain lines in *Sephestia's Song to her Child* from *Menaphon* :

> " Mother's wag, pretty boy,
> Father's sorrow, father's joy ! . . .
>
> Such a boy by him and me,
> He was glad, I was woe. . . ."

But the same cretic movement, a favourite one with Hopkins, was again used with fine effect in Beaumont and Fletcher's *Song to Pan.*

Of the other poets after Greene who sometimes used sprung rhythms, Hopkins himself quotes Shakespeare and Campbell, discusses Coleridge without any overt acknowledgment of indebtedness, but makes no mention of Donne, Blake, Shelley, Tennyson, Browning, Meredith, Matthew Arnold, and Christina Rossetti as forerunners of more or less significance in his own field of metrical emancipation.

[1] *Letters*, vol. i. p. 156.   [2] *Ibid.*   See also *Poems,* Author's Preface, p. 6.

Shakespeare's freedom is apparent in his blank verse ; he frequently omits a weak syllable or adds extra ones, thereby giving his rhythm that vigour and flexibility which is implied in the word " sprung ". What Abbott calls " lines of four accents " may often be scanned quite satisfactorily as sprung rhythm :

" Youth, | beauty, | wisdom, | courage, | all
That happiness and prime can happy call : "
> (*All's Well*, II. i. 184.)

" Is goads, thorns, nettles, tails of wasps."
> (*Winter's Tale*, I. ii. 329.)

" Letters should not be known ; riches, poverty . . .
Bourn, bound of land, tilth, vineyard, none."
> (*Tempest*, II. i. 157–9.)

The changed pronunciation of words like *riches* and *bourn* may have disguised the original rhythm of the lines ; but Hopkins would almost certainly have scanned them, by predilection, as above. Similarly, a number of lines quoted by Abbott [1] as having a syllable or foot omitted after a marked pause, could very well be treated as " sprung " : for instance,

> " Scarce an | y joy
> Did ev | er so | long live. | - | No sorrow. . . . [2]

could be effectively read as

> " Did ever so long live.   ⌃   No sorrow. . . ."

Again

> " To watch, | poor perdu !
> With this | thin helm. | × - | Mine ene | my's dog . . . " [3]

could be

> " With this thin helm.   ⌃   Mine enemy's dog . . . ."

Many editors have emended the text of Shakespeare for the sole purpose of rationalizing the metre ; but after the acceptance of Hopkins the following readings and scansions should be as practical and academic as any others :

" Our thighs pack'd with wax, our mouths with honey."
> (2 *Hen. IV*, iv. 77.)

---

[1] See *Shakespearian Grammar* (edn. of 1888), §§ 504–80.
[2] *Winter's Tale*, V. iii. 53.
[3] *King Lear*, IV. vii. 36.

" Nothing but that ; move still, still so."
> (*Winter's Tale*, IV. iii. 142.)

" Call our cares fears, which will in time."
> (*Coriol.*, III. i. 137.)

" Let fall thy lance. Despair and die."
> (*Rich.* III., V. iii. 143.)

In Volume I we have already defined Shakespeare's influence on Hopkins's development of the " outride " or " hanger ".[1]

There are two or three pre-Shakespearian poets who, whether or not Hopkins was familiar with their work, deserve to be mentioned here as technical forerunners. First is John Lydgate (1373–1460), whose " tumbling verse " has the freedom and much of the verve of the popular ballad and nursery rhyme. Mr. Aldous Huxley speaks of " Lydgate-like breakings and prolongings of the line " as one of the devices by which Hopkins, in the tense later sonnets, contrives to render (" with what terrible adequacy ") the sobbing and spasmodic extremes of unhappiness.[2] Whether the element of uncertainty in the rhythm of *London Lyckpeny* was due to a careless fluency or to a deliberate reaction against the perfected syllabism of Chaucer is a question not easily answered ; but its relationship to the sprung rhythm of Hopkins may be seen in the following scansions :

> " Unto the common place I yode thoo,
>> Where sat one with a sylken hoode ;
> I dyd hym reverence, for I ought to do so,
>> And told my case as well as I coode. . . ."

> " Then hyed I me to Belyngsgate,
>> And one cryed, ' hoo ! go we hence ! '
> I prayd a barge-man for gods sake,
>> That he would spare me my expence." [3]

---

[1] In chapter iii.

[2] *Texts and Pretexts* (Chatto and Windus), 1st edn. p. 284.

[3] *Specimens of English Literature, A.D. 1394–1599* (Skeat), pp. 24 and 27. The normal scansion of the first four lines would probably be

The nearest we have to an opinion by Hopkins on verse of this kind, ambiguous and " little calculated ", is contained in a note on a poem by Sir Thomas Wyatt :

> " Chaucer and his contemporaries wrote for a pronunciation fast changing. . . . Their versification was popular and hit the mark in its time, but soon, as far as I can see, became obsolete, and they being much read and not rightly scanned thus came to suggest rhythms which they never thought of." [1]

The " doggrel " of *Ralph Roister Doister* (*circa* 1550) is thought by Hopkins to have arisen in this way—" a shapeless thing, the corruption or degeneration of something literary misunderstood or disfigured. If it were a spontaneous popular growth it would be simpler and stronger." [2]

The last sentence is significant ; yet Hopkins's opinions on two other poets of that period are hardly what we should expect. He praises Surrey as an accomplished rhythmist who, in his couplets of alternate six and seven feet, was trying to systematize " this wretched doggrel ". He finds him a greater man than Wyatt, whose rhythm is " very French and lightsome, lighter than Surrey's and weaker ".[3] This view is strange, since Wyatt has been hailed by one critic as the forerunner, in rhythmic subtlety, of T. S. Eliot. Hopkins's comment on the metre of a poem by Wyatt shows how uncertain and tentative much of his theorizing could be ; the poem in question is *The Lover Seeking for his Lost Heart*, and begins :

> " Help me to seek ! for I lost it there ;
> And if that ye have found it, ye that be here,
> And seek to convey it secretly,
> Handle it soft, and treat it tenderly,
> Or else it will plain, and then appair.
> But pray restore it mannerly,
> Since that I do ask it thus honestly,
> For to lese it, it sitteth me near ;
> Help me to seek ! " [4]

[1] *Letters*, vol. i. p. 108. The words omitted in this quotation suggest that in 1880 Hopkins believed that even Chaucer might have intended to write in sprung rhythm : " everybody knows that final *e* for instance has often to be sounded in Chaucer, but everybody does not know that mostly it is *not* to be sounded and that the line which scans by its aid is really to be scanned another way " (*loc cit.*). This probably implies such a reading as :

> " Whan Zéphirús éek with his swét(e) bréeth . . .
> The téndre cróppes ánd the yóng(e) sónne. . . ."

By *not* sounding the final *e*'s we get monosyllabic feet. But see *Letters*, vol. ii., pp. 66–7.
[2] *Ibid.*   [3] *Letters*, vol. i. *loc. cit.* p. 109.   [4] *Ibid.* p. 107.

According to Hopkins, Bridges took the rhythm for " free triple time, iambs and anapaests say, and four feet to a line (except the refrain) ".[1] But Hopkins will not have it so ; he insists that the metre here, as in French verse, depends upon counted syllables and not upon the natural oratorical stress. The main point, he says, is the pause or caesura. Like Udall in the doggrel of *Ralph Roister Doister*, Wyatt " thinks himself at liberty to give each wing of the line two or three stresses at pleasure, but not more than two syllables, a stress and a slack, to each foot." The second half of line 8 he scans :

" it sitteth me near "

. . . that is really, ' it sitteth me near ' or as I would like to write it

" it sitteth me near '

the black ball marking the real or heard stress, the white the dumb or conventional one." [2]

The truth seems to be that Wyatt, like Bridges himself, wavered between a strict syllabic metre and a freer stress-rhythm, though Bridges's intention is never so obscure as Wyatt's. Hopkins concedes an important point when he says :

" I should add that as both parts of [Wyatt's] line may begin with the stress or slack at option he gets an effect of sprung rhythm, which however from the weakness of the stresses is slight."

But how was either Hopkins or Bridges to know the precise *weight* of Wyatt's stresses ? Similarly, when Mr. Matthiessen relates Wyatt's freer rhythms to those of Mr. Eliot, he probably underestimates the frequency with which the early poet gave his words a foreign accent (e.g. *harboùr, suffèr, mistrèss, dangèr*) :

" They flee from me that sometime did me seek,
    With naked foot stalking, in my chamber :
I have seen them, gentle, tame and meek,
    That now are wild and do not remember,
    That sometime they put themselves in danger
    To take bread at my hand ; and now they range
    Busily seeking with a continual change." [3]

[1] *Letters*, vol. i. p. 107.   [2] *Ibid.* p. 109.
[3] The following opinion by Prof. F. O. Matthiessen affords an interesting comment on the Bridges-Hopkins controversy over Wyatt :
" What fascinated [Eliot's] ear in the early seventeenth century poets was the ' constant evasion and recognition of regularity ', the reliance on the iambic penta-

That is fine poetry ; and if this passage and the rest of the poem are read with the natural speech rhythm of to-day we have a remarkable anticipation of the freer rhythms of both Bridges and Eliot.

If the uncertainty of Wyatt's stressing makes his metre " French and lightsome ", the same cannot be said of that thoroughly English measure of forty years later—the Skeltonian ' rigmarole '. Here we have something like the forthright vigour and flexibility of sprung rhythm—that popular if less subtle form of it which derives from the nursery rhyme and weather saw (' Red at night, Shepherd's delight '). In the normal two-stress line, monosyllabic feet are rare but paeons are common ; and sometimes the torrent of syllables makes the addition of a third full or secondary stress almost unavoidable :

> " Why come ye nat to court ?—
>   To whyche court ?'
>   To the kynges court : "

> " Thus royally he dothe deale
>   Vnder the kynges brode seale ;
>   And in the Checker he them cheks ;
>   In the Ster Chambre he noddis and beks. . . ." [1]

Saintsbury's words on Skelton might, with a little modification, be applied to Hopkins :

> " With his quicker, more restless, more subtle wit and intelli-
> gence, he feels constantly and acutely the *gêne*, the constraint and
> irksomeness of these [i.e. syllabic] metres. . . . He wants to run
> up and down all the gamut from aureate to familiar diction ;
> to get quick changes of verse and rhyme and cadence ; to have
> elbow-room and finger-openings." [2]

The reaction of Lydgate and Skelton against the metrical smoothness of the Chaucer-Gower school was repeated when Coleridge, in *Christabel*, turned away from the faultless syllabism

---

meter form and yet the continual skilful withdrawing from it. What strikes him as an essential quality in the most interesting verse is this very hesitation between regularity and irregularity, in subtle correspondence to a pyschological perception of the precarious balance that constitutes life itself : ' It is this contrast between fixity and flux, this unperceived evasion of monotony, which is the very life of verse.' " *The Achievement of T. S. Eliot* (Oxford University Press), pp. 79 and 87.)

[1] *Why Come Ye Nat To Courte ?* ll. 398–400 ; 333–6.
[2] *History of English Prosody*, vol. i. p. 242.

of most eighteenth-century verse—from what Hopkins called the absurdity of " fond mem'ry's voice " and " th'umbrageous grove ". Coleridge, like Hopkins, had been fascinated by the *Samson Agonistes* choruses. After some experimental verses in one of his note-books, he writes :

" Drūnk wĭth Ĭ—dŏlātrў—drūnk wĭth Wīne

A noble metre if I can find a metre to precede and follow :

Sūmptŭoŭs Dălĭlă floātĭng thĭs wăy . . ."

The fruit of this rumination was the accentual verse of *Christabel*, of which he writes in his Preface :

> " The metre is founded on a new principle, namely that of counting in each line the accents, not the syllables. Though the latter may vary from seven to twelve, yet in each line the accents will be found to be only four. Nevertheless this occasional variation in number of syllables is not introduced wantonly, or for the mere ends of convenience, but in correspondence with some transition in the nature of the imagery or passion."

This anticipates, though not completely, the rationale of Hopkins's sprung and expressional (or " imitative ") rhythm. In actual practice, lines like

" 'Tis the míddle of the níght by the cástle clóck
And the ówls have awákened the crówing cóck. . . ."

may be reduced in syllabic length to

" Ís the níght chílly and dárk ?
The níght is chílly but nót dárk. . . ." [1]

which are pure sprung rhythm.

Dixon pointed out this resemblance to Hopkins,[2] who replied that the note to *Christabel*

> " . . . was drawing a distinction between two systems of scanning, the one of which is quite opposed to sprung rhythm, the other *is not, but might be developed into*, that."

Although, he adds, it was but a step from many popular and literary cadences then in being to sprung rhythm, and nature even without that help seemed to prompt it of itself, yet the step had never, as far as he knew, been taken. The *Christabel* metre

---

[1] The stresses are so marked by Bridges in *Milton's Prosody* (1921), pp. 87 and 89.
[2] *Letters*, vol. ii. p. 18.

7*

was a " mixed rhythm " arising from the substitution of three-syllabled for two-syllabled feet without strict regard for *time* or *quantity*—a " logaoedic " measure. This, he says, " is freely done in ballad-measures and Coleridge does it in *Christabel*." [1]

The " new principle " differs from that of sprung rhythm in two essential features : in the former the stressed syllable has not sufficient weight or time-value to allow of paeons or of a sequence of three or more monosyllabic feet. Bridges has shown,[2] moreover, that the *Christabel* verse is not even strictly *accentual*. In a line like

" How drowsily it crew ",

there are only two real accents, whereas Coleridge's system demands three. Similarly the following lines can each have four stresses, but only when the metre, which is virtually syllabic, supplies one conventional secondary accent :

" From her kennel beneath the rock
She maketh answer to the clock. . . ."

Hence the rhythm falls between two principles : it is neither wholly syllabic nor wholly accentual but a mixture of both. Actually *Christabel* shows an easy preponderance of standard iambic lines ; but the discrepancy we have noticed is similar to that which marred Hopkins's own early efforts at sprung rhythm.[3]

The logaoedic measure was caught up by Scott and Byron and passed on to Shelley, Tennyson, and Swinburne, with the last of whom it reaches a perfection which, after the first flush of enthusiasm, leaves in us a sense of limitation and disappointment. Shelley was nearer to the elusive tradition of sprung rhythm when, in *To the Night*, he varied the opening lines of the lyric—

" Swiftly walk over the western wave
Spirit of Night ! "

with

" Thy brother Death came and cried
Wouldst thou me ? "

Bridges bestows great praise upon the cumulative rhythm of Shelley's " Away ! the moor is dark beneath the moon " (1814).

[1] *Letters*, vol. ii. p. 21.   [2] *Milton's Prosody* (1921), p. 88.
See above, chap. i. p. 95.

The poem is important technically, as it shows that Bridges's own most successful rhythms (in *London Snow*, for instance) were not wholly derived from those of Hopkins. The use of alexandrines and of longer lines which are related to the shorter lines by a fiction of double-stressing produces a kind of musical scheme— that which used to be called *Alla breve*,

> " . . . four minims to the bar, with some secondary accent on the third of them and liberty to introduce triplets. The variant rhythms which this scheme allows are purposely elaborated towards the end with a great effect of luxuriance." [1]

Shelley consciously uses various stress-rhythms to counterpoint his original measure and so destroy its sing-song framework :

> " Away ! the moor is dark beneath the moon,
>
>   Rapid clouds have drunk | the last pale beam of even : "

The effect of paeons and longer feet is produced in

> " And profoundest midnight shroud the serene lights of heaven. . . .
>
> Some respite to its turbulence unresting ocean knows ; "

This system of double-stressing reappears in the trochaic alexandrines of George Meredith's *Love in the Valley*, the first version of which appeared in 1851. The metre seems to be derived partly from the Galliambic, partly from the Saturnian measure. The normal, slightly sing-song movement of

> " Every woodland tree | is flushing like the dogwood,
>
>   Flashing like the whitebeam, | swaying like the reed," [2]

is varied by such lines as

> " Soon will she lie | like a white frost sunrise. . . ."
>
>   Large and smoky red | the Sun's cold disk drops ",

in which the quantitative spondee and the monosyllabic foot of sprung rhythm seem to jostle each other. The rhythm is, in effect, sprung. The four or five main oratorical stresses take

---

[1] *Milton's Prosody* (1921), p. 104.
[2] Cf. Hopkins's " wind-beat whitebeam " (No. 8). Meredith repeats the image three lines later :

> " Flashing as in gusts the sudden-lighted whitebeam ".

Had Hopkins read *Love in the Valley* ?

control of it ; yet since the hexametric base is constantly re-asserting itself, the application of the time-principle forces us to fill out the shorter lines with heavy monosyllabic feet which are roughly equal in length to the accentual trochees and dactyls. The metrical uncertainty has disturbed some critics :

> " It becomes almost an annoyance to find here and there a verse that violates the very laws on recognition of which the whole significance of the melody depends." [1]

And indeed a line like

" Úp lānes, thröugh wōods, they tröop in jöyful bånds,"

may be read with four, five, or seven stresses but in no way with six. Yet the metre of the poem as a whole is less supple than the true sprung rhythm. Meredith attempts no striking changes in tempo, no powerful cumulative effects. Nevertheless, it marks an important step towards the innovation of Hopkins.

All our English logaoedic or ' mixed ' measures owe much to the classical hexameter, the influence of which upon our native metres was strengthened by the recurrent attempts, since the time of Gabriel Harvey, to establish the quantitative hexameter in English. But the real tradition of " sprung rhythms " in modern English is to be traced rather in those examples of rough, seemingly uncouth rhythms which are found in Donne, Blake, and occasionally in Browning

A characteristic of Hopkins's verse is the close " over-reaving ", as he called it, of consecutive lines ; [2] and it is signi-ficant that in Donne's *Satires*, where the rhyming couplet is always straining towards or even beyond the freedom of late Shake-spearian blank verse, this *élan* is accentuated by a bold defiance of the conventional stress-points, by the occasional splitting of a rhyme-word at the end of a line,[3] and by a synatactical tightness which packs the line with emphatic syllables and a huddle of urgent ideas :

[1] Basil de Selincourt in Sturge Henderson's *George Meredith* (Methuen, 1907), p. 237. But contrast the following opinion :
" In the face of this poem, as nowhere else in Mr. Meredith's enchanted woods, criticism drops its weapons. One can only be thankful that so great an inspiration has been clothed in a form so nearly perfect." (*George Meredith*, by G. M. Trevelyan, Constable, 1912 ; p. 41).

[2] See *Poems of G. M. H.*, Author's Preface, p. 4.

[3] Cf. Hopkins, *Poems*, Nos. 12, 17, 32, 38, 41, 44 and 48. The same device is to be met with in Campion, Herbert of Cherbury and others.

" Líke a wédge in a blóck, wríng to the bár
　　Béaring like ásses. . . ."　　　　　　　　　(II. 71–2).

" So doth, so is religion ; and this blind-
　　ness too much light breeds.　But unmoved thou
　　Of force must one, and forced but one allow ;
　　And the right."　　　　　　　　　　　　　(III. 68–71).

" He knóws who hath sóld his lánd, and nów doth bég
　　A lícence, óld íron, bōots, shóes, and égg-
　　shélls to transpórt, etc."　　　　　　　　　(IV. 103–5).

Double reversal (' counterpoint ') and resolution are frequent :

" Frées from the stíng of jésts áll whō in extréme
　　Are wrétched or wícked ;　of thése twō a théme
　　Chárity and líberty gíve me."　　　　　　　(V, 5–7).

The next passage, like many in Hopkins, needs a few stress-
marks to save the unpractised reader from floundering.　By
marking the natural speech-rhythm with large accents and the
normal metrical stress with dots we find an extreme case of that
" counterpoint " which Hopkins illustrated from Ovid :[1]

" Hów múch wórse àre súitors, whó tò men's lúst

　　Are máde préys ?　Ó, wórse thàn dúst òr wórms' méat,

　　For theý do ēat yòu now whose sélves worms shall eat."
　　　　　　　　　　　　　　　　　　　　(V, 20–32.)

　　It is remarkable that nowhere in his writings does Hopkins
mention Donne ;　yet it is difficult to believe that he had not
read a poet who in personality, intellect, and style was so like
himself.　That Hopkinsian felicity of syntax which ensures the
closest union between the semantic and audible rhythms is
anticipated in many passages of Donne ;　and there is a psychological significance in this tendency of two poets, each passionately
intellectual and morally earnest, to unite similar unconventional
modes of rhythm and grammar :

" To stand inquiring right, is not to stray ;
　　To sleep, or run wrong, is.　On a huge hill,
　　Cragged and steep, Truth stands, and he that will
　　Reach her, about must and about must go,
　　And what th' hill's suddenness resists, win so."
　　　　　　　　　　　　　　　　　　　　(III. 78–82.)

[1] See above, chap. ii. p. 114.　Donne's intention of imitating the roughness of
Persius would account for this metrical irregularity.

The quality of tense, excited diction and syntax in Donne is, as in Hopkins, integral to the total rhythmical effect. The lyrics and sonnets are less rugged, but of one characteristic sonnet Mr. Aldous Huxley has said,[1] with obvious truth : " Donne's ' Batter my heart, three-person'd God ' is simply Hopkins without the rhythmical subtleties." Yet perhaps it is only a half-truth to imply that the resemblances to Hopkins are restricted to emotive thought and syntax : there are, also, certain rhythmical affinities.[2] The heavy long monosyllables noticeably control the tempo ; the stressing in lines 6, 7 and 8 is the natural pulse of a rising emotion :

" Batter my heart, three-person'd God ; for you
As yet but knock ; breathe, shine, and seek to mend ;
That I may rise, and stand, o'erthrow me, and bend
Your force, to break, blow, burn, and make me new.
I, like an usurp'd town, to another due,
Labour to admit you, but O, to no end.
Reason your viceroy in me, me should defend,
But is captived, and proves weak or untrue. . . ." [3]

That is the language and rhythm of what is called ' passion '. In a later poet, Browning, whose handling of rhythm, diction, and syntax often shows resemblances to those of Donne and Hopkins, we seldom meet this deep personal emotion ; yet his passion, though more objective, rhetorical, or (as Hopkins said) " blustering ", frequently expresses itself in similar rhythms. In his most vigorous, heroic mood is *Hervé Riel* :

" For up stood, for out stepped, for in struck amid all these
—A Captain ? A Lieutenant ? A Mate—first, second, third ?
No such man of mark. . . ."

In *Master Hugues of Saxe-Gotha* there are two passages which, though highly characteristic of Browning's hearty, earnest-facetious, conversational and exclamatory style, might well have suggested the rhythmical trick and fantasy of two passages in Hopkins :

" What with affirming, denying,
Holding, riposting, subjoining,
All's like . . . it's like . . . for an instance I'm trying. . . .
There ! See our roof, its gilt moulding and groining
Under those spider-webs lying ! "

.   .   .   .

[1] In a letter to the present writer.
[2] Miss L. I. Guiney, in *The Month* (March 1919) spoke of the " counterpointed intricacy " of Donne's rhythms.   [3] *Holy Sonnets*, XIV.

" While in the roof, if I'm right there,
　. . . Lo, you, the wick in the socket !
Hallo, you sacristan, show us a light there,
　Down it dips, gone like a rocket ! "

Hopkins uses the same broken logaoedic measure in

" But how shall I . . . make me room there !
Reach me' a . . . Fancy, come faster—
Strike you the sight of it? look at it loom there,
Thing that she . . . there then ! the Master . . ." [1]

And in the later poem of shipwreck :

" Too proud, too proud, what a press she bore !
Royal, and all her royals wore.
　　Sharp with her, shorten sail !
Too late ;　lost ;　gone with the gale." [2]

Sporadic instances of sprung rhythm are to be found in a
number of the major Victorian poets.　The bold effect in
Tennyson's line, "Break, break, break", was repeated in Matthew
Arnold's *Forsaken Merman* (line 85) and in Christina Rossetti's
Goblin Market (line 542) ; but Hopkins was puzzled by the
apparent inability of these poets to see how that principle of
strong stress and long pause could be given a much wider application, and could be still further set off by the ' musical ' equivalence
of four semiquavers to the crotchet—the paeonic foot.　Nevertheless, without Swinburne, Tennyson, and other contemporaries,
Hopkins would possibly not have been the master of poetic
rhythm that he was.　Swinburne's command of the "blessed
trisyllabic swing and swell " and of a wide range of logaoedic
measures ; Tennyson's equal skill in the irregular metres of some
early poems like *All Things Will Die*, and in such a rhythmical
tour de force as *The Revenge* ; Matthew Arnold's bold experiment
with ' free verse ' in *The Strayed Reveller*, and Christina Rossetti's
fine metrical verve and variety in *Goblin Market* and *A Ballad of
Boding*—all these provided Hopkins with a solid contemporary
tradition of metrical virtuosity upon which he could innovate
with confidence.
　　Yet in all the nineteenth century there was, perhaps, no
piece of verse so close in form and spirit to the sprung rhythm of
Hopkins as the early poem by Blake which Father Lahey has
already quoted.　In the absence of stress-marks, we cannot be

---

[1] *The Wreck of the Deutschland*, stanza 28.　　[2] *The Loss of the Eurydice*, stanza 9.

quite certain of Blake's rhythmical intention in every line ; but
the following is a scansion for which Hopkins, if no other, could
have found ample justification :

> " Thou fair-haired Angel of the Evening,
>   Now whilst the sun rests on the mountains, light
>   Thy bright torch of love—thy radiant crown
>   Put on and smile upon our evening bed !
>   Smile on our loves : and while thou drawest the
>   Blue curtains of the sky, scatter thy silver dew
>   On every flower that shuts its sweet eyes
>   In timely sleep." [1]

Blake, like Campbell, was one of those poets who, as Hopkins
put it, " took up sprung rhythm and mislaid it again ".[2]   The
Battle of the Baltic, in spite of a line so strong and majestic as

> "And her arms along the deep proudly shone ",

is not in sprung rhythm : Campbell, Browning, Arnold, and
Christina Rossetti were all " burning, but they missed it ".[2]
Coventry Patmore, an acute critic of rhythm and metre, could
himself come as near to sprung, imitative rhythm as the following :

> " And so the whole
> Unfathomable and immense
> Triumphing tide, comes at the last to reach
> And burst in wind-kissed splendours on the deaf'ning beach." [3]

Yet he was unable to recognize in Hopkins's rhythms the consummation, or at least an authentic development, of his own
admirable theories.[3]

Robert Bridges, as we have seen, was more clearly though
still not fully aware of what Hopkins had achieved. If anyone
should accuse Bridges of withholding the Hopkins poems so that
he might himself capitalize on sprung rhythm, R. B.'s preface to

---

[1] *To the Evening Star*, in *Poetical Sketches* (1783). There are similar rhythmical
effects in *To Winter*, *To Autumn*, *Fair Eleanor*, and *Samson*.

[2] *Letters*, vol. i. p. 156.

[3] From the ode *Wind and Wave*. As Mr. Herbert Read points out in his essay
on Patmore (*In Defence of Shelley and Other Essays*), there is a curious discrepancy
between the free variation of his lines, with their occasional vigorous assertion of
speech rhythm, and such a meticulous care for a syllabic base as is shown in the
syncope of " deaf'ning ".

his own *Poems*, Third Series, 1880, could be adduced in his favour :

> "The poems in the smaller type, like those similarly distinguished in the author's last series [1879], are written by the rules of a new prosody, which may very well exist by the side of the old. It is left to the judgment of the reader : but the author hopes that these verses will be read with attention to the natural quantity and accent of the syllables,—for these are the interpretation of the rhythm,—and not with the notion that all accents in poetry are alternate with unaccented syllables, nor with the almost universal prejudice that when two or more unaccented syllables intervene between two accented syllables the former must suffer and be slurred over : a prejudice which probably arises from the common misuse of unaccented for short syllables.
>
> "The use of feet which correspond to pæons, and the frequent inversions of feet in these new rhythms, render it possible for four or five unaccented syllables to follow on each other.
>
> "The author disavows any claim to originality for the novelty : this is almost entirely due to a friend, whose poems remain, he regrets to say, in manuscript.
>
> "Christmas, 1879." [1]

The inference to be drawn from that is plain enough, and it redounds to the credit of both the friends.

Writing to Patmore nearly four years later, Hopkins refers to Bridges's poems " in the smaller type " and neatly sums up the prosodic aspect of the " new rhythm " :

> "About that new prosody according to which I think English verse might be written and by which Bridges has written parts of *Prometheus*, as well as some earlier poems, the most beautiful, I think, ' Snow in London ', [2] I do not know that Bridges shares all my views ; he would, I think, treat it as less strict than I should say it ought to be and has been freer in putting strong syllables in weak places and weak in strong than always pleases my ear. As I look at it, it is a simple thing and capable of being drawn up in a few strict rules, stricter, not looser than the common prosody. But though the rules would be few and strict, the freedom of motion in the rhythm gained under them would, as I believe, be very great. The converse at all events you will agree to and would insist on, that where there is much freedom of motion the laws which limit it should be strict." [3]

It is difficult to imagine Hopkins stating finally, to say nothing of keeping consistently, those " few strict rules " (for his own

---

[1] Quoted in *Letters*, vol. i. p. 310.
[2] I.e. ' London Snow.' See also *Letters*, vol. i. p. 111.   [3] *Further Letters*, p. 187.

Preface says nothing about syllabic quantity). Certainly the "new rhythm" as he practised it, with its Greek 'phrasing' and irregular *cynghanedd*, was something far too complex and personal to be reduced to a few strict rules. It was given only to Hopkins to achieve the maximum "freedom of motion" which is compatible with the most elaborate poetic *inscape*.

Yet too much freedom of motion can be as irksome as too little. Hopkins never adopted sprung rhythm exclusively, for his last sonnets were in a modified form of standard rhythm. Freedom to be as prosodically free or self-restricted as his muse required at any given time—that was the reasoned but uncompromising demand which Hopkins made on Tradition.

CHAPTER IV

HOPKINS AS READER AND CRITIC

THE majority of Hopkins's letters to Bridges, Dixon, and Patmore (with a much smaller proportion of those to Baillie) [1] are taken up with literary matters—chiefly theories of poetry and opinions on the work of his friends and of other poets, ancient and modern. Many of the theories and principles have already been discussed in earlier chapters, where they were necessary to throw light upon the form and meaning of his own verse. The remaining pronouncements, both general and particular, should enable us to build up a fairly complete picture of his creative personality : they furnish a profile, as it were, to be set beside the full-face of the *Poems* against the background of the whole English tradition.

All his critical observations are, moreover, intrinsically interesting. His appreciations reveal hidden beauties ; his fault-finding is, with rare exceptions, both just and shrewd ; his diatribes divert us with their wit and force us to revise our standards. As a whole, they lack the cohesion and direction of a ' body of criticism ' ; but by collation, selection, and arrangement we have tried to reduce them, in this chapter, to a convenient logical and chronological order.

We shall first deal with some interesting general principles and then pass on to a summary of Hopkins's opinions on individual poets.

" Criticism," said Hopkins at the age of nineteen, " is a rare gift, poetical criticism at all events, but it does exist." [2] His friend Baillie had " impaired his reputation for judgment." by indulging in a half-truth or paradox to the detriment of all critics. If, Hopkins continues, the existence of feeble critics precludes the possibility of fine ones, we might as logically say that because Dr. Watts, Dr. Johnson, and Eliza Cook supposed themselves to be poets, good poetry has never been written.

---

[1] The letters to Patmore and Baillie are all included in *Further Letters of Gerard Manley Hopkins* (1938).

[2] *Further Letters*, pp. 56–7 (Sept. 6, 1863).

Baillie had spoken with " horror " of Shakespearian criticism ; but Hopkins will not allow this :

> " It appears to me that among Shakspere's critics have been seen instances of genius, of deep insight, of great delicacy, of power, of poetry, of ingenuity, of everything a critic should have. I will instance Schlegel, Coleridge, Charles Lamb, Mrs. Jameson."

Insight, delicacy, power, poetry, ingenuity—that is an array of qualities which should make real critics proud of their vocation and the criticasters ashamed of their presumption. Yet Hopkins was surely both exact and comprehensive in his estimate of the critical faculty. No one was more disgusted than he by " bad criticism "—that is, illiberal, insensitive, politically biased fault-finding :

> " How I have hated *The Quarterly*, *The Edinburgh* and *Blackwood* ! How I have longed for their utter extinction ! And How exasperated I have felt with Dr. Johnson, or in our times with the snarls of *The Athenaeum* ! "

In later life, Hopkins himself emitted something resembling a snarl in the direction of Swinburne ; and we must agree with him when he says, " A perfect critic is very rare ". Yet almost every critic of real power snarls at something, for a " gentlemanly feebleness " is not an attribute of the penetrative, divining intellect. What really matters is the quality of the snarl—and its rational justification. The rare snarls of Hopkins have at least the merit of gentlemanly vigour and a logical regard for obvious facts and Christian principles.

Hopkins clinches the matter with an observation which is highly significant in the light of his later practice as a poet :

> " The most inveterate fault of critics is the tendency to cramp and hedge in by rules the free movements of genius, so that I should say, according to the Demosthenic and Catonic expression, the first requisite for a critic is liberality, and the second liberality, and the third, liberality."

He was already aware of the shortcomings of " general rules ", of the " dangers of generalization ". But having heard him formally demur to the tyranny of the " general rule ", we shall now see to what effect he himself could generalize.

A convenient starting-point is to determine Hopkins's conception or general criterion of *style*, as that term is usually applied to standard or ' classic ' authors. His friend, Robert Bridges, was for him the leading contemporary representative of the Classical tradition in English poetry—a line beginning with Milton and passing through Gray, Landor, Campbell, and Matthew Arnold :

> " Style seems your great excellence ; it is really classical. What fun if you were a classic ! "

So few people, he adds, have style, except individual style or manner—" not Tennyson nor Swinburne nor Morris, not to name the scarecrow misbegotten Browning crew." [1] The inclusion here of Tennyson is unfortunate : in its combination of superb craftsmanship and poetic magic, the best of Tennyson (*Morte d'Arthur*, *Ulysses*, etc.) can be denied *style* only if that word is deprived of all significant meaning.[2]

Of all the poets who have kept their eyes upon the Greek ideals of diction and form, Milton was held to be supreme. Hopkins quotes Matthew Arnold, whom he calls " a rare genius and great critic " :

> " Matthew Arnold says Milton and Campbell are our two greatest masters of style. Milton's art is incomparable, not only in English literature, but, I should think, almost in any ; equal, if not more than equal, to the finest Greek or Roman." [3]

This high opinion of Milton was, and still is, orthodox. Dixon considered, however, that Campbell was too small a writer to be put after Milton ; but Hopkins persisted in calling Campbell " a perfect master of style " [4] :

> " Cold and dull as the *Pleasures of Hope* is and much more that he wrote, there is always the ' freehand ' of a master in his work beyond almost all our poets."

In Campbell's finest ballads, *The Battle of the Baltic* and *Hohenlinden*, Hopkins detected " an inspired felicity seen nowhere else that he himself could not have analysed or justified ". The examples he adduced are interesting but not overwhelming :

> " An inversion and a phrase like ' On the deck of fame that died ' or the lines ' But the might of England flushed / To antici-

---

[1] *Letters*, vol. i. p. 111. Fortunately he concludes with : " The Brownings are very fine too in their ghastly way." (See below, pp. 207–9.)

[2] Elsewhere, Hopkins recognizes Tennyson's " workmanship and infallibly telling freedom of stroke " (*ibid.* p. 139). For further comments, see below, p. 205.

[3] *Letters*, vol. ii. p. 13. Matthew Arnold's opinion was found in the *Quarterly Review*, January 1877, pp. 186–204. Reprinted in *Mixed Essays*, 1879.

[4] *Ibid.* p. 99.

pate the scene ' seem to me as if the words had fallen into their places at a magical signal and not by any strain and continuance of thought." [1]

In relation to this Classical tradition of poetic *style*, the great Romantic innovators, Wordsworth and Coleridge, together with other prolific writers of the same period (Southey, Byron, Shelley, etc.) are mentioned with a qualified respect :

> " The Lake poets and all that school represent the mean or standard of English style and diction, which culminated in Milton but was never very continuous or vigorously transmitted, and in fact none of these men unless perhaps Landor were great masters of style, though their diction is generally pure, lucid and unarchaic." [2]

According to Hopkins, the outward visible signs of a perfect style are three : it must be " of its age " ; it must have sufficient rhetorical verve to carry the heightened mood of poetry ; in the combination of all its formal qualities, it must be distinctive. But certain inward spiritual graces, or ethical qualities, were also indispensable : " A true humanity of spirit, neither mawkish on the one hand nor blustering on the other, is the most precious of all qualities of style " ; [3] and allied to this was " earnestness of spirit " or high seriousness.[4]

In Aeschylus, for instance, Hopkins found not only a fiery vein of poetic energy akin to his own, but also a deeper sincerity and a more conscious moral purpose than in any other ancient poet. " How noble is his style ! " he exclaims, and later :

> "What a noble genius Aeschylus had ! Besides the swell and pomp of words for which he is famous there is in him a touching consideration and manly tenderness ; also an earnestness of spirit and would-be piety by which the man makes himself felt through the playwright. This is not so with Sophocles, who

[1] *Letters*, vol. ii. p. 23. Yet the late Prof. C. H. Herford could say : " . . . one of these otherwise magnificent songs is marred by false notes like that which tells how the ' might of England flushed to anticipate the scene '. . . ." (*The Age of Wordsworth*, 1899, p. 200). Hopkins, surely, was the better critic.

[2] *Ibid.* p. 98-9

[3] *Ibid.* p. 74. This " humanity of spirit " he prized in the poems of Bridges and Dixon. On the other hand, mawkishness and bluster marred the work of Swinburne, Tennyson and Browning. Byron, too, is implicated : " the *sentimental* school of Byron, Moore, Mrs. Hemans . . ." (p. 98) ; " Tennyson has some jarring notes of Byron in *Lady Clara Vere de Vere*, *Locksley Hall* and elsewhere " (p. 98. See below, pp. 205-7).

[4] See above, Introduction, p. 24.

is only the learned and sympathetic dramatist ; and much less Euripides." [1]

Not all critics will agree with this estimate of Sophocles ; and the relegation of Euripides to third place is in marked contrast to the general modern preference for " sad Electra's poet ".[2] Hopkins's opinion, however, is consistent with that fundamental distinction between his own poetry and the bulk of modern literature—a literature in which the emphasis, in moral questions, has been shifted from divine law to human casuistry. Whatever attitude we may adopt towards Hopkins's religious beliefs, we are bound to admire the consistency with which he demanded that literature, and especially poetry, should be either " morally neutral " or a recognized medium for the propagation of the highest moral ideas.

In practice and theory, Hopkins everywhere advocates the principles of true Classicism, but only as regards style or manner. The *matter* of modern poetry should, he thought, be based upon the deeper spirituality of the Christian tradition and not upon an effete mythology. He condemns Bridges's play, *The Return of Ulysses*, on the ground that for the modern poet to introduce, " in earnest ", the goddess Athene among the human characters was a gross error of taste. It revolts him. " Being an unreality ", he says, " she must talk unreal ". He then delivers a stern lecture on the depravity of the Greek deities, their lack of majesty or even dignity—" old bucks, young bucks, and Biddy Buckskins ". They are totally unworkable material, the merest frigidity which must chill and kill every living work of art they are brought into. His moral revulsion breaks into " griggish " humour :

> " What did Athene do after leaving Ulysses ? Lounged back to Olympus to afternoon nectar."

But he strikes home with greater force in the sequel :

> " The background of distance and darkness and doom which a tragedy should always have is shut out by an Olympian drop-

---

[1] *Letters*, vol. i. p. 256.

[2] Witness the popularity of Prof. Gilbert Murray's verse translations of this dramatist, and their frequent performance. But cf. Jebb : " Aeschylus has an element of Hebrew grandeur, Euripides has strong elements of modern pathos and romance ; these things easily come home to us. But in order fully to appreciate Sophocles, we must place ourselves in sympathy with the Greek mind in its most characteristic modes of thought and with the Greek sense of beauty in its highest purity " (*Greek Literature*, 1886, p. 88).

scene ; the characters from men become puppets, their bloodshed becomes a leakage of bran." [1]

That is the finality of truth. It implies a principle which in no way invalidates the use of ghosts, witches, and fairies in Shakespeare ; for whereas Bridges was merely hiring properties from a Classical ' Wardour Street ', Shakespeare was drawing upon the realities of popular belief and superstition. The witches in Macbeth, moreover, are symbols of the forces of evil postulated in Christian theology, and the success of their dramatic handling (if we reject the impertinent Hecate) is universally acknowledged. Again, what Hopkins calls the " background of distance and darkness and doom " is conspicuous in all the really great tragedies (and there are too few) from the Œdipus to Macbeth, from King Lear to The Mayor of Casterbridge.

Hopkins's criticism was not merely destructive. He showed real acumen when he turned from his second attack on Olympus to admit that the Greek mythology was still susceptible of fine treatment—

> " allegorical, for instance, and so treated gives rise to the most beautiful results. No wonder : the moral evil is got rid of and the pure art, morally neutral and artistically so rich, remains and can be even turned to moral uses." [2]

Such allegorical treatment had been exemplified by Dante in the Inferno ; but as Dante's conception was not altogether to Hopkins's taste, the latter may have had in mind the method of his own sonnet Andromeda. [3]

As a Classicist and a Roman Catholic, Hopkins had put his aesthetic and moral worlds in order. He insisted on " principles ", deplored inconsistency, and hated a manifest hybridism in a writer's philosophical presuppositions. For the latter reason he calls Canon Dixon to account : Dixon's poem, Life and Death, he says, contains very subtle and original speculations, yet because they take no account of the supernatural they have " a quite heathen air ". [4] Hopkins was justified in asking why an Anglican clergyman should, when writing about death, deliberately

---

[1] Letters, vol. i. pp. 216–7. Cf. the equally severe and witty criticism in vol. ii. p. 146–7.
[2] Ibid. vol. ii. p. 147.
[3] See Vol. I. of the present work, pp. 185–6.
[4] Letters, vol. ii. p. 61. Life and Death is in Selected Poems of R. W. Dixon, 1909, p. 110.

exclude the Christian doctrine of resurrection and immortality. In Dixon's poem, Death says :

> " I am the brother of Life . . .
> I ruin what she rears."

The poet stops short at the pain and horror of physical disintegration ; whereas Hopkins himself, in *The Echoes*, *The Heraclitean Fire* and elsewhere, fervently denies this apparent finality. To Hopkins it seemed as though Canon Dixon had one set of values and beliefs for his congregation and another set for the more ' liberal ' and sophisticated readers of his poetry. Hopkins makes a similar animadversion on Bridges's *Elegy on a Lady* [1] : the Lethe mythology of the last stanza, he says, is " a fall-off and unrealizes the whole ".[2]

The same professional scrupulosity caused Hopkins to rebuke Dixon for his use of the word ' angel ' :

> " Though it is often done I can never be reconciled to calling men or women angels ; there seems something out of tune in it." [3]

Again, after praising certain images in *Love's Consolation* :

> " ' Each drop more precious than the gems that stud An angel's crown ' strikes me as poor, indeed vulgar ; I think angels are the very cheapest things in literature." [4]

This would seem to be aimed not so much at those famous works in which angels have been introduced with precise theological purpose and reverence (the *Paradiso*, *Paradise Lost*, *The Dream of Gerontius*) as at lesser effusions in which angels were employed like Greek goddesses or used, as in Dixon's poem, to give romance a dash of piety.

Without actually quoting Matthew Arnold's well-known criterion, Hopkins was equally emphatic on the importance of " high seriousness " :

> " This leads me to say that a kind of touchstone of the highest or most living art is seriousness ; not gravity but the being in earnest with your subject—reality." [5]

---

[1] *Poetical Works*, 1914, vol. ii. bk. i. 14.
[2] *Letters*, vol. i. p. 109. Bridges speaks of " banks of the forgetful streams " where " pale indifferent ghosts wander ".
[3] *Ibid.* vol. ii. p. 65.   [4] *Ibid.* p. 77.   [5] *Ibid.* vol. i. p. 225.

In some contexts, this " seriousness " or " reality " is practically synonymous with Catholicism ; Bridges, for instance, is accused of falling short of absolute sincerity :

> " To have a turn for sincerity has not made you sincere nor a turn for earnest / in earnest." [1]

The same touchstone leads Hopkins into some bold and perverse judgments :

> " It seems to me that some of the greatest and most famou works are not taken in earnest enough, are farce (where you ask the spectator to grant you something not only conventional but monstrous). I have this feeling about *Faust* and even about the *Divine Comedy*, whereas *Paradise Lost* is most seriously taken. It is the weakness of the whole Roman literature." [2]

Why Lucretius and Virgil should be denied the credit of taking their work seriously is far from obvious. In *Faust*, however, there are indeed farcical and gratuitous elements—a want of unity (as Hopkins says elsewhere) in both the dramatic action and the ethical purpose, which give some grounds for Hopkins's doubt about Goethe's absolute seriousness.[3] To one trained, as every Jesuit is, to fight daily against the subtle, baleful Enemy of the *Spiritual Exercises* (a Spirit who cannot be conceived aright except as the negation of anything tending to risibility), Goethe's Mephistopheles, with his superficial cynicism and waggish tricks, must appear a figure of farce.[4] Yet Goethe had ample precedent for his conception of " Old Iniquity in his Fool's clothing " ; and to deny him " earnestness " is a paradox which suggests no alternative explanation of the undeniable power and prestige of *Faust* as a whole. Again, in the *Inferno* there are things, including Satan, which are monstrously obscene and grotesque if not actually farcical ; but the almost fanatical seriousness of the poet can hardly be questioned. According to Dean Church, Dante was " the restorer of seriousness in literature. He was so by the magnitude and pretensions of his work and by *the earnestness of his spirit*." [5] Such flirting with paganism as we find in

" Minerva spira e conducemi Apollo " [6]

---

[1] *Letters*, vol. i. p. 96. " Sterne ", he adds, " had a turn for compassion, but he was not compassionate."   [2] *Ibid.* p. 225.

[3] " The incidents for instance of Goethe's *Faust* are fascinating, but the unity of action, the bearing of all these on one common lesson the play is to teach or effect it is to produce, is not telling at first sight and is perhaps—I have no opinion really defective " (*Letters*, vol. ii. p. 113).

[4] Cf. *Further Letters*, p. 212 : " it is really farce."

[5] *Dante*, 1849.   [6] *Paradiso*, ii. 7

would be utterly distasteful to Hopkins and would compare unfavourably with the practice of Milton, who is always faithful to his " Heavenly Muse " and everywhere subordinates the Classical epos to the Christian ethos.[1]

These adverse criticisms of Dante and Goethe were due to a self-imposed rather than a natural limitation in the field of imaginative vision. To this limitation we must attribute his failure to complete the *St. Winefred's Well* tragedy and other works which required a sustained imaginative invention : his insistence on the highest degree of moral integrity in the artist, together with his fear of being misunderstood if he treated of crime and lust, deprived him of rich stores of human motive and action. Nevertheless, in the interests of Christian faith and culture the appearance from time to time of stringent criticism like that of Hopkins is highly salutary : it reminds professed believers of those undefined frontiers where broad-mindedness merges into a self-deluding hypocrisy.[2]

From the aesthetic as from the ethical point of view, Hopkins was a shrewd detector of the insincere and the counterfeit. Matthew Arnold denounced *affectation* as fatal to the Grand Style and high seriousness ; and Hopkins must have been one of the first critics to attack the prevalent archaism of much Victorian poetry. Bridges's *Nero* seemed to Hopkins one of the finest plays ever written, yet (he adds) " it is sicklied o'er a little with an Elizabethan diction, and this is its defec ." [3] He considered Bridges not so culpable in this respect as Swinburne, Morris, Simcox, and others of the medievalist school ; and he made a special reservation in favour of Dixon's long " poetical history ", *Mano* (1883). This work, being written from a strictly medieval point of view, is frankly but not excessively tinged with archaism, which at first displeased Hopkins. At the second reading, however, he found that

" the archaism of the diction did not stand in the way of powerful effects, but allowed of vigorous and homely language." [4]

[1] It is worth noting that Matthew Arnold's definition of the Grand Style, and standard of " high seriousness ", were derived from three poets—Homer, *Dante*, and Milton. Commenting on this, Saintsbury says : " Nobility . . . severity and seriousness . . . who will deny these things to the *Commedia*? " (*History of English Criticism*, 1925, p. 478).

[2] Cf. *Further Letters*, pp. 81 (bottom)–82.

[3] *Letters*, vol. i. p. 275. Cf. p. 218 : " *Ulysses* . . . is sicklied o'er as by a blight."

[4] *Ibid*. vol. ii. pp. 113, 116.

Dixon, he says elsewhere,

> " employs sometimes the archaic style now common, but with such a mastery and dramatic point as justify a practice otherwise vicious." [1]

There is a touch of unconscious partiality in his pronouncement that Dixon's archaism was the most learned of any modern poet's [2]—" a living beauty in the style " ; for having said so much, he straightway retracts : " still I cannot think even so that it is right : *I look on the whole genus as vicious.*" [3]

Doughty's *Arabia Deserta* (1888) he knew by reviews and extracts only. But when Bridges observed that Doughty's style was free from the taint of Victorian English, his retort was vigorous :

> " Hm. Is it free from the taint of Elizabethan English ? Does it not stink of that ? for the sweetest flesh turns to corruption. Is not Elizabethan English a corpse these centuries ? No one admires, regrets, despairs over the death of the style, the living native masculine rhetoric of that age more than I do ; but 'tis gone, 'tis gone, 'tis gone." [4]

He supposed that Doughty wrote in that style because it was ' manly ' : but affectation, he insists, is not manly.

Hopkins's position in this matter of archaism requires some elucidation. As we have seen, his own style contains a considerable admixture of archaic and especially Elizabethan elements [5] ; and when he says to Bridges, " we do not speak that way ; therefore if a man speaks that way he is not serious ", [6] Bridges might have replied that the critic's own poetic language was hardly current idiom, even when allowance had been made for drastic ' heightening '. Any dispute based on the vague expression " speak that way " would be unprofitable ; the important truth is that Hopkins cast all his ingredients into the melting pot and produced a style which has the coherent actuality of living speech, whereas the poets he arraigned were often content with an extrinsic and palpable archaism which seems to us to-day, as it seemed to Hopkins, detrimental to " earnest " and " nature ". [7]

---

[1] *Letters*, vol. ii. pp. 177–8.
[2] Like Rossetti, he seems to have read old ballads and romances to find " stunning words for poetry ".   [3] *Letters*, vol. ii. p. 156.
[4] *Ibid.* vol. i. p. 284.   [6] See Vol. I. chap. iv. of the present work.
[4] *Letters*, vol. i. p. 218.   [7] Cf. *Further Letters*, p. 82.

Hopkins showed a similar fastidiousness in his frequent application of the word "keepings", by which he meant those furnishings, paraphernalia, and artistic appurtenances of an age which, when accurately reproduced in a work of art, give to the whole "nature" and a peculiar felicity. Keepings go with background and local-colour ; but to be perfect they must, like style, be of their own age :

> "There ought to be the sense of beauty in the highest form both in the artist and the age, the style and keepings of which the artist employs."

Hopkins commends Dixon for the excellence of his keepings ; but he falls heavily on Bridges for using the word "domeless" to describe the courts of Olympus : "it is not archaeologically right." [1]

Again Hopkins becomes "griggish" :

> "Courts can seldom be domed in any case, so that it is needless to tell us that those on Olympus are domeless. No : better to say kamptuliconless courts or Minton's-encaustic-tileless courts or vulcanizèd-india-rubberless courts. This would strike a keynote at once and bespeak attention. And if the critics said those things did not belong to the period you would have (as you have now with *domeless*) the overwhelming answer that you never said they were but the contrary."

The offending word was changed to "aetherial". But Hopkins's stricture was really of wide application, striking at the nineteenth-century weakness for vaguely Romantic or conventionally Classical words and keepings.[1]

He finds keepings the best guide for the classification of schools of poets : [2] Keats's school chose medieval keepings, not pure but drawn from the middle ages indirectly through the Elizabethan tradition. The school of Rossetti or the Pre-Raphaelites is descended from the Romantic school ("'Romantic' is a bad word ") of Keats, Leigh Hunt, Hood, and Scott ; keepings, therefore, betray them as imitators twice removed from their object, a fact which partly accounts for Hopkins's limited respect for them.

Keepings are "the weak point " in the Lake poets—"a sort of colourless classical keepings "—

> "When Wordsworth wants to describe a city or a cloudscape

[1] *Letters*, vol. i. pp. 165, 167.   [2] *Ibid.* vol. ii. pp. 98–9.

which reminds him of a city it is some ordinary rhetorical stage effect of domes, palaces and temples." [1]

In Wardour Street we hardly expected to find Wordsworth ; but we are not surprised to meet Byron, Southey, and Moore :

" Their keepings are any gaud or a lot of Oriental rubbish "

—a sentence which to many modern ears will sound like the healthy swish of the scavenger's hose. Byron's genius cannot be dismissed so lightly ; but Hopkins saw that Southey in *Thalaba*,[2] Moore in *Lalla Rookh*, and Byron in his melodramas of oriental crime were all attracted by the glitter of Eastern keepings because of their value as exotic literary decoration ; and such art, unless touched by the high seriousness of genius, was to him a specious art.

To illustrate the shrewdness of Hopkins's ear and eye for pastiche and the second-hand in literature, there is an interesting piece of textual criticism on Dixon's poem *Too Much Friendship* : [3]

> "The language is a quaint medley of the Middle-Ages and ' Queen Annery ', a combination quite of our age and almost even of our decade, as we see in Morris and that school (to which, I suppose, you belong), having a charm of its own that I relish and admire but as a thing alien to me. Here is a pleasing instance :
>
>> ' Rattled her keys, unfavourable sign,
>> And on her turning wheel gan to decline.'
>
> The first line is like *The Rape of the Lock* :
>
>> ' Spadillio first, unconquerable lord——'
>
> and the second is like Spenser." [4]

Dixon repudiated, and justly, the affiliation to the school of Morris ; but with something like an abashed air he quickly rewrote the " pleasing " pastiche :

---

[1] *Loc. cit.* Hopkins was probably thinking of *On Westminster Bridge* and the following from *The Excursion*, Book II :

> " Clouds of all tincture, rocks and sapphire sky . . .
> Each lost in each, that marvellous array
> Of temple, palace, citadel, and huge
> Fantastic pomp of structure without name. . . ."

[2] For Hopkins on Newman's preference for the metre of the opening of *Thalaba* to that of *Samson Agonistes*, see *Letters*, vol. ii. p. 13.

[3] *Last Poems*, pp. 1–21.

[4] *Letters*, vol. ii. p. 83.

" The instance you give is a glaring one : & I was wondering whether you would notice it : tho' I did not know there was so pat a parallel in Pope." [1]

In all his judgments on style and presentation, Hopkins emphasizes the importance of spontaneity, immediacy of appeal. Another coinage bearing on these qualities is the word " bidding ", which he applies to oratory and drama. While praising the beauty and action of Bridges's *Prometheus the Firegiver*, he has doubts about the play's acting : it lacks *bidding*, " the art or virtue of saying everything right *to* or *at* the hearer, interesting him, holding him. It is difficult, he says, to combine this bidding, such a fugitive thing, with a monumental style ; and " your style is monumental." The Greek and Shakespeare, he adds, achieved this combination, though Shakespeare had more bidding and was less monumental.[2]

Here Hopkins puts his finger on one of the major faults of nineteenth-century poetic drama from Coleridge and Byron to Swinburne and Bridges.[3] Much of the poetry of Browning and Hopkins has this dramatic bidding in a high degree, yet the rare perfect combination of poetic genius and dramatic imagination was not in them. Beddoes had said that the man who was to awaken the drama would have to be a bold trampling fellow— no mere reviver however good. Attempted reanimations based on Shakespeare and Schiller were numerous ; but it was the new verse-form and bidding of Caradoc's soliloquy in Hopkins's *St. Winefred's Well* fragment that provided the most significant hint to future dramatic poets.[4]

Hopkins saw clearly that " bidding ", concentration and other

[1] *Letters*, vol. ii. p. 90. On Morris he (Dixon) says : " So far as I can judge his touch is entirely different from mine : very powerful, even sledge-hammery : but not over subtle, by no means intellectual, and what I call desolately limited " (p. 92). Bridges remarks : " Dixon is of a very different calibre from Morris. . . . I think that Dixon exhibited far higher poetic gifts " (*Selected Poems of R. W. Dixon*, p. xxxi.).

[2] *Ibid*. vol. i. p. 160.

[3] Of Swinburne's *Locrine*, for instance, Hopkins says : " It is scarcely to be called a play . . . but for music of words and the mastery and employment of a consistent and distinctive poetic diction, a style properly so called, it is extraordinary. But the diction is Elizabethan or nearly : not one sentence is properly modern, except where there could in no case be any difference to be made. I should think it could only be in Persian or some other Eastern language that a poetical dialect so ornate and continuously beautiful could be found. But words only are only words." (*Letters*, vol. ii. pp. 156–7.)

[4] Cf. the freer metres in Mr. T. S. Eliot's theatrically successful *Murder in the Cathedral* (1935).

rhetorical virtues could not be attained without a certain structural quality which he calls " centrality or reference to one point ".[1]   Some of Dixon's songs are criticized as being like " chance glimpses of landscape seen through a square window in passing ".   Again, this lack of centrality " injures the general effect of Mano " [2] : Hopkins could not find the " clew " to the story, and Patmore voiced the same objection.[3]   In dealing with this reference-to-one-point in drama, Hopkins puts forward a paradox which throws light upon his own method as a poet of vividly dramatized thought and personal experience ; he says, no doubt with Shakespeare in mind :

> " . . . other things being alike, unity of action is higher the more complex the plot ; it is more difficult to effect and more valuable when effected.   *We judge so of everything.*" [4]

The complex plots of *King Lear* and *Hamlet* are, despite their immeasurably greater scope, analogous to the complex of emotions precariously poised in *The Wreck of the Deutschland* or *The Windhover* ; as Shakespeare imposed upon his material the unity, cohesion, and symmetry of a spoked wheel, so the conflicting and subsidiary motives in Hopkins's poems are drawn in and variously related to one central point in Christian faith and doctrine—the moral value of suffering and sacrifice.[5]

The esemplastic power of the poetic imagination shows itself in two stylistic devices which Hopkins calls respectively " sequence of phrase " and " sequence of feeling ".   Milton, he says, is the great master of sequence of phrase ; but Bridges " excels in both sequence of phrase and sequence of feeling on feeling ".

> " By sequence of feeling I mean a dramatic quality by which what goes before seems to necessitate and beget what comes after —at least after you have heard it it does." [6]

This dramatic quality—contributory, but not essential, to the more comprehensive " bidding "—is the equivalent in emotive experience of rhyme in versification : the poetic mind's antennae are so sensitive that they catch up every relevant suggestion

---

[1] *Letters*, vol. ii. p. 64.   [2] *Ibid*. p. 177.
[3] *Further Letters*, p. 171.   [4] *Letters*, vol. ii. p. 113 (our italics).
[5] Akin to this insistence on a clear central motive is his demand for absolutely precise images. Bridges, Dixon and Browning were all criticized for want of precision or " perspective " in their imagery (*Letters*, vol. i. pp. 94, 110, 111 ; *Letters*, vol. i. pp. 55–6).   [6] *Letters*, vol. ii. p. 8.

The result is an intense actuality of the kind evoked by great drama.   Hopkins points out an example in Dixon's *Love's Consolation* :

> " And I remember, sleeping in my bed,
>   A mighty clap of thunder shook my head
>   About laburnum time ; and I awoke
>   And watched the lightning make a great white stroke
>   Three hours above the poplar tops, and then
>   Came morning and the writing of a pen
>   Telling me that my love and reverence
>   Three days before had sold herself for pence
>   Unto a clown who riches had in store ;
>   Yea, sold herself for that three days before.
>   *Ah !   Lord, thy lightnings should have wakened me*
>   *Three nights before they did. . . ."* [1]

The italicized words are " seeming necessary and yet unforeseen " : [2] the feeling has the inevitability of psychological truth. It is identical in kind with Lear's more poignant

> " What, have his daughters brought him to this pass ? " [3]

In Bridges, sequence of feeling produces a peculiar tenderness :

> " In spite of the Miltonic rhythms and some other points, your sonnets remind one more of Shakespeare's.   Milton's sonnets are not tender as Shakespeare's are." [4]

In Patmore and Dixon the outcome of sequence of feeling is an intense pathos.   Hopkins found Patmore's pathos " harrowing " ; [5] and certainly no one could read this poet's *The Azalea, The Departure, Tired Memory*, or Dixon's *Ode on Advancing Age* without realizing how subtlety of form and depth of emotion are bound up with the sequence of feeling on feeling, the chime of image on image.[6]   In Hopkins's own poetry, this calculated sequent chiming of images contributes much towards the total impression of inevitability : in *The Deutschland*, for instance, the " combs of a smother of sand " (stanza 14) hark back to the sand in the hourglass—" it combs to the fall " (stanza 4) ;   and

---

[1] See *Letters*, vol. ii. p. 177 and *Selected Poems* of R. W. D. pp. 28–9.   Hopkins cites also *Mano*, Book I, Canto xiv, lines 25–7 and 61 : " She would have answered underneath the boughs "—a passage of great beauty and pathos.

[2] *Letters*, vol. ii. *loc. cit.*   [3] III. iv. 62.

[4] *Letters*, vol. i. p. 38.   Cf. p. 39 : the sonnets " are all full of manly tenderness and a flowing and never-failing music."   [5] *Ibid.* p. 106.

[6] For Hopkins's appreciation of Dixon's deep thoughtfulness, earnestness, pathos, and humanity, see *Letters*, vol. ii. pp. 117 and 177.

8

we should mark the sequence in " Gertrude, lily " . . . " lily showers ", " Storm flakes " . . . " rose-flake ", " seal of his seraph-arrival " . . . " sisterly sealed ".[1]

Of that other quality, " sequence of phrase ", Dixon gives the following explanation :

> " There is in Milton, as I think, a sort of absolute precision of language that belongs to no other poet : a deliberate unrolling as if of some vast material, which is all there already, and to which the accident of the moment in writing can add nothing : a material which his mighty hands alone can grasp, unroll and display. If I am right, this is what you happily call ' sequence of phrase '. His matter is more external to himself than in other poets." [2]

To this Hopkins replied :

> " I quite agree with what you said about Milton. His verse as one reads it seems something necessary and eternal." [3]

The secret of Milton's amazing fluency and continuity is, as Dixon says, his " self-sufficiency " ; it partly accounts for that conventional or generalized diction to which some recent critics have objected.[4] Milton's refusal or inability to be influenced, as Shakespeare so frequently was, by the " accident of the moment " deprives his epic style of those vividly dramatic and human touches which Hopkins included under his new critical term, " sequence of feeling ". Yet this want in Milton is inseparable from the great virtue of his style—its perfect suitability for his lofty supernatural theme.[5]

We pass now to a brief conspectus of Hopkins's weighed opinions and *obiter dicta* on individual English poets. Naturally, his numerous comments on the poetry of Bridges, Dixon, and Patmore were as much the expression of friendship as of any spontaneous desire to appraise and rectify ; hence a sub-conscious wish to be encouraging caused him to expatiate on many poems (especially of Dixon's) which now seem unworthy of so much thought. On the other hand, certain poets who must have

---

[1] Stanzas 20–23.   [2] *Letters*, vol. ii. pp. 10–11.   [3] *Ibid.* p. 13.

[4] E.g. Dr. F. R. Leavis in his essay on Milton in *Revaluation* (1936) and Mr. T. S. Eliot in *A Note on the Verse of John Milton* (*Essays and Studies* by Members of the English Association, vol. xxi. 1935).

[5] Mr. C. S. Lewis, in his admirable *Preface to Paradise Lost* (1942), expresses with amplitude and finality a view of Milton's epic style which is similar to that of Dixon and Hopkins.

exerted an influence on his own work are either completely ignored or violently attacked.[1]

Of the pre-Shakespearian poets, Chaucer is mentioned only as a metrist " extremely smooth and regular " ; for, he adds, when the law of his versification is understood and one finds

> " that it is all a matter of obsolete accent the quaintness, the rude but pleasing counterpoint, the irregularity, and the interest have all disappeared." [2]

Langland, tackled late in life, was found to be a bore. Surrey was somewhat extravagantly praised as " a great writer and of the purest style "[3] and was unaccountably preferred to the more rugged, subtle, and passionate Wyatt. Even Spenser, whom Hopkins must have read with some application, is contemptuously labelled as a writer of " Parnassian ", and the lost books of *The Faerie Queen* are included in a list of " fortunate losses of literature ".[4]

For his ignorance of Marlowe, Hopkins could " flog " himself ; and indeed of all Shakespeare's contemporaries in drama, Ben Jonson alone had won this poet's ear : *Volpone* is justly declared to be " one of the richest and most powerful plays ever written ". Ben Jonson, moreover, is said to have more real poetry in him than Browning.[5]

Hopkins acknowledged without reserve the supreme quality of Shakespeare, the " breadth of his human nature ", knowledge, and technical skill. Like Keats, Hopkins entertained the ambition of writing one or two fine poetic plays ; but, he complains,

> " In reading Shakespeare one feels with despair the scope and richness of his gifts, equal to everything ; he had besides sufficient experience of life and of course practical knowledge of the theatre." [6]

Anticipating Mr. Stephen Potter (*The Muse in Chains*), Hopkins deprecated the fact that the poet whose universality and humour were unrivalled should be fastened on by the leeches of scholastic pedantry. When some learned lady and Mr. Furnivall argued

---

[1] E.g. Donne, Crashaw, Francis Quarles and Meredith are not mentioned ; of Shelley he records only " specious liberal stuff" and certain verse-forms ; the insidious attraction of Whitman was deliberately avoided (*Letters*, i. 155) ; for his opinions of Browning and Swinburne, see below.

[2] *Letters*, vol. ii. pp. 66–7. (Cf. vol. i. p. 108.)

[3] *Ibid.* p. 87.

[4] *Note-books*, pp. 29, 33.

[5] *Letters*, vol. i. p. 237 ; vol. ii. p. 75.

[6] *Ibid.* i. p. 92–3.

about the seasonableness of the glow-worm in Hamlet, Hopkins called it " great trifling " :

> " Shakespeare had the finest faculty of observation of all men that ever breathed, but it is ordinary untechnical observation, neither scientific nor even like a farmer's professional ; and he might overlook that point of season." [1]

Hopkins's main affinities being with Shakespeare and those poets of subtle metaphysical insight who immediately followed him, the absence from the *Letters* of any mention of Donne and Crashaw is both strange and disappointing. Since the death of Hopkins, both poets have risen high in critical estimation ; and another ' Metaphysical ' who has recently emerged from obscurity is Edward Benlowes, the diction of whose long divine poem, *Theophila* (1652), frequently anticipates the characteristic compounds and condensed, inverted phrases of Hopkins [2] : yet of Benlowes also there is no mention. It is safe to say that Hopkins's own poetic reputation will always be closely bound up with that of Donne and the other ' Metaphysicals ' ; and it would have been instructive to know his reactions to poetic natures (at once intellectual and emotional, sensuous and ascetic) to which his own complex personality was so closely related.

Donne he might have avoided on moral grounds, but no such scruples could arise with regard to Herbert, Vaughan, and Marvell. Of the latter two he says :

> " Marvell . . . is a most rich and nervous poet. Vaughan . . . has more glow and freedom than Herbert but less fragrant sweetness."

While appreciating the subtle imaginative overtones in Vaughan, he did not consider him Herbert's equal. [3]

For Hopkins, the seventeenth century produced only two

---

[1] *Letters*, vol. ii. p. 140.

[2] In an excellent article called " G. M. H., His Literary Ancestry " (*English*, Spring, 1940), Mr. Terence Heywood quotes the following ' Hopkinsian ' passages : " Wrack'd is with bitter-sweet extremes my mind, / Shell'd, sheath'd, cag'd, coffin'd in her treacherous friend " ; " How from the rock, rod-struck in ire, / Did cataracts gush out ? How did the seas retire ? " ; " Deprav'd of vice, depriv'd of grace ". Mr. Heywood adds : " His imagery is glaringly and overwhelmingly dynamic ; he loves storms, shipwrecks, forcible verbs like ' shoot ', ' sprout ', ' unbowel '. . . . Compound words are very frequent (' woolly-curdled clouds ', ' shot-bruis'd mud-walls ', ' bough-cradles ' ,' hope-blades ') ; there are double possessives (' sin's asp's womb '). . . ."

[3] *Letters*, vol. ii. pp. 23-4.

other poets—Milton and Dryden. While overtly professing to imitate Milton,[1] he tacitly acknowledges Shakespeare's ascendancy by being, in effect, more like him. And a similar discrepancy is found in his attitude towards Dryden.

In the first place, it is fitting that the writer who is often called the father of modern prose style should be acclaimed by Hopkins as one who could transmute the material of prose into genuine poetry by some peculiar power :

> " He seems to take thoughts that are not by nature poetical, —stubborn, and opaque, but under a kind of living force like fire they are powerfully changed and incandescent." [2]

That was written as early as 1865. Twenty-two years later, Hopkins is reproving Bridges for not liking Dryden :

> " I can scarcely think of you not admiring Dryden without, I may say, exasperation."

Dryden, he insists, is the most masculine of our poets :

> " . . . his style and his rhythms lay the strongest stress of all our literature on the naked thew and sinew of the English language, the praise that with certain qualifications one would give in Greek to Demosthenes, to be the greatest master of bare Greek." [3]

The sinewy vigour, directness and intellectual force of Dryden are beyond question ; but placing him above Shakespeare and Donne, even in masculinity alone, is a judgment which, without further elaboration, fails to be convincing.

Hopkins presents us with another enigma when he says that his own style " tends always more towards Dryden ". Such progress reminds us of Hamlet's crab, which grew backwards. Admittedly in *Epithalamion* he was working, however remotely, in the tradition of *Alexander's Feast*, and there are some resemblances between Dryden's diction and that of Hopkins's later sonnets ; but the differences, surely, are far more striking. In his prose style, certainly, Hopkins often displayed a satiric vigour quite in the vein of *MacFlecknoe*. There is one passage where he regrets the obscurity and laboured diction of his own

---

[1] *Letters*, vol. i. p. 66.
[2] *On the Origin of Beauty, Note-books*, p. 88.
[3] *Letters*, vol. i. pp. 267–8.

sonnet *The Sea and the Skylark* (original version) and tilts, incident-ally, at Browning :

> " There is, you see, plenty meant ; but the saying of it smells
> I fear of the lamp, of salad oil, and, what is nastier, in one line
> somewhat of Robert Browning." [1]

Dryden's successor, Pope, was admired for the epigrammatic finish and make-believe pathos of *The Rape of the Lock*. Yet Hopkins's use on two occasions of the word " Popery " shows that he regarded Pope as an original poet whose influence on a swarm of later ' coupleteers ' was stultifying.[2] Crabbe he approved for his " strong and modern realistic eye " ; [3] but the pale imitativeness of the eighteenth-century poetry as a whole repelled him, and only the other transitional or pre-Romantic poets—Gray, Collins, Burns, and Blake—attracted his notice.

He was again orthodox in his appreciation of Gray's *Elegy*. Reproving Bridges for echoing some of its lines, he speaks of the poem's " faultless and canonical beauty " ; it is a work which " may be outdone but, if you understand, it cannot be equalled." [4] (Thus, admiring but doing otherwise, Hopkins wrote *The Wreck of the Deutschland*.) He is, moreover, at great pains to refute Wordsworth's adverse criticism of Gray's sonnet *On the Death of Mr. Richard West*.[5] Having remarked on its rhythmical beauty, " due partly to the accent being rather trochaic than iambic ",[6] he pronounces the poem an exquisite piece of art, and by implica-tion discredits Wordsworth's theory of poetic diction. Words-worth held that only five lines of Gray's sonnet have any value, and Hopkins's retort would be an effective answer to some of his own critics :

> " Such a criticism is rude at best, since in a work of art
> having so strong a unity as a sonnet one part which singly is less
> beautiful than another part may be as necessary to the whole
> effect, like the plain shaft in a column and so on." [7]

---

[1] *Letters*, vol. i. p. 164.　Dryden might have put it thus :
> Sure, when with words and numbers he is playing,
> Plenty is meant, I grant ye, but the saying
> Smells of the lamp and four pair attic fog,
> Of salad oil and, nastier still, of Og.

[2] *Ibid.* pp. 100–1 ; vol. ii. pp. 83, 99.　　[3] *Ibid.* vol. ii. p. 99.　　[4] *Ibid.* vol. i. p. 69.
[5] Preface to the Second Edition (1800) of *Lyrical Ballads*.
[6] E.g. " In | vain to | me the | smiling | mornings | shine——"
and not
> " In vain | to me | the smil | ing morn | ings shine,"
[7] *Letters*, vol. ii. pp. 87 and 137.

To the "heavenly beauty" of Collins's *Ode to Evening* Hopkins paid the further compliment of trying to set it to music :

> "I groped in my soul's very viscera for the tune and thrummed the sweetest and most secret catgut of the mind." [1]

Campbell's *Battle of the Baltic* moved him to a similar endeavour.[2] These musical efforts were unfortunately abortive ; but they do at least underline the fact that Collins and Campbell, like Hopkins himself, struck out a new music in English poetry.

After the precise, rhetorical diction and subtle rhythms of Gray and Collins, the "richness and beauty of manly character" in Burns was, for Hopkins, vitiated by "a great want in his utterance". Looking at the unprincipled amorist with the eyes of the "unco guid", Hopkins could yet admire the independence of spirit which enabled Burns, like Goethe ("scoundrels" both !), to speak out "the real human rakishness" of his heart—"a really beating though rascal vein." Burns did not court popularity as Tennyson did ; yet whereas Tennyson's utterance was "truly golden", Burns had no eye for pure beauty :

> "he gets no nearer than the fresh picturesque expressed in fervent and flowing language. . . . Between a fineness of nature which would have put him in the first rank of writers and a poverty of language which puts him in the lowest rank of poets he takes, when all is balanced up, about a middle place."

We may agree with the final estimate while demurring at the opinion that Burns's utterance is never really beautiful. There are passages in *Winter Night, Address to the Unco Guid, Tam o' Shanter, Auld Brig*, etc., which have much of the laconic vigour and lively colour of Hopkins's own diction.[3]

Again, Hopkins is guilty of nothing less than a critical solecism when he declares that there is more true poetry in William Barnes, the Dorset poet, than in Burns :

> "I do not say of course vigour or passion or humour or a lot of things, but the soul of poetry, which I believe few Scotchmen have got." [4]

Barnes, he says, is a perfect artist of a most spontaneous inspiration. It is as though Dorset life and landscape had taken flesh

---

[1] *Letters*, vol. i. p. 199.　　　　　[2] *Ibid.* pp. 201-2.

[3] *Ibid.* pp. 95-6. Cf. Carlyle on Burns : "Who ever uttered sharper sayings ; words more memorable, now by their burning vehemence, now by their cool vigour and laconic pith ? "　　　　　[4] *Ibid.* p. 162.

and tongue in man.   True, he lacks fire ; " but who is perfect all round ? " [1]   It is enough for Hopkins that Barnes comes

> " like Homer and all poets of native epic, provided with epithets, images, and so on which seem to have been tested and digested for a long age in their native air and circumstances and to have a *keeping* which nothing else could give ; but in fact they are all of his own finding and first throwing off." [2]

Barnes's epithets and images are not " far-fetched or exquisite ", but they are straight from nature and quite fresh.   His rhythms, too, are charming, most characteristic, and smack of the soil.

There is an interesting opinion on dialect :

> " I think the use of dialect a sort of unfair play, giving, as you say, ' a peculiar but shortlived charm ' . . . but its lawful charm and use I take to be this, that it sort of guarantees the spontaneousness of the thought. . . ." [3]

The last thought may be doubted ; but we sense a definite threat to ultimate values when Hopkins claims that Barnes is " nearly as good " when rendered in standard English, whereas Burns " loses prodigiously by translation ".   Admittedly it would often be as difficult to translate Burns into Southron English as to turn Hopkins himself into Ayrshire Scots ; whereas Barnes can usually be ' standardized ' with ease.   Tenderness and truth to nature must be allowed to both poets ; but the originality of Burns is not diluted, like that of Barnes, by large draughts of emotional commonplace.[4]   Hopkins had been stirred by Barnes's " Westcountry instress "—a phrase which suggests a sentimental predilection for the objects of the critic's own experience.[5]

That unshakable moral criterion which underlies Hopkins's critical attitude towards the rakish Burns is again apparent in

[1] *Letters*, vol. i. p. 221. On this subject, Hopkins was in agreement with Gosse and Patmore but at loggerheads with Bridges : " I hold your contemptuous opinion an unhappy mistake " . . . " You are quite wrong about Barnes's poems—— ".

[2] *Further Letters*, p. 222. He adds : " However his employment of the Welsh *cynghanedd* or chime I do not look on as quite successful. To tell the truth, I think I could do that better, and it is an artificial thing and not much in his line."

[3] *Letters*, vol. i. p. 87. Cf. p. 88 : " Now the use of dialect to a man like Barnes is to tie him down . . . " ; it narrows his field but heightens his effects.

[4] Cf. George Saintsbury (*A Short Hist. of Eng. Lit.*, V. v. 720) : " We must not rule a man out because he writes ' smilen feäce ' for ' smiling face ' ; but in those who are jaded with ' smiling face ' there is perhaps a dangerous readiness to take ' smilen feäce ' as necessarily poetry."

[5] Hopkins associates this instress with popular airs, Worcestershire and Welsh landscape, the smell of oxeyes and applelofts. (*Letters*, vol. i. p. 88.)

his qualified approval of " crazy Blake ", as he calls him. The best of his poems

> " are of an exquisite freshness and lyrical inspiration, but there is mingled with the good work a great deal of rubbish, want of sense, and some touches of ribaldry and wickedness." [1]

The animadversion is a just one which, since Swinburne's study of 1868, a kind of awe-struck adulation has tended to suppress. There is much crudity and ill-informed fanaticism in Blake's attacks on organized religion, in his wanton confusion of Christian dogma with his own sometimes flagrantly anti-Christian ethics. A glance at *The Poison Tree, Earth's Answer, A Little Girl Lost, To Tirzah,* and *The Garden of Love* will reveal doctrines which to a sincere Christian, as Hopkins was, are as morally vicious as the poetic method of some of these poems is, to the fastidious critic, aesthetically dubious. Yet in spite of Blake's vagaries, Hopkins could acknowledge in him " a most poetically electrical subject both active and passive ".

Hopkins recalled with satisfaction the occasion on which Blake, on hearing someone read Wordsworth's *Ode on the Intimations of Immortality,* fell into an hysterical excitement at the words " The pansy at my feet ".

> " Now commonsense forbid we should take on like these unstrung hysterical creatures : still it was a proof of the shock "

Hopkins is earnestly remonstrating with Dixon for calling this ode " not particularly good " : this, he says, is one of the half dozen finest odes of the world. Blake's vision was probably delusive, but not so Wordsworth's : he was one of the few men of all time who, like Plato, have *seen something* :

> " Human nature in these men saw something, got a shock ; wavers in opinion, looking back, whether there was anything in it or no ; but is in a tremble ever since." [2]

Nevertheless Wordsworth was, he maintained, an imperfect artist. Despite the divine philosophy and the lovely gift of verse, there is yet *beaucoup à redire.*[3] He had a profound insight of some things and little of others ; but in the *Immortality*

---

[1] *Letters,* vol. ii. p. 153.   [2] *Ibid.* pp. 147–8.
[3] Of *The Excursion* he asks : " is it not fairly true to say ' This will never do ' ? There does seem to be a great deal of dulness, superfluity, aimlessness, poverty of plan " (*Letters,* vol. i. p. 141).

Ode his insight was at its deepest.   The execution, also, is masterly :

> " The rhymes are so musically interlaced, the rhythms so happily succeed (surely it is a magical change ' O joy that in our embers '), the diction throughout is so charged and steeped in beauty and yearning (what a stroke ' The moon doth with delight ' !) " [1]

Why, he asks, should Wordsworth-worship be a difficult thing ?

> " What I suppose grows on people is that Wordsworth's particular grace, his *charisma*, as theologians say, has been granted in equal measure to so few men . . . to Plato and who else ? I mean his spiritual insight into nature." [2]

Hopkins saw that the best of Dixon's poetry owed much to Wordsworth. Speaking of that charming short lyric, " The feathers of the willow ", he says :

> " I do not think anywhere two stanzas so crowded with the pathos of nature and landscape could be found (except perhaps there are some in Wordsworth). . . ." [3]

There is, indeed, a *pathos of nature* in Wordsworth—particularly in *The Small Celandine* and *Composed at Neidpath Castle*. But unlike Dixon's, Wordsworth's type of pathos is never the main motive of a poem ; it is always subservient to some dominant human theme, as in the last two lines of the great *Ode*. Dixon is perhaps overpraised when he is told that the " pathetic imagination " of the graceful but slight *Wayward Water* [4] is unmatched in our literature except by some of Coleridge.[5] A more poignant and imaginative handling of nature is to be found in Dixon's fine *Ode on Advancing Age*,[6] to say nothing of Hopkins's own *Binsey Poplars* and *Ribblesdale*. Blake, Shelley, and even Byron have all expressed very beautifully that close relationship between the forms and moods of nature and the most poignant emotions of man.[7]

This " pathetic imagination " is essentially an outcome of the

---

[1] *Letters*, vol. ii. p. 148.   [2] *Ibid.* p. 141.
[3] *Ibid.* p. 3.   See Dixon's *Selected Poems*, p. 74.   [4] *Ibid.* p. 143.
[5] *Ibid.* vol. i. p. 250.   [6] *Selected Poems*, p. 132.
[7] Influenced by Wordsworth (the master in this kind), Byron wrote, in *The Island* (1823), II. xvi :

> " Are the dropping caves
> Without a feeling in their silent tears ?
> No, no ;—they woo and clasp us to their spheres. . . ."

The modern master of this *pathos of nature* is Thomas Hardy.

so-called Romantic revival ; but we should note in passing that Hopkins did not always use the word *imagination* with the Wordsworthian and Coleridgean sense of deep perception and significant combination.   Dixon's lyric called *Fallen Rain* [1] (in which the rain complains that owing to the coquettish smile of the rainbow it is now trampled by the feet of the clown) was extravagantly hailed by Hopkins as " the most delicate and touching piece of imagination in the world " :

> " I do not think it would be possible to find, for a work of pure imagination, anything anywhere more beautiful. . . ."

Wordsworth and Coleridge would have classed it as a minor work of *fancy* ; and many modern critics would dismiss it as a mere *pathetic fallacy*.   Even Hopkins himself complained of false perspective in the image :

> " While on the one hand delighting in this play of imagination a perverse over-perspectiveness of mind nudges me that the rain could never be wooed by the rainbow which only comes into being by its falling nor could witness the wooing when made. . . ." [2]

Despite the nudging, Hopkins was still nodding when he used the word *imagination* in a way which renders nugatory a valuable critical term.

In the explicit or implicit opinion of Hopkins, the influence of Byron and Shelley upon the poetry of the nineteenth century was on the whole unfortunate : we see this in his criticisms of Tennyson, Browning, and Swinburne.   On the other hand, the influence of Wordsworth, Coleridge, and Keats was held to be mainly good.   Of Coleridge he says little, but on Keats he writes with deep interest and percipience.

In the first of two letters to Patmore on this subject [3] he dissents from that poet's view that Keats was one of the feminine geniuses among men, that he was not the " likest " but the " unlikest " of our poets to Shakespeare :

> " His poems, I know, are very sensuous—and indeed they are sensual.   This sensuality is their fault, but I do not see that it makes them feminine.   In this fault he resembles, not differs from Shakspere."

Comparing the early work of Keats with the early work of a much older Shakespeare (who had, moreover, the advantage of

---

[1] *Selected Poems*, p. 148.   [2] *Letters*, vol. ii. pp. 20 and 47–8.
[3] See *Further Letters*, pp. 233-39.

a more unified tradition), Hopkins finds the extravagance o
Endymion no worse than the same abandon in parts of *Romeo an*
Juliet—e.g. County Paris compared to a book of love, etc., in
Act I, iii, which has " some kind of fantastic beauty like an
arabesque " but in the main is " nonsense ".

Hopkins had read " something good in Matthew Arnold '
about the true masculine fibre in Keats's mind ; [1] but in his
next letter he has modified his view. Having re-read Keats a
little he is struck by the force of Patmore's criticism :

> " It is impossible not to feel with weariness how his verse i
> at every turn abandoning itself to an unmanly and enervating
> luxury."

The " Life of Sensations rather than of Thoughts " desiderated
by Keats [2] was naturally obnoxious to Hopkins : the " impressions " (as he misquotes " Sensations ") were not likely to have
been innocent. Yet although Keats had not begun to dedicate
his powers to one of the great causes, and although he lived in
mythology and fairyland the life of a dreamer, he had nevertheless given promise of an interest in higher things. Hopkins's
remarks from this point anticipate, within discreet limits, the
sanguine speculations of Mr. Middleton Murry : Keat's genius

> " would have taken to an austerer utterance in art. Reason
> thought, what he did not want to live by, would have asserted
> itself presently and perhaps have been as much more powerful
> than that of his contemporaries as his sensibility or impression
> ableness, by which he did want to live, was keener and richer
> than theirs."

All this tallies with what Keats proposed for his own future
in a letter of April 1818.[3] Indeed, Hopkins saw in the poems
themselves a fine judgment already able to restrain but unable
to direct,—a judgment which prevented Keats from flinging
himself blindly on " the specious Liberal stuff that crazed Shelley
and indeed, in their youth, Wordsworth and Coleridge." This
echoes Matthew Arnold on the ineffectual Shelley, and anticipates what Mr. T. S. Eliot has recently been saying about tha

---

[1] " But the thing to be seized is, that Keats had flint and iron in him, that he
had character. . . ." (Essay on Keats, Prefatory to the selection of Keat's poems
in Ward's Poets : reprinted in *Essays in Criticism*, Second Series, 1925, p. 112).

[2] *Letters of John Keats*, ed. M. Buxton Forman, 1931, vol. i. p. 73.

[3] " I have been hovering for some time between an exquisite sense of the luxurious
and a love for philosophy. Were I calculated for the former I should be glad, but
as I am not I shall turn all my soul to the latter." (*Ibid.* p. 146.)

poet's adolescent mind.[1]   Keats, moreover, had a " deeply
observant turn " ; he was made to be a thinker as much as a
singer, but his thoughts were still those

> " of a mind very ill instructed and in opposition ; keenly sensible
> of wrongness in things established but unprovided with the
> principles to correct them by."

The principles Hopkins had in mind we of course know ; but
he seems to have overlooked the great obstacle to their acceptance
—Keats's admiration of what he calls the " negative capability "
of Shakespeare.   Even Keats's principles of art, says Hopkins,
were in many ways " vicious ", though he was correcting his
faults ' eagerly " (a happy word).   He knew nothing of construction to the last, as witness the palpable confusions of *Lamia* ;
yet even when misconstructing he showed a " latent power—for
instance the way the vision is introduced in *Isabella*."

The broad truth of Hopkins's strictures has been tacitly
acknowledged by all those who have deplored the worst effect of
Keats's vague cult of Beauty—namely, the enervating ' escapist '
Romanticism and aestheticism of the later nineteenth century.
Yet by the light of Truth in the imagination—that other essential
element in Keat's intuitive creed—he " had found his way right
in his odes ".   Poetry of such vision and concentrated beauty, allied
to a deep religious faith and purpose, would have made Keats
the ideal poet of the supernatural as well as of the natural order.

On Keats's chief successor, Tennyson, Hopkins is somewhat
ambiguous : now he calls him a " glorious poet " and " one of
our greatest poets " ; at another time he accuses him of faults
which are scarcely compatible with either greatness or glory.
When Dixon rather presumptuously dismisses Tennyson as " a
great outsider ", Hopkins is grieved to hear the great man so
depreciated ; but he knows what Dixon means—an outsider " to
the soul of poetry ".[2]   Contrasting Tennyson with Burns, he finds
the genius of Tennyson " uninformed by character ".   The word
" character " in such a context is sadly in need of definition ;
but Hopkins goes on to say that Tennyson's thought was commonplace while his utterance was golden : [3] like Swinburne and " the
popular poets, he was weak where that age was weak—in thought
and insight : [4]

> " To me his poetry appears ' chryselephantine ' ; always
> of precious mental material and each verse a work of art, no

[1] *The Use of Poetry and the Use of Criticism* (1933), p. 89.
[2] *Letters*, vol. ii. p. 24.   [3] *Ibid.*, vol. i. p. 95.   [4] *Further Letters*, p. 189.

botchy places ; not only so but no half-wrought or low-toned ones, no drab, no brown-holland ; but the form, though fine, not the perfect artist's form, not equal to the material." [1]

There is truth in this, despite the apparent confusion.

The epithet " chryselephantine " (derived from ancient sculpture in wood overlaid with plates of gold and of ivory) is the precise term to describe Tennyson's verse. Yet we cannot at once reconcile the " precious mental material " with the " commonplace thought " and " vulgarity " mentioned in the same and later criticisms. " Mental material " must mean imagery and fanciful embroidery—what John Drinkwater called Tennyson's " missal-like illumination " ; [2] and H. J. C. Grierson made the same point as Hopkins when he said, of *The Princess*, that the style " is still elaborated and brocaded out of all proportion to the theme ".[3] What is true of the Gilbertian plot of *The Princess* is true also in varying degrees of *Locksley Hall*, *Maud*, and the *Idylls* : Dixon called *Locksley Hall* " an unpleasant and rather ungentlemanly row ", to which Hopkins replied that not only that poem but *Maud*, *Aylmer's Field*, and *The Princess* were all ungentlemenly rows.

Hopkins foresaw that Tennyson's blaze of glory would die down to a much smaller but still intense point of light :

> " When the inspiration is genuine arising from personal feeling, as in *In Memoriam*, a divine work, he is at his best, or when he is rhyming pure and simple imagination, without afterthought, as in the *Lady of Shalott*, *Sir Galahad*, the *Dream of Fair Women* or *Palace of Art*." [4]

Tennyson lacked two qualities essential to the highest art—" form in the imagination " and " temper " :

> " But the want of perfect form in the imagination comes damagingly out when he undertakes longer works of fancy, as his *Idylls*."

Each scene of the *Idylls* is " a triumph of language and of bright picturesque, but just like a charade " : the trumpery Galahad of *The Holy Grail*, for instance, is " merely playing the fool over Christian heroism ".[5]

In praising the " temper " of Dixon's ode *The Spirit Wooed*,[6]

---

[1] *Letters*, vol. ii. p. 24.   [2] *Victorian Poetry*, p. 58.
[3] *Cambridge History of English Literature* (1932), xiii. pp. 31–2.
[4] *Letters*, vol. ii. pp. 24–5.   [5] *Ibid.* p. 24.
[6] *Selected Poems*, pp. 113–15 ; and *Letters*, vol. ii. pp. 55–6.

Hopkins says that most modern poets, including Tennyson and Browning, are lacking in this quality. By " temper " he means that emotional intensity which derives from the concentration and perfect balance of the spiritual, intellectual, and sensual elements in poetry. It is allied to what Ruskin called " repose " in the plastic arts ; it implies tension, calm in the midst of stress, a style in which every word is fastidiously weighed. Common in all the great moments of Shakespeare's plays, it also appears eminently in *Lycidas* and in the best odes of Wordsworth, Coleridge, Keats, and Patmore.

If " temper " implies a significant fusion of form, tone, and content, two of the chief enemies of this quality are metrical facility and bluster. In *Locksley Hall*, Tennyson had cried : " Well—'tis well that I should bluster "—a loss of *temper* in more than one sense of the word. Again, in his " rhetorical pieces " like *The Lord of Burleigh* and *Lady Clara Vere de Vere* he is " at his worst . . . downright haberdasher ".[1]

Hopkins should have been fair to Tennyson and Browning by noting that an exactly right *temper* is to be found in such perfect poems as *Ulysses* and *The Grammarian's Funeral* ; but in Browning he finds many frigidities, including a want of fine spiritual insight, balance, and restraint :

> " Any untruth to nature, to human nature, is frigid. Now he has got a great deal of what came in with Kingsley and the Broad Church school, a way of talking (and making his people talk) with the air and spirit of a man bouncing up from table with his mouth full of bread and cheese and saying that he meant to stand no blasted nonsense." [2]

Browning's position as a very considerable poet is not to-day in question ; yet in the above homely analogy Hopkins has stigmatized a weakness in Browning which debars much of his verse from comparison with the highest.

As an example of this " frigid bluster " (which to many of Browning's admirers has seemed nothing worse than bluff, healthy honesty), Hopkins quotes the repetition of " My friend " in *The Flight of the Duchess*, a poem of which the learned-facetious and heavily Gilbertian manner is particularly oppressive. *Mr. Sludge the Medium* and *Bishop Blougram's Apology* are both interest-

[1] *Letters*, vol. ii. p. 25 ; cf. p. 55.
[2] *Ibid.* p. 74. Cf. *seqq.*—" There is a whole volume of Kingsley's essays which is all a kind of munch and not standing of any blasted nonsense from cover to cover."

ing and original works which contain little of what Hopkins understood by the ' soul of poetry ' ; and as a *locus classicus* of the " no blasted nonsense " vein the *Soliloquy of the Spanish Cloister* springs to mind :

> " ' St, there's Vespers ! *Plena gratiâ*
> *Ave, Virgo !* Gr-r-r—you swine ! "

This, Hopkins seems to say, is *one* mood or vein of human nature ; but Browning and Kingsley would have us look at all human nature through it ;

> " And Tennyson in his later works has been ' carried away by their dissimulation ' ".[1]

Browning therefore lacks that " true humanity of spirit " which makes Shakespeare so profound and universal a poet and gives a minor distinction to the work of Dixon and Bridges.

Dixon put forward the paradox that Browning seemed " not thoroughly educated ", with the less startling submission that Browning had not taken poetry at the highest point at which it had been left by others.[2] Hopkins's depreciation went farther, indeed too far :

> " I hold with the old-fashioned criticism that Browning is not really a poet, that he has all the gifts but the one needful and the pearls without the string ; rather one should say raw nuggets and rough diamonds." [1]

In assessing Hopkins's valuation, we must remember that there is much in Browning, from *The Confessional* to *Fifine* and *The Ring and the Book*,[3] to offend the susceptibilities of a Catholic priest. Hence he wrote to Bridges :

> " I always think that your mind towards my verse is like mine towards Browning's : I greatly admire the touches and the details, but the general effect, the whole, offends, I think it repulsive." [4]

Yet even the details could sometimes be displeasing. He dismisses the account of the market-place in *The Ring and the Book*

---

[1] *Letters*, vol. ii. pp. 74-5.   [2] *Ibid.* p. 70.

[3] Of this poem he says (*op. cit.* p. 74) : " I read some, not much, of the *Ring and the Book*, but as the tale was not edifying and one of our people, who had been reviewing it, said that further on it was coarser, I did not see, without a particular object, sufficient reason for going on with it. So far as I read I was greatly struck with the skill in which he displayed the facts from different points of view ; this is masterly, and to do it through three volumes more shews a great body of genius."

[4] *Letters*, vol. i. p. 137.

as " a pointless photograph of still life . . . minute upholstery description ".[1]   Again, Browning is arraigned for a serious " want of perspective " in one image of *Instans Tyrannus* : [2] it is ridiculous, Hopkins says, to call the sun the " visible boss " of a heavenly shield protecting the victim of a human oppressor, since the sky is concave towards us and the tyrant himself is under it, just as much as his victim.   This he calls " frigid fancy with no imagination ", and it is true that Browning's rapid, fluent manner was subject to such lapses :   there is another example in *How They Brought the Good News*, where the shoulders of the galloping horse butting away the haze are compared to a stationary object—a " bluff river headland ".

If the general effect of Browning's verse was repulsive, that of Swinburne evoked in Hopkins a far stronger feeling—a mixture of abhorrence and scorn.   With his usual fairness, Hopkins acknowledges the superficial fascination of Swinburne's " astonishing genius " ; [3] but before Mr. T. S. Eliot he also realized that it was a genius that had more to do with the manipulation of words than with the evocation of meanings :   " words only are only words ".[4]   Morally, much of Swinburne was anathema (e.g. the blasphemous *Hymn of Man* in *Songs Before Sunrise*, 1871) ; he had " no principles ",[5] was classed with Victor Hugo as a " plague of mankind "—and to laud such writers

" . . . is often wicked and in general is a great vanity and full of impious brag and a blackguard and unspiritual mind." [6]

Formally, everything Swinburne wrote was " rigmarole ".[7]   He was a master of word-music, but his genius could do " only one thing " ; [8] his alliteration, like his metres, became more and more mechanical.

Few poets have ever written about a contemporary with more savage exactitude than Hopkins did in his remarks on the second and third series of *Poems and Ballads* :

" . . . a strain of conventional passion, kept up by stimulants and crying always in a high head voice about flesh and flowers, democracy and damnation." [9]

" Swinburne has a new volume out, which is reviewed in its own style : ' The rush and rampage, the pause and the pull-up

[1] *Loc. cit.*   [2] vii. 1–8. See *Letters*, vol. ii. p. 56.
[3] *Letters*, vol. i. p. 79.   [4] *Ibid.* vol. ii. p. 157.
[5] *Ibid.* vol. ii. p. 136.   [6] *Ibid.* vol. i. p. 39.
[7] *Ibid.* vol. ii. p. 135.   [8] *Ibid.* vol. i. p. 79.   [9] *Ibid.* p. 73.

of these lustrous and lumpophorous lines '.   It is all now a ' self-
drawing web ' ;   a perpetual functioning of genius without truth,
feeling, or any adequate matter to be at function on." [1]

He finds that Swinburne has no real understanding of rhythm ; [2]
in *The Armada*, for instance, there is " heavydom " and " water-
logged lines ", and though Swinburne sometimes hits brilliantly
at other times he misses badly.

Not only are the poems on babies found to be " blethery
bathos " (" His babies make a Herodian of me "), but Swinburne
shows no ability to observe nature.   Of a poem on sunset Hopkins
says :

> " Either in fact he does not see nature or else he overlays the
> landscape with such phantasmata, secondary images and what
> not of a delirium tremendous imagination that the result is a
> kind of bloody broth . . . at any rate there is no picture." [3]

In *Evening on the Broads* (undoubtedly the poem referred to)
sunset is described in the well-known Swinburnean formulae of
loves, ghosts, shadows, glories, memories, and *spirits.*

> " Glad of the glory of the gift of their life and the wealth of
> its wonder. . . ."

Secondary images are thus woven into a woolly stocking-stitch
of this and of that and of something else.   There is too much
" transparent rapture " ;   it is all a " molten music of colour ",
which comes very near to Hopkins's " bloody broth " in the
line—

> " Darkness and lightness darkens and lightens the sea that
> is thickened and thinned."

It is necessary (or perhaps superfluous) to add that to Swinburne, as to Browning, Hopkins did much less than justice.
There *are* poems in Swinburne which present vivid, concrete
pictures—of the sea, for instance, in the splendid *Tristram of
Lyoness* ;   there is much morally neutral and highly individual
lyric poetry which glows with truth and genuine feeling.   Yet
after long draughts at his ebullient springs one is left with the

----

[1] *Letters*, vol. i. p. 304.

[2] Cf. John Drinkwater in *Victorian Poetry* (1923) : " Swinburne . . . had little
rhythmic subtlety. . . . We have only to take any characteristic passage from one of
the supreme creators of rhythmical life (Shakespeare, Milton, Wordsworth, Keats,
Tennyson and Arnold), and to see how nervously the phrasing line runs through it,
to realize how little of this line there is in Swinburne . . ." (p. 110).

[3] *Letters*, vol. i. p. 202.

uncomfortable sensation of having drunk unhealthy quantities of gassy mineral water.

Of four outstanding poetic personalities of the century— Matthew Arnold, Rossetti, William Morris, and Meredith— Hopkins says little or nothing. In 1873 Arnold's " Empedocles volume " seemed to Hopkins to have " all the ingredients of poetry without quite being it ".[1] Morris's *Earthly Paradise* he considered " fine in colouring and drawing " ; [2] but otherwise Morris's artificial Romantic medievalism and prolix narration had little to attract a fellow-poet so completely dedicated to religion, actuality, and terseness. The other artificial school of the 'eighties—those poets like Lang, Dobson, Gosse, and Marzials who " fumbled with triolets, villanelles, and what not "—was treated as an exotic growth of little vitality and of no permanent value.[3]

We have now to consider in more detail Hopkins's criticism of those poets whom he knew personally, namely (in order of familiarity) Bridges, Dixon, and Patmore. His faithful and dis- interested encouragement of these men, together with his practical help in the final polishing of some of their works, constitutes one of Hopkins's claims to the title of critic ; yet we could wish that some of the time he spent in suggesting improvements which were not adopted had been more profitably utilized by his own muse.

Patmore, the oldest, had begun the publication of *The Angel in the House* as early as 1854. The *Unknown Eros* odes first appeared in collected form in 1877, although nine of them had been printed privately in 1868. Hopkins first met Patmore in the summer of 1883, when the latter was fifty and already regarded his life-work as practically completed ; his influence on the older poet was therefore restricted to conscientious textual criticism of the final version of *The Angel in the House* and the later Odes. Whenever Hopkins suggested structural alterations or modifications of concept Patmore always replied that since he could never again recapture the original mood such changes would be impossible.[4]

Hopkins first mentions Patmore in a letter to Dixon of 1878 : Patmore's fame, like Dixon's, was " deeply below his great merit ".[5] At a time when *The Angel* could be dismissed as

---

[1] *Further Letters*, p. 43.   [2] *Letters*, vol. ii. p. 3.

[3] *Ibid.* vol. i. pp. 49–50, 276. Popular poets like Lewis Morris, Edwin Arnold, and Alfred Austin were also dismissed with polite disapproval or indifference (*Letters*, vol. i. pp. 275–6).   [4] *Further Letters*, p. 164.   [5] *Letters*, vol. ii. p. 6.

" goody-goody dribble ",[1] and the Odes won little praise, Hopkins was one of the few who recognized Patmore's true poetic stature. In 1879, he reproves Bridges for some strictures on Patmore's " period-building " :

> " The faults I see in him are bad rhymes ; continued obscurity ; and, the most serious, a certain frigidity when, as often, the feeling does not flush and fuse with the language. But for insight he beats all our living poets, his insight is really profound, and he has an exquisiteness, far fetchedness, of imagery worthy of the best things of the Caroline age." [2]

Again, in a later post-script :

> " How can you speak of Patmore as you do ? I read his *Unknown Eros* well before leaving Oxford.[3] He shows a mastery of phrase, of the rhetoric of verse, which belongs to the tradition of Shakespeare and Milton and in which you could not find him a living equal nor perhaps a dead one either after them." [4]

Hopkins was grieved to find that in a competition to ascertain the best grading of English writers in prose and verse, Patmore was not even in the running :

> " And when I read *Remembered Grace*, *The Child's Purchase*, *Legem Tuam Dilexi* and others of this volume I sigh to think that it is all one almost to be too full of meaning and to have none and to see very deep and not to see at all, for nothing so profound as these can be found in the poets of this age, scarcely of any. . . ." [5]

Hopkins aptly summed up Patmore's poetic gift when he spoke of his " insight and delight in paradox on, so to say, the Tory side of everything ".[6] Like Hopkins himself, Patmore was a convert to Catholicism (1864) ; hence the profound insight with which he was accredited was both the measure and the result of certain mental and emotional affinities between the two poets. There was a further link in their common interest in the subtleties of metrical law.[7] Yet Hopkins, ever consistent in his moral approach to poetry, could on one occasion qualify his attribution of " insight " to Patmore with remarkable candour,

---

[1] See review by the Positivist, Frederic Harrison, quoted in *Further Letters*, p. 221.
[2] *Letters*, vol. i. p. 82.
[3] As Hopkins left Oxford in 1867, this was hardly possible, for the first group of odes was not issued until 1868.
[4] *Letters*, vol. i. p. 93   [5] *Further Letters*, p. 201.   [6] *Letters*, vol. ii. p. 63.
[7] See above, p. 159 ; also *Further Letters*, p. 178 *et seqq.*

and he several times brought his friend to book for using words which might " disedify " and mislead. In criticizing the " exaggeration and sophistry " of a piece called " *The Comparison* ",[1] Hopkins admits that it is full of insight :

> " but if it is not fair, then all the insight in the scorched world does not make up for the want of judgment and of truth. . . . Ruskin, it seems to me, has the insight of a dozen critics, but intemperance and *wrongness* undoes all his good again." [2]

The distinction made here between genius and good sense is nowadays too infrequent.[3]

Altogether, Hopkins's praise of Patmore as a consummate poetic artist does not strike us to-day as exaggerated ; rather it tends to swell that body of critical opinion which would place Patmore among the major poets of his age. His poems fulfilled Hopkins's two highest poetic desiderata—perfection of form and " high matter ". They were, moreover, " a good deed done for the Catholic Church and another for England ".[4] Of Patmore's Odes on Psyche, which divided his admirers into two camps, Hopkins wrote :

> " This poem and the two next are such a new thing and belong to such a new atmosphere that I feel it as dangerous to criticize them almost as the ' Canticles '." [5]

Again, Hopkins's deep veneration for the sacrament of Christian marriage and the sanctity of the married state—an attitude which made him, as he says, grow " spoony " over married couples—predisposed him to accept Patmore's most

---

[1] *The Angel in the House*, Book I, Canto V, Preludes, I.

[2] *Further Letters*, pp. 165–6.

[3] Cf. *ibid.* p. 225, where, criticizing W. B. Yeats's first separate publication, *Mosada* (1886), Hopkins calls it " a strained and unworkable allegory " and adds : " commonsense is never out of place anywhere, neither on Parnassus nor on Tabor nor on the Mount where our Lord preached ". He then adduces the " consummate and penetrating imagination " of Ariel's ' spiriting ' in *The Tempest* : " you cannot lay your finger on the point where it breaks down ".

Another example of criticism from moral standards is when Hopkins makes the serious and just objection that in two passages of *The Angel* Patmore had " given incidentally some countenance to the vice of vanity in women " (*Further Letters*, pp. 159–64). Here again, Shakespeare is the pattern : " It is the same in literature as in life : the vain women in Shakespeare are the impure minded too, like Beatrice . . . those whose chastity one would have trusted, like Desdemona, are free from vanity too " (p. 161). Cf. also p. 169 (14) : pp. 174–5—on *The Scorched Fly* ; p. 195— ' Their Jew '.   [4] *Ibid.* p. 218.   [5] *Ibid.* p. 199.

popular work, *The Angel in the House*, as a philosophic and religious poem of the highest importance :

> " To dip into it was like opening a basket of violets. To have criticized it looks like meddling with the altar vessels ; yet they too are burnished with washleather." [1]

> " The *Angel in the House* is in the highest degree instructive, it is a book of morals and in a field not before treated and yet loudly crying to be treated. It cannot indeed ever be popular quite with the general, but I want it to be popular as a classic is, read by many, recognized by all." [2]

The excellence of Patmore's Odes has never been seriously questioned ; but neither these nor *The Angel* have yet received their due.   In the words of a recent critic :

> " Justice has never been done to the subtlety of Patmore's thought nor to the poetic strength with which it is expressed." [3]

Hopkins reacted like a typical Victorian, however, in not noticing that weakness of *The Angel* which strikes most modern readers—the too frequent intrusion, especially in the earlier parts, of facile sentiment and trivial incident.

What Hopkins could not do for himself he tried in all earnestness to do for Patmore : he sought to persuade the latter to carry out his projected poem on the ' Marriage of the Blessed Virgin ', with the plea that where there is high excellence in a poet's work, " volume, amount, quantity tells and helps to perpetuate all :

> " Are Virgil's Georgics and Bucolics read more or less for his having written the Aeneid ? · Much more.   So of Shakespeare's and Dante's sonnets." [4]

He used similar arguments with Bridges and Dixon, urging that a generous output and a desire to be known were the necessary conditions of that universally beneficent influence which poetry ought to exert.   But not even as an act of devotion would Patmore

---

[1] *Further Letters*, p. 214. Of the fifty-six alterations to this poem suggested by Hopkins, Patmore acted on only twenty-two, and many of these were slight matters of punctuation and spelling. Of the thirty-five strictures on the shorter poems, all but eleven were rejected, often against Patmore's own better judgment. Hence his statement that he had acted on " at least two-thirds " of Hopkins's hints is inaccurate : he acted on just over one-third.

[2] *Ibid.* p. 215.

[3] B. Ifor Evans in *English Poetry of the Later Nineteenth Century* (1933), p. 139.

[4] *Further Letters*, p. 211. Cf. *Letters*, vol. i. p. 231.

" strain against nature " to write a poem : he was one of the few considerable Victorian poets who knew when to stop.

Over Richard Watson Dixon, a man eleven years older than himself, Hopkins exercised a longer and more effectual tutelage. His first letter to his former schoolmaster—a frank outpouring of praise, gratitude, and friendly criticism—is one of the most moving documents in English literary biographia.[1] The neglected author of *Christ's Company* (1861) and *Historical Odes* (1864) was deeply stirred : such encouragement, coming in a dry season, was a fresh beginning ; had it never been given, we might have lacked half a dozen of the best lyrics, two of the very finest odes, and one of the more interesting longer narrative poems in the language.

Yet taken as a whole, Hopkins's estimate of Dixon's poetry is too favourable. Dixon himself, a man of noble character and engaging modesty, felt the element of exaggeration in Hopkins's first letter, and said so. Hopkins remonstrated with him, but later admitted that he had lost the mood for enjoying some of the pieces in *Christ's Company*.[2]

Inequality, a frequent vagueness of form and obscurity of expression—these faults in Dixon were candidly stated ; but against them were set " extreme beauties—

> " imagery inheriting Keats's mantle, the other-world of imagina-
> tion (constructive imagination is rare even among poets), the
> ' instress ' of feeling, and a pathos the deepest, I think, that I
> have anywhere found."

Dixon's *Ode to Summer* was considered worthy to be placed beside Keat's *Autumn*, *Nightingale*, and *Grecian Urn* :

> " This richness of image, matched with the deep feeling which
> flushes his work throughout, gives rise to effects we look for
> rather from music than from verse."[3]

There is truth here ; but we must qualify it by saying that whereas the greater masters show a natural fecundity and sustained inspiration, Dixon's best is revealed only in flashes.[4] His *Summer*, for instance, though delightfully phrased, is comparatively commonplace beside Keats's *Autumn*. In the longer works, moments of brilliant clarity are " lost in wildernesses ".

---

[1] June 4, 1878 ; *Letters*, vol. ii. p. 1.
[2] *Letters*, vol. ii. pp. 35-7.   [3] *Ibid.* p. 177.
[4] " The last line of *Love's Consolation* is a wonderful touch of genius." (*Letters*, vol. i. p. 74).

Hopkins himself complained of lapses into a gibberish, of a frequent " meagreness or want of flush and fusedness " [1] in his diction.

Nevertheless, when full allowance has been made for friendship, contemporaneity, a similar vein of " humanity ", and a close kinship in faith, Hopkins's criticism stands as a valuable tribute to an undervalued poet.

With the narrative poems influenced by the school of Morris and Rossetti Hopkins betrayed only an imperfect sympathy. He saw that Dixon's most profound and original poems were those in which are evinced, separately or in combination, a Wordsworthian insight into nature,[1] a metaphysical apprehension of the significance of human suffering, and a Blake-like intuition of the intimate life and human affinities of the visible world. The fusion of imagination and intellect comes out best in the finest of the early poems, *Love's Consolation*, and in the best of the later works—three splendid odes and parts of *Mano*.

The first of these odes, *The Spirit Wooed*, is " a lovely piece of nature and imagination all in one, in a vein peculiarly yours ".[1] The stronger *Ode on Conflicting Claims* is, in execution, " nearly perfect " : in thought and feeling Dixon is here " always a master and never makes a false note ".[2] Again, after reading the *Ode on Advancing Age*, Hopkins says :

> " Please write more odes. The ode ' Thou goest more and more ' seems to me one of the very grandest ever written in anything." [3]

Formally these odes assert the influence of Keats modified by the irregular rhythms of Patmore. In their close-knit poignancy they display, like the poems of Hopkins, " a feeling for the tragedy that is kneaded up in human life ".[4] In the bulk of his work, Dixon resisted the fascination of his friend's rhythms and diction as completely as he admired their originality : in the last-named ode, however, there are successful touches of sprung rhythm.

After the *Historical Odes*, which Hopkins rightly called dull, and a few poems in the macabre vein, the weirdness of which

---

[1] *Letters*, vol. ii. p. 55.

[2] *Ibid.*, vol. i. p. 139. Cf. vol. ii. p. 68 : " . . . to me a poem of an immortal beauty."   [3] *Ibid.* vol. ii. p. 157.

[4] *Ibid.*, vol. ii. p. 155. The sky-images of *The Spirit Wooed* owe something to Shelley.

pleased him,[1] we find in a number of others a subtle metaphysical quality which amply justifies Hopkins's enthusiasm : the best of these are *Nature and Man* (" One of the most perfect of all, both in thought and expression "), *The Soul's World*, and *To Shadow*.[2]

Some of Dixon's shorter lyrics (songs ' for music perhaps ') are, as both Hopkins and Bridges claimed, among the best in the language.[3]   Hopkins, moreover, was the first to point out the resemblance between Dixon and Blake.   Very Blake-like is the opening of *Death and Victory* :

> " He wept, he wept : there came a wind
>   Out of the cloud heavy and blind :
>   The angel of human thoughts had joy—
>   And water dropped from the cloud's hair. . . ."

A lyric we have already mentioned, *Fallen Rain* (for which Hopkins composed an air of real distinction),[4] is, as Saintsbury remarked, " Blake himself." [5]   This facile identification is in one respect a token of Dixon's weakness as a poet : he assimilated and sometimes enriched the vein of a Blake, a Wordsworth, a Coleridge, a Shelley, a Keats, and a Morris, but he failed to make that total fusion of influences which reveals the strong and undivided personality.

At his first reading of Dixon's most ambitious work, *Mano*, Hopkins felt some doubts about its quality and success.   His " riper thoughts " (expressed in a letter which is unfortunately lost) were more reassuring to Dixon ; his appreciation stood somewhere between that of Bridges, who thought the poem " marvellous ", and that of Patmore, who was frankly disappointed.   We may, however, sum up Hopkins's attitude to Dixon's work as a whole by quoting from the critique which the former contributed to Thomas Arnold's *Manual of English Literature* (1885) :

> " In his poems we find a deep thoughtfulness and earnestness, and a mind touched by a pathos of human life, of which *Mano* is, in a strange but a typical case, the likeness ; noble but never

[1] E.g. *The Wizard's Funeral* (S.P., p. 14) and *The Secret Execution. (Letters*, vol. ii p. 171).

[2] *Selected Poems*, pp. 116, 16, and 52 respectively.

[3] The titles of two, *Wayward Water* and *Ruffling Wind*, were supplied by Hopkins.

[4] See *Letters*, vol. ii. Appendix iii. p. 169. Also below, Appendix A, p. 389.

[5] This lyric, he adds, is " not a *pastiche* or an imitation but a poem, Blake's authorship of which . . . no one would have doubted for a moment."   (*Camb. Hist. of Eng. Lit.*, ed. cit. xiii. p. 197.)

highflown, sad without noise or straining—everything as it most reaches and comes home to man's heart." [1]

A compliment to Hopkins's critical acumen was paid by Bridges when, in his Memoir and the Notes appended to Dixon's *Selected Poems* (1909), he quotes freely from the *Letters* ; moreover, most of the pieces chosen had previously received the cachet of Hopkins's particular approval.

Hopkins tolerated the archaic style of *Mano*, and the well-worn classical themes of *Ulysses and Calypso, Cephales and Procris,* etc., for the sake of their quiet grace and " instress " of feeling. But many of the more academic poems of both Dixon and Bridges he admired, we feel, with a certain reserve, as things alien to himself—backwaters in the stream of Reality.

Bridges, nevertheless, he held to be a very considerable poet. When the candour of some of his criticisms caused his dejected friend to ask whether there was any good in his continuing to write poetry, Hopkins replied :

> " You seem to want to be told over again that you have genius and are a poet and your verses beautiful." [2]

Of the sincerity of this opinion he gave practical proof in the " marketing " of Bridges's books among friends and even strangers. He never tired of praising his fellow-poet's pure style and " constant music ". The feeling for beauty in Bridges is called " pure and exquisite " ; he is not so rich in imagery as Tennyson, Swinburne, or Morris, but (and here the eulogy is prejudiced by a note of exaggeration)—

> " but in point of character, of sincerity or earnestness, of manliness, of tenderness, of humour, melancholy, human feeling, you have what they have not and seem scarcely to think worth having (about Morris I am not sure : his early poems had a deep feeling)."

There were, of course, radical differences in temperament and outlook between the Jesuit poet and the free-lance who heartily disliked Jesuitry. With his own philosophical position so clearly defined, Hopkins looked with disapproval at Bridges's spiritual errantry, a want of firm outline in his fundamental

---

[1] *Letters*, vol. ii. p. 177.

[2] *Ibid.* vol. i. pp. 95–6. Addressing his friend as " my dearest ", Hopkins admits that he is " biassed by love ", but later says : " If I were not your friend I should wish to be the friend of the man that wrote your poems."

beliefs ; he deprecated his friend's vague theism, his fondness for the Greek Pantheon, his indefinite pagan *cultus* of Truth and Beauty.   The long narrative *Eros and Psyche*,[1] for instance, is warmly commended for stylistic qualities, but is virtually condemned in the following :

> " The story you have not elevated but confined yourself to making it please.   Eros is little more than a winged Masher, but Psyche is a success, a sweet little ' body ' rather than ' soul '." [2]

When Hopkins adds that the characters " say all the right things and so on " and that the poem should be widely and lastingly admired, we seem to be reading a sarcastic review of the latest ' best seller '.   The ode " O my vague desires " evokes a little homily :

> " What then is the meaning of those yearnings or aspirations in the mind ? . . . This poem as well as that sonnet . express your belief that the mind is immortal. . . . You cannot wisely neglect that world of being to which you imply that you will come.   In it or above it is the sovereign spirit God, to whom you should at once make your approach with the humblest and most earnest prayers." [3]

Still, this preoccupation with the " man within " did not prevent Hopkins from criticizing the rhythm and diction of this poem with some thoroughness ; and when later he praised it, somewhat extravagantly perhaps, as " a unique and wonderful creation ",[4] we feel that he valued it mainly as the symptom of a desirable spiritual change in its author.

Hopkins realized that his own rhetorical intensity was not the only medium of poetic beauty ; that the real strength of Bridges lay in a restrained and melodious subtlety of direct statement, relieved at times by imagery of a delightful quaintness and ingenuity.   To the *Growth of Love* sonnets, with their " grave and feeling genius ", their admirable sequence, turn, and recoil of thought—to these noble poems he yielded a measure of praise which later times, if not our own, will fully endorse.   Yet frequently, when criticizing Bridges's text, he suggested alterations which, though stronger in the Hopkinsian manner, could not have been adopted by Bridges without loss of artistic

---

[1] From the Latin of Apuleius ; *Poetical Works of R. B.* (1914), p. 87.
[2] *Letters*, vol. i. p. 206.
[3] *Ibid.* pp. 117–8. For the ode, see *ibid.* Note N, p. 311.
[4] *Ibid.* p. 160.

integrity.[1] Hopkins had no conscious wish to make Bridges a poetic proselyte : the former admitted that it was " d——d impertinence " on his part to rewrite ten lines of one of R. B.'s sonnets ; and as we shall see, Hopkins almost resented his friend's incursions into sprung rhythm. He advised Bridges to use his suggestions as shoelasts on which to shape his own final handiwork, and that, in the main, is what Bridges did.

The association of these two poets was a state of tension between two impressionable but wise and independent personalities. By gentle ridicule, Hopkins sought to dissuade Bridges from writing and printing Latin verse (" a waste of time and money ") and also from dabbling too seriously in the French verse forms then popular. In return, Bridges was always warning his friend of the dangers of indulging his idiosyncrasy too freely.

Hopkins forestalled modern opinion by finding the best of Bridges in his shorter idylls, nature poems, and song-lyrics. He admired particularly the simple beauty of the songs—their Caroline delicacy and vocal effectiveness :

" Your poetry is highly songful and flies into tunes." [2]

The poems of Bridges are frequently composed of commonplace thoughts and sentiments which produce nevertheless a truly magical effect of freshness and originality. Hopkins notices how in *The Water Party*. [3]

" the feeling of ' business ' (in the dramatic sense) given by scattering in touches of landscape between the stages of landing, stripping, and so on is in the highest degree bright and refreshing." [4]

Among the most musical and satisfying of Bridges's shorter poems are those written under the influence of Hopkins in a

[1] E.g. for Bridges's " 'Tis joy the foldings of her dress to view " (original *Growth of Love*, v.), Hopkins wants

" Her fall of fold is daylight in my view——" (*Ibid.* p. 35).

Cf. also the suggested change from

" I heard great Hector sounding war's alarms "

to

" I heard great Hector *hurling* war's alarms " (p. 91)

and from

" When, parched with thirst, astray on sultry sand
  The traveller faints, upon his closing ear . . ."

to

" All drawn with thirst, all lost on sultry sand,
  The traveller fainting finds into his ear . . ." (p. 70).

[2] *Letters*, vol. i. p. 105.   [3] *Poetical Works*, p. 250.   [4] *Letters*, vol. i. p. 81.

modified form of sprung rhythm. About these Hopkins was strangely diffident :

> " The pieces in sprung rhythm—do not quite satisfy me. They do read tentative, experimental ; I cannot well say where the thought is distorted by the measure, but that it is distorted I feel by turning from these to the other pieces, where the mastery is so complete." [1]

Two of the poems thus depreciated were the well known *A Passer By* and the no less successful *The Downs*. Another popular anthology piece, *London Snow*, was acknowledged to be unique and charmingly fresh. Yet Hopkins felt that the rhythm was still not perfect, and proffered suggestions for emendation, which were wisely ignored. Bridges was unshaken also by adverse criticism of the pathetic lines *On a Dead Child*. Having called the poem " Browningese ",[2] Hopkins admits that it is fine, but

> " I do not think the rhythm or the thought flowing enough. The diction is not exquisite as yours can be when you are at ease." [3]

To Bridges's defence that the piece is deliberately severe Hopkins replies, " perhaps it is bald ". He condemns the words " wise, sad head " and " firm, pale hands " as sentimental commonplace. On such questions opinions will always differ ; but the epithet " wise " could be justified for its visual truth and for its suggestion of knowledge acquired through death. But we could hardly expect Hopkins to be pleased with the total impression left by a poem which ends, as this one does, on a note of agnostic despair : " Ah ! little at best can all our hopes avail us. . . ." [4]

A more detailed account of Hopkins's influence on the rhythm and diction of these poems by Bridges (with their significant echoes of the stronger, more original poet) has already been given in Volume I.[5] But before we leave Bridges, there is one apparent inconsistency in Hopkins's criticism which calls for explanation. Supposing that the words " he may hear " in one

---

[1] *Letters*, vol. i. p. 71.

[2] *Ibid.* p. 111. As an example of Browningese, Hopkins quotes stanza 6, line 2 :

> " To a world, do I think, that rights the disaster of this ? "

[3] *Ibid.* p. 122.

[4] For the above poems see *Poetical Works of R. B.* (1914). *A Passer By* and *The Downs* are Nos. 2 and 7 of *Shorter Poems*, Book II (Dedicated to G. M. H.) ; *London Snow* and *On a Dead Child* are Nos. 2 and 4 of Book III (To R. W. D.).

[5] Chapter vii.

of Bridges's sonnets mean nothing but " he *can* hear ", Hopkins adds : " But the meaning should be felt at once." To this Professor Abbott supplies a footnote : " Not a rule that G. M. H. wished to be judged by." [1]   Now although Hopkins is more often obscure than either Bridges or Dixon, we must not forget his earlier statement :

> " Obscurity I do and will try to avoid *so far as is consistent with excellences higher than clearness at a first reading.*" [2]

The ambiguity of Bridges's " he may hear " does not subserve a higher excellence : " if it means *He perhaps hears* it is feeble and downright padding." Hopkins himself is not impeccable in this matter, but as we have tried to show in other chapters, most of the uncertainties and obscurities in Hopkins are (like those of Donne and Patmore) strictly compatible with an unusual richness of thought and originality of perception.

To sum up, Hopkins's critical remarks, with their vigorous style and constant preoccupation with definite ethical and aesthetic standards, frequently remind us of the honest and trenchant manner of Dr. Johnson. If his praise of his friends' verses was sometimes coloured by personal feeling, both Dixon and Bridges could have said, with Patmore :

> " Your careful and subtle fault-finding is the greatest praise my poetry has ever received." [3]

Though he could at times be harsh and hypercritical, Hopkins's taste was more catholic, his perception more versatile than that of Johnson, who had not enjoyed the advantage of early enlightenment at the feet of Wordsworth, Coleridge, and Keats. With Hopkins as with Johnson, however, it is usually difficult if not dangerous to disagree ; in either case, disagreement always entails an exhilarating mental exercise, a salutary revision and reaffirmation of our own principles.

---

[1] *Letters*, vol. i. pp. 70 and 72.   [2] *Ibid.* p. 54.   (Our italics.)
[3] *Further Letters*, p. 177.

PART II

MATURITY AND ACHIEVEMENT

" . . . we should explain things, plainly state them, clear them up, explain them ; explanation—except personal—is always pure good ; without explanation people go on misunderstanding . . . therefore always explain."

(G. M. H., *Letters*, vol. i. p. 275.)

CHAPTER V

POEMS OF NATURE AND GOD
(1876–1879)

THE first manifestation of Hopkins's maturity was, of course, *The Wreck of the Deutschland*, which has already been discussed at length. Of the poems that followed it only a few have, in the present work, been subjected to an adequate *aesthetic* criticism ; that is to say, only *The Windhover, Andromeda, The Blessed Virgin, That Nature is a Heraclitean Fire*, and one or two more have been fairly examined as complete, self-contained works of art. In this and the next two chapters all the poems written after 1876 will be surveyed, for the most part in chronological order, against the background of the poet's changing circumstances and developing thought ; we shall also consider some of the richer fragments. Familiarity with the biographical facts given in our introductory chapter will be assumed, and our main purpose will be to estimate the value of the experience communicated by each poem, and so lead naturally to the summing up, in the Epilogue, of the poet's whole achievement.

An organic growth, like that of a poet's mind, can hardly be cast into rigid categories. Hence the titles of this and the next two chapters are not strictly inclusive or exclusive ; we have usually preferred the natural sequence of the poems to a more logical scheme. Nevertheless it will be found that the verses written between January 1876 and April 1879 (the period treated in the present chapter) are mostly nature poems expressing joy, positive faith, and mystical perception ; whereas those composed between October 1879 and August 1885 (the scope of Chapter vi.) show that although God is still the centre of interest (and to this poet the spiritual was always supreme), the general or secondary emphasis has shifted from nature to man—" life's pride and cared-for crown " who is as dogged in sin as in his heroic attempts to adjust himself to a difficult world. In this middle group of poems Hopkins tells us much about his own spiritual struggles, so that Chapter vi. forms a natural transition to the last phase (1885–9), the subject of Chapter vii. Certain poems which belong chronologically and thematically to one

9

group have been transposed for purposes of comparison—for example, *The Candle Indoors* and *Spelt from Sibyl's Leaves*. If *Inversnaid*, a pure 'nature poem', happens to fall among the 'poems of man', it shows that Hopkins was never entirely obsessed by one theme. Moreover, the verses reviewed in Chapter vii. are not all 'terrible': the poet is still able to get outside himself, to recover much of the joy and assurance of the year 1877.

The strenuous composition and immediate 'failure' of *The Deutschland* would account for the otherwise meagre output of 1876—two 'presentation pieces', the unfinished *Moonrise* and *The Woodlark*, and an interesting attempt at a Welsh *cywydd*. *The Silver Jubilee*, though it was published and is still of interest to Catholics, is poetically slight. Yet it has points of technical merit. The "high-hung". bells which did *not* celebrate the Bishop's anniversary are replaced by the symbolic chiming of the sprung rhythm :

> " Whát is sóund ? Náture's róund
> Makes the Silver Jubilee."

The second stanza refers to the restoration of the Catholic hierarchy in England and Wales :

> ·' Five and twenty years have run
>   Since sacred fountains to the sun
>   Spráng, that bút nów were shút,
>   Shówering Silver Jubilee."

The first word in the third line holds the clue to the mystery of the term " *sprung* rhythm " : the juxtaposition of the two stressed syllables (where the traditional ear would expect a strong and a weak) imparts a ' spring ' or rhetorical impetus to the verse.

Penmaen Pool was composed in a mood half playful but none the less wholly sincere in its enjoyment of natural beauty. The sub-title, " For the Visitor's Book at the Inn ", has misled some critics into ignoring or depreciating this daintily forceful effusion ; but how many other Victorian poets could match the clear, sharp yet still sensuous tones of ?—

> " You'll dare the Alp ? Yóu'll *dart* the skiff ?—"

> " The Mawddach, how she trips ! though *throttled*
>   If floodtide teeming *thrills* her full,
>   And mazy sands all *water-wattled*
>   Waylay her at ebb, past Penmaen Pool."

The " (who'll not honour it?) ale like goldy foam " has a Neo-Georgian smack which suggests that Hopkins would have been quite at home in the company of those hearty fellow-ultramontanes, Belloc and Chesterton.

As Hopkins left it, *The Woodlark* was a mere jumble of attractive *motifs*. Now, as skilfully rearranged and in three places very sensitively " patched " by Fr. Geoffrey Bliss, it has become a satisfying and even lovely piece of verse.[1] In this poem, with all the naïve glee of a child, Hopkins has gone straight to nature, to the " pure wild volition and energy ", as Ruskin enjoined. Yet from an opening of extreme Wordsworthian simplicity this amazing poet conjures a diction of the most elaborate artifice. Here we have a frank study in onomatopoeia, from the " *Teevo cheevo cheevio chee* of the first line to the " sweet—sweet—joy " of the close ; more than that, the effects of varying line-lengths, as produced by sprung rhythm upon the four-stress verse, have been successfully combined with the richest effects of Welsh *cynghanedd* and sensuous suggestion.

From line 11 to the end the poem purports to be the utterance or ' message ' of the song-bird. Its charm is in the beauty of the setting provided for the " little woodlark " (though the bird Hopkins observed so lovingly was probably the tree-pipit) and no less in the ornitho-biographic accuracy of the picture. Some critics will say that the following passage is too lush, impressionistic ' late Turner ', in its riot of visual and tonal colour ; that the centre of interest has been ponderously shifted from the small bird to the cornfield :

> " To-day the sky is two and two
> With white strokes and strains of the blue.
> The blue wheat-acre is underneath
> And the braided ear breaks out of the sheath,
> The ear in milk, lush the sash,
> And crush-silk poppies aflash,
> The blood-gush blade-gash
> Flame-rash rudred
> Bud shelling or broad-shed
> Tatter-tassel-tangled and dingle-a-dangled
> Dandy-hung dainty head."

[1] See Vol. I. of the present work, pp. 288-9, or *Poems of G.M.H.*, Third Edition.

Yet before condemning (and while we are puzzling over the " *blue* wheat acre ") we should listen to Fr. Bliss :

> " Obviously to enjoy this poem to the full more is necessary than to be interested in the technique of poetry. You must have kept open eyes in the fields : have stared at the poppied wheat, delighting in the wind-confused petals coloured deep as blood and ' rash ' as flame, or lifted the drooped buds to see where the crimson breaks through the pale lipped wounds between the green : have pulled the half-plumped wheat-ears from their soft lush sash or sheath (as you surely did if you were ever a boy) and bitten on them till the milky juice of the unripe grain oozed out." [1]

To this we may add : what a precise epithet is " braided " ! What a delicate word is " sash ", with its three combined meanings—silk-scarf, cincture, and frame ! How admirably does " crush-silk " give the texture of the poppy petal ! [2] The very lightness of the stresses on the rhyming syllables of " lovely " and " fumitory " (pronounced " fumit'ry ") is in keeping with the nature of the lace-leaved foam-tuft flower.

The three poems we have just considered, together with the ten sonnets which are dated 1877, were written while Hopkins was reading Theology at the Jesuit college of St. Beuno, near Tremeirchion, North Wales. This noble house, standing on a hillside overlooking the Vale of Clwyd, was set in the midst of the type of landscape which was most pleasing to Hopkins. The distant mountains with their " violet-sweet " hues and bold but not forbidding contours ; the silent stretches of pastureland ; the whitewashed cottages nestling amid clumps of bushy trees ; the majestic cloudscapes massing and disintegrating above the summits, and after rain the white rills which streak the slopes— all these left their impress upon the poems we are now to examine.

These sonnets were written by a man who was immersed in the Latin syllogisms of St. Thomas Aquinas's *Summa*, preparing himself for the priesthood of a religion which is popularly associated with the Dark Ages, superstition, penance, and gloom —with anything rather than a lusty pagan enjoyment of the material world. But in 1865 Hopkins had read Arnold's *Essays*

---

[1] *The Month*, June, 1936 ; pp. 530–1.
[2] Cf. Francis Thompson's poppy :

> " Like a yawn of fire from the grass it came,
>   And the fanning wind puffed it to flapping flame."
>
> (*The Poppy*).

in Criticism, and a passage from the essay on *Pagan and Medieval Religious Sentiment* might well have prepared the ground for this Jesuit's poetic harvest :

> " Medieval Christianity is reproached with its gloom and austerities ; it assigns the material world, says Heine, to the devil. Yet what a fulness of delight does St. Francis manage to draw from the material world itself, and from its commonest and most universally enjoyed elements—sun, air, earth, water, plants ! His hymn expresses a far more cordial sense of happiness, even in the material world, than the hymn of Theocritus. It is this which made the fortune of Christianity,—its gladness, not its sorrow ; not its assigning the spiritual world to Christ, and the material world to the devil, but its drawing from the spiritual world a sense of joy so abundant that it ran over upon the material world and transfigured it."

The tradition of St. Francis was carried on in poetry by the Spanish Augustinian, Luis de León, by the Carmelite mystic, Fray Juan de la Cruz, by the English poets, Vaughan and Traherne.[1] From this line of joyous visionaries was Hopkins descended—at least, a part of him was, for like Hamlet he was a man of many worlds and moods : he was as much disturbed by the conflicting creeds and theories of his own age as he was consoled and reassured by the serene faith of the thirteenth century.[2]

The first poem of 1877, *God's Grandeur*, is written in " standard rhythm counterpointed " :

> " The world is charged with the grandeur of God.
> It will flame out, like shining from shook foil ;
> It gathers to a greatness, like the ooze of oil
> Crushed. Why do men then now not reck his rod ? "

---

[1] Of Luis de León (b. 1527) Mr. Aubrey Bell says : " It became his mission to recreate the external world for his soul in the light of a new psychology and sensibility, to transform in a freshly awakened curiosity and love of beauty the common things, rain, a leaf, a cloud, into miracles that revealed the glory and presence of God." (*Luis de León*, p. 239). Similarly of St. John of the Cross (b. 1542) we read : " He had learned to take the keenest and loftiest delight in Nature ; for it was always leading him to contemplation." (Robert Sencourt in *Carmelite and Poet*, p. 118.) Vaughan's deeply spiritual *Regeneration* had the same natural origin ; and in Traherne's *Nature* we find an apt epigraph for the mature nature-poems of Hopkins :

> " His Works He bid me in the World admire.
> My Senses were Informers of my Heart,
> The Conduits of His Glory, Pow'r, & Art."

[2] Cf. Hopkins's *Nondum*, stanza 6.

In the opening line the reversed feet or " counterpointing " may be ignored by any reader who is not afraid of docking the line of a full stress ; yet Hopkins wanted the half-stress on " with " to give the statement a slow weightiness, a suggestion of intoned solemnity.

In our approach to the meaning of this sonnet we follow Dr. Pick by quoting a passage from the *Note-books* :

> " All things therefore are charged with love, are charged with God and if we know how to touch them give off sparks and take fire, yield drops and flow, ring and tell of him." [1]

That is a beginning ; but the poem has deeper implications. In the first verb, " charged ", Hopkins accosts the scientific materialists in their own language : the world is a thundercloud charged with beauty and menace, with the electricity of God's creative love and potential wrath. The dynamism of this poet's imagery is shown in the sudden merging of the image of lightning (" It will flame out ") into the more concrete and curious image of " shook foil ".   Here there is a technical blemish, for the reader has no means of ascertaining the exact sense of " foil " without the poet's own explanation :

> " I mean foil in the sense of leaf or tinsel, and no other word whatever will give the effect I want.   Shaken gold-foil gives off broad glares like sheet lightning and also, and this is true of nothing else, owing to its zigzag dints and creasings and network of small many cornered facets, a sort of fork lightning too." [2]

The whole sonnet, Hopkins says, might have been written expressly for the sake of that image.

The *direct* meaning, that the world is a vast reservoir of Divine power, love, and beauty, is immediately obvious.   But the poet must have been aware, if only subconsciously, of the deeper, less explosive symbolism in his carefully chosen images. The shaking of the foil signifies an important doctrine : life itself must be shaken, disturbed, jarred, before the deepest instress can be felt and the heroic virtues (the highest beauty) can appear.   And is it not in their movement, their natural

---

[1] *Comments on the Spiritual Exercises, op. cit.* p. 342.

[2] *Letters*, vol. i. pp. 168–9.   A reader of our first volume (a Brigadier and " fervent admirer of Hopkins since 1918 ") writes : " I am horrified that Hopkins intends this to mean ' shaken goldfoil '.   That takes me to Drury Lane or the Transformation Scene. . . .   He should have meant—as I thought he did—the sun glint on a sabre in action."

activity, that most creatures reveal their characteristic splendour ?
Moreover, God's grandeur strikes through the cosmic natural
order and penetrates even to the complex minutiae, the creasings
and cornered facets of the most artificial civilization ; though
here it may be obscured or adulterated. The Elizabethan
" shook " is a better word than " shaken " : it is more sudden
and acute ; and its very archaism suggests, however faintly, the
eternal *Now*. Apt, too, is the next similitude, the crushing of
oil-seed ; for here the Divine effluence, normally obscured by
industrialism, is richly re-communicated in terms of an industrial
process. " Crushed " is the verbal link between the omnipotent
World-Wielder and the pitiful, obtuse human agent, who so
easily forgets both the source and the true purpose of all this
power (" Wring thy rebel . . . ", " Melt him but master him
still "). The last words of the quatrain, " his rod ", are reminis-
cent of the " lashed rod " of *The Deutschland*. The price of
folly is pain and defilement :

> " Generations have trod, have trod, have trod ;
>   And all is seared with trade ; bleared, smeared with toil ;
>   And wears man's smudge and shares man's smell : the soil
> Is bare now, nor can foot feel, being shod."

We are suddenly reminded that not all human activity is
natural and beautiful. In 1881 Hopkins wrote to Bridges :

> " While I admired the handsome horses I remarked for the
> thousandth time with sorrow and loathing the base and bespotted
> figures and features of the Liverpool crowd."

Norwegian emigrants, by comparison, seemed " fine and
manly " ; and in the above Swiftean observation we see why
this Jesuit, who in the classroom dramatically re-lived the scenes
in Homer, could attribute the British defeat at Majuba Hill to
a cowardice engendered by that grievous degradation of the
human body.[1]

Hopkins saw the daily processions of factory operatives in
the north almost as Dante saw the hosts of the damned in Hell :
' I had not thought *toil* had undone so many ' ; and here again
this Victorian anticipated T. S. Eliot and other modern poets.[2]

---

[1] *Letters*, vol. i. pp.127–8, 131–2 ; also *Further Letters*, pp. 146 and 289. It is
said that Hopkins, while lecturing on Homer, gave a practical illustration of the
spite of Achilles against the slain Hector by dragging a supine student feet-foremost
round the room.

[2] Cf. T. S. Eliot's *The Waste Land*, l. 63 and Note.

Harold Monro's " Under the pavement the live earth aches " [1] is a sensitive variation on " the soil / Is bare now " ; and Hopkins's regret that the foot can no longer feel, " being shod ", reminds us of Tagore's assertion that a child, at one stage of its education, should roam about and climb trees—barefooted. In believing that something vital could be learnt through the soles of the feet, Hopkins was close in spirit to Whitman, D. H. Lawrence, and the primitive ' dark gods ' ; but while he saw that men were losing all sense of space and time, he was more concerned about their indifference to first and last things— Eden, Original Sin, and Salvation.

The octave of this sonnet is a statement of the poetic *motif* in obverse and reverse. The poet presents a factual antinomy and then, in the sestet, tries to remove the contradiction and balance the account :

" And for all this, nature is never spent ;
    There lives the dearest freshness deep down things ;
And though the last lights off the black West went
    Oh, morning, at the brown brink eastward, springs—
Because the Holy Ghost over the bent
    World broods with warm breast and with ah ! bright wings."

Man, who sullies the " sweet earth " with his smudge and smell, seems here to be deliberately slighted. Despite the worst efforts of collective humanity, inanimate nature still speaks directly of that informing Spirit which, as Milton said, was present from the first :

    " and with mighty wings outspread,
    Dove-like sat'st brooding on the vast abyss
    And mad'st it pregnant." [2]

Consciously or not, Hopkins has echoed Milton ; and if the whole sonnet is not properly understood, the charge of plagiarism will be coupled with the more serious charge of exalting nature at the expense of man. The truth is that Hopkins was so deeply concerned about the salvation of man that he was trying to lead him back to God " through his natural senses ", trying to restore to him his lost vision of the Kingdom of Heaven, explicit news of which was all around him. Despite man's increasing indifference to eschatology, his crass mistaking of means for ends, he may still derive by intuition from what Shelley called the ' spirit of Nature ' the power of renewing contact with first and last things.

[1] *Real Property.*   [2] *Paradise Lost*, I. 19 22.

Just as the dayspring is continually renewed, so the Holy Ghost (the creative Spirit), the Paraclete (the defender, the giver of hope and encouragement) is constantly crying out to man " Come on, come on ! " [1] Hopkins echoes Milton, but with a set purpose and with a significant change of tense : the process of creation, he says, *is still going on*. " The proper function of the Holy Ghost," says another writer, " is to complete Creation, to finish and to make all things perfect." [2] And in the sermon just quoted Hopkins himself, having spoken of the Holy Ghost as " struggling with the world ", concludes with the words :

> " . . . the Holy Ghost has followed and will follow up this first beginning, convincing and converting nation after nation and age after age till the whole earth is hereafter to be covered, if only for a time, still to be covered, with the knowledge of the Lord." [3]

The last lines of the sonnet are not concerned with the evangelizing of the world in the conventional sense, but rather with the direct " instress " of God through nature. Nothing in the poem is more important than that seemingly unimportant " ah ! " in the last phrase of all ; it expresses the surprise and delight with which the man of single eye and pure heart greets every new manifestation of " the dearest freshness ", the immanence of God, " deep down things ".

Ever since Vaughan and Marvell (with a hint, perhaps, from Duke Senior's " tongues in trees, etc.") first developed a Romantic delight in the perception of an ideal spiritual relationship between man and external nature, the mystical reading of earth has proved more and more fruitful in English poetry. After Wordsworth, this visionary gleam has found a specifically Catholic expression not only in Hopkins but also in Alice Meynell and Francis Thompson. As Hopkins penetrates beneath appearances to discover God's grandeur everywhere in nature, so Thompson finds the Kingdom of God " in no Strange Land " :

> " O world invisible, we view thee,
> O world intangible, we touch thee. . . " [4]

Asiatic, ritualistic, half pagan in the splendour of its imagery, his vision is more apocalyptic, less trammelled than that of

---

[1] See Hopkins's sermon on the two Paracletes, based on *John* xvi. 5–14, and in particular 8–11. He compares the Paraclete to a batsman in cricket, crying to his partner " Come on, come on ! " (*Note-books*, pp. 285–94.)

[2] B. Delany, O.P., in the *Introduction* to Bede Jarrett's *The Holy Ghost* (C.T.S. Pamphlet), p. iv.   [3] *Loc. cit.* p. 294.   [4] *The Kingdom of God.*

Hopkins by the murk and miasma of prevailing conditions ; ye
the same element of delighted surprise is there :

> " Turn but a stone, and start a wing ! "

Moreover, he too reproaches man for those mundane attachmen
which induce spiritual blindness :

> " 'Tis ye, 'tis your estrangèd faces
> That miss the many-splendoured thing." [1]

Both Hopkins and Thompson reacted powerfully again
pagan nature-worship and pantheism. Of " Lady Nature
Thompson says :

> " This Lady is God's Daughter, and she lends
> Her hand but to His friends," [2]

and this thought, expressed in quite different terms, " caps, clear
and clinches " the rhapsodic poetry of Hopkins's next sonne
The Starlight Night.

The subject of this poem, as a brilliant illustration of th
truth stated with metaphysical breadth in *God's Grandeu*
immediately kindles the poet's fancy :

> " Look at the stars ! look, look up at the skies !.
> O look at all the fire-folk sitting in the air !
> The bright boroughs, the circle-citadels there !
> Down in dim woods the diamond delves ! the elves'-eyes !
> The grey lawns cold where gold, where quickgold lies !
> Wind-beat whitebeam ! airy abeles set on a flare !
> Flake-doves sent floating forth at a farmyard scare !—
> Ah well ! it is all a purchase, all is a prize." [3]

Childlike reminiscence and faery lore tumble out with visions
city lights, embattled heavenly hosts and the diamond-gleam
glow-worm or ferine eyes in " forests of the night ". " Down
dim woods the diamond delves " can hardly be paraphrased
yet the line opens magic casements. A field of buttercups in th
chill of after-dawn, when the grass is grey with dew, is an a
similitude for major stars sprinkled about the Milky Way ; b

---

[1] *The Kingdom of God.*　　　　　　[2] *Of Nature : Laud and Plaint.*
[3] The rhythm is " standard, opened and counterpointed ". " Opened " mea
that the first line in octave and sestet alike is " sprung ". Cf. *Spring* (No. 9).

we require the dynamic image of " where quickgold lies " to give the whole picture the quality of newly discovered reality. This sense of quivering movement and freshness is kept up by the poet's delicate exploitation of two of our rarer trees—white-beam and the abele or white poplar—which kindle and sparkle when the winds turns up the white undersides of their leaves. Finally, with his flake-white doves Hopkins seems to bring the whole firmament down to earth for our closer inspection. Across the lens of this poet's fancy the heavenly bodies do not glide but dance and pause and flutter ; and with ocular correctness they appear to become more animated the longer they are stared at.

The last line of the octave ushers in the deeper metaphysical *motif*. These riches of the night sky must not be just idly looked at ; they must be understood, rightly valued, actually possessed. To see them (as Alice Meynell said of the daisy) from " God's side " is a privilege to be bought by devotion and good works :

" Buy then ! bid then !—What ?—Prayer, patience, alms, vows."

Then, as though expecting a protest that the cost is too high, this poetic and apostolic auctioneer volubly reaffirms the rarity and attractiveness of the lot under consideration :

" Look, look : a May-mess, like on orchard boughs !
    Look ! March-bloom, like on mealed-with-yellow sallows ! "

This is the sacramental view of nature : heavenly grace is offered, but a sacrifice is demanded in return. And man is prepared for this : the highest reaction to beauty is a feeling of exalted humility —the desire to imitate, to create in terms of one's own talents an equivalent beauty. For most people there is but one field for such activity—the field of moral and social endeavour. For the true Christian there is also the sphere of devotions, rites, obser-vances which intensify religious experience and perpetually signalize the divine origin of Christian morals. Ultimately, to those who interpret aright nature's hieroglyphs, the mysteries of Death and Judgment will prove no more mysterious than Christ's image of the wheat and the tares : " and in the time of harvest I will say to the reapers, Gather up first the tares and bind them into bundles for burning ; but gather the wheat into my barn." [1]

" These are indeed the barn : withindoors house
    The shocks. This piece-bright paling shuts the spouse
        Christ home, Christ and his mother and all his hallows."

[1] *Matthew*, xiii. 30.

The "underthought" is rich in reference—not only to the image of the wheat and the tares but also to the parable of the Sower. Implicitly, too, the aesthetic aspect of behaviour is identified with the ethical—beauty comes home to Beauty.[1] Christ's 'harvest-home', the Ascension, was the promise of a similar reward for his spouse, the 'soul' of the Church. In using "shocks" for "stooks" the poet may have intended (or at least did not avoid) an ominous undertone—a suggestion of the awful disillusionment of those who had carelessly misread Christ and His Creation; those who, like the defaulting guests in the parable of the Marriage Feast, had gone about their merchandise, or had come without a wedding garment. It is fitting, however, that the sonnet should end with a serene altar-piece, a subject for Mantegna.

In *The Starlight Night* Hopkins was close in spirit to his Christian predecessors of the sixteenth and seventeenth centuries. In his *Noche Serena*, Luis de León begins :

> " Ay levantad los ojos
> A aquesta celestial eterna esfera. . . ." [2]

and goes on to describe the ' numinous ', the sense of eternity, the transience of human life ; but he concludes, as Hopkins begins, with a series of ecstatic images :

> " O campos verdaderos
> O prados con verdad frescos y amenos
> Riquísimos mineros !
> O deleitosos senos
> Repuestos valles de mil bienes llenos." [3]

Henry Vaughan and William Habington were two more of those numerous religious men who have declared the stars to be " of mighty use ". The former anticipates Hopkins :

> " They are that City's shining spires
> We travel to." [4]

[1] Cf. the *Journal*, Aug. 17, 1874 : " As we drove home the stars came out thick I leant back to look at them and my heart opening more than usual praised our Lord to and in whom all that beauty comes home." (*Note-books*, p. 205).
[2] " O lift up your eyes to this heavenly eternal sphere. . . ."
[3]   " O fields of truth
         O meadows, yes, with truth freshly adorned
         Mines full of riches !
         O breasts of delight
         Deep valleys replete with a thousand blessings."
[4] " Joy of my life while left me here "(*Stars*).

And Habington, in his *Nox Nocti Indicat Scientiam*,[1] is equally sensitive to the *moral* instress of natural beauty ! those celestial fires, he says, reveal the permanence of beauty and virtue, the impermanence of sin and ugliness.

In 1874, the very year in which Hopkins gazed up at the stars and praised God, James Thomson published *The City of Dreadful Night*,[2] that poem of magnificent frustrated sensibility. Here the stunning impact of science has produced an atheistic melancholia which is belied (as Hopkins would have said) by the inscaped richness of sound and imagery :

> " Cold windows kindle their dead glooms of glass
> To restless crystals ; cornice, dome, and column
> Emerge from chaos in the splendour solemn ;
>   Like faëry lakes gleam lawns of dewy grass." [3]

We feel that Hopkins must have read that passage : he looks at the stars with the same eye but with a different mind.   Similarly, Thomson gives the lie direct to Luis de León :

> " The spheres eternal are a grand illusion."

Our last comparison is with George Meredith, who was not uninfluenced by Spanish mysticism.   In *Meditation under Stars* (1888) he sees men as motes of dust dwarfed by the universe ; yet he accredits man with the supersensuous power of perceiving some metaphysical relationship between himself and the stars :

> " To deeper than this ball of sight
>   Appeal the lustrous people of the night."

The spirit, he says,

>   " leaps alight
>   Doubts not in them is he
>   The binder of the sheaves, the sane, the right."

This " binder " or harvester, according to Trevelyan, means Deity or Reason ; but how strange that Meredith, eleven years after Hopkins, should light upon the same image ! [4]

---

[1] *Castara* (1634).   Habington's reaction against ' profane ' poetry was similar to that of Robert Southwell.

[2] In the *National Reformer*.   [3] XVII, 2.

[4] It is just possible that Meredith had seen *The Starlight Night* in manuscript.   In 1881 Dixon sent this poem and *The Caged Skylark* to Hall Caine, who must have known Meredith through Rossetti and Watts-Dunton.   (See *Letters*, vol. ii. p. 46.)

Hopkins's high religious seriousness between 1877 and 1879 finds telling proof in a letter to Bridges :

> " When we met in London we never once, and then only for a few minutes before parting, spoke on any important subject, but always on literature.   This I regret very much." [1]

Indeed, the first-fruits of his consummated priest- and poet-hood, though they will seem to Freudians an interesting example of what is called ' an escape from sex ', are even more strikingly an illustration of the doctrine enunciated by John Keble while he was Professor of Poetry at Oxford.[2]   Poetry, says Keble, lends Religion her wealth of symbols and similes : Religion restores these again to Poetry—" clothed with so splendid a radiance that they appear to be no longer merely symbols, but to partake (I might almost say) of the nature of sacraments."   True poetry, like earnest prayer, is the effort of the soul to enter into direct communication with its Maker, to derive and partake of knowledge denied to the merely rational mind.

To Arnold's " the strongest part of our religion to-day is its unconscious poetry " Hopkins would have demurred, scenting a heresy ; he would also have rebutted the claim that poetry would more and more take the place of religion.   Yet for many readers of Hopkins the strongest part of *his* religion is that spontaneous poetic utterance which makes him (despite his comparative failure as a preacher) a powerful Christian evangelist.

Nowhere does the combination of prayer, poetry, and predication seem more like a spontaneous fusion than in the sonnet called *Spring* :

> " Nóthing ís so beáutifúl as spríng—
>   When weéds, in wheéls, shoot lóng and lóvely and lúsh ; "

The " sprung leading " suggests the crisp freshness of the air, the poet's sudden ecstasy—like a burst of applause.   Prominent among the weeds that shoot " in wheels " are the wild blackberry stems, the regular arcs of which are so characteristic of English commons and hedgerows.   Next, the naïve comparison of thrush's eggs to " little low heavens " anticipates the ' heavenly meaning ' of this earthly parable—the Christian exegesis in the sestet ; and the song of the thrush, with its lightning flash of sound rinsing

---

[1] *Letters*, vol. i. p. 60.
[2] 1831–41.   The lectures were in Latin.   See *Lectures on Poetry*, translated by E. K. Francis (1912), vol. ii. Lecture XL.

nd wringing the aural sense, is like purgative holy water : it
eminds the adult, soiled by time and sin, that an instress from
rimal nature has the power of restoring the quick responses, the
nsophisticated delight of the age of innocence. Then, as the
bserving eye passes up the " glassy " bark of the blossoming
ear tree to the intense blue of the sky, which seems close enough
ɔ be brushed by the foliage, the childish habit of staring fixedly
ɪto the ether reveals a ferment of oleaginous particles, an active
hrism clear but rich in colour, above or through which are
hevying the small, white, ruffled clouds :

> " that blue is all in a rush
> With richness. . . ." [1]

ɪere, truly, God's grandeur " gathers to a greatness like the ooze
f oil ". This *kinesis* of light and beauty is the medium for the
iffusion of solar energy and Divine love : it imbues the very
ɪmbs with an ecstasy of being, expressed now in the dumb
ɔetry of movement :

> " the racing lambs too have fair their fling."

The sestet opens with a curt question—

> " What is all this juice and all this joy ? "—

Eden had not been revealed, Hopkins would have deduced it
om a child and a May morning. No thorough-going secularist
he poet seems to imply) could ever completely penetrate to the
ɪeaning of all this freshness—unless he were rediscovering the
ɔctrine of the Fall :

> " A strain of earth's sweet being in the beginning
> In Eden garden."

ɪke Wordsworth, Hopkins sees the Fall re-enacted in most men's
ɪes : the morning glory fades into the light of common day ;

[1] Miss E. E. Phare quotes very aptly from the *Journal* (April 22, 1871) : " But
ɪh a lovely damasking in the sky as to-day I never felt before. The blue was
ɪarged with simple instress, the higher, zenith sky earnest and frowning, lower more
ɪht and sweet. High up again, breathing through woolly coats of cloud or on the
ɪains and branches of the flying pieces it was the true exchange of crimson, nearer
ɪ earth / against the sun / it was turquoise, and in the opposite south-western bay
ɪow the sun it was like clear oil but just as full of colour, shaken over with slanted
ɪshing ' travellers ', all in flight, stepping one behind the other, their edges tossed
ɪh bright ravelling, as if white napkins were thrown up in the sun. . . ." (*Note-
ks*, pp. 143–4.)

the ' single eye ' is dulled and divided.   Hence the invocation to
Christ, son of the immaculate Mary, on behalf of that vulnerable
innocence :

> " Have, get, before it cloy,
>   Before it cloud, Christ, lord, and sour with sinning,
>   Innocent mind and Mayday in girl and boy. . . ."

The " juice and joy " are virtually one—the energizing sap of an
idealism which is both Platonic and Christian. Many readers
who give no absolute credence to the Garden of Eden and the
Virgin Mary are nevertheless mystically stirred by this sestet ; by
a momentary suspension of disbelief, or by imaginative adaptation, they accept them both—as ideal ' forms ', or as symbols of
purity, aspiration, perfection.

Some non-Christians, however, will enjoy the naturalistic
octave but dislike the sequel : they will find there the ' typical
Jesuit ' striving to gain control over the minds of the young,
straining to cramp their lives in the strait-jacket of a ' narrow '
dogma. But for Hopkins, we must remember, Christ was *truth* ;
and in one of his sermons he explains his preference for this
particular Teacher :

> " No stories or parables are like Christ's, so bright, so pithy,
> so touching ; no proverbs or sayings are such jewellery : they
> stand off from other men's thoughts like stars, like lilies in the
> sun ; nowhere in literature is there anything to match the
> Sermon on the Mount : if there is let men bring it forward." [1]

Many have rushed, as many more will, to answer this challenge.
To those, however, who are not completely blind to portents,
Hopkins's sonnet called *Spring* may have a greater doctrinal
value to-day than at any other conceivable time.   They will
suspect, perhaps, that a materialism which is diametrically
opposed to Christianity is rapidly strangling not only the soul
but the very body of *homo sapiens* ; that unless the sphere of love
is extended beyond the present social and political frontiers our
civilization will perish.   A reformed humanity, sufficiently
detached from material interests to allow all men to " have fair
their fling " as God's favoured creatures, would be very close to
the moral standards of Christ, would indeed be

> " Most, O maid's child, thy choice and worthy the winning."

If one part of Hopkins was like St. Francis, rejoicing in all
creatures, loving all men, another part of him (the Hamlet-strain

[1] *Note-books*, p. 264.

showed a certain affinity with the austere Diogenes looking for an honest man in a world darkened by folly and vice. Even in the comparatively joyous poems which we are now examining there is an undertone of sadness—a deep dissatisfaction with the moral and even physical shortcomings of mankind. In the sermon just quoted he describes his standard ; beginning with the body, he says that beyond any Greek conception

> " There met in Jesus Christ all things that can make man lovely and lovable. In his body he was most beautiful. . . .. They tell us that he was moderately tall, well built and slender in frame, his features straight and beautiful, his hair inclining to auburn. . . ." [1]

He goes on to say that the graces of mind, and above all of *character*, are far higher than physical beauty in the scale of excellence ; and it was natural that the aesthete and true humanist in Hopkins should desire for all men a balanced perfection of qualities. Though in his letters he sometimes associated too closely the physical and the moral " scaping " in a person, he was right in his general assumption that poverty, squalor, and overwork would produce a degraded human type.[2]

Another sonnet, *The Lantern out of Doors*, deals with the higher, beneficent order of humanity. It presents first a dramatic symbol, which throws a light before it and prepares the mind for the main subject—those men of distinctive, unforgettable personality whom the poet had once known :

> " Sometimes a lantern moves along the night,
>   That interests our eyes. And who goes there ?
>   I think ; where from and bound, I wonder, where,
> With, all down darkness wide, his wading light ?

> " Men go by me whom either beauty bright
>   In mould or mind or what not else makes rare :
>   They rain against our much-thick and marsh air
> Rich beams, till death or distance buys them quite."

At the first reading that lantern suggests many things : a little touch of Diogenes in the night ; that casual passer-by about whom Wordsworth, Whitman, and D. H. Lawrence felt so passionately curious ; Christ, the Light of the World (that comely, wistful figure with the lantern in Holman Hunt's famous picture) moving from one " heart's vault " to another. This

---

[1] *Loc. cit.* pp. 261–2.   [2] E.g. see above, pp. 25–7 and 231.

last idea, being the fittest, prevails : this is Christ, who " plays
in ten thousand places—

> " Lovely in limbs, lovely in eyes not his
>   To the Father through the features of men's faces." [1]

Hopkins does not merely ask, " What *is* this beauty ? What is
its value for *me*—here and now ? " He yearns to know its pro-
venance and final goal, its ultimate *spiritual* value ; whether it
will flower into " immortal beauty " or go, as we say, the way of
all flesh.   In the fourth line there is, in " wading ", a hint of
difficulty, as though these rare personalities are obliged to move
in an unfriendly element.

Hopkins probably had in mind certain complete or partial
strangers as well as men with whom he had been in close contact.
The latter would include Riddell, Liddon, Dolben, Addis, and
Coles ; there was also R. W. Dixon, whom he had seen only for
a few months at Highgate School and whose poems had affected
him so deeply that, on becoming a Jesuit, he had copied some of
them out for future reference.   Hopkins's first letter to Dixon
(June, 1878), like many he wrote to Bridges, testifies to the
strength and purity of his gift for admiration—a quality which
in his case must be defined as a feeling of oneness ' in Christ '.[2]
Thus in the sestet of this elegiac sonnet Hopkins declares his faith
in Christ's supernatural tutelage :

> " Death or distance soon consumes them : wind
>   What most I may eye after, be in at the end
> I cannot, and out of sight is out of mind.

> " Christ minds ; Christ's interest, what to avow or amend
>   There, eyes them, heart wants, care haunts, foot follows kind,
> Their ransom, their rescue, and first, fast, last friend."

From the rational point of view this sestet presents, under a
bold affirmation of faith, nothing more than a pious hope ; for,
granted Christ's interest, the care of the Good Shepherd for his
sheep ; granted the " gospel proffer, a pressure, a principle,
Christ's gift ", how was Hopkins to know that his choice spirits
would co-operate with Divine grace ?   Without that willing co-

---

[1] *Poems*, No. 34.
[2] Cf. line 8 of Bridges's dedicatory sonnet to G. M. H. : " For love of Christ
will win man's love at last."

operation their ransom, their rescue, could not be effected. The last line of the sonnet is, in fact, a ' conditional prolepsis '.

As we have already remarked,[1] the locution " *wind* / What most I may eye *after* ", though dramatically precise, is inexcusably awkward and cacophonous ; and the rhythm of the closing line is forceful rather than elegant. [2] But against these blemishes we should set the admirable matching of octave and sestet in such words as " interests " (line 2) and " interest " (line 12) ; " eyes " and " eye " (lines 2, 10 and 13) ; " mind " and " minds "— subtle modulations which emphasize the central *motif*, the shift from ' watching ' to ' watching over '. Noteworthy, too, is the change from the commonplace " buys " (line 8) to the lordly " ransom " (line 14) : our enforced sale, at a loss, is redeemed by an enforced purchase, for a gain ; for what death or distance " buys ", Christ can *buy back*.

The interest here shown in rare persons of " favoured make and mind " was later transferred to the more commonplace people : in *The Candle Indoors* (1879) Hopkins produced, against his original intention, " a companion to the Lantern ". The parallelism is striking : the lantern becomes the Biblical candle ; the " wading light " is replaced by the liquid luminosity of " yellowy moisture " ; the " much-thick and marsh air " is toned down to " mild night's blear-all black ", while the " rich beams " which rain upon the earlier murk suffer a time-change into the " to-fro tender trambeams " that " truckle at the eye " of the still wistful beholder.

The last image has frequently been quoted as a bad example of this poet's oddity ; [3] yet there will always be readers who will appreciate its stimulating far-fetchedness and inherent truth. Those delicately wincing rays of light which are reflected from the eyelashes and converge on the bright object are indeed like shining tramlines ; they truckle at the eye because they are obedient to that organ, responsive to the slightest movement of the eyelid. Mr. Dylan Thomas, a modern poet who shows some affinity with Hopkins in his concentrations of bold, obscure images, might have thrilled his numerous admirers by putting it thus :

" Or wincing tramlines glitter in the lash."

[1] See Vol. I of the present work, pp. 146–7, and *Letters*, vol. i. p. 66.

[2] The reading in MS " B " is " Their ransom, their rescue and . . ."

[3] See *Introduction* to the Poems (Second Edition), p. xiii.

This candle, which Hopkins had casually observed in some
living-room, conjures up the homely interior with some rustic
Jessy or Jack plying an evening task. With exquisite art the poet
makes both diction and rhythm ' expressional ' :

> " By that window what task what fingers ply,
>
> I plod wondering, a-wanting, just for lack
>
> Of answer the eagerer a-wanting Jessy or Jack [1]
>
> There   God to aggrandise, God to glorify.—"

In the second line the slow counterpointed opening is quickened
by the dialectal " a-wanting " ; and this sudden quickening of
the poet's curiosity, his priestly imitation of " Christ's interest "
is rhythmically emphasized by the ripple of short syllables in the
next line—as though thought and emotion were made audible.
Moreover, the gap after " There " is no mere typographical
freak : it indicates a transitional pause in thought which no
conventional comma or dash would suggest.

The traditional *volta* after the octave (always carefully
observed in these earlier sonnets and in most of the later ones) is
here a complete *volte face* : from the imagined stranger who ought
to be glorifying God, the poet's anxious thought turns suddenly
home to himself ; the wax candle has become the symbol of
sanctifying grace :

> " Come you indoors, come home ; your fading fire
> Mend first and vital candle in close heart's vault ;
> You there are master, do your own desire ; "

St. Paul, St. John of the Cross and other mystics have constantly
repeated Christ's warning against hypocrisy in his dedicated
followers : " they must beware ", says Fray Juan, " of complacency, spiritual pride, judgment on others."   Hopkins himself
was not entirely free from this fault : his judgments on Whitman
and Gladstone as men were not charitable.   We may perhaps see
now why Hopkins began this sonnet with such a vividly idiosyncratic representation of a lighted candle : he wanted to plant in
our minds an image that would ' stick ', like a barbed arrow
rankling or tickling a little, making us smile or grimace ; but

---

[1] The rhythm of this sonnet is " standard, counterpointed " ; but only by the
most arbitrary elision can this line be scanned as a standard pentameter.   This is
really sprung rhythm.

unforgettable   Whenever we see such a light blissfully putting
back the darkness, throwing out " trambeams " to explore the
encircling gloom, we shall think of " the heart of light, the
silence ", the spirit of God dwelling in man—" in close heart's
vault ".   Christ (as Hopkins said in the *Deutschland*[1]) is " our
heart's charity's hearth's fire " ;   only by constant vigilance can
we prevent this fire from fading into " blue-bleak embers ".[2]
Grace is the fuel and free will the stoker : what, then, hinders ?
The answer is in the following rhetorical questions : ' You
hypocrite, your nimble fingers itch to remove a mote from a
neighbour's eye ; but what of the beam in your own ? You are
a living lie, condemned by your own conscience.   You who
should be the salt of the earth have lost your savour and are fit
only to be cast out and trodden underfoot.' [3]   The mild in-
quisitiveness with which the sonnet opened has become a stern
self-inquisition :

> " are you that liar
> And, cast by conscience out, spendsavour salt ? "

The Wordsworthian and Ruskinian strains in Hopkins produced four other sonnets which may be paired off as complementary variations on a basic theme.   All four are offshoots of
God's Grandeur : they present, under varying aspects, the contrast
between the graceful, seasonal renewal of vegetative life and that
" graceless growth " which unregenerate man calls ' material
civilization '—between " news of God " and rumours, so to speak,
of the Devil.   *The Sea and the Skylark*,[4] composed at Rhyl in 1877,
should be compared with *Duns Scotus's Oxford*, written in 1879
while Hopkins was preacher at the church of St. Aloysius in that
city.   The Lancashire sonnet *Ribblesdale* (1882) was expressly
labelled " companion " to *In the Valley of the Elwy*, which belongs
to St. Beuno's and 1877.

The octave of *The Sea and the Skylark* is pure idiosyncratic
description.   The first quatrain is dedicated to the sea, the second
to the lark, and both subjects are richly " inscaped " :

> " On ear and ear two noises too old to end
>   Trench—right, the tide that ramps against the shore ;
>   With a flood or a fall, low lull-off or all roar,
>   Frequenting there while moon shall wear and wend."

---

[1] Stanza 35.   [2] *The Windhover.*
[3] Cf. *Matthew*, v. 13–16 and vii. 5.   [4] Called originally " Walking by the Sea."

The sheer word-music of these lines, from the repetition with sense-variation of *two—too—to* in the first to the onomatopoeic climax in the third and the quiet lapse in the fourth, is to this reader's ear perfect. The diction will bear close scrutiny : " Trench " is unexpected—and trenchant ; " lull-off " is a happy coinage ; while " Frequenting " is such a word as only a true poet would use, it conveys so pregnantly the *notion* of regularity, age-old habit, and the *feeling* or ' prepossession ' of familiarity and pleasure.

With the entry of the bird the rhythm becomes more crisp and rapid, the phonal pattern shows more " quaining ", " margaretting " :

> " Left hand, off land, I hear the lark ascend,
>   His rash-fresh re-winded new-skeinèd score
>   In crisps of curl off wild winch whirl, and pour
> And pelt music, till none's to spill nor spend."

Depreciating the earlier version of this quatrain,[1] Hopkins called it a product of his " salad days ", his Welsh days. In 1882, five years after it was written, its baroque imagery and elaborate " lettering " seemed to smell of the lamp : as in the Welsh *englyns*, he added, " the sense gets the worst of it ".[2] But does it ? There is " plenty meant ", as he claimed, though the sense is not glaring ; and in any case he thought well enough of the sonnet to recast the second quatrain while leaving the rest almost unaltered.

The immediate feeling of the subject is conveyed by such vivid word-pigments as " rash-fresh ", " crisps of curl ", " pour and pelt music ". The images of skein and winch become lucid and are surely effective as soon as we recognize their synaesthesia, and visualize the regular curl or kink in twine which is rapidly paid out from a tightly wound reel or card :

> " The *skein* and *coil* are the lark's song, which from his height gives the impression (not to me only) of something

[1] In MS. " A " :

> " Left hand, off land, I hear the lark ascend
>   With rash-fresh more, repair of skein and score,
>   Race wild reel round, crisp coil deal down to floor,
> And spill music till there's none left to spend."

[2] An *englyn* is a four-line epigrammatic stanza, the form of which is bound l strict *cynghanedd*.

falling to the earth and not vertically quite but tricklingly or wavingly. . . ."[1]

The laps or folds, as the poet says, are the notes or the short measures or bars of them, and the whole effect is of a musical score written up and down " a liquid sky trembling to welcome it ". The synaesthesic modulation occurs at the word " re-winded " (pronounced " -wīnded "), which means ' sounded again with recovered breath, with second wind ', and also suggests ' re-wound ', as in the re-winding and re-playing of, say, a pianola record. The key thought is one of renewal, resumption : the lark in wild glee races the reel round, paying his musical score down to the earth ; there, in Fancy's eye, it is all re-wound on to another winch, reel or what you will, ready for its " rash-fresh " unwinding—its old, old but ever new encore—at the bird's next flight.

To Hopkins, as to Shelley and Meredith, the lark is both object and symbol : to Shelley it is freedom and the spirit of prophecy ; to Meredith it appears "seraphically free / From taint of personality "—its song is sheer truth ; to Hopkins it sings of something man has lost—purity. Whether nature sing high with the lark or sing low with the sea, she eternally puts man to shame :

> " How these two shame this shallow and frail town !
> How ring right out our sordid turbid time,
> Being pure ! We, life's pride and cared-for crown,
>
> Have lost that cheer and charm of earth's past prime :
> Our make and making break, are breaking down
> To man's last dust, drain fast towards man's first slime."

Hopkins, who has been blamed for being too persistently Christian and moralistic, must here face the charge of being too much of an aesthete. Though the 1870's were in many ways sordid and turbid, no town at that time or to-day could *ethically* be described as " shallow and frail " unless the criteria of depth and strength were clearly indicated. Hopkins, who knew the

---

[1] *Letters*, vol. i. p. 164. (Nov. 1882). " Not to me only " suggests that Hopkins had seen George Meredith's *The Lark Ascending* (1881), which begins :

> " He rises and begins to round,
> He drops the silver chain of sound
> Of many links without a break,
> In chirrup, whistle, slur and shake . . ."

value of human courage and endurance, was in this sonnet less respectful towards human personality than he was later in *Ribblesdale*, where the ontological relationship between nature and man is more sensitively stated :

> " And what is Earth's eye, tongue, or heart else, where
>   Else but in dear and dogged man ? "

To stigmatize as shallow and frail a whole townful of dear and dogged Welsh folk seems almost a sin against the brooding presence of the Holy Ghost.

In getting at the real meaning of this offending sestet we should first note that despite Evolutionism Hopkins was not the only Victorian poet who believed in " the cheer and charm of earth's past prime ".   Arnold wrote nostalgically of the days when " life ran gaily as the sparkling Thames ", and the concept was even dearer to Meredith :

> " Leave the uproar : at a leap
>   Thou shalt strike a woodland path,
>   Enter silence, not of sleep,
>   Under shadows, not of wrath,
>   Breath which is the spirit's bath
>   In the old Beginnings find."
>
> *(Nature and Life)* [1]

The " weeds and the wilderness " of Inversnaid could regenerate the natural piety of Hopkins ; but because of that the Gospels of Christ were not, as Wordsworth had unconsciously implied, " barren leaves ".[2]   And perhaps Hopkins's condemnation of that modern town may be justified by the basic Christian *motif* of his sonnet—the horror which he shared with Pascal at the general negligence in matters which concern all men intimately, namely, the issues of eternity.   From the Christian standpoint, any form of materialism is desperately frail and tragically shallow. Man is " life's cared-for crown " because he alone among creatures has been given the reason, grace, and free will by which to achieve sainthood and immortality.   The statement, in the last line of the sonnet, that man is returning to his " first slime " is a challenging inversion of the Darwinian thesis and at the same time a bitter taunt : ' this, it seems, is the only destiny man is fit for.'

---

[1] Cf. his *A Faith on Trial* and *Ode to the Spirit of Earth in Autumn* ; in the latter poem ' Eden ' is mentioned.

[2] See Wordsworth's *The Tables Turned*, stanzas 1 and 8 : " Up ! up ! my Friend, and quit your books. . . . Close up those barren leaves."

The whole sonnet anticipates the mood of Mr. T. S. Eliot's *The Waste Land* and *The Hollow Men*. As critic and poet Mr. Eliot has stood in much the same relation to our own age as Arnold and Hopkins did to theirs; and either of the earlier men might have written the following passage, which serves admirably to explain the sestet of *The Sea and the Skylark* :

> " A moment of Jansenism may naturally take place, and take place rightly, in the individual ; particularly in the life of a man of great and intense intellectual powers, who cannot avoid seeing through human beings and observing the vanity of their thoughts and their avocations, their dishonesty and self-deception, the insincerity of their emotions, their cowardice, the pettiness of their real ambitions." [1]

As we have said, the " cowardice " should not be stressed, for there is plenty of courage and dogged endurance in any community of men ; but the sordid and finite pettiness of their real ambitions—that was the harrowing fact for Hopkins and Eliot. *The Sea and the Skylark* is not cynicism ; but to be understood it must be read in conjunction with the ' cynical ' sonnet, " The shepherd's brow, fronting forked lightning, owns . . ."

Although it has long been fashionable to seek in the work of a poet what is called a social philosophy, lyric poetry is still as much the expression of moods and impulses as of reasoned emotions. It is futile to expect poets to be logically consistent. Thus when we turn to another of Hopkins's poems of 1877, *Pied Beauty*, we find that he was not antipathetic to man's workaday world. Having sung " Glory be to God " for all those varied forms and hues of creation which have traditionally appealed to lovers of beauty (yet how *strange* as well as familiar are those " fresh-firecoal chestnut falls " !), he gives us the Whitmanesque line :

> " And all trades, their gear and tackle and trim."

The last phrase evokes the more picturesque village crafts and seaport avocations ; yet the strongly emphasized " all trades " can hardly exclude all the pit-head and factory appurtenances which spoilt the landscape and befouled the air and water of Widnes and St. Helens. Perhaps the little aesthetic word " trim " rules out the uglier manifestations of industrialism. But why should it ? At the right time and in a suitable light a belching chimney or a blast furnace is as beautiful—dapples the chance

---

[1] *The ' Pensées ' of Pascal (Essays Ancient and Modern*, by T. S. Eliot ; p. 155).

install of a townscape as effectively as clouds and trawlers brindle
the sunset scaping of Brixham harbour. In his letters Hopkins
manifests a touch of Ruskin's anti-industrial ' fanat-aestheticism ' ;
and although modern art has effected some sort of compromise
with the Satanic mills, we can hardly blame those sensitive
Victorians for their strong reactionary feeling. In the closing
quintet of *Pied Beauty* there is a capacious Whitman-like acceptance of *natural* pieings and perversities, a flux of Heraclitean
opposites which culminates in praise for the super-Heraclitean
God :

> " All things counter, original, spare, strange :
>> Whatever is fickle, freckled (who knows how ?)
>> With swift, slow ; sweet, sour ; adazzle, dim ;
> He fathers-forth whose beauty is past change :
>> Praise him." [1]

Hopkins liked the forms and activities of the material world
to be as varied, curious, and irregular as the God of inexhaustible
invention chose to make them ; moreover, men too, as artists,
were bound to be original, spare, strange. But in the moral
sphere, the " counter " (like Swinburne) and the " fickle " (like
Carlyle)—all those who had " no principles " or who flourished
anti-Christian banners—these were anathema. For Hopkins
there was no beauty in change and diversity unless the mind held
a clear concept of permanence and unity. As he says in *The
Starlight Night* and elsewhere, it is by means of morality that we
apprehend permanence, that we see through the life of things
into the life of God. Morality, the Christian ethic, is the um-
bilical cord connecting the soul to its Source ; if that cord is
severed man can still live—but only with a detached, finite and
foredoomed existence.

A more subtle treatment of the principles of flux and per-

---

[1] Hopkins describes the rhythm of *Pied Beauty* as " sprung paeonic ". Sprung it
certainly is, but the term " paeonic " is misleading : if every line is to have five
stresses there are only *two* paeons in the whole poem :

> " Glory be to God for dappled things—
>> For skies of couple-colour as a brinded cow ;
>> For rose-moles all in stipple upon trout that swim ; "

In line 9, half-stresses and pauses compensate for the absence of five equally marked
stresses :

manence is to be found in another poem of the same fruitful year —the bold and resilient *Hurrahing in Harvest*. In its fusion of sensuousness and imagination (as Blake used that word), this sonnet incorporates more successfully than any other short poem we know the doctrine of God's immanence and transcendence.

This doctrine, like that of the Incarnation and the Holy Trinity, is what is called a ' mystery ' ; and perhaps the best introduction to such poems as *Hurrahing in Harvest* and *The Caged Skylark* will be a brief summary of what Hopkins says in a letter touching the ' mysteries ' of his religion. Bridges, he says, does not mean by ' mystery ' what a Catholic does :

> " You mean an interesting uncertainty : the uncertainty ceasing, interest ceases also. This happens in some things ; to you in religion. But a Catholic by mystery means an incomprehensible certainty : without certainty, without formulation there is no interest." [1]

A doctrine, he claims, has a greater value than mere " interestingness " ; but speaking now of that quality only he adds that at bottom the source of interest for both Bridges and himself was the same ;

> " it is the unknown, the reserve of truth beyond what the mind reaches and still feels to be behind."

Now this *feeling* of the mind for what lies beyond its ken happens to be the ever-flowing source of mystical speculation. Perhaps we should say that it was, rather than is, such a source : it was active for Plotinus, St. Augustine, St. Francis, St. John of the Cross—men who mounted by the steps of created things to the Uncreated, deriving spiritual knowledge and certainty from sensory experience and finally shedding that experience in a Union which transcended all symbols. Pascal, though not a mystic, was close to this metaphysical certainty when he said, " Le cœur a ses raisons dont la raison ne sait point." It was the mystic Blake who best understood the modern stultification of the mystical consciousness, who condemned the growing materialistic scepticism which had locked man up in the prisonhouse of his five senses. " Man's perceptions," said Blake, " are not bounded by the organs of perception, he perceives more than sense (tho' ever so acute) can discover." [2]

To the narrower scientific and secular consciousness of to-day the psychology of the great mystics, with its extraordinary sensi-

---

[1] *Letters*, vol. i. pp. 187–8 (Oct. 1883).　　　[2] *Of Natural Religion*.

tiveness to supra-rational intimations, is almost a closed book.
Yet the difference between the perception of the mystic and the
faith of the ordinary Christian believer in the ' mysteries ' is
probably one of degree only, not of kind.   Hopkins knew this,
and he tried to explain the fascination of the unknowable Known
by means of subtle analogies drawn from chess and music.
Dealing next with the mystery of the Trinity he says :

> " to some people this is a ' dogma ', a word they almost chew,
> that is an equation in theology, the dull algebra of the schoolmen ;
> to others it is news of their dearest friend or friends, leaving them
> all their lives balancing whether they have three heavenly
> friends or one—not that they have any doubt on the subject,
> but that their knowledge leaves their minds swinging ; poised
> but on the quiver." [1]

Such a phrase as " the dull algebra of the schoolmen " shows
that Hopkins understood, though he did not share, the position
of the ' natural ' religionists ; and it may be doubted whether
any great religious or mystical poetry was ever written save by
those whose minds were " poised but on the quiver ".   These
words, which describe so aptly the sensitive hair-spring of poetic
inspiration, may be taken as the Christian mystic's equivalent for
Keats's " negative capability ".   Hopkins did not regard a
Christian dogma as a plain fact, emotively and intellectually
finite : to him it was like an ever-living flower, full of sap, colour,
and inscape ; he turned it over and over in his mind, exploring
all its metaphysical possibilities.   For example, in Christian
theology Christ, the second Person of the Trinity, is often identified
with the Word ; therefore Hopkins says that the nun in *The
Deutschland*

> " Read the unshapeable shock night
>   And knew the who and the why ;
> Wording it how but by him that present and past,
> Heaven and earth are word of, worded by ?—" [2]

That is to say, past and present, heaven and earth are all " news "
of Christ, and conversely all these things are best understood
through Him.   Revolving this concept and fusing it, so to speak,
with an " install " or " instress " of Welsh landscape in August,
he struck out, in *Hurrahing in Harvest*, a symbolization of Immanence which is analogous to Blake's aphorism : " Everything on
earth is the word of God, and in its essence is God." [3]   Perfect

---

[1] *Letters*, vol. i. pp. 187–8.   [2] Stanza 29.   [3] *Notes to Lavater*.

identity is precluded by the pantheistic assumption in the words
" *is* God " ; moreover nothing to Hopkins was a direct manifestation of God unless by its nature and function it was either
" morally neutral " or morally justified.

> " The Hurrahing Sonnet was the outcome of half an hour of
> extreme enthusiasm as I walked home alone one day from fishing
> in the Elwy." [1]

One is reminded of Keats's letter to Reynolds, in which he tells
how the chaste weather, Dian skies, and the warm stubble fields
struck him so much in his Sunday walk that he composed his
ode *To Autumn*. Keats, like all great poets, was feeling towards
the supreme spiritual Reality ; but whereas Keats was often
content to rest in physical sensation, to find an uneasy peace or
psychic harmony in the acuteness of his perception of the present
material world, Hopkins could not rest until his imagination had
boldly transcended the limitations of sense and logic. What the
humanistic poets dimly apprehended he saw and grasped : his
aspiration took him through and beyond Dian skies to the
Absolute.

In *Hurrahing in Harvest*, therefore, we meet four elements in
fusion—the senses, aspiration, the Incarnation, and Beatitude ;
and the catalyst that brings about this combination is the mystery
of Immanence—the immanence of the transcendent God :

> "Summer ends now ; now, barbarous in beauty, the stooks arise
>
> Around : up above, what wind-walks ! what lovely behaviour
>
> Of silk-sack clouds ! has wilder, wilful-wavier
>
>   rall.
> Meal-drift moulded ever and melted across skies ? " [2]

In the first line we hear an echo of Jeremiah : " summer is
ended, and we are unsaved " ; yet this poem is no jeremiad.
The pivotal word, for both rhythm and meaning, is " barbarous ", with its " great stress " and succeeding slight pause. It is
pagan : in the shadowy pun of *barb-* there is a hint of bearded
Pan ; and the whole phrase " barbarous in beauty " epitomizes

[1] *Letters*, vol. i. p. 56.
[2] The rhythm is " sprung and outriding ". The notation is from MS. " A ",
except for the " hurried foot " (" moulded ever "), which is the present writer's
reading. Above l. 4 ' rall.'=*rallentando*.

both the shaggy tidiness of stooked corn and the graceful disarray of fluctuant, disintegrating clouds—in fact, all the apparently capricious energy in nature.

Perception leads to appetency : Hopkins now looks for the informing spirit, the unifying principle, the deeper reality :

" I walk, I lift up, I lift up heart, eyes,
  Down all that glory in the heavens to glean our Saviour ;
  And eyes, heart, what looks, what lips yet gave you a
Rapturous love's greeting of realer, of rounder replies ? "

The metaphor in " glean " links the natural to the supernatural harvest. The mystical imagination follows in the track of natural forces and picks up vestiges of God—no matter how small ; but the gleanings prove an abundant reward, as the sudden shift from metaphor to personification makes clear. The whole physiognomy of the welkin is bright with the play of expression : beauty becomes articulate and voluble—" garrulous of the eyes of God " as Francis Thompson said later of a field-flower.[1] Re-turning the tables on Wordsworth's *The Tables Turned*, Hopkins seems to say : ' One instress from the love of Christ will teach you more of nature than all the pantheists and nature-worshippers can.'

Two truths cannot conflict : indeed, they must be reconcilable. God is in the visible universe ; and Christ is God : hence when our moral and physical powers are rightly attuned (" heart, eyes ") we preceive Christ :

" And the azurous hung hills are his world-wielding shoulder
  Majestic—as a stallion stalwart, very-violet-sweet !—"

In this moment of insight the poet assimilates the unmoved Mover and that which is moved : he sees the muscular, gracefully rounded hills, with their veils of tranquilizing vapour, as part of the mystical anatomy of Christ ; it is as though matter resolves itself into spirit, or conversely as though Spirit has materialized in an Incarnation which embraces inanimate as well as human

---

[1] *Field-flower.* Thompson's affinity to Hopkins comes out in the synaesthesia of his description of the flower :

" Musical of the mouth of God
  To all had ears to hear it ;
Mystical with the mirth of God,
  That glow-like did ensphere it."

nature—a naturalistic Beatific Vision. But naturalism and pantheism were far from Hopkins's thought ; this passage may be accepted as ' figurative ', without metaphysical subtlety : ' As these hills, though softly bloomed with haze, remind me of a powerful stallion, so they remind me of the supernatural beauty of Christ—colossal, but not forbidding ; majestic, yet still comforting, nostalgic, gentle and attractive.' Images of this kind must be interpreted in the light of traditional Catholic naturemysticism, like that of San Juan de la Cruz. In the *Cantico Espiritual*, the Creatures, asked whether the Beloved has passed their way, reply :

> " Mil gracias derramando,
> Pasó por estos sotos con presura.
> Y yéndolos mirando,
> Con sola su figura
> Vestidos los dejó de hermosura." [1]

As Mr. Robert Sencourt has said, such poetry

> " is a spontaneous revelation of a mystery by which created things are a living, visible garment of God ; and *everything, if looked at rightly*, is but a symbol, and therefore a disclosure, of things unseen, and of the underlying reality which is the mind of God." [2]

The close of *Hurrahing in Harvest* leaves no doubt about the transcendence of God, the completely spiritual nature of the real, ultimate Beatitude :

" These things, these things were here and but the beholder
   Wanting ; which two when they once meet,
 The heart rears wings bold and bolder

   And hurls for him, O half hurls earth for him off under his feet."

Eyes have we and we see not : the " beholder " was wanting until Hopkins (like Plato, Wordsworth, and all the mystics) had " seen something "—that " something far more deeply interfused " whose dwelling, as Wordsworth said, is everywhere in nature and in the mind of man. For Hopkins, Beatitude was more than

---

[1] Stanza 5 :   " Scattering a thousand gifts,
He passed by these groves apace,
And looking at them in passing,
He, only with his face,
Bequeathed to them garments of beauty."

[2] *Poet and Carmelite* (1943), p. 139. San Juan, says Mr. Sencourt, " was a combination of a theologian and a poet." That was equally true of Hopkins.

vision ; it was love. The " heart " which rears wings implies the concentrated moral force of the disciplined affections, intellect, and will ; and the " *half* hurls " means that Hopkins was too much of a realist to believe that man, as a finite being, could dispense with the symbolic physical world to which he belongs. Both Aquinas and Scotus maintained, as Hopkins does in this poem, that the supernatural order is not the antithesis of the natural order ; rather it is the τέλος, the fulfilment of that order.

Very properly did Bridges, when arranging the *Poems*, follow up *Hurrahing in Harvest* with *The Caged Skylark* ; for whereas both poems deal with " man's mounting spirit ", the second seems at first to deny that holy joy in the bodily senses which is so marked in the eight preceding sonnets. A half an hour of extreme enthusiasm had convinced Hopkins of the essential freedom of the spirit ; but what is half an hour of inspired recreation among so many days and weeks of unremitting and apparently thankless toil ? He would not be a man who did not at times acutely feel, as St. Augustine did, the spirit's bondage to the flesh :

" As a dáre-gále skýlark scánted in a dúll cáge
        Man's móunting spírit in his bóne-house, méan house, dwélls—
        Thát bird beyónd the remémbering his frée félls ;

    Thís in drúdgery, dáy-labouring-óut life's áge." [1]

The significant phrase is " beyond the remembering " ; for just as the caged skylark seems at most times to have grown accustomed to his bondage, to have forgotten his natural habitat, so that other bird, the spirit of .man, is enslaved by the material world, seems to have forfeited its birthright, to be cut off from its natural (that is, supernatural) regions. Rare enough is the artist's " muse of mounting vein " ; very much rarer is that power of wing which enables the mystic to hurl the earth off under his feet.

The second quatrain develops these two themes—resignation and frustration :

" Though aloft on turf or perch or poor low stage,
        Both sing sometimes the sweetest, sweetest spells,
        Yet both droop deadly sometimes in their cells
    Or wring their barriers in bursts of fear or rage."

[1] The rhythm is " falling paeonic, sprung and outriding ". The outrides marked in the text are from MS. " A ".

The first line is skilfully made to apply to both captive bird and human spirit : the lark's cage is hung " aloft " for safety, and a " turf " (preferably ' full of clover ') is placed in it for a dietetic purpose ; but that same turf suggests also, to our mind, Thomas Gray's " upland lawn " and Wordsworth's " free fells ". Again, the " perch " (pulpit, rostrum ?) and " poor low stage " indicate clearly enough those moments of joy or vision which relieve the tedium of cage-bound and earth-bound existence. Moreover, " stage " turns our thoughts back to that passage in Webster's *Duchess of Malfi* which probably supplied the original *motif* of this sonnet ; Bosola says to the Duchess :

> " Didst thou ever see a lark in a cage ?   Such is the soul in the body : this world is like her little turf of grass, and the heaven o'er our heads, like her looking-glass, only gives us a miserable knowledge of the small compass of our prison." [1]

We note, in passing, other characteristic felicities of style—the complementary meanings of " spells " (' periods ' and ' charms '), of " deadly " (' deathlike ' and ' implacable ', with a hint of damnation for the spirit) ; and then the onomatopoeic vigour of the eighth line.

The sestet takes up the comparison between the free bird, the dare-gale skylark, and the human spirit which strives to mount,—and the inference is not immediately consoling ; but the closing tercet restores man's prestige by rehabilitating the human body on the supernatural plane :

" Not that the sweet-fowl, song-fowl, needs no rest—
  Why, hear him, hear him babble and drop down to his nest,

    But his own nest, wild nest, no prison.

" Man's spirit will be flesh-bound when found at best,

    But uncumbered : meadow-down is not distressed
    For a rainbow footing it nor he for his bones risen."

The Catholic doctrine of the resurrection of the body, here sensuously epitomized, is best explained in the words of an approved theologian :

> " When we die, the body and soul are separated for a time ;
> the soul goes to be judged by God, and is rewarded or punished

---

[1] Act IV, sc. ii.   The resemblance between this passage and Hopkins's sonnet was first pointed out by Mr. Geoffrey Grigson in *New Verse*, No. 14 (April, 1935).

according to its works ; the body is buried, and in course of time falls away into dust. . . . At the end of the world the body rises and comes to life when the soul enters into it. It will be the same body that we have had on earth, but a spiritualized body like our Lord had after His resurrection from the dead." [1]

The soul in heaven, Hopkins believed, will be happy but will not know complete Beatitude until it is reunited with its body ; when that state has been achieved, and not before, the words of Browning's Rabbi will be fulfilled :

> " All good things
> Are ours, nor soul helps flesh more, now, than flesh helps soul ! "

Hopkins's analogy between the beatified body and soul and a rainbow resting on thistledown is sufficiently delicate and ' metaphysical ' to tease us, very pleasantly, into wistful thought.

Traditional Christianity is based on three cardinal virtues—Faith, Hope, and Charity. Modern secularization, however, tends more and more to deprive Faith and Hope of their supernatural origin and purpose, to bring the Kingdom of God down to earth and to lay all the stress on Charity, which has come to mean philanthropy. In his own life and work, Hopkins tried to give Faith and Hope their pristine values. Theoretically Hope for him, as for all Catholics, was " a supernatural gift of God, by which we firmly trust that God will give us eternal life and all the means necessary to attain it if we do what He requires of us." [2]

In an undated fragment he interprets the dogma in his own fashion and somewhat in the .poetic manner of Quarles or Crashaw ; but instead of emphasizing the firm trust, the note of certainty, he dwells upon the pains and frustrations incident to human imperfection, the impossibility of gaining a perfect knowledge of that in which we trust—in short, the difficulty of meriting the full gift of Faith and Hope :

> " Hope holds to Christ the mind's own mirror out
> To take His lovely likeness more and more.
> It will not well, so she would bring about
> An ever brighter burnish than before
> And turns to wash it from her welling eyes
> And breathes the blots off all with sighs on sighs.

[1] *The Catechism Simply Explained*, by H. T. Cafferata ; § 129.
[2] Cafferata, *op. cit.* § 136.

> Her glass is blest but she as good as blind
> Holds till hand aches and wonders what is there ;
> Her glass drinks light, she darkles down behind,
> All of her glorious gainings unaware.
>
> .   .   .   .   .
>
> I told you that she turned her mirror dim
> Betweenwhiles, but she sees herself not Him.
>
> .   .   .   .   .   [1]

The whole ' conceit ' has an intricate beauty which is suggestive ; but its uncertain metrical pattern and unfinished state may have been due to a felt weakness, a lack of logical " perspective " in the palpably artificial image. The mind is represented as the mere instrument or retinal organ of an extra-mental appetency ; whereas Hope is actually a sensation, desire, or concept which the mind itself must help to create. The subtle image is not quite subtle enough. Yet having called it " artificial " we almost regret that epithet ; for Hopkins's fragment, like the famous pictorial allegory by Watts entitled *Hope* (1885), is a sincere poetico-philosphical attempt to elucidate what is in fact a mystery : as Chesterton said in his profound comment on the picture, it is something beyond the scope of either paint or language.[2] The blindfold and apparently dejected figure in Watt's painting strains her head downwards as though to catch the note of the last unbroken string on her lyre ; similarly Hopkins's allegorical figure, " as good as blind ", is yearning to behold, in the mind's dim mirror, the clear image of Christ—her lodestar, her very *raison d'être*. In the picture, which is pagan, a solitary star symbolizes the ultimate goal or ideal ; and in a poem of 1886 Hopkins speaks of Christ as the " soul's star " :

> " There's none but truth can stead you.   Christ is truth." [3]

Nevertheless, to adapt the query of W. Loftus Hare concerning Watts's painting—who but a man who knew the melancholy of despair could have written that fragment on Hope ? The ' welling eyes " and the " sighs on sighs " should not be interpreted as disillusionment or loss of faith but rather as contrition for sin, for failure to keep the mind clear of mundane interests and fit for God's entry. The whole image is elucidated by a passage in Hopkins's sermon called *The Principle or Foundation* :

> " . . . Are we his pipe or harp ? we are out of tune, we grate upon his ear.   Are we his glass to look in ? we are deep

[1] *Poems*, No. 57.   [2] *G. F. Watts* (1904), pp. 94-108.
[3] *Poems*, No. 54—*On the Portrait*, etc.

in dust or our silver gone or we are broken or, worst of all, we misshape his face and make God's image hideous. . . . If we have sinned we are all this." [1]

The above fragment might have been written as late as 1885 or 1886 and has been dealt with here for the obvious purpose of illustrating the poet's individual treatment of Christian dogma.

To return now to the poems of 1877, we must first remind the reader that *The Windhover*, which ought to be reviewed in this context, has been fully examined in Volume I, chapter v. The remaining sonnet of that fruitful year stands appropriately as an example of the fusion of that Pauline trinity—Faith, Hope, and Charity : it is *In the Valley of the Elwy*. [2]

Christian charity comprehends not only human kindness and compassion but also a deep concern for the salvation of souls. Hopkins remembers a family (" the Watsons of Shooter's Hill ") who were once kind to him beyond his deserts. Then comes a curious echo of Wordsworth—a confluence of the sweetness of charity and the sweetness of uncontaminated nature :

> " Comforting smell breathed at very entering, [3]
> Fetched fresh, as I suppose, off some sweet wood.
> That cordial air made those kind people a hood
> All over, as a bevy of eggs the mothering wing
> Will, or mild nights the new morsels of spring :
> Why, it seemed of course ; seemed of right it should."

Wordsworth had said that " one impulse from a vernal wood will teach us *more* of moral right and wrong than all the doctrine of the wise ; but Hopkins does not fall into this error of unbalanced enthusiasm. He merely asserts the reasonableness of his feeling that in the Watsons' home there was a significant correspondence between the people and their environment. It seemed only right that the beauty of God's utterance of Himself in the material world should foster and set off the highest moral beauty in man. He implies more, but no more than this : that people who have the right attitude towards God and His creatures will be sensitive to the cordial air, will instinctively respond to the dumb exhortation of inanimate nature, which (as he says in *Ribblesdale*) can only *be* but does that long and well, which gives praise to God without knowing it.

[1] *Note-books*, pp. 303–4.   [2] *Poems*, No. 16.   [3] The stressing is from MS. " B

But does man always instinctively respond to the tongues in trees and sermons in stones ? By no means ! Man is a fallen creature, " unteachably after evil ". Mild nights and fragrant copses may sometimes help to incubate the knowledge of " moral evil and of good " ; but without some rational and more coercive argument to engage his mind and will, man would discover to his cost that the ' influences of nature ' can be ambiguous if not subversive. Wordsworth himself, in *Ruth* [1] and elsewhere, acknowledged this fact. So in this sonnet, after a whole octave of preamble concerning the ideal relationship between man and nature, Hopkins comes down, in the sestet, to his real motive— the contrast between the beauty of Wales and the relative moral imperfection of its inhabitants :

> " Lovely the woods, waters, meadows, combes, vales,
>   All the air things wear that build this world of Wales ;
>   Only the inmate does not correspond : "

It is a pity, and a blemish, that this poem gives the impression that the Welsh are less righteous than other peoples. Hopkins, we may be sure, had no uncharitable intentions, and the fact that he found the people of Ribblesdale no more amenable to God's law than the folk in the valley of the Elwy makes the whole question of nationality adventitious. The last tercet is really a plea to God on behalf of *all* people who fall short of complete spiritual fulfilment :

> " God, lover of souls, swaying considerate scales,
>   Complete thy creature dear O where it fails,
>   Being mighty a master, being a father and fond."

The poet begs for Divine intervention ; but he believes that this must normally come about through the agency of the Christian Church ; for without the " mothering wing " of a moral theology based upon faith and hope, the charities will seldom be hatched from the heart of wayward man.

The modern materialistic conception of faith and hope seems to have arisen from a humanistic gloss on the words of St. Paul : " but the greatest of these is charity ". Hopkins, however, while faithfully preserving the supernaturalism of St. Paul, by no means underrated the Love which is " the fulness of the Law ". In its

[1] Stanzas 21–5.

plainest doctrinal form it appears in the two fragments printed
last in the *Poems* ; No. 73 (1885 ?) ends thus :

> " But thou bidst, and just thou art,
> Me shew mercy from my heart
> Towards my brother, every other
> Man my mate and counterpart." [1]

Such earnest effusions are mainly utterances of the priestly character. For the powerful collaboration of the poetic personality
we must turn to poems of which the prime *motif* is human, personal
and natural rather than pietistic or doctrinal. Piety and doctrine
are usually present in warp and woof ; but the actual loom of his
great poems is the pulsing life in man and nature.

After completing his theological studies at St. Beuno's
Hopkins was ordained priest on September 23, 1877 ; and from
October of that year till the following April he was sub-minister
at Mount St. Mary's College, Chesterfield. In the latter month
he wrote to Bridges :

> " It was pleasing and flattering to hear that Mr. Pater
> remembers and takes an interest in me.
> " My muse turned sullen in the Sheffield smoke-laden air and
> I had not written a line till the foundering of the Eurydice
> [March 24, 1878] and that worked on me and I am making a
> poem—in my own rhythm. . . ." [2]

We could wish that Hopkins had shown less interest in Pater (and
Aestheticism) and had looked more earnestly for suitable poetic
subjects, even amid the Vulcan-stithies of Chesterfield and
Sheffield. However, his stay at Mount St. Mary's produced, in
The Loss of the Eurydice, a semi-didactic lyrical ballad which is like
a new species in poetry. It has not the rich variety, personal
revelation, and mystical depth of its greater companion poem
The Wreck of the Deutschland. Though it is more objective, its
occasional blemishes are not so easily assimilated in the sweep of
emotion, for the style is often staccato, Browningesque : until it
is perfectly mastered the rhythm is not plangent or compelling.
There are one or two strained images and awkward ambiguities,
one clumsy inversion,[4] one lapse into sentimentality,[5] and in a
few of the rhymes a bold resourcefulness (misnamed ' preciosity '

---

[1] No. 74 might well be entitled *Charity*. Cf. *Poems*, Nos. 30 and 61.
[2] *Letters*, vol. i. p. 48.　　　　[3] E.g. stanzas 12, 13 and 14.
[4] Stanza 13.　　　　[5] Stanza 18.

which is not to everyone's taste.[1] Even less to the taste of many readers will be the mordant but sincere Catholic propaganda in stanzas 22–26. Nevertheless, the poem deserves greater appreciation than it has yet received.

The training ship *Eurydice* had been overturned off Ventnor by a sudden squall from land, and there had been only two survivors. In treating this subject Hopkins's aim was firstly to make us experience the incident in imagination and feel the pathos of the disaster, and secondly, to use it as a symbol of that spiritual shipwreck which threatened all Christendom, and England in particular.

To dispel a technical difficulty, we remind the reader that in every quatrain the first, second, and fourth lines carry four full stresses apiece, while the third indented line carries only three. The first mistake Hopkins made was in opening with a stanza which is rhythmically ambiguous. Yet the second and third make the intention quite clear, and we now transcribe the first two, with our own stressing and expression marks:

" The Eurydice—it concerned thee, O Lord :

Three hundred souls, O alas ! on board,

   Some asleep unawakened, all un-

warned, eleven fathoms fallen

Where she foundered ! One stroke

Felled and furled them, the hearts of oak !

   And flockbells off the aerial

Downs' forefalls beat to the burial."

The wave-like effect of surge and lapse in these lines is characteristic of the expressional and dramatic vigour of the whole work.

---

[1] The present writer *likes*, or cheerfully accepts, *all* the rhymes except *portholes— mortals* (stanza 10).

We should notice, too, how the sheep-bells on the neighbouring downs provide a dying fall of poignant irony.

Here again, as in *The Deutschland*, the diction conveys a satisfying general meaning and word-magic before the subtlety or " far-fetchedness " of a particular image has been grasped. Quite naturally, Bridges queried " furled " in stanza 2. Hopkins replied :

> " How are the hearts of oak furled ? Well, in sand and sea water. . . . You are to suppose a stroke or blast in a forest of ' hearts of oak ' (=, ad propositum, sound oak timber) which at one blow lays them low and buries them in broken earth. *Furling* (*ferrule* is a blunder for *furl*, I think) is proper when said of sticks or staves." [1]

Hardly satisfactory as an explanation ; but almost by accident the image in " furled " is .poetically right if we take it to mean bunched together like trees after felling and lopping : there is also the moving suggestion of the furled hopes of drowned men huddled in the womb of the sunken ship, like young in their dead mother. In stanza 4 the ' heart of oak ' metaphor embraces the whole ship with its complement of mature seamen and lads in training :

> " She had cóme from a crúise, tráining séamen—
>   Mén, bóldboys sóon to bé men :
>   Múst it, wórst wéather,
>   Blást bóle and blóom togéther ? "

After this introduction the poet gives us a vivid description of the actual foundering (stanzas 5–11). It includes some great poetry—condensed, astringent, appealing directly to the senses but at the same time keeping the mind alert and " on the quiver ". As Hopkins himself said, when the work is competently *read aloud* there is no raw nakedness or violence in the style.[2] This poetic body is that of an athlete—spare, muscular, agile, yet suitably clad :

> " No Atlántic squáll óverwróught her
>   Or rearing billow of the Biscay water :
>   Home was hard at hand
>   Ánd the blów bóre from lánd.

---

[1] *Letters*, vol. i. p. 52. *Furl* is probably from the obsolete ' furdle ', a variant of fardle ', bundle (akin to O.F. ' fardeler ', to make into a bundle).

[2] See *Letters*, vol. i. p. 79.

> "And you were a liar, O blue March day.
>   Bright sun lanced fire in the heavenly bay ;
>   But what black Boreas wrecked her ? he
>   Came equipped, deadly-electric,

> "A beetling baldbright cloud thorough England
>   Riding : there did storms not mingle ? and
>   Hailropes hustle and grind their
>   Heavengravel ? wolfsnow, worlds of it, wind there ? "

Reminiscences of Greek epic and Teutonic elegy are spontaneously merged in a living present ; in such an imaginative synthesis the neologisms and occasional archaisms are easily absorbed.

As we have said, the poet's aim was to bring the disaster right home to the English imagination and then work on the English religious sensibility ; hence a Miltonic use of familiar proper names :

> "Now Carisbrook keep goes under in gloom ;
>   Now it overvaults Appledurcombe ;
>   Now near by Ventnor town
>   It hurls, hurls off Boniface Down." [1]

The real horrors of the scene are given with poetic circumstance : the sea " Raced down decks, round messes of mortals " ; the plight of the seamen trapped in the plunging vessel or sucked down in the vortex is *felt* in the insistent internal rhyme of

> "But she who had housed them thither
> Was around them, bound them or wound them with her."

The third section of the poem (stanzas 12-21) falls into three parts, all of which deal with personnel of the ship : first, Marcus Hare, the brave captain, who is involved somewhat ambiguously in a moral reflection about the physical courage even of wrongdoers ; second, the Bristol-bred Sydney Fletcher, one of the two survivors ; third, a typical yet deliberately symbolic corpse washed up by the tide. The personification of Right in stanza 13 must be understood as follows : ' Duty—stern, unattractive, remorseless—seemed to whisper, " You too, captain, must follow your ship." ' Of Fletcher we read :

> "Now her afterdraught gullies him too down ;
>   Now he wrings for breath with the deathgush brown ;
>   Till a lifebelt and God's will
>   Lend him a lift from the sea-swill."

[1] Contrast the bald opening of stanza 15 : " Sydney Fletcher, Bristol-bred. . . ."

10*

The last two lines have been called " as bathetical a couplet as ever a religious poet concocted." [1] But what, pray, is wrong ? Does God's mercy scorn the humble instrumentality of a lifebelt ? Are not " lift " and " sea-swill " both precise and vivid ? The sylleptic " Lend " is strictly true in both the natural and theo-logical senses ; for as " lend a lift " is a variant of " lend a hand ", so the special mercy was a new " lease of grace ". Frank atheism and a sense of humour might have produced *real* bathos :

> " Till a lifebelt and blind Chance
> Lend him a lift from the Davy-dance."

The elegiac beauty of the last two of the following stanzas could hardly be surpassed :

> " They say who saw one sea-corpse cold
> He was all of lovely manly mould,
>   Every inch a tar,
> Of the best we boast our sailors are.

> " Look, foot to forelock, how all things suit ! he
> Is strung by duty, is strained to beauty,
>   And brown-as-dawning-skinned
> With brine and shine and whirling wind.

> " O his nimble finger, his gnarled grip !
> Leagues, leagues of seamanship
>   Slumber in these forsaken
> Bones, this sinew, and will not waken."

The last three words are the key to the fourth section (stanzas 22–26), for Hopkins is not only distressed at the loss of valuable lives : he is far more concerned about the foundering of immortal souls :

> " He was but one like thousands more,
>   Day and night I deplore
>   My people and born own nation,
>   Fast foundering own generation."

Here, after a curt apology for reviving old grievances, he laments the ' theft ' of Catholic churches and the neglect of shrines since the English Reformation ; and the mention of " hoar-hallowèd shrines unvisited " brings him back to the once breathing and now ruined temple of the spirit—the dead body of the sailor, and

---

[1] Alan Pryce-Jones in *The London Mercury*, May 1931.

thence to the whole crew of " dare-deaths " cut off without grace
and absolution.   He wonders with some bitterness not so much at
this particular act of God but rather at God's inscrutable purpose
in allowing heresy to infect the whole English race—people who
were once so Catholic and Marian that " Walsingham Way was
a name for the Milky Way, as being supposed a fingerpost to our
Lady's shrine at Walsingham, in Norfolk : " [1]

> " Deeply surely I need to deplore it,
>> Wondering why my master bore it,
>>> The riving off that race
>>> So at home, time was, to his truth and grace

> " That a starlight-wender of ours would say
>> The marvellous Milk was Walsingham Way
>>> And one—but let be, let be :
>>> More, more than was will yet be.—" [2]

The " one " was Duns Scotus, the great English champion of the
Immaculate Conception.   Wisely, Hopkins checks the Pindaric
urge to elaborate the pedigree of merit, and closes this section with
a bold prophecy : " Patience, my heart.   England will return to
the true Church ; there will be deeper devotion, greater saints
than ever before."

The last section (stanzas 27–30) opens with an inferior variation on a theme from *The Deutschland* : " Why, tears ! is it ?
tears ; such a melting, a madrigal start ! " Mothers, wives, and
sweethearts, he says, do well to weep for their dead : it shows
that the heart is " right ".   But without grace they are impotent ;
only self-abasement in prayer will do them and theirs any good :

> " But to Christ lord of thunder
>> Crouch ; lay knee by earth low under ; "

With priestly thoroughness, he gives the mourners a prayer to offer :

> " Holiest, loveliest, bravest,
>> Save my hero, O Hero savest."

We wish Hopkins had written " O Hero who savest ", for whatever is gained by omitting the relative pronoun is in this instance

---

[1] *Letters*, vol. i. p. 53.
[2] " Of ours " means ' one of our communion '—a Roman Catholic.   If " let be "
is stressed with the greater weight of voice on " be ", the discordant stress of " yet
be " makes a Welsh rhyme, as in a *cywydd*.   See above, pp. 146-7.

more than nullified by the resulting awkwardness. It is otherwise, however, with the unusual but forceful perfect-imperatives of the next stanza, which clearly means : ' And I pray that when my man is finally overtaken, overhauled, by the Day of Judgment, you will have heard this my prayer and will have granted retro-spectively that grace which he lacked and which is so necessary for his salvation.' In the last stanza the poet holds out the hope of Purgatory : those who have died in mortal sin, he says, are past redemption ; but for " souls sunk in seeming " (the dead who had sinned venially or without wilful malice)—for these the intercessory prayers of the faithful can still win remission of punishment and ultimate beatitude :

> " Fresh, till doomfire burn all,
> Prayer shall fetch pity eternal."

Inevitably, our opinion of the artistic quality of the last nine stanzas will be closely bound up with our reactions to the poet's beliefs : any final judgment must therefore be a personal one. We believe, however, that the true universality of the poem, the moral " overthought " significant for all men, may be indicated thus : the problem of contingent evil and pain must be faced earnestly, devoutly, hopefully ; admitting the inscrutability of God's total plan, we must find our peace and fulfilment in faith, purity, and self-surrender : " In sua voluntade è nostra pace."

A sensation of genuine bathos is experienced when we turn from the " raw nakedness " and " unmitigated violence " of Hopkins's poem to the unimpeachable mediocrity of Sir Noel Paton's *The Last of the ' Eurydice '* :

> " The training ship *Eurydice*—
> As tight a craft, I ween,
> As ever bore brave men who loved
> Their Country and their Queen—
> Built when a ship, sir, *was* a ship,
> And not a steam-machine."

The ballad, as a piece of terse semi-poetical reporting, is not without merit and has a few fine touches ; [1] but it makes no attempt to recreate the experience or to relate the episode to the spiritual sum of things. We feel that but for Hopkins this would indeed have been the " last " of the Eurydice.

In May 1878 Hopkins was back at Stonyhurst, where he wrote *The May Magnificat*. During the Lady Month it was the custom

---

[1] E.g. the " sprung " line : " And broadside the great ship went down . . ."

at Stonyhurst to hang polyglot verses in honour of the Virgin
before her statue : Hopkins wrote four, possibly five such poems,
two being in Latin [1] and another, as we have seen, in imitation
(with a difference !) of Swinburne.[2] In *The May Magnificat*,
which is ' Horatian ' in stanzaic form, Hopkins himself professed
to see little good " but in the freedom of the rhythm " ; he was
not surprised to hear that Bridges disliked it : there is something
about it, he adds, " displeasing to myself." [3]

From the narrowly or even jealously Christian point of view,
it may seem that the poem is marred by a discordant note of
pagan naturalism ; even Professor Abbott has suggested that

> " the lush, yet fresh, beauty of the descriptive writing, which
> conveys the very ' feel ' of May-time, clashes inevitably with
> praise of the Virgin Mary." [4]

But why should Hopkins regard this juxtaposition as an injurious
clash ? As we have seen, his poetic sensibility was mystically one
with his sense of the numinous, with his instinct for offering praise
and prayer to God ; his perception of the divine in humanity
was spontaneously fused with his apprehension of God through
every other window of reality. In the sonnet *Spring*, thrushes and
peartrees speak to him of " Innocent mind and Mayday in girl
and boy ", and he immediately describes such perfection as
" Most, O maid's child, *thy* choice." Where, then, is the discrepancy in his present comparison between " This ecstasy all
through mothering earth " (the joy of growth in nature), and the
ecstasy all through mothering Mary at the growth within her
finite nature of the infinite Creator of nature itself? In each
case he is objectifying or projecting his own joy ; but why not?
He is only giving back what he has received. Even if nature, or
Mary either, lived " in our life alone " (their perfection being an
emanation from the soul itself—

> " A light, a glory, a fair luminous cloud
>   Enveloping the Earth—") [5]

still the elevating effect on the consciousness and character would
be the same. When Hopkins wrote that " Growth in everything " reminded Mary of

> " How she did in her stored
>   Magnify the Lord ",

[1] See *Note-books*, p. 255, and *Poems*, 3rd edn., Nos. 138 and 139.
[2] See above, chapter i. p. 93.   [3] *Letters*, vol. i. pp. 65 and 77.
[4] *Op. cit.* p. 77 (note).   [5] *Dejection : an Ode*, by S. T. Coleridge.

he meant that he himself had perceived the analogy and had wondered at the amazing humility of God. Hopkins was possessed with the "beauty-making power" of faith and imagination, and might well have addressed Mary in the words of Coleridge :

> "Joy, virtuous Lady ! Joy that ne'er was given,
>   Save to the pure, and in their purest hour,
>   Life, and Life's effluence, cloud at once and shower,
>   Joy, Lady ! is the spirit and the power,
>   Which wedding Nature to us gives in dower
>   A new Earth and new Heaven. . . ."[1]

In the joyous poems of Hopkins it is through "Christ and his mother and all his hallows" that nature is wedded to humanity, for only the pure in heart shall see God, whether in a bluebell or on the Throne of Glory. In another poem Hopkins says that "Sorrow's springs are the same" ; [2] conversely in this poem he tells us that the springs of holy Joy must all ultimately draw from one founthead—Christ.

The something displeasing to the poet himself was probably the prosaic tone and substance of the first two stanzas, or even more probably the indecorous suggestion in the last stanza that Mary might need to be reminded of her "mirth" and of her

> "exultation
> In God who was her salvation."

Yet even here the fancy could be defended ; for Mary, in spite of the fact that through her Son's intercession she was exempt from the stigma of Original Sin, was still human. And in passing we should remind the general reader that true Catholics do *not* deify the Blessed Virgin or practise idolatry before her image. In this poem and elsewhere, Hopkins's attitude towards her is strictly and correctly one of the highest *veneration*.

From July to November 1878, Hopkins was stationed as ' select preacher ' at Mount Street, Grosvenor Square, London. To Bridges he wrote :

> "I am at present writing 3 sermons to be preached in August ; I have little else to do (of duty) and so employ myself in making up my theology, but my work will soon thicken." [3]

---

[1] *Dejection : an Ode.*   [2] *Spring and Fall ; Poems*, No. 31.   [3] *Letters*, vol. i. p. 55.

Care and even anxiety over his sermons precluded other interests, and this period seems to have produced no new poems. In December he was moved to St. Giles, Oxford, where for the next nine months he worked as preacher and missioner. Here he saw Pater again and was kindly welcomed by his university friend Paravicini, who eventually erected to the poet's memory that first monument—the inscribed font still to be seen in St. Aloysius' Church.

Hopkins found the atmosphere of his Alma Mater congenial to his muse; for though, as he said, " I have parish work to do, am called one way and another, and can find little time to write," [1] this Oxford period in 1879 was comparatively fruitful, yielding nine finished poems.

Like Arnold, Clough, and Dixon before him, Hopkins drew spiritual nourishment from the surrounding countryside, the beauty of which had been given something of a mystical significance by Arnold's two great pastoral elegies; and even for Dixon's sake Hopkins loved " the Wytham and Godstow landscape (as I take it to be) of ' Love's Consolation ' and ' Waiting ' " In March he writes to Dixon :

> " I have been up to Godstow this afternoon. I am sorry to say that the aspens that lined the river are everyone felled." [2]

As reparation for this loss of inscape, Hopkins wrote *Binsey Poplars*, one of the most delightful irregular lyrics in the language. The " sprung " lines vary in length from a norm of four stresses to others of two, three, five and six, so that the rhythm wavers and shimmers like the very leaves of the white poplar. The number of stresses in each line is clearly indicated by the indentation :

> " My aspens dear, whose airy cages quelled,
>   Quelled or quenched in leaves·the leaping sun,
>   All felled, felled, are all felled ;
>   Of a fresh and following folded rank
>   Not spared, not one
>   That dandled a sandalled
>   Shadow that swam or sank
> On meadow and river and wind-wandering weed-winding bank." [3]

---

[1] *Letters*, vol. ii. p. 20. [2] *Ibid.* p. 26. [3] Outrides from MSS. " B " and " H ".

In this first section the picture is atmospheric, impressionistic
—like a small canvas by Monet. Behind the leafy meshes of the
aspens, the sun seems to flash up and down, like a hopping
canary ; but the full significance of " leaping sun " is not brought
out until the wind-motive is stressed in the later image (" dandled
a sandalled / Shadow ").[1]   Then, stimulated by the fluctuant yet
carefully controlled rhythm, we *see* the swinging leaves and the
chequered pattern of light and shade dancing on the ground.
Purely impressionistic too is the " fresh and following folded
rank " ; for unless we see the trees as Hopkins did (that is, from
one end of the foreshortened row, each trunk protruding from
behind its predecessor) we cannot appreciate the truth of
" folded " (' like the rounded folds of a heavy curtain ').[2]

The second part is the rationale of the poet's regret. It is
saved from sentimentality by the sharp fascination of physical
horror in the central image ; without this and the neologisms,
" beauty been " and " unselve ", the repetitive incantation of
the close would be jejune :

> " Ó if we but knew what we do
>   When we delve or hew—
>   Hack and rack the growing green !
>   Since country is so tender
>   To touch, her being so slender,
>   That, like this sleek and seeing ball
>   But a prick will make no eye at all,
>   Where we, even where we mean
>   To mend her we end her,
>   When we hew or delve :
>   After-comers cannot guess the beauty been.

[1] By what seems to be a curious coincidence, George Meredith wrote and
published nine years later, in 1888, a poem called *The South-Wester*, which contains
the same image :

> " Day of the cloud in fleets ! O day
> Of wedded white and blue, that sail
> Immingled, with a footing ray
> *In shadow-sandals* down our vale ! "
>   (*A Reading of Earth.*)

Again, the wedded, immingled white and blue recalls Hopkins's *The Woodlark* (1876)
and *Ashboughs* (1885 ?) : " May / Mells blue and snow white through them . . ."

[2] For this suggestion I am indebted to my friend, Mr. E. L. Hillman.

> Ten or twelve, only ten or twelve
> Strokes of havoc unselve
>   The sweet especial scene,
> Rural scene, a rural scene,
> Sweet especial rural scene."

This poet's concern is all for distinctive beauty, not at all for immediate economic necessity ; and since our men of affairs have too frequently reversed these considerations, we need not blame Hopkins's almost feminine sensibility.

To understand nature aright, Thoreau once said, our regard for her must be almost a personal one. It was so with Hopkins in *Ribblesdale* (1882), where the spoliation of natural beauty is bracketed with man's moral delinquency : nature is like a devout woman married to a selfish waster.[1] Wordsworth had warned the Traveller that the " holy pleasure " imparted by nature implied a sacred obligation :

> " Yea, all that now enchants thee, from the day
>   On which it should be touched, would melt away." [2]

Posterity has not been wholly converted ; as Mr. Herbert Palmer's coal miner complained in 1934 :

" We've been mucking up this country for a hundred bleeding years." [3]

It was in the 1870's that this process became appreciable in the purlieus of the old university town which still nestles unchangeably in the crooked arm made by the Cherwell and the Isis. It was around the irritant of a base and graceless modernity that Hopkins deposited the pearl of his sentiment for medieval Christianity, as represented by the great Schoolman, Duns Scotus. The first quatrain of *Duns Scotus's Oxford* deals spaciously with the old city ; the second, restricted in length by fifteen syllables,

[1] Lines 5–8 :   " . . . strong
>   Thy plea with him who dealt, nay does now deal,
>   Thy lovely dale down thus and thus bids reel
>   Thy river, and o'er gives all to rack or wrong."

The poet is addressing nature ; " him " means God. It is significant that in his great poems Hopkins never writes " He " or " Him " for the Deity. This implies that he aims at poetry, not conventional devotional verse ; he is addressing the agnostic as well as the Christian : ' Your God, as well as mine.'

[2] *Admonition to a Traveller.*

[3] ' The Coal Miner's Disgust ' (*Summit and Chasm*).

deplores the abridgment and souring of beauty by the new utilitarian suburbs : [1]

" Towery city and branchy between towers ;
  Cuckoo-echoing, bell-swarmèd, lark-charmèd, rook-racked, river-
      rounded ;
  The dapple-eared lily below thee ; that country and town did
  Once encounter in, here coped and poisèd powers ;

" Thou hast a base and brickish skirt there, sours
  That neighbour-nature thy grey beauty is grounded
  Best in ; graceless growth, thou hast counfounded
  Rural rural keeping—folk, flocks, and flowers." [2]

The first two lines complete the banquet for eye and ear—the strong towers and all the live murmur of an Oxford day. The " dapple-eared lily " is eloquent of waters unpolluted by trade. Time was when town and country were severally perfect ; merged but distinct ; balanced and set-off one against the other —in short, " coped and poisèd powers ". Now, however, this ideal marriage of nature and nurture has been disturbed by an interloper, the *leitmotif* for whose entry is the only penny-plain ' legitimate ' pentameter in the whole sonnet (line 5) ; indeed, " bri*ckish skir*t " seems deliberately cacophanous. The com- mercial Philistine, having no interest in either nature or culture, has confused the old harmony existing between God's handiwork and man's.

The sestet is one of the noblest tributes ever paid to Scotus— a great and neglected thinker :

" Yet ah ! this air I gather and I release
  He lived on ; these weeds and waters, these walls are what
  He haunted who of all men most sways my spirits to peace."

That conscious, deliberate gathering and releasing of the very atmosphere in which Scotus wrote his *Opus Oxoniense* is an intensification of joy and gratitude ; for had not Duns given Hopkins the philosophic rationale of his own intuitive knowledge of " realty " (reality)—of the universal in and through the

---

[1] Cf. *Letters*, vol. ii. p. 20 : " . . . that landscape the charm of Oxford, green shouldering grey, which is already abridged and soured and perhaps will soon be put out altogether . . ."

[2] The outrides are from MS. " B ".

individual ?[1] But joy is intensified by submerged pain ; even as he wrote, Hopkins felt and deplored the trend of Oxford and the whole world away from the teaching of this Schoolman, who for him was still

> " Of realty the rarest-veinèd unraveller ; a not
> Rivalled insight, be rival Italy or Greece ;[2]
> Who fired France for 'Mary without spot."

There is a tradition (impugned by some) that Scotus, specially summoned to Paris, had there defended with resounding success his belief in the Immaculate Conception of the Blessed Virgin—a dogma which was not made *de fide* for all Catholics until 1854.[3] To many readers the last-line reference to Mary will seem a sudden flying-off at a tangent, a freezing of the emotional current. On the other hand, those who share the poet's beliefs will be aesthetically warmed by it, for its justification is almost entirely Catholic. Mary is ' Mother of Divine Grace ', and as such is honoured by Hopkins in *Poems*, No. 37. When he spoke of the new suburbs of Oxford as a " graceless growth " he meant by that epithet something more than ` uncomely ' ; he meant nothing less than ' lacking in spiritual grace ', devoid of social decency : for those unsightly accretions were to him symbolic of an age which allowed the whole inverted pyramid of material progress to bear oppressively upon what should be the apex of human life—the spirit of man.

We see therefore that as Charles Kingsley gave us ' muscular Christianity ', so Hopkins gives us ' aesthetic Christianity '. The above sonnet contains elements which are Hellenistic or humanistic rather than Christian ; yet neither the sensuous beauty nor the vigorous ' criticism of life ' is antagonistic to a generous politico-social concept of ' applied ' Christianity.

Written at the same time as *Duns Scotus's Oxford* was the splendidly idiosyncratic *Henry Purcell*, the Scotist motivation of which has already been discussed.[4] Bridges seems to have

---

[1] See Volume I of the present work, chapter i.

[2] Cf. *Further Letters*, p. 201 : " Scotus . . . saw too far, he knew too much ; his subtlety overshot his interests ; a kind of feud arose between genius and talent, and the ruck of talent in the Schools finding itself, as his age passed by, less and less able to understand him, voted that there was nothing important to understand and so misquoted and then refuted him."

[3] See Hopkins's sermon " *on the Immaculate Conception* " (*Note-books*, pp. 267–70).

[4] Volume I of the present work, chap. i. p. 25. The full text of this sonnet, with outrides from MS. " A ", is set out in *ibid*. chap. iii. (p. 101).

found this sonnet unusually difficult. Although Hopkins had in 1879 given his friend an elaborate explanation of the sestet (conceding that it was " not so clearly worked out as I could wish "),[1] yet as late as 1883 Bridges was still asking questions about the octave. Obviously he was fascinated as well as puzzled by the *embarras de richesses* ; but in all probability he never quite recovered from what he termed " the rude shocks of Hopkins's purely artistic wantonness ". In this poem Hopkins was linguistically wanton in the interests of art—though the intelligibility of his art would have been enhanced if he had modified the singularity of the opening quatrain and made a slight concession to the normal English mentality by using a regular perfect-optative instead of his own peculiar " imperative of the past " (" Have fair fallen "). Hopkins tells us plainly that following Shakespeare he took " fair " to be the substantive governing the verb (*'fair* fortune be-*fall'*) ; but for obvious reasons he could not have begun with

' May fair fortune have befallen . . . so arch-especial a spirit. . . .'

though he might have compromised with

' Fáir may the sóul, O fáir, | faír have fállen so déar
  To me, so árch-espécial a spírit | as héaves in Hénry Púrcell. . . .'

Mr. Stephen Spender has said recently that he cannot think in the tense Hopkins uses without " a mental contortion ".[2] Coming from such a poet-critic, this reaction must be taken as fairly general : as Mr. Spender says, most readers will mistake " Have fallen " for a third person plural indicative or else will misread it as " Has fallen ". Hopkins is to be blamed for a hyperaesthetical disregard for the linguistic habits of the average Englishman—a fact which makes the present writer tremble to admit that he is still inclined to agree with Hopkins's final comment :

> " I am unwilling to alter that line, for if it will only stand, and it will, it pleases me much." [3]

Similarly, by all the rules of syntax and style lines 3 and 4 are unpardonably loose and ambiguous :

[1] *Letters*, vol. i. p. 83.
[2] Review of our first volume in *Tribune* (Nov. 17, 1944).
[3] *Letters*, vol. i. p. 173.

> " . . . spirit as heaves in Henry Purcell,
> (3) An age is now since passed, since parted ; with the reversal
> (4) Of the outward sentence low lays him, listed to a heresy, here."

To what verbs do these limiting clauses and phrases belong ? As the poet's own paraphrase shows, " An age, etc. " qualifies " spirit ", while " with the reversal, etc. " harks back to " fair have fallen " :

> " May Purcell, O may he have died a good death and that soul which I love so much and which breathes or stirs so unmistakeably in his works have parted from the body and passed away, centuries since though I frame the wish, in peace with God ! so that the heavy condemnation under which he outwardly or nominally lay for being out of the true Church may in consequence of his good intentions have been reversed." [1]

Knowing, as we do now, the full weight of logical or ' prose ' meaning which this quatrain is expected to bear in only just over half the number of words, we are not surprised at its partial failure in communication. Who would have perceived that " since passed, since parted " could refer to any word but " age " ?—that the whole double clause could be equivalent to : ' which spirit (an age has now elapsed) passed away, parted from the body ', or perhaps rather ' which spirit is now, for an age since, passed away, parted from the body ' ? The clause asks to be taken as an adverbial limitation of " heaves ", and on the whole it is not easy to convince oneself that there is a poetic gain to compensate for the lack of clarity. Yet we find in the last clause of this quatrain a significant ambiguity—a proleptic suggestion that the prayer now being uttered has already been answered.

The rest of the sonnet, with its bold analogue of the seabird which is elucidated in a magnificent climactic simile (and we should mark the giant *charpente*, the colossal grasp of its esemplastic syntax—" so some great stormfowl . . . fans fresh our wits with wonder "), is no more difficult than metaphysical poetry legitimately may be. Hopkins seems to say : ' Although Purcell's spirit may now be among the damned (which I can hardly believe), that spirit, as manifested in his music, is *for me* among the archangels (" so *arch*-especial . . . with his air of *angels* "),—for in theology every angel is a separate species—a species, that is, in super-nature ; and I have always believed

[1] *Letters*, vol. i. pp. 170-1.

that in our human nature every true artist is like a species, and can never recur. As we know, nature and super-nature meet in prayer : they also meet in the greatest art, which is always transcendental, a mode of mystical experience.'

Hopkins praised Purcell for his clear fidelity to two principles —his individual make (" sakes of him ", *haecceitas*) and his specific make (*humanitas*). Purcell's " own abrupt self " was not the deliberate flaunting of a conceited selfhood or of a pathologically introverted nature. Bridges seems to have suspected that Hopkins's words implied something violently ' broken off ', anti-social ; but the latter quickly protested :

> " . . . your remark on Purcell's music does not conflict with what my sonnet says, rather it supports it. My sonnet means ' Purcell's music is none of your d——d subjective rot ' (so to speak). Read it again." [1]

Now Hopkins could not have meant to stigmatize all subjectivity in art ; by so doing he would have condemned himself no less than his favourites, Herbert and Patmore. He would not have condemned the healthy *universalized* subjectivity of these poets or of Lamb ; or, in music, of a Schumann or Elgar. It is not easy to say what music he regarded as " d——d subjective rot " (was it Wagner ?) ; it is however at this date easy to survey retrospectively the growth of that morbid ' egomania ' which came in with naturalism and Rousseau's *Confessions*, developing with the seamy side of Romanticism (' the Romantic Agony ') from a rational deism to an irrational satanism, from a generous plea for equality among men to a disproportionate exaltation of Man and the eventual dethronement of God. Hopkins's phrase was prophetic, for to-day we have seen a plethora, in poetry, fiction, music, and painting, of what may be called extreme *Mon-cœur-mis-à-nu*-ism, of the modern Pelagian heresy that whatever comes out of Man must be good—except the laws of propriety or decency that may condemn it. [2]

The moral of the Purcell sonnet is that a healthy, valuable individuality is not a self-conscious exhibitionism but, like Hopkins's own " oddness ", a natural accident of the personality. The artist, " but meaning motion "—intending only to express normal emotions and values—unconsciously betrays his mental gait. It must be admitted that Hopkins himself, whenever he

---

[1] *Letters*, vol. i. p. 84.
[2] E.g. certain works by D. H. Lawrence, James Joyce, Salvador Dali, and Picasso.

relied on private associations and solipsist locutions (such as " sakes " and " have fallen ") was getting dangerously close to a form of " subjective rot " ; but these occasional excesses were due, as Bridges saw, to " a purely artistic wantonness ", never to a serious psychic perversion. His heart was right though his judgment might falter ; such a passion for the full orchestra of language was bound to produce some unfamiliar, disturbing tones. Again, few artists have been more consistently subjective in method than Hopkins ; yet few have been more boldly objective in their interpretation of widely accepted spiritual and cultural values.

The very complexity of the idiosyncratic and emotive presentation of thought in the Purcell sonnet was in part due to the unusual vividness and permanence of this poet's " installs "—his mentally and verbally recorded impressions of varied aspects of nature, each one with its characteristic " scaping " or " inscape ". These submerged sense-data, suddenly released from the ' unconscious ' by some peculiarly comprehensive and searching experience, came crowding and jostling into the picture, modifying one another and finally merging in one striking synthetic image. We have already seen this process at work in the *Heraclitean Fire* ; [1] and something like it may be traced in the following quotations—the first from Charlotte Brontë's *Shirley*, which Hopkins had read before 1865 ; the second from his *Journal* of 1873 ; the third from the last tercet of *Henry Purcell* (the italics are ours) :

(1) " The air was now *dark* with *snow* ; an Iceland *blast* was driving it wildly. This pair neither heard the *long ' wuthering ' rush* nor saw the *white* burden it drifted. . . ." (Chap. xxxiii.)

(2) " I looked at the pigeons down in the kitchen yard. . . . The two young ones are *all white* and the *pins of the folded wings*, quill pleated over quill, are like crisp and shapely cuttle-shells found *on the shore*. The others are *dull thundercolour* or *black-grape-colour* except in the *white pieings*, the quills and the tail. . . ." (*Note-books*, pp. 175–6.)

(3) " . . . so some great *stormfowl*, whenever he has walked his while
     The *thunder-purple seabeach plumèd purple-of-thunder*,
     If a *wuthering* of his palmy *snow-pinions* scatter a colossal smile
     Off him, but meaning motion *fans fresh* our wits with wonder."

[1] See Volume I. chapter v.

Dark, plumy, lowering clouds and the white or cloudy plumage of birds ; snow and the rush of a cold wind ; the shapely pleatings on the white pinions of the wildfowl walking tamely on the stormy shore ; the scatter of snowflakes and the sudden scatter of wing-feathers flung out palm-wise, fan-wise ; the whiff of wind from the wild motion giving unaware a whiff of knowledge about the neatly packed plumage on the underside of the wing—it was only the sharp instress of Purcell's music that could unify these diverse elements and cause the underlying pattern to break, like a broad smile of recognition, upon the poet's imagination. Rightly did Shelley say that imagination respects the similitudes of things, that τὸ ποιεῖν is the principle of synthesis, having for its object " those forms which are common to universal nature and existence itself."

This poem gives us a considerable gust of knowledge about Hopkins, the stormy petrel of the English poetic tradition. It is *his* " forgèd feature " that finds *us*. So vigorously and stormily at times does it thrust on and throng our ears that it stuns our comprehension. No poet can lift us so dizzily, waft us and lay us down again more soothingly ; yet by none have our mental muscles been more exquisitely racked and loosened.

In 1879 Hopkins reached the first climacteric of his maturity. He had now for two and a half years and with many an anvilding hammered out the bright and battering sandals of a fiery Pegasus which he alone could turn and wind ; but the effort of being thus true to himself without the stimulus of publication and adequate recognition had, despite his own scrupulous detachment from worldly ambitions, severely taxed his powers. With the single exception of the undated fragment on Hope, all the poems we have treated in the present chapter have borne the stamp of a mind and faith imbued with " the power / Of harmony and the deep power of joy ". In at least half the poems written after the middle of 1879 this power of harmony and faith, which enabled him to see into the life of things, is still active ; but in this period there is no mistaking the presence of a new note—a sharper contrast between consolation and anxiety, pain and delight, resignation and protest ; a gradual then sudden steepening of the " cliffs of fall " between the *instress of self* and self-disgust, between the triumph of beauty in the human spirit and a sense of undisguised (though never quite absolute) defeat.

The causes of this change, as far as they can now be ascertained, will be the first concern of our next chapter.

CHAPTER VI

POEMS OF GOD AND MAN
(1879–1885)

If the shift of emphasis from Nature to Man, in the poems written after 1879, admits of any rational explanation, it is probably this—that Hopkins had become more conscious of himself as a suffering mortal, more acutely aware of his own personal dilemma. The crisis in his case amounted to a partial or sub-conscious realization that he was destined not to achieve a *permanent* balance and harmony between his conflicing desires and impulses.

In June 1878 he had written his first letter to Canon Dixon, by whose poems he had once been deeply impressed. There he says :

> " I knew what I should feel myself in your position—if I had written and published works the extreme beauty of which the author himself the most keenly feels and they had fallen out of sight at once. . . ."

Hopkins certainly felt the extreme beauty of his own un-published poems ; yet neither his problem nor Dixon's was exclusively one of personal ambition. As he says in the same letter :

> " It is not that I think a man is really the less happy because he has missed the renown which was his due, but still when this happens it is an evil in itself, and a thing which ought not to be and that I deplore, *for the good work's sake* rather than the author's.[1]

The words we have italicized are important. No one knew better than Hopkins that artistic creation is not purely a private and personal act. As he demonstrated when he urged Bridges and Patmore to write more poetry for the glory of God, England and the Empire, he realized that the making of a poem is also, in effect, a *social* act. According to Shelley and others, the poet does not desire merely to show how clever he is or to find emotional relief in self-expression. Because some divine spirit is working

---

[1] *Letters*, vol. ii. p. 2.

through the medium of his personality, he desires, consciously or subconsciously, to make a necessary adjustment between himself and the world—a psychological adjustment which he believes to be equally valid for other people. The measure of his success, and incidentally of his own happiness, is the praise which the beauty and truth of his work evokes. In 1886 Hopkins put all this in his own way :

> " I say it deliberately and before God, I would have you and Canon Dixon and all true poets remember that fame, the being known, though in itself one of the most dangerous things to man, is nevertheless the true and appointed air, element, and setting of genius and its works. What are works of art for ? to educate, to be standards. Education is meant for the many, standards are for public use. To produce then is of little use unless what we produce is known . . . by being known it works, it influences, it does its duty, it does good. We must then try to be known, aim at it, take means to it." [1]

In 1878 he had consoled Dixon and himself too by saying that " the only just literary critic is Christ ",[2] that the praise of one's fellows is at best but a token of the judgment which Christ passes on our doings.

Bridges saw that in such a man as Hopkins worldly hopes and ambitions, though rigidly controlled, are inevitably bound up with spiritual aspirations and desolations :

> " Thy sainted sense trammel'd in ghostly pain,
> Thy rare ill-broker'd talent in disdain. . ." [3]

Bridges, knowing the sense of fulfilment which comes with publication, urged Hopkins to allow a few friends to move on his behalf ; but the Jesuit's professional scruples were insurmountable :

> " No, do not ask Gosse anything of the sort. (1) If I were going to publish, and that soon, such a mention would be the ' puff premilinary ',[4] which it would be dishonourable of me to allow of. . . . (3) When I say that I do not mean to publish I speak the truth. I have taken and mean to take no step to do so beyond the attempt I made to print my two wrecks in the *Month*."

[1] *Letters*, vol. i. p. 231. For " *true* . . . air " (l. 4) G. M. H. first wrote " necessary . . . air ".　　[2] *Ibid*. vol. ii. p. 8.

[3] Dedicatory sonnet by R. B. in *Poems of G. M. H.*

[4] Spelt so in MS. Does the mis-spelling expose a repressed desire to withhold the objection ?

That was written in February 1879 ; *The Wreck of the Deutschland* and *The Loss of the Eurydice* had been rejected by the Jesuit magazine in 1876 and 1878 respectively.   Hopkins continues :

> " If some one in authority knew of my having some poems printable and suggested my doing it I should not refuse, I should be partly, though not altogether, glad. But that is very unlikely." [1]

Despite its restraint, such an admission, with its curious reservation in " not altogether ", is charged with neuropathic possibilities.   The clue to its real meaning is in those three words " my two wrecks "—written so, with a casual ambiguity. In an earlier letter he had called them " my two almost famous Rejected Addresses " ; but although he had not lost his sense of humour and proportion, he must have felt that as a people's poet, a *vates*, he was either a failure or (dare he hope ?) before his time.   Even if his poems could be published there and then, would they be understood ?   He answered the question himself when he deprecated Dixon's expressed intention of sending all or part of *The Eurydice* to a Carlisle newspaper :

> " You will see that your warmhearted but much mistaken kindness will be unavailing : if the paper takes the piece (which it is sure to misprint) few will read it and of those few fewer will scan it, much less understand or like it." [2]

This vein of defeatism is very different from the mood in which the poem had been written : he had hoped that the work would prove ' popular '.

That same letter to Bridges, of February 1879, reveals a different aspect of his psychic malady :

> " I cannot in conscience spend time on poetry, neither have I the inducements and inspirations that make others compose. Feeling, love in particular, is the great moving power and spring of verse and the only person I am in love with seldom, especially now, stirs my heart sensibly and when he does I cannot always ' make capital ' of it, it would be sacrilege to do so.   Then again I have of myself made verse so laborious." [3]

The " only person " could have been none other than Christ ; yet as we have seen, Christ had on many occasions stirred his

---

[1] *Letters*, vol. i. pp. 65-6. He wrote in exactly the same strain to Dixon : " I have no thought of publishing until all circumstances favour, which I do not know that they ever will, and it seems to me that one of them should be that the suggestion to publish should come from one of our own people." (*Letters*, vol. ii. p. 28.)

[2] *Ibid.* vol. ii. p. 31.   [3] *Loc. cit.* p. 66.

heart or received his homage in poems that were the reverse of sacrilegious. Those less frequent and as it were less negotiable heart-stirrings may suggest an even more intimate communion with the Divine Lover. Now that the poet's 'spiritual diary' has been destroyed,[1] we cannot be certain of the nature and significance of these mystical states ; we can feel sure, however, that the above confession indicates no falling off in the reality and intensity of his religious experiences.

With his conscious will he put aside all desire for fame as a poet, calling it the least of his mortifications : " There is more peace," he wrote in 1881, " and it is the holier lot to be unknown than to be known." [2]   If there is a sour grape in that it is one which he was prepared to burst, with a fierce and holy joy, against his palate fine (he had already symbolized the process in *The Deutschland*, using a ripe sloe for a grape !).[3]   Any rancour he felt against life was repressed. His ostensible renunciation of success as an artist was really unavoidable, so imperative was his desire for moral justification, for sanctity. That he would suffer he knew ; yet he chose self-immolation. For one who believes implicitly, as he did, in the heavenly Reward, all joy is an anticipation and all pain is a promise :

" Ah well ! it is all a purchase, all is a prize."

" Father and fondler of heart thou hast wrung :
Hast thy dark descending and most art merciful then."

What we have said concerning Hopkins's personal inhibitions does not imply that from 1879 onwards he was subject to an unremitting melancholia. His moods varied with his physical condition. The parish work in Liverpool was so wearying to mind and body, leaving him " nothing but odds and ends of time ", that he wrote no more than twenty-six lines of verse in seven months.[4]   Had it not been for the interest in his work steadily maintained by Bridges, and the great joy he felt at Dixon's generous praise, he would probably have relinquished his modest hope of having a few pieces gathered up and published after his death. As it was he could lament, in 1881 :

" Every impulse and spring of art seems to have died in me, except for music, and that I pursue under almost an impossibility of getting on." [5]

---

[1] See Preface to the present volume, p. viii.
[2] *Letters*, vol. ii. p. 89.   [3] Stanza 8.
[4] *Letters*, vol. ii. p. 33.   Cf. p. 42 : " Liverpool is of all places the most museless."
[5] *Ibid*. vol. i. p. 124.

In his great overture, *The Wreck of the Deutschland*, he had already given out (by a sort of empathy or projection of the self into another) a personal *motif* which was to undergo many poignant variations :

> " The jading and jar of the cart,
> Time's tasking, it is fathers that asking for ease
> Of the sodden-with-its-sorrowing heart. . . ." [1]

In *The Windhover*, of 1877, this feeling of weariness and despair had been transvaluated into a spiritual triumph. But the first poem to dwell unequivocally upon the theme of a persistent personal unrest is the Curtal Sonnet called *Peace*,[2] which was first drafted in 1879 :

> " When will you ever, Peace, | wild wooddove, shy wings shut,
> Your round me roaming end, and under be my boughs ?
> When, when, Peace, will you, Peace ? I'll not play hypocrite
> To own my heart : I yield you do come sometimes ; but
> That piecemeal peace is poor peace. What pure peace allows
> Alarms of wars, the daunting wars, the death of it ?

> " O surely, reaving Peace, my Lord should leave in lieu
> Some good ! And so he does leave Patience exquisite,
> That plumes to Peace thereafter. And when Peace here does house
> He comes with work to do, he does not come to coo,
> He comes to brood and sit."

Having regretted, as most critics will, the affected inversion of " own my heart " and the uncomfortably weak ending of line 6 (" . . . the death of *it* "), we can still pronounce this poem a success. The second line, which at first presents " an irritating grammatical tangle," resolves itself with familiarity into a thought-dramatization of subtle precision. The modified gerund " round me roaming " is a complete poetic word, the delicate exactitude of which would have been destroyed if Hopkins, in deference to conventional idiom, had written " Your roaming round me end " or " End your roaming round me " ; for in these locutions " round me " becomes syntactically confused with " end ", whereas it must exclusively limit " roaming ". Similarly, " under *be* my boughs " (on the analogy of ' under*lay* ', ' under*lie* ', ' under*prop* ', etc.) carries an elemental sense of passive *being* which would be excluded by some more specific an

---

[1] Stanza 27.   [2] *Poems*, No. 22.   The rhythm is ' standard alexandrines '

facile word, such as ' rest ', ' dwell ', or ' live '.   Again, the
alliterative punning in line 5 is not mere musical ingenuity ; it is
an earnest ' running logic ' of feeling linked with sound, other
examples of which we have noted in Sophocles, Shakespeare,
Sidney, and Rilke.[1]

The first part of the poem ends with the adumbration of a
state of peace which, being " pure ", can be nothing less than
the peace of heaven.   Then with the *volta* comes a transition from
negative to positive, from deprivation to enrichment, from the
personal heart-cry to the personal surrender.   The soul must
protest against its exile from heaven ; but the man of faith does
not lose his head.   He may release a head of emotional steam,
but as a result the human ' machine ' (as Wordsworth called it)
attains a more even stroke—a poise of emotion and intellect
which enables it to expend itself in productive action.   So
Hopkins turns round upon himself and corrects his first wrong
impression.   The Peace he had desired had been an idle consummation of ease, a gentle cooing of the undisturbed spirit ;
but the Peace he is now prepared to accept, " piecemeal " if
God so ordain, must be an active ' will to work '—a readiness to
share in the continuous Divine act of Creation.

The final image of the sitting bird intent on its progenitive
function points back to the Dove of the New Testament and
the brooding Holy Ghost of *God's Grandeur*.   As the " bright
wings " were suggested by Milton, so the restive wooddove
here may have owed something to the dove which for Wordsworth symbolized the unquiet starts and incubations of the
poetic imagination :

> " his mind, best pleased
> While she as duteous as the mother dove
> Sits brooding, lives not always to that end,
> But like the innocent bird hath goadings on
> That drive her as in trouble through the groves." [2]

As Keats felt the essential relationship between Joy and
Melancholy, so to Hopkins it was axiomatic that ends which
are *right* as well as *good* are seldom attained without a struggle.
The military image, " alarms of wars ", anticipates the later
sonnets *Patience* and *St. Alphonsus* ; and on the virtue of patience
St. Ignatius had said :

[1] See above, pp. 125, 126, 141, and Vol. I, p. 272.
[2] *The Prelude*, Book I, ll. 139–43.

" Let him who is in desolation labour to hold on in patience, such patience as makes against the vexations that harass him : let him consider that soon he shall be consoled, using diligent efforts against desolation, as is enjoined in the Sixth rule." [1]

Hopkins adds therefore that God, in " reaving " Peace, leaves in its place the changeling-virtue—

> " Patience exquisite,
> That plumes to Peace thereafter."

The archaic " reaving " has just the right suggestion of bereavement by a gentle but decisive taking away. And " exquisite " is the exact epithet for Patience, combining the acute pain of deprivation with the keen satisfaction of self-mastery. The metaphorical " plumes " can denote two opposite ideas : first ' fledge ', ' furnish or adorn with plumes ', with the added suggestion of winging away to the Reward ; but under this and prior to it is the idea of renunciation, ' to strip of feathers '. Then there is the secondary connotation, ' to plume oneself ' on an achievement, for it is the proper pride of the justified soul which converts the dubious nestling, Patience, into the full-fledged dove of Peace. Thus the opposites in the poem (loss and gain) are reconciled in the various meanings of " plumes ", just as the metaphysical fulcrum of *The Windhover* is the ambiguous verb " Buckle ".

Although Hopkins believed that no man should expect to find peace in this world without doing some work of vital importance to the community, he could still admire the drone who was not cast down by poverty. In the fragment called *Cheery Beggar* he says :

> " The motion of that man's heart is fine
>   Whom want could not make pine, pine
> That struggling should not sear him, a gift should cheer him
> Like that poor pocket of pence, poor pence of mine." [2]

Hopkins's intense love for common humanity is revealed in most of the poems of the period 1879–80—in *The Bugler's First Communion*, *The Candle Indoors*, *The Handsome Heart*, *Felix Randal*, and *Brothers* ; but before looking at these works it will be well to consider the deep earnestness of the man behind them.

While labouring somewhat thanklessly among his parishioners at Oxford, he was equally concerned about *uncommon* humanity

---

[1] *Spiritual Exercises*, First Week, Rules 6–8.   [2] *Poems*, No. 61.

in the person of Robert Bridges, for whose soul he was assiduously angling. If only Bridges would say something about his religious beliefs Hopkins would be glad :

> " You understand of course that I desire to see you a Catholic, or, if not that, a Christian or, if not that, a believer in the true God (for you told me something of your views about the deity, which were not as they should be)." [1]

Being a " gentleman ", he adds, is not enough. He allows that to be a true gentleman may be a thing essentially higher than to be a great artist or thinker. But since " to be a gentleman is but on the brim of morals, is rather a thing of manners than of morals properly ", how much greater (he adds) than art, philosophy, manners, and everything else must be the least degree of true virtue :

> " This is that chastity of mind which seems to lie at the very heart and be the parent of all other good, the seeing at once what is best, the holding to that, and the not allowing anything else whatever to be heard even pleading to the contrary." [2]

That passage of 1883 shows how deliberate had been Hopkins's own sacrifice—his refusal to make an unprofessional bid for success as a poet : " You would not, I hope, (he had asked R. W. Dixon) think I secretly wished to steal a march upon my superiors : that would be in me a great baseness."

" Chastity of mind " and Sacrifice are the basic themes of two didactic poems of 1879, *Morning Midday and Evening Sacrifice* and *The Handsome Heart*.[3] In the former, as befits the theme, the metrical unit is the most solemn in English verse—the trimeter. Diction, tone, and thought are all neatly developed in three regular stanzas, which represent the three stages of life—the morning of childhood and youth, the midday of maturity, the evening of advanced age. The first, addressed *virginibus puerisque*, is light and winsome :

> " The dappled die-away
> Cheek and wimpled lip,
> The gold-wisp, the airy-grey
> Eye, all in fellowship—
> This, all this beauty blooming,
> This, all this freshness fuming,
> Give God while worth consuming."

[1] *Letters*, vol. i. p. 60.   [2] *Ibid.* pp. 174–5.   [3] *Poems*, Nos. 24 and 27.

The epithet " die-away " is subtle : it suggests simultaneously (1) the red of the young cheek delicately fading into the white, and (2) the more serious ' fading ' implied in the rhymes—*blooming, fuming, consuming.*

The answer to the question ' How are the young to give their fresh beauty " back to God " ? ' may be deduced from the poet's work as a whole : by leading pure and devout lives, not least by heeding the admonition of that short poem in which Hopkins's confessed " spooniness and delight " over married couples finds a dignified expression—*At the Wedding March* : [1]

> " Each be other's comfort kind :
>   Deep, deeper than divined,
>   Divine charity, dear charity,
>   Fast you ever, fast bind."

This realist knew that Christian marriage is, among other things, a spiritual battlefield on which merit may be won or lost. Believing the sacrament of marriage to be the medium of a special grace, he would regard any breach of the bond as a blasphemous denial of man's holiness. Hence " with tears "—of anxiety as well as joy—he turns to God,

> " Who to wedlock, his wonder wedlock,
>   Deals triumph and immortal years." [2]

Life's forenoon has its responsibilities ; but it is usually the mid-day—the successful, self-confident prime of life—that proves to be the period of moral sclerosis :

> " Both thought and thew now bolder
>   And told by Nature : Tower ;
>   Head, heart, hand, heel, and shoulder
>   That beat and breathe in power—
>   This pride of prime's enjoyment
>   Take as for tool, not toy meant
>   And hold at Christ's employment."

---

[1] *Poems*, No. 28.

[2] So great was Hopkins's veneration for the marriage bond that he would tolerate no jokes on the subject. In a humorous poem by Bridges an " old salt "

> " Seeing the ' Anne ', his boat, was lost,
>   And Anne his wife was saved alone,
>   Slipped from his moorings, and has gone."

Hopkins condemned the passage as vulgar, " leaving a bad taste . . . suggestive of hornjokes, Benedicks, and that kind of thing, tedious when not odious." (*Letters*, vol. i. pp. 71 and 75.) Many who secretly agree with Hopkins would rather be thought a little vulgar than slightly priggish. As a priest, Hopkins was in a privileged position.

When a man has taken the measure of his faculties, knows how to co-ordinate them under his will, seems to his fellows ' a tower of strength '—that is the time when Self-indulgence is apt to take the helm of a gilded vessel manned by the carnal sins, proudly riding the azure realm (as Gray put it)

> " Regardless of the sweeping Whirlwind's sway,
>   That, hush'd in grim repose, expects his evening prey." [1]

The sacrifice which Hopkins (*vice* Christ) demands of achievement is that which he asked of Bridges—giving alms " paying, heavily for a virtue ", an act which " changes the whole man . . . . not his mind only but the will and everything." [2]

Stanza 3 is like a frankly Christian variation on Gray's theme. By evening, the sacrifice may be long overdue and the time for redemption short.   Under the white hair, the fully matured mind glows like a core of heat protected by ash. If such a man says, " I acknowledge no God ; I am self-sufficient ; I have nothing to regret "—woe betide him ! Life is ebbing ; retribution stalks nearer. Yet even now one evening prayer would rob the Devil of his evening prey. The last three lines must be spoken with a crescendo of fierceness : they explain the sharp vocative used later in *Carrion Comfort*—" O thou terrible " ; they show what the Christian author of *Gerontion* meant by his startling image—" Came Christ the tiger " :

> " What life half lifts the latch of,
>   What hell stalks towards the snatch of,
>   Your offering, with despatch, of ! "

As poetry, the *Sacrifice* is a minor work. Yet that " naked encounter of sensualism and asceticism " which Miss Phare [3] pronounced " a serious defect " in the poem is surely the very quality of stark realism which gives it a peculiar force—a positive value for our day. Hopkins, in his glad acknowledgment of the life of the senses, was a balanced Christian : but in the world as he saw it there was little evidence of that nice poise between sensualism and asceticism which Christianity advocates under the term ' detachment '. And can we affirm that in the present age self-denial and altruism are any more widely esteemed and practised ? If a greater measure of social equity has been established it is because men as blunt as Hopkins, nakedly confronting the Nietzschean ' will to power ' with a higher ideal of mutual

---

[1] *The Bard*, stanza 4.   [2] *Letters*, vol. i. p. 61.   [3] *Op. cit.* pp. 121-22.

aid, have seized politically what was politically denied, forcing upon the sensual and selfish a few hundred years of overdue ' asceticism '.

A purely psycho-analytical study of what would be called the ' religious complex ' and ' neurosis ' of Hopkins would no doubt deliberately ignore, or by implication discredit,[1] the religious values in his life and work, laying all the stress upon the physiological and emotional factors. It would probably be asserted that his abiding consciousness of sin had a sexual origin, that his later pathological condition, as revealed in the *Letters* not to say the ' terrible ' sonnets, was due in no small measure to his celibate state, to the repression or imperfect ' sublimation ' of strong sexual and paternal instincts.

To admit the possible, partial truth of such a diagnosis is not to range oneself with those who believe that psycho-analysis, or some other possible synthesis of scientific data, is capable here and now of revealing the whole significant truth about such a man as Hopkins. Inhibitions like his have many times been proved to be the immediate endo-psychic causes of accidie (one of the ' seven deadly sins '), of a sense of failure, of nervous prostration, of a deep sadness bordering (as Hopkins says his own did) on madness.[2] He himself spoke of the celibate life in the following terms :

> " The reason why I like men to marry is that a single life is a difficult, not altogether natural life ; to make it easily manageable special provision, such as we have here, is needed, and most people cannot have this." [3]

Elsewhere, as we have already shown, he says that the man who has denied himself and followed Christ receives from God a special guidance, a more particular providence.[4] Hopkins and his co-religionists would say that the extent to which God accorded this protective grace was God's own concern, just as the degree to which the priest ' co-operated ' with grace depended upon the man's active will. It is all a ' mystery ', a spiritual transaction between the Divine Master and the dedicated servant, and any additional, unexpected suffering imposed upon the latter would be in the nature of purgation or probation. To call self-denial ' masochism ' or ' sado-masochism ' is often, if not

---

[1] E.g. the *Psycho-analytical Study of the Neurosis of Charles Baudelaire* (1932), by René Laforgue. [2] *Letters*, vol. i. pp. 221-2 (1885).

[3] *Ibid.* p. 194 (1884). [4] See above, Introduction, p. 44.

usually, a gross perversion of language ; [1] and in any case the psycho-analytic position does not confute the claim of faith, as made by Hopkins. Such a claim has never yet been confuted by any form of scientific investigation.

Historically, and in spite of the once numerous examples of priestly incontinence, Hopkins's belief in " special guidance " has on the whole been justified. For centuries before Freud appeared, the wisest preceptors of the Jesuit order had understood the necessity of something very like ' sublimation ' ; they had appreciated the beneficent effects of a careful conditioning of the physical and psychic being of those who renounced the full secular life. The long and varied training to which Jesuit priests are subjected has for one of its main purposes the testing of the candidates' aptitude for this very transmutation of raw emotional energy into the higher spiritual and socially useful activities.

In sending to Bridges, in 1879, the sonnet called *The Handsome Heart : at a Gracious Answer*,[2] Hopkins remarked that he was then finding within his professional experience a good deal of matter to write on. That was a hopeful sign, and the sonnet itself seems to indicate a successful sublimation of the paternal instinct. This poem and *The Bugler* have, moreover, as a kind of submerged but irrepressible theme, that same encounter of sensualism and asceticism which we have just been discussing.

Bridges liked the sonnet, but Hopkins himself thought it " not very good ". It is, he explained, " historical autobiographical ", and the story

> " was that last Lent, when Fr. Parkinson was laid up in the country, two boys of our congregation gave me much help in the sacristy in Holy Week. I offered them money for their services, which the elder refused, but being pressed consented to take it laid out in a book. The younger followed suit ; then when

---

[1] See Flugel, *Man, Morals and Society* (1945), p. 100 : " Masochism, however, he [McDougall] would probably have considered, is a word that should be used only when the sexual component is clearly manifest." Cf. *ibid*. p. 104: " How far we are to follow Freud in regarding moral masochism as sexual (and therefore perhaps correctly described as masochism at all) depends of course to some extent upon our willingness to follow him also in adopting a wide view of the ' sexual ' and also upon our agreement with him as regards the existence and importance of unconscious factors." We believe, as many others do, that Freud adopted *too* wide a view of the ' sexual '.

[2] *Poems*, No. 27. (' Common rhythm counterpointed '.)

some days after I asked him what I should buy answered as in
the sonnet."—[1]

"'But tell me, child, your choice; what shall I buy
 You?'—'Father, what you buy me I like best.'
 With the sweetest air that said, still plied and pressed,
 He swung to his first poised purport of reply.

 What the heart is! which, like carriers let fly—
 Doff darkness, homing nature knows the rest—
 To its own fine function, wild and self-instressed,
 Falls light as ten years long taught how to and why.

 Mannerly hearted! more than handsome face—
 Beauty's bearing or muse of mounting vein,
 All, in this case, bathed in high hallowing grace . . .

 Of heaven what boon to buy you, boy, or gain
 Not granted!—Only . . . O on that path you pace
 Run all your race, O brace sterner that strain!'"

The tenderness and intimacy of the conversation are felt in
the lift and cadence of the first two lines. The first, Hopkins
says,

" should be so read, with a rising inflection, after which the next
line, beginning with the enclitic, gracefully falls away."[2]

The first quatrain has two technical flaws—the repetition of the
rhyme-word " buy " and the clash of " plied " and " reply ".
Moreover the whole poem contains four *whats*, and this tendency
on the part of Hopkins to repeat words (cf. the three *times* in
Andromeda) would be a serious fault in verse of less subtlety and
rhetorical power. As it is, the repetition of " buy " seems
inevitable; and the assonantal clash of " plied " and " reply "
heightens the effect of a swing back to the first spontaneous
equilibrium of the boy's moral nature (a balance between the
desire to be gratified and the desire to please): the poise which
was disturbed by the priest's plying and pressing is restored by

---

[1] *Letters*, vol. i. p. 86.
[2] *Ibid.* p. 86. Hopkins continues " And in like manner with proclitics and so on :
if a strong word and its epithet or other appendage are divided so that the appendage
shall end one line and the supporting word begin the next, the last becomes emphasised
by position and heads a fall-away or diminuendo. These little graces help the ' over-
reaving ' of the verse at which I so much aim . . ."

the counterpoise of the lad's dogged return to the same
" *re*ply "

The second quatrain develops, in a beautifully apt image, the
Wordsworthian concept of the natural goodness of the young
heart. Yet the thought is not Rousseauist or Pelagian. *Home* is
God, the Source of moral perfection, so that " homing nature "
means the soul doing God's work. But before this can happen
the soul must " doff darkness ", be released by baptism and
other " high hallowing " graces from the prison-house of Original
Sin. (Though in one sense the child is " father of the man ",
the child has a responsible father or guardian who must see that
he is allowed to ' come unto Christ '). This boy had received no
long and elaborate training in the moral virtues, but he had
taken the *charisma*, the infused spiritual grace of his religion.
Father Gerard himself had quietly released the catch and let
this bird go free ; and the fine function of self-instressed or
intuitive piety (called " wild " because the will had not been
unduly tamed by instruction) had brought the young spirit in
full circle back to the sacerdotal hand.

Such beauty of character, the poet says, is worth more than
any beauty of body or mind. This boy seemed well equipped
for life ; yet there was one heavenly gift which the priest could
still solicit on his behalf—and here the poet's mood of consolation changes suddenly to a spasm of anxiety : may the boy's
eyes be opened to the need for perseverance ; may he brace his
will to the enormous task of resisting evil, of co-operating with
divine grace !

In its own *intimiste* and Christian manner, this poem deals
with one of the great archetypal problems of humanity. Blessed
are those, says Hamlet,

> " Whose blood and judgment are so well commingled
> That they are not a pipe for fortune's finger
> To sound what stop she please." (III. ii.)

This antinomy of blood and judgment, impulse and law, sensualism and asceticism, harks back to what we have already said, in
Volume I, concerning Hopkins himself and the state of tension
between *personality* and *character*. Of " blood ", impulse, sensualism considered as the biological driving force, the raw material of
the higher culture, Hopkins was no enemy. Yet few Victorians
of strict principles would have gone so far as he did when, in a

letter to Patmore, he recognized and commended in most men a streak of atavistic " tykishness " :

> " But about the ' tyke ' you did not altogether understand me. If I had said that you had less than anyone else of the Bohemian, though that is not the same thing, the meaning would have been plainer. As there is something of the ' old Adam ' in all but the holiest men and in them at least enough to make them understand it in others, so there is an old Adam of barbarism, boyishness, wildness, rawness, rankness, the disreputable, the unrefined in the refined and educated." [1]

A tyke, he explains, is " a stray sly unowned dog ". Tykishness is a quality which a man like Patmore must survey without sympathy and " wholly from without " ; but

> " I thought it was well to have ever so little of it and therefore it was perhaps a happy thing that you were entrapped into the vice of immoderate smoking, for to know one yields to a vice must help to humanize and make tolerant."

Such an attitude in Hopkins could be traced to his Jesuit training—which might also account for his opinion that *Dr. Jekyll and Mr. Hyde* is a highly significant human allegory. All this anticipated the Id-doctrine of psycho-analysis, and we adduce it here to show that Hopkins was no ' proud Jack ' among the religious. Yet in proportion as he understood the power of the unruly Id, the natural urge to pursue egocentric desires (and " my Hyde," he said, " is worse ") so he understood the need for control, imposed from within as well as from without. His poetry at this period turns on two fundamental beliefs—(1) the ultimate freedom of the will in all moral questions, and (2) the efficacy of prayer, the self-ameliorative impulse of Wordsworth's

> " Give unto me, made lowly wise,
>   The spirit of self-sacrifice ;
>   The confidence of reason give ;
> And in the light of Truth thy bondman let me live." [2]

It was his deep and philosophic veneration for the spirit of self-sacrifice which caused Hopkins to be attracted by the pro-

---

[1] *Further Letters*, p. 244 (1888). His illustration from Shakespeare is interesting : " Ancient Pistol is the typical tyke, he and all his crew are tykes, and the tykish element undergoing dilution in Falstaff and Prince Hal appears to vanish, but of course really exists, in Henry V as king."   [2] *Ode to Duty*.

fession of the soldier. If Wordsworth had not written *The Happy Warrior*, this Jesuit, we feel, would have attempted it. The two boys whose moral nature awakened his muse in 1879 were both marked out for a life of danger and struggle :

> " The little hero of the Handsome Heart has gone to school at Boulogne to be bred for a priest and he is bent on being a Jesuit.
> " I enclose a poem, the Bugler. I am half inclined to hope the Hero of it may be killed in Afghanistan." [1]

Such a hope is not demonstrably ' sado-masochism ' (for the sexual component is by no means clearly manifest) : it is, however, Hamlet's disease of extreme sensitivity—that revulsion and deep despair at the wickedness of the world. " Get thee to a nunnery " has almost become " Get thee to a cemetery ". To the inveterate Christian in Hopkins the premature death of the body was as nothing in comparison with mortal sin and perdition.

The Bugler's First Communion [2] contains enough eccentricities of style to alienate many readers who would not be disconcerted by the undisguised Roman sacramentalism ; on the other hand, many will accept the oddity and reject the doctrine. The reader who is not entirely possessed by the central emotive theme will find more than one bold device (or ' tykish ' trick) to irritate him ; but the reader who is drawn to the quick of the flame will find few breaches of literary decorum which are not integral to the poem's peculiar excellence. Hopkins risked too much when, with half an eye on Browning or W. S. Gilbert, he indulged the mongrel perversity of rhyming " boon he on " and " Communion " ; but all the other rhymes are good—or passable. The transposition in " least me quickenings lift " (stanza 10) may be pure Latinate folly ; but the starts and involutions of syntax do as a rule express tortuously the tortuous turns and recoils of living thought and genuine emotion. [3] It is this feeling of eager, inchoate expression which saves the poem from sentimentality ; it is our sense of its being immediate, unconventional, unpolished, that shows up to such advantage the beauty

---

[1] *Letters*, vol. i. p. 92. Below the latter poem in MS. " A ", Hopkins wrote : " ordered to Mooltan in the Punjaub ; was to sail Sept. 30."

[2] *Poems*, No. 23. For an account of the rhythm, see Volume I of the present work, p. 89.

[3] A fanatically puritanical and unsympathetic modern poet is reported to have called Hopkins " a posturing ecclesiastical fop ".

of the feeling and word-music, the felicity of the more lucid and
luminous phrasing. In no poem by Hopkins does the conversational and dramatically spontaneous style combine more successfully with the grand style of resonant yet imaginative declamation.
We must admit, however, that the perception of these qualities
depends to a large extent upon the rightly attuned mood and
sensibility which the reader brings to the poem.

The first two stanzas are deliberately low-pitched : the ' over-
reaving ', parentheses, and elusive rhymes (and if read properly
they *are* elusive) are all calculated to loosen and disguise the
verse-form without destroying it altogether. It is a half-casual,
Lamb-like buttonholing of the reader : ' A bugler boy from the
Cowley barracks—over the hill there (when I was stationed in
Oxford part of my work lay at that building).[1] Anglo-Irish, he
tells me. Have you ever reflected,' this laconic, ultramontane
Elia seems to ask, ' that the piety of the Irish and the practical
efficiency of the English ought to make a very good combination ? ' So at least Hopkins hopes for this Bugler, who

" Shares their best gifts surely, fall how things will. . . ."

If that " fall how things will " has any political implications they
are quickly submerged in the flood of more personal emotions ;
but those four words clearly anticipate the diffident, somewhat
querulous note on which the poem closes.

In the third stanza the poetic tone rises as the Bugler, humble
for all his red-coated glory, kneels at the altar rail :

" Here he knelt then in regimental red.
  Forth Christ from cupboard fetched, how fain I of feet
          To his youngster take his treat !
  Low-latched in leaf-light housel his too huge godhead.

" There ! and your sweetest sendings, ah divine,
  By it, heavens, befall him ! as a heart Christ's darling, dauntless ;
          Tongue true, vaunt- and tauntless ;
  Breathing bloom of a chastity in mansex fine.

  Frowning and forefending angel-warder
  Squander the hell-rook ranks [that] sally to molest him ;
          March, kind comrade, abreast him ;
  Dress his days to a dexterous and starlight order."

---

[1] *Letters*, vol. i. p. 97.

The sensuous beauty and lofty ethical meaning of such expressions as " Breathing bloom of a chastity in mansex fine " and " Dress his days to a dexterous and starlight order " require no commentary. But to understand the poet's full meaning we have to realize the strength and far-reaching significance of his belief in the Real Presence, in the efficacy of the sanctified wafer as a spiritual prophylactic. To call the Host a " treat " was to face boldly the charge of triviality or exaggeration ; but no other word in the language has a " prepossession of feeling " so rich, apt, and immediate as this one. The wholly or largely sensual pleasure of a child before a dish of strawberries or a day's outing was for Hopkins the right image (when duly exalted by context) to express the keen spiritual delight of the true believer in the *latens deitas* of the Eucharist. We must realize, too, that the whole poem embodies the emotions, hopes, and fears of a sincere and unusually sensitive Catholic priest in the very act of administering the Sacrament to an unusually promising communicant. The priest's emotion is, of course, being recollected in comparative tranquillity, and three of the stanzas refer to antecedents ; but the unique quality of the poem is in its subtle yet sincere analysis of what was for Hopkins an apical experience, a moment of profound ontological import. " That brow and bead of being " as he calls the boy—might he not become " An our day's God's own Galahad " ? In one sense, that ministration was a supreme test of the efficacy of the Eucharist. The style has an almost clinical air ; we seem to be watching a delicate spiritual operation, of which we are made to feel the sharp actuality :

> " There ! and your sweetest sendings, ah divine,
>   By it, heavens, befall him ! "

Thought is streaked, stabbed with emotion, as it is in reality ; as Miss Phare has said, the two elements have not been kneaded into a smooth consistency.

No less convincing is the priest's joy at finding up at the barracks a disciple who, like the Italian boy of *The Handsome Heart*, was tractable by reason of a " self-instressed " devotion :

> " How it does my heart good, visiting that bleak hill,
>   When limber liquid youth, that to all I teach
>   Yields tender as a pushed peach,
>   Hies headstrong to its wellbeing of a self-wise self-will ! "

This well deserved gratification at seeing one's own earnest efforts rewarded is like the luxury of walking on soft springy turf :

> " Then though I should tread tufts of consolation [1]
> Days after, so I in a sort deserve to
>   And do serve God to serve to
> Just such slips of soldiery Christ's royal ration.
>
> Nothing else is like it, no, not all so strains
> Us : "

None of the priest's work is so exciting, exacting, or when successful so rewarding, as this task of watching over the spiritual welfare of the young.

How apposite, in these passages, are the military images : " hellrook *ranks* [that] [2] *sally* to molest him " (where " -rook " suggests blackguardly swindlers and seducers : Hopkins was no sentimentalist in dealing with the Army), " *March*, kind comrade, *abreast* him ", " *Dress* his days ", " Christ's royal *ration* " (the last word rhyming, in sense as in sound, with " consolation ") ! Christ is at once private soldier, sergeant, quartermaster, and monarch ; as the poet says elsewhere :

> " Mark Christ our King. He knows war, served this soldiering through ; "

and we shall see by and by how this hierarchy of being is clinched in the one divine Person.

The moral crux of the poem is that unforgettable line,

> " Dress his days to a dexterous and starlight order."

This was probably the first subliminal *motif* ; for as we have seen before in our analysis of Hopkins's poetry, one thought may be like an artesian well tapping reserves of unconscious memories and desires. There is a poem by Henry Vaughan, *The Constellation*, which is radically related and in many ways complementary to *The Bugler* : it supplies, in fact, the " underthought " of Hopkins's poem.

Having observed how the stars move " with exact obedience ", the Silurist turns his eyes down to describe that same

---

[1] The stressing of this line is from MS. " B ".

[2] We have restored the relative pronoun here and on p. 297 because we wish it had never been omitted. See *Preface to Notes* by R. B. in *Poems of G. M. H.*

materialism and spiritual disunity in the life of man which later gave Hopkins grounds for such deep disquiet :

> " He gropes beneath here, and with restless care
>   First makes, then hugs a snare ; "

he adores " dead dust ", broad acres and rich crops, but " seldom doth make heav'n his glass ".[1]   (So Hopkins, standing before his youthful communicant, thought of the snares *he* might hug ; thought too, as Vaughan did, of the phenomenal courage that holiness demanded : " Who kneels, or sighs a life, is mad ".) Vaughan then addresses the stars :

> " But seeks he your obedience, order, light,
>   Your calm and well trained flight,
>   Where, though the glory differ in each star,
>   Yet is there peace there, and no war ? "[2]

This anticipates Hopkins's view that mankind may be, nay, should be, richly diverse in personality yet spiritually united by faith and moral principle.   As Vaughan's poem reveals a passionate anxiety for the spiritual chastity and unity of the English nation, so Hopkins's poem is a prayer for the steady promotion ' in Christ ' of this Bugler and all such " slips of soldiery ", such " beads of being ". Like the " lily-showers " and " rose-flakes " of *The Deutschland*,[3] all these May blossoms of humanity are seen as petals showered in homage before the feet of Christ as He journeys to Calvary and Paradise :

> " . . . fresh youth fretted in a bloomfall all portending
>   That sweet's sweeter ending ;
>   Realm both Christ is heir to and there reigns."

The " sweeter ending " is the beatified state described in *The Golden Echo* : it is the " flower of beauty " perpetuated ; " O it is an all youth ! " Christ shows how the Reward is to be earned and bestows it in person on those who follow Him. So the

---

[1] Stanza 5.

[2] Stanza 8 ; cf. Wordsworth's *Ode to Duty* :

> " Thou dost preserve the stars from wrong ;
> And the most ancient heavens, through thee, are fresh and strong."

[3] Stanzas 21 and 22.

hierarchy of ' all ranks ', the diapason of human life, closes full in the Man-God.[1]

From stanza 9 to the end of *The Bugler*, Hopkins wavers between a firm missionary faith and a Hamlet-like shuddering and shrinking from reality :

> " O now work well that sealing sacred ointment ! "

So eager is he to exorcize evil that his words forestall and by-pass one another :

> " O for now charms, arms, what bans off bad [2]
>   And locks love ever in a lad !
> Let me though see no more of him, and not disappointment

>   2   3   4   1   5   6   9   7   8
> Those sweet hopes quell whose least me quickenings lift
>   9a   10a   11a   12a   5a   6a   7a   8a
> In scarlet or somewhere of some day seeing
>   9b   10b   11b   12b
>   That brow and bead of being
> An our day's God's own Galahad."

The numbers from 1 to 9 suggest the normal word-order. The similar numbering of certain word-groups indicates the inter-locking of thoughts (e.g. 5a can follow 4, 9a and 9b can both follow 8a), as though the explosive force of barely contained emotion had disrupted the logical sequence. This is the " passionate emotion which seems to try and utter all its words in one " [3] ; for such emotion, the ideal written language would

---

[1] The connexion we have traced between Vaughan's *Constellation* and Hopkins's *Bugler* is substantiated by other resemblances and verbal echoes. Vaughan deprecates both the Civil War and the wars between Christian sects in terms which to Hopkins must have seemed like an indictment of all Protestantism :

> " But here, commission'd by a black self-will,
>   The sons the father kill, etc. " (st. 10).

" Our guides," he says, " prove wand'ring stars " ; and Hopkins feared that his Bugler would " rankle and roam / In backwheels though bound home "—would be seduced by heresy as well as carnal sin. Moreover Vaughan's " black " (used twice) becomes in Hopkins's poem " hellrook " ; his " self-will " is reformed as " self-wise self-will ". He also uses the words " that hill (st. 1), " slips " (st. 4) and " dress " (" Give to Thy spouse her perfect and pure dress, / Beauty and holiness ")—all of which are found in *The Bugler*, the last two with a reversal of grammatical function.

[2] I.e. ' O now there is need for that grace which charms, arms, etc.'

[3] Charles Williams, in Introduction to *Poems of G. M. H.*, 2nd edn. p. xv.

be two-dimensional, not one-dimensional, so that co-ordinate ideas could spring simultaneously from their common base :

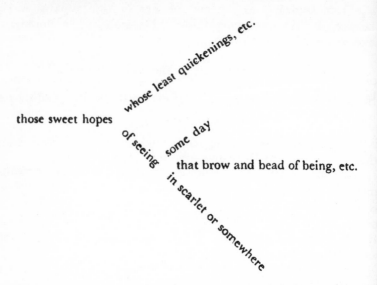

those sweet hopes

whose least quickenings, etc.

of seeing some day

that brow and bead of being, etc.

in scarlet or somewhere

Whether such licentious transpositions should ever have been indulged in is certainly a debatable point.   Here they seem successful, because the poet has boldly grasped white-hot iron with his bare hands and wrought it into a pleasing pattern. The perfect consonancy and assonance weld the ill-sorted parts into a flowing design, imposing the harmony of truth upon timorous hope and tortuous aspiration.   Hopkins has *inscaped* his own experience; but other poets will "do likewise" at their peril.

Like Hamlet again, Hopkins now seeks comfort in the idea of predestination :

> "Though this child's drift
> Seems by a divine doom channelled, nor do I cry
> Disaster there ; "

yet he cannot help thinking of the degradation and profanity this boy may be dragged through on his devious journey to heaven.   'Discipline, both military and moral, is apt to be resented.   What sins may fester in his conscience' ("rankle" means all this.)   May God spare him the trouble I foresee ! Ready to resign the lad's fate to Christ, and at the same time to battle with Omnipotence if prayer should "go disregarded"

Hopkins, still " poised but on the quiver ", lapses grudgingly into a sort of emotional stalemate :

" Forward-like, but however, and like favourable heaven heard
      these."

Hopkins could not have maintained the extreme moral and pietistic sensitivity of this poem. The position of Mr. T. S. Eliot's *Ash Wednesday* :

" Teach me to care and not to care ",

is a paradox which every Christian must solve emotionally, though the intellectual solution may elude him.

At times, no doubt, Hopkins was bored or irritated by his parishioners ; [1] but his fastidious brooding care for the young is apparent in *The Bugler*, and it reappears in *Brothers*. This poem, based on a real incident, was conceived in 1879 while Hopkins was sub-minister at Mount St. Mary's, Chesterfield, but was not completed until 1880.

Henry, a reserved, sensitive boy, is waiting for the curtain to rise on a school play in which his younger brother, the impulsive John, has been given a part. Would the young rogue make a fool of himself ?—

" . . . then fear, then joy
Ran revel in the elder boy."

Noticing Henry's unusual empathic concern, the priest watches him closely, preferring the " tender by-play " of this real-life performance to the stage fiction which provokes it. Such natural curiosity may have a deep psychic origin : in this case the boy Henry, who is " wrung all on love's rack ", is virtually the symbol, the ' objective correlative ', of the poet's own intense and slightly neurotic solicitude for all young ' bloods ' and impulsive Johns. Thus Hopkins observes, precisely and minutely, such " truth's tokens " as lip-biting, blushing and the character-istically impatient driving of " Clutched hands down through clasped knees ".

Awaiting his cue in the wings and almost bursting with what is now called ' exhibitionism ', the brass-bold imp, young John,

---

[1] Of his Oxford parishioners he wrote : " And I believe they criticized what went on in our church a great deal too freely, which is d——d impertinence of the sheep towards the shepherd, and if it had come markedly before me I should have given them my mind." (*Letters*, vol. i. p. 97.)

is the symbol of that adventurous side of Hopkins's nature which we have already identified with the Windhover and the " dare-gale skylark ".

After two tedious acts John's cue comes at last, and Henry

" heart-forsook,
Dropped eyes and dared not look."

But the little Roscius scores a resounding success :

" Eh, how all rung !
Young dog, he did give tongue ! "

In just the same manner Hopkins the poet, " barbarous in beauty ", throwing decorum to the winds, had proclaimed the glory and terror of God in the " presumptuous jugglery " of his new rhythm.

In the elder brother's attitude towards the younger there was none of the usual rivalry and jealousy : the self-effacement of the one was complementary to the self-assertion of the other ; and so it was (though not absolutely and finally so) with the priest-and-poet duality in Hopkins.

Pathos, said the latter, " has a point as precise as jest has " and the climactic point of this poem is in line 37 :

" But Harry—in his hands he has flung
His tear-tricked cheeks of flame
For fond love and for shame."

Schoolboy emotions have undergone a change since the days of Dean Farrar ; but the sentiment here, though extreme and possibly exaggerated, is true in kind. Obliquely, moreover, it signifies that the priest who could not perform his sacred duties to his own satisfaction was half-ashamed of his poetic muse ; yet because he knew that his poetry was dedicated to the same great cause, flowed from and returned to the same transcendent source, he loved that too with the overmastering, supra-rational love of Henry for young John.

The poem may thus be read as a psycho-neurotic symptom but because the conflict in Hopkins between ' character ' and ' personality ',[1] between ' extravert ' and ' introvert ', had not yet reached the pathological stage, the poem can and indeed

---

[1] As defined in Vol. I, chap. i. of the present work.

should be read first of all as a straightforward description of an admirable brotherly affection.   The last image,

> " There's comfort then, there's salt ",

links the piece with *The Candle Indoors*, in which a tender concern for the spiritual welfare of others turns suddenly to self-denunciation.   The salt of Henry's tears is the very salt of Christ, whereby men become ' the salt of the earth ' ; and the savour of that salt (despite the acidic reactions of a Nietzsche) is not yet entirely lost :

> " Nature, bad, base, and blind,
> Dearly thou canst be kind ;
> There dearly then, dearly,
> I'll cry thou canst be kind."

It was possible for Hopkins to treat this subject without morbid sentimentality or cynicism because the conflict between his own real and ideal selves was not so devastating as some critics have maintained.   His ideal self was in fact neither all saint nor all artist, but rather a combination of the two—the saintly artist or the artistic saint.   That is partly the reason why he disliked Goethe, Swinburne, and Victor Hugo and praised Savonarola, George Herbert, and Carl Maria von Weber.[1]

Hopkins's poems about childhood and adolescence spring from something deeper than the mere accidents of professional duty. These poems reveal an important affinity with Vaughan, Traherne, Blake, and Wordsworth.   Vaughan, in a piece called *Childhood*, speaks of

> " the short, swift span
> Where weeping virtue parts from man ;
> Where love without lust dwells, and bends
> What way we please without self-ends."

That, when set against the premature sophistication of the modern child, may seem untrue ; yet it stands with Hopkins's " fine function wild and self-instressed " and " Yields tender as a pushed peach " as a picture of what childhood should be and still largely is.   Hopkins saw that a right conception of childhood, of its immediate and symbolic value, is one of the main ontological roots of the Christian faith.   In a child, even more than in a bluebell, he found the key to the mystery of Christ's

---

[1] Of Weber he said : " He was a good man, I believe, with no hateful affectation of playing the fool and behaving like a blackguard." (*Letters*, vol. i. p. 98.) For his opinion of Hugo and Swinburne (" those plagues of mankind ") see *ibid*. p. 39.

beauty. How profoundly Vaughan was to influence Wordsworth, and how close the latter was to the child-concept of Christianity, can be felt in the Silurist's

> " An age of mysteries ! which he
>   Must live twice that would God's face see."

Confined to the edges and bordering light of that symbolic age of innocence, Vaughan cried, " O for thy centre and midday ! " And the same aspiration made Wordsworth commit the bold psychic hypallage of projecting his own mature mystical cognition into the " six years' darling " of the *Immortality* ode.

Between such insight (which is more comprehensible than Coleridge believed) and the " blethery bathos " of Swinburne's babies (which made " a Herodian " of Hopkins),[1] there is the pure ' infant eye ' with which Traherne looked at childhood. This reappears in Blake's *Songs of Innocence*, but develops an alarming doctrinaire twist in the *Songs of Experience*. Hopkins, for all his idealism and Trahernian moments, takes for the most part a more normal view of this particular subject. He knew that nature, even in children, could be bad, base, and morally blind ; yet Childhood was always sacred. Because of his own intellectual subtlety and the more distracted, sceptical age in which he lived, he was unable or unwilling to maintain the fresh and salutary but somewhat monotonously repetitive vision of a Traherne. Nevertheless his attitude to the child was very close to the profound simplicity of Christ's injunction : " Suffer little children to come unto Me."

In another poem of 1880, written amid the " charming heartiness " of his working-class Liverpool parishioners, Hopkins brings out the childlike passivity and natural piety which subsist, though often precariously, at the core of human personality. *Felix Randal* has recently been called " the best short poem in the language ",[2] and the praise is not extravagant. A full transcription of the poem, with all its outrides, has been given in Volume I ; [3] in the present chapter, therefore, we shall merely attempt to show the skill with which the emotive and dramatic potentialities of the Italian sonnet-form have here been utilized and even extended.

The first quatrain opens colloquially with the announcement

---

[1] *Letters*, vol. i. p. 304. Hopkins is a little unfair to Swinburne.
[2] Mr. George Orwell in his review of our first volume, *The Observer*, Nov. 12, 1944.
[3] Chapter iii.

of the farrier's death and a reminiscence of his sickness and decline. This rises to a swift minor climax at " big-boned and hardy-handsome " (words which already anticipate the close) and sinks to a *rallentando* and *diminuendo* as the man weakens under his " fatal four disorders ". The last word, " contended ", strikes the keynote of the next ' act ' or quatrain.

" Sickness broke him. Impatient | he cursed at first, but mended
    Being anointed and all : "

The short opening sentence, the caesural pause, the sharp rhyme of " cursed at first "—all combine to produce an expressional rhythm which suggests those staccato bursts of rage, all-too-familiar tokens of deadly warfare between the failing body and the proud, resentful spirit. Hopkins, with that Elian technique already mentioned, now takes a quick leap forward to show how resigned Felix had become by the time he had received the last sacrament of Extreme Unction (the anointing of the eyes, ears, mouth, etc., with consecrated oil), and then as quickly retraces his steps to explain that " a heavenlier heart " (a mood of sincere repentance and resignation) had set in some months before, when the priest had taken the Holy Eucharist to his bedside. Before receiving that " sweet reprieve and ransom " Felix must have made his confession ; but as his statement was possibly not as complete an unburdening as it should have been, the generous priest implores a total pardon on the strength of the dead man's good intention : " Ah well, God rest him all road ever he offended ! "

The sestet rises to the universal without diminishing—nay, by actually heightening our sense of the individual. It recapitulates the two contrasted themes of the octave—triumphant strength and pathetic weakness : but here, fittingly, the order is reversed. The love given and received by the dying springs from a deep intuitive sense of common origin and fate. Like the climax of pure pathos in the fourth act of a Shakespearian tragedy, the first tercet belongs to those most poignant things which are summed up in three words of Virgil—*sunt lacrimae rerum* :

" My tongue had taught thee comfort, | touch had quenched thy
        tears,
" Thy tears that touched my heart, child, | Felix, poor Felix Randal ; "

In the last tercet the motivation is both direct and oblique. The sheer force and beauty of the poetry will be felt at once ;

but its subjective and theological implications might easily be misunderstood. This tone-picture of the physical prowess and carefree swagger of the younger Felix (appropriate name!) is a necessary contrast to his later sad helplessness. Yet if the poem had ended on the 'note of line 11 it would surely have failed—from sheer sentimentality. As it stands, the last tercet is at once a funeral panegyric and (on the text of ' How are the mighty fallen!') a prudential warning. There is a neurotic element, perhaps, in the fact that this unpractical priest of tender constitution so admired muscular strength; and *Felix Randal* is not primarily a page from the spiritual diary of a professional soul-hunter. True, the priest's gratification at the sick man's change of heart is there, plainly enough; but Hopkins was also mortal man, and felt as a man. He meant the reader to hold in equipoise both the pain of dissolution and the joy of salvation. In heaven, as he says in *The Golden Echo* (1882), " whatever's prized and passes of us . . ." is fastened with the tenderest truth " To its own best being and its loveliest of youth ". Hence the poet concludes with a picture of Felix, his hammers and his horses, which is a veritable apotheosis, or at least an apocalypse :

" When thóu at the rándom grim fórge, | pówerful amídst péers,

Didst fettle for the great gray drayhorse | his bright and battering sandal."

Morally, the young Randal was haphazard, like the brickwork of his forge. The clumping assonance and thumping alliteration are to our ears magically transformed by the evocative mythopoeic words—" peers " and above all " sandals ". Horse-shoes are heavy but sandals are *light*. Hence for one reader the above lines are both reminiscence and promise. He would rather be a pagan suckled in a creed outworn than fail to catch, in these lines, the suggestion of angel-postilions—of hooves, lightning-shod, beating aerially the golden macadam of some translunary paradise.

Since the twentieth-century climate of opinion is (perhaps temporarily) inimical towards metaphysics and religion, it is only to be expected that many present-day readers of *Felix Randal* will attach more importance to what they consider Hopkins's spontaneous, natural, pagan brooding over the fact of dissolution than to the dogmatic Christian elements—the redeeming qualities of humility, repentance, and the Sacraments. Hence the general agnostic approval of that remaining poem of 1880, *Spring and Fall : to a young child*, for this piece seems wholly pagan in its handling of an age-old fascinating theme. Like the stoicism, pity, and alleged ' realism ' of Thomas Hardy and A. E. Housman, it seems to indicate a courageous ' facing of the facts ', a tacit acknowledgment of the triumph of science over ' illusion '. But let us examine this episode of young Margaret (" not founded on any real incident ") [1], for which Hopkins intended to compose some plainsong music : to write ' churchy ' music for a conscious lapse into materialism would have been for him a strange undertaking.

The plain, direct meaning of the poem is as follows :

' Child, are you sad because all the beautiful leaves in Golden-grove are falling ? Have you the unspoilt vision, the natural piety, to care for leaves just as you would care for dolls, picture-books and the like ? When you are older you will not be so sensitive to such ordinary changes in your environment : even though the lovely foliage of whole forests will drop to earth and rot away, you will remain unmoved. Nevertheless you will shed plenty of tears hereafter, and as time goes on you will understand your grief. In this life, sorrow takes many forms ; we are saddened by all kinds of losses and disappointments. Yet all sadness springs from one and the same source, and that is the knowledge (which you, already, have vaguely and intuitively divined) that we human beings, just like leaves, must all wither and die. In grieving for leaves falling you are virtually lamenting, in advance, your own inevitable death and dissolution.'

As no young child could possibly understand this poem, it is obviously intended for the adult eavesdropper. Moreover no mere prose paraphrase can do justice to the overtones of ambiguity in such a line as " And yet you will weep and know why." The last line but one, " It is the blight man was born for," seems to give the lie to Hopkins's belief in the pristine perfection and immortality of Adam and Eve ; for it was man's first disobedience that " brought death into the world and all our woe." But we must remember that Hopkins felt, with Duns Scotus, that man's free will is really compatible with ' necessity '—that is, with God's foreknowledge : man was born

---

[1] But the name " Goldengrove " will be found on the ordnance map of North Wales : several miles N.W. of St. Beuno's is ' Goldengrove Farm '.

to sin and die, though had he chosen he could have remained immaculate. Thus the doctrine of the Fall of Man is suggested in the title of the poem, and the ' underthought ' is derived from *Isaiah*, lxiv. 6–7 :

> " But we are all as an unclean thing, and all our righteous-nesses are as filthy rags ; *and we all do fade as a leaf ; and our iniquities, like the wind, have taken us away.*"

And at the close of the passage the same thought is hammered home : " Thou hast consumed us because of our iniquities."

In verse 7, moreover, Isaiah introduces another thought : " for Thou hast hid Thy face from us " ; and this element in the underthought of *Spring and Fall* harks back to the sub-title of *Nondum* (1866), " Verily Thou art a God that hidest Thyself ", which also comes from Isaiah, and which helps to explain the poet's attitude towards death in the later poem : ' Every man is doomed to confront the fact of death. There are moments when faith in survival, in the resurrection of the body, is not strong enough to mitigate the natural horror of " tombs and worms and tumbling to decay " '. *Spring and Fall* is like ' detail from ' the natural setting of that larger picture, *That Nature is a Heraclitean Fire and of the comfort of the Resurrection.*

The poem which asks to be treated next is one which was begun five years later, *Spelt from Sibyl's Leaves*. Like *Spring and Fall*, this " longest sonnet ever made " [1] contains no explicit reference to Christian doctrine ; in both, however, we can discern an ' underthought ' which is pagan as well as Hebraic. That image of death in the eye and heart of Margaret is reminis-cent of that passage in Book vi of Virgil's *Aeneid* where the boys and maidens crowd down to the bank of Styx, " as numerous as withered leaves fall in woods with the first cold of autumn." Similarly the title, *Spelt from Sibyl's Leaves*, is a reference to the Cumaean Sibyl, prophetic votaress of Apollo, who conducted Aeneas into Avernus in the same book of the Aeneid.

' Sibyl ' means ' will of God '. Hopkins appreciated the deep piety of Virgil (*anima naturaliter christiana*), whose account of Avernus contains an anticipation of Catholic eschatology. Pro-vided the pagan conception of God, Heaven, and Hell seemed to be " in earnest ", the scrupulous Hopkins was prepared to

---

[1] *Letters*, vol. i. p. 245 : " I have at last completed but not quite finished the longest sonnet ever made and no doubt the longest making. It is in 8-foot lines and essays effects almost musical." (Nov. 26, 1886.)

admit an implicit reference even to Apollo. Hence for a distinctly moral purpose he " spells " (interprets a mystery) from the imaginary and symbolic book of the Sibyl, into whom, as Virgil says, " prophetic Apollo breathes an enlarged mind and spirit, disclosing to her the future." [1] Hopkins, too, claims to disclose and interpret the future, and his choice of a pagan title would seem to suggest that he wanted, in this poem, to point out the highest common factor in the religion of pagan antiquity and in his own Catholicism.

At the very beginning of Virgil's account of the descent into Avernus occurs a passage which might have suggested to Hopkins the central image of his own poem :

> " Ibant obscuri sola sub nocte per umbra,
>
> .   .   .   .
>
> quale per incertam lunam sub luce maligna
> est iter in silvis, ubi caelum condidit umbra
> Iuppiter, et rebus nox abstulit atra colorem."

> (They moved along darkling, under the solitary night through the shade . . . as is a journey in woods beneath the unsteady moon, *under a scanty light*, when Jupiter has wrapped the heavens in shade and black night *has stripped objects of colour*.) [2]

In *Sibyl's Leaves* objects are stripped of both colour and individual form with the approach of night ; and under the symbol of nightfall, ' judgment ' and ' damnation ' are fused in the self-torment of a sensitive soul. The poem's culminating point, the division into *two*—" black, white ; right, wrong," contains another probably unconscious reference to Virgil : " Nox ruit, Aenea ", night comes on apace,

> " while we waste hours in lamentations. This is the place where the path divides itself *in two* : the right is what leads beneath great Pluto's walls ; by this our way to Elysium lies ; but the left carries on the punishments of the wicked and conveys to cursed Tartarus." [3]

It is interesting to note also the resemblance between Hopkins's " ware of a world where but these two tell " (line 13) and the function of Virgil's Rhadamanthus, a judge in hell who extorts confession of secret sins hugged in a vain impunity until the late hour of death :

> " quae quis apud superos, furto laetatus inani,
> distulit in seram commissa piacula mortem." [4]

---

[1] *Aeneid*, vi. lines 11-12. cf. also stanza 73 of Marvell's *Upon Appleton House*.
[2] *Aeneid*, vi. lines 268-72.   [3] *Ibid*. lines 539-43.   [4] *Ibid*. lines 568-9.

But before we consider the full implications of Hopkins's last two lines we should go back and trace the development of the moral theme from a naturalistic beginning.

The opening is *adagio* :

" Eárnest, eárthless, équal, attúneable, | vaúlty, volúminous, . . stupéndous

Evening strains to be tíme's vást, | womb-of-all, home-of-all, hearse-of-all night."

Much meaning is packed into those epithets in the first line. Evening is "earnest" because it is quiet and conduces to solemn thought : this attribute strikes the keynote of the poem. Evening (from *even*=level, equal) is "earthless" and "equal" because it smooths out the varied aspects of day ; because the eye of man, drawn upwards as the light is drained from the landscape, tends to lose itself in the tranquillity of space, in the *equally diffused* lingering luminosity of the zenith. It is "attuneable" because the expanse of clear sky harmonizes with the mood of the soul, or (by synaesthesia) peals out in unison with our thought at such a time. In four epithets Hopkins has concentrated the mystical feeling of Wordsworth's "The holy time is quiet as a nun" and Leopardi's *L'Infinito*. In the latter poem the mind creates for itself "sovrumani silenzi", unearthly silences, whereby it remembers the eternal [1] ; but now, as in Leopardi's poem, the mind retains its connexion with earth. The next words, "vaulty" and "voluminous", denote shape and size. We feel the earth turning and slowly unrolling the vast dim tapestry of the gloaming sky ; but there is also a suggestion of *light* (note the concealed ' luminous ') and of *tone* (' vault ', ' volume ', ' strains '). Thus if we take these words with the foregoing aural image in "attuneable" we seem to hear a swelling voluntary under a vast cathedral roof. No wonder the poet catches his breath before summing up the experience in that comprehensive "stupendous" !

The poet describes, or rather suggests, the progressive *scapes* of evening—sunset, twilight, and dusk. There is a tenseness of

---

[1] E.g. the lines :

> " Ma sedendo e mirando, interminati
> Spazi di la da quella, e sovrumani
> Silenzi, e profondissima quiete
> Io nel pensier mi fingo. . . ."

expectancy in the atmosphere (and also in the diction) as evening "strains" to become night. Anticipating the darkness which engulfs all objects, Hopkins feels night to be the all-engrossing symbol of birth, life, and death—of the whole mystery of our being. The triple image is pre-Christian, atavistic; the poet's imagination is trying to embrace all time, all experience.

In the next *scape* of evening, Hopkins seems to be remembering Milton's "hornèd moon" among her "spangled sisters bright"; [1] but *this* horn is *heard* as well as seen:

"Her fond yellow hornlight wound to the west, | her wild hollow
    hoarlight hung to the height
Waste; her earliest stars, earl-stars, | stars principal overbend us,
Fire-féaturing heaven."

There can be no doubt that *hornlight* means the moon; in an early draft (Dublin Note-book) the epithet "lean" is bracketed with "fond". There is, however, a discrepancy in the fact that whereas the fading "hoarlight" in the zenith can truly be said to *waste*, the moon would surely grow brighter as the night deepened; and the setting of the moon (the early draft has "low with the west") could hardly be called 'wasting'. For these reasons we still hanker, though perversely, after the reading already suggested in Volume I [2]—that "hornlight" means the last saffron "horny rays" of the sunset. The tender nostalgic associations of "fond" would apply to either phenomenon, and the clockwise mechanical motion in "wound to the west" indicates the inexorable march of time whichever way we take it.

The compound "earl-stars" chimes with "earliest", but not in sound only. The original meaning of *earl* was probably 'quick, active, keen', and if we combine this with the later sense ('noble, chief') the compound is like an antiphonal echo from the past. In the vault of space the stars limn the features of heaven in points of fire; as they do so they "overbend us"—suggesting remote superhuman powers which draw nearer to man as his familiar world becomes less distinct:

"For earth | her being has unbound, her
    dapple is at an end, as—
tray or aswarm, all throughther, in throngs; | self ín self steepèd and
    páshed—quíte
Disremembering, dísmémbering | áll now."

[1] Paraphrase of Psalm cxxxvi., stanza 9.   [2] Chapter v. pp. 166-7.

Ostensibly these words mean that with the fading of daylight earth's individual features and variegated forms are either lost to the eye completely or merged in shadowy neutral masses, driven all through one another ; but the hint of something more violent and catastrophic than a mere visual transformation is already there in " pashed " and " dismembering ".

It is at this point, as Dr. Leavis says,[1] that the poet is suddenly struck with nature's parable. The whole " warpèd world " will one day be undone,[2] dismembered ; all its variety will be " unbound ", its richness of *selving* utterly forgotten. At the last day will come the Judgment ; but even before that event the poet must think of his own spiritual state :

> " Heart, you round me right
> With : Our evening is over us ; our night | whelms, whelms, and will end us.
> Only the beak-leaved boughs dragonish | damask the tool-smooth bleak light ; black,
> Ever so black on it. . . ."

His heart tells him quietly but roundly that he must give heed to the signs. Earth's brightness and dapple have been resolved into atavistic images charged with menace—the beaks of vultures and the claws of dragons, symbolic shapes fiercely etched on the cold steely sky, like patterns damascened on a sword-blade (the sword of Justice). There is a note of almost childish dread in " black, *ever so* black on it " ; those beak-leaves are truly Sibylline, prophetic :

> " Our tale, O our oracle ! | Let life, waned, ah let life wind
> Off her once skeined stained veined variety | upon, all on two spools ; part, pen, pack
> Now her all in two flocks, two folds—black, white ; | right, wrong. . . ."[3]

The chiasmus in " black, white ; right, wrong " (a deliberate emendation of " wrong, right ") suggests the difficulty which even a just man may encounter in distinguishing and choosing between good and evil.

Estimate therefore, Hopkins concludes, take heed of and keep constantly in mind just these two opposites :

---

[1] *New Bearings, loc. cit.* [2] See *Lines for a Picture of St. Dorothea*, stanza 7.
[3] Note that " wind " (l. 10) harks back to " wound " (l. 3).

" reckon but, reck but, mind

But these two ; ware of a world where but these | two tell, each
   off the other ; of a rack

Where, selfwrung, selfstrung, sheathe- and shelterless, | :houghts
   against thoughts in groans grind."

Beware of the Judgment ; anticipate that spiritual world in
which only these two attributes count, each unmistakably set off
by the other. For unless you heed this oracle your punishment
will be total and eternal separation from God, the unremitting
torment of contemplating your own sins.

Confirmation of this reading is found in some notes made by
Hopkins during a retreat at Beaumont in 1883 : [1]

> " But after death the soul is left to its own resources, with
> only the *scapes* and *species* of its past life ; which being unsupple-
> mented or undisplaced by a fresh continual current of experience,
> absorb and press upon its consciousness. . . .
>
> " God is good and the stamp, seal, or instress he sets on each
> scape is of *right, good* or *bad, wrong*. Now the sinner who has
> preferred his own good, as revenge, drunkenness, to God's good,
> true good, and God, has that evil between him and God, by his
> attachment to which and God's rejection of it he is carried and
> swept away to an infinite distance from God ; and the stress
> and strain of this removal is his eternity of punishment."

The sharp terrifying beauty of *Sibyl's Leaves* was separated by
twenty hardening and chastening years from the slightly languid
asceticism of *The Habit of Perfection*. But although the former
was written at the time and in the mood of " life, waned "—the
period of the agonizing " I wake and feel the fell of dark "—its
subjectivity admits of a more impersonal and universal interpretation ; it does not record the same acrid self-disgust, and is
rather an admonition than a lament.

Its style, with its clotted consonants, harsh staccato and
brusque emphasis, makes it one of the hardest of all the poems
to appreciate. To produce the best effect it should be spoken
by several voices, like a Greek chorus, some parts in unison,
other parts antiphonally. It is hard to believe that such impassioned Euphuism could be the expression of one heart and
brain ; shared out, it produces the effect of statement and
corroboration—of tone, overtone and echo ; it becomes credible.

This powerful inner rhythm working through a progression

[1] Unpublished MS. in " H " ; the notes are dated Sept. 3-10.

of ideas in binary and ternary groups was not achieved all at once. Going back to the poems of 1881–2 we find in the sonnet " As kingfishers catch fire " a bold and successful experiment in closely patterned texture and expressional rhythm.

The vocalic quantities in the first line tell us that whereas the kingfisher darts and is gone, the dragonfly draws its zig-zag flight less rapidly across our vision :

" As kíngfishers catch fire, dragonflies draw flame. . . ."

In the next three lines internal rhyme sets up onomatopoeic cross-rhythms, which may be analysed thus :

(1) As tumbled over rim

in roundy wells

(2)   Stones ring ;
like each tucked string

tells,
bell's,

each hung

(3)

Bow swung
finds tongue

to fling

out broad its name :

In this interlacing of rhymes the resonant *ng* sound occurs six times. The amazing craftsman has also managed to weave into the fabric four groups of triple alliteration :

*t*umbled,	*t*ucked,	*t*ells
*r*im,	*r*oundy,	*r*ing
*S*tones,	*s*tring,	-*s t*ongue
*b*ell's,	*B*ow,	*b*road

Yet all this art is not unduly obtrusive when the poem is read aloud, and indeed the fulness of harmony would be lost if these correspondences were not submerged in the regular flow of the five-stress lines. Such an analysis as the above is not a requisite of appreciation, but it seems to bear out what Hopkins was always thinking and saying about the close connexion between art and mathematics.[1]

It would take much space to exhaust the beauties of this sonnet. The whole octave is a cunning synthesis of archaic and

[1] E.g. *Letters*, vol. ii. pp. 71–2, 135 ; *Further Letters*, p. 129.

popular elements : *roundy* is a nursery word to suit a childish action, and "bell's/Bow (the curved interior of the cup) vaguely but sweetly suggests ' Bow bells '. In line 5 " each mortal thing " is a reminiscence of *Who is Sylvia ?* [1] and is also a common expletive ; but its meaning here is precise and important : for just as all finite things proclaim their individuality, flash or ring out their particular *selving*, so the infinite or immortal parts of human personality should do this too, by virtue of the grace and all-engrossing godhead in Christ. Then the sestet gives an example ; the just man " justices "—

" Acts in God's eye what in God's eye he is—
  Christ—for Christ plays in ten thousand places. . . ."

All physical beauty in human beings moved Hopkins to reverence, for it reminded him of the perfection of Christ, " beauty's self and beauty's giver ". But beauty of character, which can be made to shine through even deformed features, testifies to the higher beauty of Christ's soul, the Holy Spirit. Unfortunately, as the poet said in his Welsh *cywydd* and as he repeats now in the next sonnet, *Ribblesdale*, even the humblest things of Earth, like water, trees and " louchèd low grass ", bear greater testimony to God's goodness and his true religion than man himself, for all his special gifts.

The sonnet just examined shows an advance in thought beyond the simple admiration and ' wishful-thinking ' of *The Lantern Out of Doors*, and the poet gives us another variation on the same theme in the alexandrine sonnet which Miss E. E. Phare has rightly described as " a delicately balanced piece of work "—*To what serves Mortal Beauty ?* (1885). Developing from a tense, elliptical opening into a comparatively regular rhythm and elegantly conversational manner of exposition, this poem is no mere pattern of words to be apprehended irresponsibly by the auditory and visual imagination. It more than satisfies our aesthetic judgment, yet its direct appeal is to our *reason*. As Hopkins vigorously asserted against Patmore and Newman, man is a rational or reasoning and not merely a seeing, feeling, contemplating, acting animal.[2]

Mortal beauty in the human being is that which sets dancing

---

[1] *Two Gentlemen of Verona* :
> " She excels *each mortal thing*
> Upon the dull earth dwelling.

[2] *Further Letters*, pp. 239-40.

the blood of the poet, the painter, the sculptor and the lover.
The artist longs to ' seal it so ', to baffle Time's tyrannic claim
to quench it. The beauty itself, and the possessor's longing to
keep it, had been described three years earlier in *The Golden Echo* :

> " . . . whatever's prízed and passes of us, everything that's
>
> fresh and fast flýing of us, seems to us sweet of us and swiftly
>
> awáy with, done away with, undóne,
>
> Ŭndone, done with, soon done with, and yet déarly and dangerously
>
> sweet
>
> Of us, the wimpled-wáter-dimpled, not-by-mórning-matchèd face,
>
> The flower of beauty, fleece of beauty, too too apt to, ah ! to
>
> fleet. . . ." [1]

The ethico-poetic purpose of the *Maidens' song from St. Winefred's
Well* is to *in*stress and stress the doctrine that mortal beauty can
be repossessed, at a price, on the supernatural plane. The
subjective point of view in *The Leaden Echo* (the utterly hopeless
anguish of personal loss) is felt even in *The Golden Echo*, where
the consolation is plangently delivered by those Christian Sibyls,
the virgins who, at the instance of St. Winefred, had dedicated
their lives wholly to God. *To what serves*, on the other hand,
treats the theme of living loveliness more objectively, showing
how we must use it on the earthly plane if we are not to lose it
for ever.

   In the epithet " dangerous " Hopkins defines accurately the
toxic elixir, the vitalizing poison (so to speak) of our keenest and
richest sensory experience. Such experience is good only as it is
assimilated in small doses which are nicely adapted to our
psychic needs. Beauty, like a stimulant taken in moderation,
" keeps warm / Men's wits to the things that are." Manifested
in many objects, but most of all in " World's loveliest—men's
selves ", this natural good keeps us in mind of that total reality
or Absolute of which the phenomenon is but one *scape* or *species*.
Hence, because of its divine function, the impact of beauty is
electric : one swift glance at it may stir more reverence, devotion,
or desire in the beholder than a long, disconcerting gaze at forms
or features less rarely endowed. We are then given an historic
example of this sudden mastering of the heart—Pope Gregory

---

[1] The double-stresses are copied from MS. " A ".

encounter with *non Angli sed angeli*, a "dear chance" which led to the evangelizing of Britain.

Without conscious polemic, the poem is directed equally against extreme aestheticism and extreme puritanism. Without force or protest, the sensualist and the ascetic in Hopkins are intellectually reconciled. As it is foolish to reject natural blessings, so it is sinful to become 'attached' to them, for such indulgence will cloud and stupefy the finest intelligence. No, not the *finest*; for the climax of the poem implies that the highest intelligence is inseparable from the soundest moral judgment—that of the person who, confronted with beauty, can

> "Merely meet it; own,
> Home at heart, heaven's sweet gift; | then leave, let that alone." [1]

The repetition of "that" in the last line of the sonnet is a little ambiguous, but in no damaging sense:

"Yea, wish that though, wish all, | God's better beauty, grace."

"Yea, wish *that* though" seems at first to contradict the foregoing "leave *that* alone", but the following "wish all" clarifies the meaning: 'Then let beauty alone. Not altogether, as I have said. Beauty is justly desirable, but it is only a part of the total Good. Wish for the all-embracing higher beauty, God's grace; for that brings an insight which will show you how mortal beauty, undiminished in its essence, falls into its proper place in the scheme of things.'

In spite of this clear-eyed compromise, the ascetic in Hopkins, the priest of Loyola's meiny who for theological reasons once refused a peach offered him by Bridges,[2] was never far below the

---

[1] "Own" is, of course, the imperative of the verb, governing "gift".

[2] In *The Testament of Beauty*, IV—Ethick, 423 *et seqq.*, Bridges speaks of the extreme Moralists:

> "whence pleasure with them,
> instead of being an in-itself absolute good
> as nature would have had it, and which men would wish
> to be always present and with his perfection increase,
> came to be bann'd as the pollution of virtue;—And so,
> when the young poet my companion in study
> and friend of my heart refused a peach at my hands,
> he being then a housecarl in Loyola's menie,
> 'twas that he fear'd the savor of it, and when he waived
> his scruple to my banter, 'twas to avoid offence.
> But I, upon that day which after fifty years
> is near as yesterday, was no stranger to fear
> of pleasure, but had grown fearful of that fear. . . ."

Cf. *Letters*, vol. i. pp. 145 and 152. The latter page suggests that G. M. H. was chary of eating *stolen* fruit. or fruit 'bought' without permission.

surface. The idea and necessity of Sacrifice were always present to him, and we feel at times that the poetic personality was saved from complete self-immolation only by sudden divagations from the steep highway of moral duty into quiet by-paths of natural beauty, as in *Inversnaid* (1881) and *Ash-boughs* (1885). Moreover, as a force tending to preserve Hopkins's psychological balance, the lifelong influence of Robert Bridges must never be underrated.

We shall now briefly consider the psychological basis of Hopkins's two unfinished works on martyrdom—verses in which human life is treated mainly as " one spell and well that one "—a battlefield on which the saint fights for Christ to the death.

The interest shown by Hopkins the celibate in three female Catholic martyrs—St. Dorothea, St. Winefred, and the Venerable Margaret Clitheroe—will be thought by some critics to admit of only one interpretation : here, they will say, is a plain case of sexual sublimation. The element of truth in that view seems to be borne out by the fact that his projected poems on the Jesuit male martyrs—Campion, Sherwin, and Bryant—were as far as we know not even seriously begun. One critic, however, has made some thoughtful comments on Hopkins's interest in martyrdom generally. Starting with a quotation from Freud which, in this context, implies that Hopkins was *not* one of " the most select and balanced minds ", the critic suggests that this poet's preoccupation with physical suffering, though not exactly pathological, was still not quite normal. From the boy-poet's description, in *The Escorial*, of the martyr's " crush'd flesh hissing on the grate ", right up to some curious epistolary allusions of 1888, Hopkins, actively as well as passively,

> " was interested in pain. He was interested in the gash, the bloody flow, the bloody hour of the martyrs. Self-humiliation and pain in others, did not obsess him, but they were always important to him." [1]

The assertion is true, and properly qualified. Even in the nature poems we find such expressions as " Speared open lustrous gashes ", " blood-gush, blade-gash ", " drop-of-blood-and-foam-dapple ". Again, the flogging of two spread-eagled

[1] Mr. Geoffrey Grigson in *Blood and Bran* (*New Verse*, No. 14, April, 1935, pp. 21–32).

sailors in Dana's *Two Years Before the Mast* (read on vacation at Lochaber in 1888) is described by Hopkins as

> "terrible and instructive *and it happened*—ah, that is the charm and the main point." [1]

That word "charm" is unexpected; but in the very next letter he again yields to the fascination of a gruesome real-life episode. Having complained about his own distress of body and mind he goes on :

> "in mind or body or both I shall give way—and all I really need is a certain degree of relief and change; but I do not think that what I need I shall get in time to save me. This reminds me of a shocking thing that has just happened to a young man well known to some of our community. He put his eyes out. He was a medical student and probably understood how to proceed, which was nevertheless barbarously done with a stick and some wire. The eyes were found among nettles in a field." [1]

In its full context, this symptom of morbid interest appears less alarming. Hopkins (grandson of a doctor) proceeds to inform his medical friend that his own eyes are " very, very sore and ", asks :

> " Can there be gout or rheumatism in the eyes? If there can I have it."

There is an obvious association of ideas, first between Hopkins and the young Oedipus (who had been subject to delusions), then between both men and the Scriptural injunction, ' If thy right eye offend thee, pluck it out.' Hopkins, probably, was unaware of the connexion : he adds simply, " I mention the case because it is extraordinary : suicide is common."

As a priest Hopkins had a particular, professional interest in pain. Part of his training as a novice had been to make ' mind-paintings ' or intense visualizations of scenes in the life of Christ, and especially for the various phases of the Crucifixion. The Atonement had for him both a real and symbolic aspect : it was the supreme type of all human suffering. While visiting the sick, Hopkins saw this principle put to the test. From being interested in the degree of pain which could be borne for a fixed idea or belief it was but a step, for one so insatiably curious as he was, to be ' intrigued ' by the infliction and endurance of pain as a pure human anomaly. You may call this ' sado-masochism ' or ' algolagnia ', as some critics have ; but the

[1] *Letters*, vol. i. pp. 279 and 282-3.

sexual component is not clearly manifest. From the Christian and common-sense point of view there is no serious perversion.[1]

In 1879 Hopkins had proposed to write a tragedy on the martyrdom of Margaret Clitheroe, whose story he found " terrible and heartrending ". No vestige of the play has survived, but we have an unfinished poem of sixty-one lines which we, judging by the autograph, would place within the period 1879–82, though another critic has adjudged the style alone to be late, austere, and mature.[2]

Hopkins was moved by certain resemblances between the trial and slow death of Margaret and the trial and Passion of Christ. She, too, foresaw, feared, yet accepted her agony ; she, too, refused to plead, and thereby incurred a more terrible fate. Hopkins's opening images are tense and promising :

> " God's counsel columnar-severe
> But chaptered in the chief of bliss
> Had always doomed her down to this—
> *Pressed to death*. He plants the year ;
> The weighty weeks without hands grow,
> Heaved drum on drum ; but hands also
> Must deal with Margaret Clitheroe."

That " also " (line 6) seems to be illogical ; and from here onwards, despite arresting passages, the poem shows a steady deterioration. True, the second stanza, with a few bold strokes and shadows, makes us feel the " Christ-ed beauty of her mind " as she " mends the way she means to go " ; and the fourth incomplete stanza tells with a grim splendour how the austere column of God's purpose with Margaret had soared up to flower into the capital of heavenly bliss—the reward of Sacrifice, highest of human accomplishments :

> " Great Thecla, the plumed passionflower,
> Next Mary mother of maid and nun
>
> .   .   .   .   .   .
>
> And every saint of bloody hour
> And breath immortal thronged that show ;
> Heaven turned its starlight eyes below
> To the murder of Margaret Clitheroe."

[1] Mr. Grigson concludes : " Hopkins would have been a more excellent poet, had he known himself better ; and those who read his poems will not be good readers unless they also examine themselves." Living to-day, Hopkins might have known himself better. But would he have preferred Freud to Christ—or been a better poet ? Extremely doubtful.

[2] Mr. Edwin Muir in *The Present Age, from 1918*, p. 91.

Certainly " Her will was bent at God ", and believing that we can appreciate this imaginative account of her spiritual triumph. But the great difficulty with poems of this sort is that the poet cannot escape the effects of special pleading. We may believe that the men who murdered Margaret were moved by " the spirit of hell " which to her virtue was " clinching-blind " ; but the spirit of history disturbs our judgment ; we cannot help feeling that this denunciation of martyr-making cuts both ways. Hear how these Protestant zealots tearfully or coaxingly besought Margaret to renounce her faith :

> " Fawning fawning crocodiles
> Days and days came round about
> With tears to put her candle out ;
> They wound their winch of wicked smiles
> To take her ; while their tongues would go
> *God lighten your dark heart*—but no,
> Christ lived in Margaret Clitheroe."

That is pure horror ; but it is also the forcing of poetry into a relatively narrow sectarian channel. Our response to the poetry is jostled by the thought that another poet might have used the same words about the burning of Latimer and Ridley.

Mr. Grigson has suggested that Hopkins discontinued this poem because of a half-realized suspicion that his poetic interest was not " in martyrdom purely ", that it had not " a full religious intention ". But we cannot believe that ' sadism ' has anything to do with it. Hopkins's attachment to the faith for which the martyr died was such that he would gladly have accepted the same fate himself : *his* values were not those of the modern psycho-analyst. It is more likely that he felt the poem to be too aggressively Catholic. His artistic instinct always aimed at a certain universality. He felt that such heroic witnesses to the ' one true faith ' [1] should be honoured as only poetry can bestow honour ; he also knew that " the highest subjects are not those in which it is easy to reach one's highest."

The above argument does not apply with equal force to his unfinished tragedy on St. Winefred, for the legendary theme of her murder by the lustful Caradoc, and her immediate resuscitation by St. Beuno, can excite no theological antagonism. Failure here was due to those inherent disabilities and external hindrances which had brought down so many of his cherished enterprises.

[1] It is important to point out that a Catholic like Hopkins would not apply the term ' martyr ' to a Latimer or Ridley.

Yet no poetic work was so close to his heart as this one. The play was to be short, probably only two acts, and the characters were to be few. A classical simplicity of structure, including the use of a chorus, was to be combined with an Elizabethan vigour of style :

> " It is a drama of passion more than of character and not at all of manners, something in what I understand to be Marlowe's treatment. . . ." [1]

Like Faustus, Caradoc was to be a man dominated by one great passion, in this case sexual desire. The tragic element in the play was apparently not centred in the virgin-martyr (whose story is really a triumph) but rather in Caradoc, the great sinner, who was " to die impenitent, struck by the finger of God."

Hopkins chose the " sprung alexandrine " measure because of its " pathos ", because it was " smooth, natural and easy to work in broken dialogue " (see the eight opening lines), and was equally suitable for intense passion. He found the metrical work arduous, but that was probably due to the fact that his purely dramatic invention was not adequate to the task :

> " I seem to find myself, after some experiment, equal to the more stirring and critical parts of the action . . . but about the filling in and minor parts I am not sure how far my powers will go. I have for one thing so little varied experience." [2]

Dramatic foreshadowing, the creation of suspense, occurs in Teryth's soliloquy in Scene 1 ; but the real heart of the play is Caradoc's great monologue, spoken immediately after the murder. It resembles a Hamlet soliloquy in its sudden but natural changes of mood and outlook, its vivid picture of a mind tormented by the struggle between good and evil. The psychology is matched by modulations in speed and tone which suggest the dazed, hectic condition of a homicidal egoist. After the first shock his mood is exultant :

> " Monuments of my earnest, | records of my revenge."

Then self-exculpation and a partial protective amnesia :

>   " I had warned her—
> Warned her ! well she knew. | I warned her of this work.
> What work ? what harm's done ? There is | no harm done, none yet ;
> Perhaps we struck no blow. . . ."

[1] *Letters*, vol. i. p. 227.   [2] *Ibid*. p. 92.

But quickly the full enormity of his crime bursts upon him ; there is a touch of Bottom and fustian in his address to his ' bloody blameful blade ' :

> " So be it.   Thou | steel, thou butcher,[1]
> I can scour thee, fresh burnish thee. . . ."

Images of Elizabethan macabre mingle with alternations of horror and pity which are in the spirit of Greek tragedy.   But the most significant feature is the way Caradoc, when faced with the furies of remorse, assumes the proud, defiant impenitence of Milton's Satan :

> " In a wide world of defiance | Caradoc lives alone. . . ."

In the axioms which follow we hear the calculated diabolical strain of perverted Selfhood (familiar to-day as the logical development of Nietzschean ' culture ' and *pseudo*-Freudian Id-worship) :

> " What is virtue ?   Valour ; | only the heart valiant.
> And right ?   Only resolution ; | will, his will unwavering
> Who, like me, knowing his nature | to the heart home, nature's business,
> Despatches with no flinching."

It has been said that Milton half-admired his own Satan ; and it is certain that Browning (perhaps in the spirit of Luther's *Pecca fortiter*) regarded his own sinners, such as Guido, with something like indulgence :

> " Let a man contend to the uttermost
> For his life's set prize, be it what it will ! " [2]

But to Hopkins such ' humanism ' was detestable.   The moral law had been firmly established ; hence Caradoc doubts his own ' will to evil ' :

> " But will flesh, O can flesh
> Second this fiery strain ? | Not always ; O no no !
> We cannot live this life out ; | sometimes we must weary
> And in this darksome world | comfort where can I find ? "

---

[1] The caesural mark in this line is not given in either of the MSS., "A" and "H". The rest of the lines quoted follow *Poems*, Third Edition, No. 105.

[2] *The Statue and the Bust.*

The love, even the maddening unrequited love which he has now sacrificed for ever, was worth far more than the self-glory he has gained :

" I all my being have hacked | in half with her neck : one part,
  Reason, selfdisposal, | choice of better or worse way,
  Is corpse now, cannot change ; "

The next three lines (if we read ' sin ' for ' murder ') might have come from one of the " terrible " sonnets :

                          " my other self, this soul,
    Life's quick, this kind, | this keen self-feeling,[1]
    With dreadful distillation | of thoughts sour as blood,[2]
    Must all day long taste murder."

The wail of an impenitent Faustus hardens at last into the savage anhedonia of a Macbeth :

" Deed-bound I am ; one deed treads all down here, | cramps all
                doing. What do ? Not yield,
  Not hope, not pray ; despair ; | ay, that : brazen despair out,
  Brave all, and take what comes—| as here this rabble is come,
  Whose bloods I reck no more of, | no more rank with hers
  Than sewers with sacred oils."

That phrase " sewers with sacred oils " unconsciously symbolizes the sharp contrast between sin and the moral law, a contrast without which no great tragedy and no true satire are possible. It is a distinction which is rapidly being lost, and this thought increases our regret that Hopkins did not finish the play. As he said himself : " I never wrote anything stronger than some of those lines."

Beuno's speech after Winefred's raising from the dead would have made a fitting conclusion to the play after the catastrophe —the striking down of Caradoc. In that speech Hopkins kept as close to Butler's *Life* of the saint as Shakespeare did to many pages in his Plutarch : the hagiographer gives copious examples, with personal details, of miraculous cures effected at St. Winefred's Well in the seventeenth century.

Hopkins said repeatedly that he did not hold with ' dramatic poems ' ; his own play was intended for performance. Yet even

---

[1] The caesural mark in this line is not given in either of the MSS., "A" and "H".

[2] Cf. " Selfyeast of spirit a dull dough sours." (No. 45.)

if his elaborate style had the quality of ' getting across ', there is nothing to show that he had the power of developing a dramatic conflict, a tense clash of personalities.   It is difficult to see what he could have made of the simple Winefred as she is described in the scanty chronicles ;   but a strong portrait of Caradoc, building up to the soliloquy—showing him at first restrained and plausible, then rasping moodily into egomania and diabolism—this would have solved the problem of Winefred and the minor characters, for they would have grown naturally as foils to the tragic protagonist.

In complete contrast to the above poems of bigotry and faith, cruelty and fortitude is that isolated lyric of 1881, *Inversnaid*, a poem in which Man and God and all the heart-throes which attend their mystical relationship seem to be forgotten.   Yet even here a strain of the poet's " duller self " enigmatically intrudes :

> " A windpuff bonnet of fáwn-fróth
>   Turns and twindles over the broth
>   Of a pool so pitchblack, féll-frówning,
>   It rounds and rounds Despair to drowning."

Apparently this pool is the deep basin hollowed out by the mountain stream at the bottom of its rugged stairs.   Looking down into those milling waters, Hopkins is fascinated :   their dance of death is beautifully sinister.   But he is in no suicidal mood.   His fancy tosses Despair into the cauldron and watches it drown ;   it then leaps up the water-stair and paints a lovely picture of the riparian scenery.   The poem concludes in the spirit of Wordsworth, Ruskin, and the National Trust :

> " What would the world be, once bereft
>   Of wet and of wildness ?   Let them be left,
>   O let them be left, wildness and wet ;
>   Long live the weeds and the wilderness yet."

As Miss Phare has pointed out, Hopkins's love of the wild and inchoate in nature is in sharp opposition to his reverence for the ordered rounded completeness of the Thomistic theology which governed his life.   It is going too far, perhaps, to suggest that in some points where Thomism and Scotism disagree Hopkins preferred the latter because it is incomplete and ' untidy ' while the former is the reverse.   Nevertheless Hopkins, with all his passion for explanation and elaboration, has also a more than usual tolerance for incompleteness in his own works. Even when allowance has been made for a keen self-criticism, he seemed to prefer hopeful travel to a possibly disappointing arrival. Mere 'becoming' was to him more painful and yet more stimulating than to most men : he was always luxuriating in the unsatisfactory position of being half-way towards something better. "All my world," he once wrote, "is scaffolding" ; and although the Thomist in him yearned for the stately edifice of absolute finality, the Scotist part of him—the intuitionalist, the mystic, the dreamer—seemed to find the lashed pole of leisurely building as congenial as the " lashed rod " of violent self-coercion. Of the stimulus of unsuccess, the fascinating uncertainty of groping towards certainty, he speaks unmistakably through the mouth of that thwarted lover, Caradoc :

" To hunger and not have, yét | hope ón for, to storm and strive and
  Be at every assault fresh foiled, | worse flung, deeper disappointed,
  The turmoil and the torment, | it has, I swear, a sweetness,
  Keeps a kind of joy in it, | a zest, an edge, an ecstasy,
  Next after sweet success."

Hopkins refused to slam the door in the face of the Mystery. Had he done so, retiring sedately and securely into the compact, well-ordered house of a finished and finite dogmatism, he would have been a more contented man ; and the poems of his last four years (about to be considered) would have been as pedestrian as the majority of Wordsworth's Ecclesiastical Sonnets or Keble's metrical devotions. That statement does not impugn Hopkins's faith in the dogma of his Church ; for there would seem to be a part of every believer which is not satisfied by faith alone.

CHAPTER VII

POEMS OF DESOLATION AND RECOVERY
(1885–1889)

TWELVE days after writing *Inversnaid* Hopkins returned to Manresa House, Roehampton, to begin his tertianship, the ' third year of noviceship ' which Jesuits undergo before being allotted their final grades and before taking their last vows. On hearing of this move Dixon wrote :

> " I suppose you are determined to go on with it : but it must be a severe trial—I will say no more." [1]

In replying, Hopkins explained that he was not, as his friend had supposed, free to withdraw from the Society ; he had taken vows which were perpetually binding at the end of his novitiate proper, in 1870, and had renewed them every six months (" not *for* every six months but for life "). He had not only made his vows publicly some twenty-two times but had made them to himself every day,

> " so that I should be black with perjury if I drew back now. And beyond that I can say with St. Peter : To whom shall I go ? *Tu verba vitae aeternae habes.* Besides all which my mind is here more at peace than it has ever been and I would gladly live all my life, if it were so to be, in as great or a greater seclusion from the world and be busied only with God." [2]

Could such a man have been happier, more vitally active and poetically productive in some secular occupation, or even as a secular priest ? Would marriage, a household and children have helped him to write those great odes on Campion and the Vale of Clwyd or indeed any others ? It is, in *his* case, more than doubtful. On the other hand we cannot believe that the man who was so quickly aware of the dangers in extra-mural duties, where " worldly interests freshen and worldly ambitions revive ",[3] would ever have been content with a purely contemplative life. He cherished the desire but lacked the aplomb

---

[1] *Letters*, vol. ii. p. 70. [2] *Ibid.* p. 75.
[3] *Ibid.* p. 76. See above, Introduction, *passim.*

and physical strength to engage simultaneously in three kinds of activity—the practical, the speculative, and the contemplative ; and the story of his successes and failures in the struggle to maintain this lofty and dangerous equilibrium was written partly in the lives of those he taught, advised, and ministered to, partly in the *Letters*, and partly in the poems—and especially in those we are about to examine.

The seven or eight sonnets of ' desolation ' (for *Patience* may perhaps be regarded as ' consolation ') are those of Hopkins's poems which above all others have captured the mind and imagination of his modern audience ; and the reason for this preference is not far to seek. Admittedly they show a concentrated art which in an age of literary formlessness, of timid or inhibited religious emotions, was bound to command a grudging or wondering respect. But that quality would not explain all the praise lavished on these poems at the expense of some of the equally fine earlier ones. The truth is (though few are aware of it and not many will care to acknowledge it) that these astringent later sonnets crystallize that sense of frustration, of separation from God, which is the peculiar psychic disease of the twentieth century.

Since the days of Voltaire, western man has progressively, grudgingly, but with a kind of good faith followed the lead of thinkers who, having ' dethroned ' and ' buried ' the supernatural God of Christianity, have failed signally (1) to find an equivalent or substitute for God as the unifying Principle, and (2) to eradicate the natural appetency which aspires to a clearly defined supernatural Absolute. Now Hopkins's ' desolation ' was the aridity, protest, rebelliousness, terror, resignation, self-pity, quasi-cynicism, self-reproach, self-disgust and renewed self-dedication of the just man of declared faith who felt that he had been deserted by his God and could not be sure why ; yet his faith continued to assert itself in a persistent humility, an underlying and unshakable conviction *either* that it was he himself who in the first place had deserted God, *or* that God would, in His own good time and way, answer the cries and prayers of His servant and eventually resolve all doubts. In a parallel if not identically similar way, modern man has for at least twenty years been wondering whether he has not been led astray by false prophets. The sociological and scientific liberalism which, a hundred years ago, began to undermine his traditional faith in God, seems to have produced not an era of enlightenment and prosperity but a veritable ' waste land ', both material and spiritual. Hence, because the sensitive, intellectual representative of modern man feels that he has been deceived by the Idea of Progress, the Life-Force, or by the universal and emergent creative Energy under whatever name it may be known, he too protests bitterly in his secret heart : " No worst, there is none ! " From every country his " cries countless " huddle in a main " world-sorrow " ; but like " dead letters " they are thrown back unanswered. The furies of retribution and destruction shriek : " Let me be fell : force I must be brief ". In speed and effectiveness, methods of ' liquidation ' and annihilation have surpassed all dreams. Baudelaire's *Une Charogne* has become the symbol of a decaying civilization : man is conscious of being nothing but a parcel of disintegrating matter : " Bones built in me, flesh filled, blood brimmed the curse." Schopenhauer, Nordau, and Spengler have expatiated on the chromatic gradations of decay and the inevitability of pessimism ; so that man is forced back on to a stoical hedonism (like Housman's) or driven into a desperate revulsion of feeling (like T. S. Eliot's) ; and Hopkins had words for both moods :

(1) " You, jaded, let be ; call off thoughts awhile
    Elsewhere ; leave comfort root-room. . . ."

(2) " Not, I'll not, carrion comfort, Despair, not feast on thee ;
    Not untwist—slack they may be—these last strands of man
    In me. . . ."

Modern man listens respectfully to the disillusioned philosopher-critic who says : ' he Tmajority of thinking people no longer believe in some future life which will redress the inevitable injustices of this one ", and straightway he feels himself to be suspended by a thread over a black pit of uncertainty or oblivion —" cliffs of fall, frightful, sheer, no-man-fathomed " ; for who can fathom the intentions of a blind, irresponsible ' unforedrawn ' creative Potentiality ? Our " small durance " cannot deal with that " steep or deep ", so Bernard Shaw pleads for an arbitrary extension of human life [1] ; but modern man, threatened only with a prolongation of puerilities (" in smooth spoons spy life's masque mirrored ") or an existence terminated not with a whimper but with a bang, rebels against the " fire and fever fussy " or wearies of " idle a being but by where wars are rife ". Why should he " die these deaths " when the end and purpose of it all is so

---

[1] See Shaw's *Back to Methuselah*.

nebulous ?   In the modern man's ordinary conversation th
expletives ' the hell of a— ' and ' What the hell ! ' indicate th
wholesale removal of Hell from the future into the presen
" Why do sinners' ways prosper ? " asks the just man.   Th
" sots and thralls of lust ", though perhaps not more numerou
than in the past, are now excused and pampered as never before
Waiting for signs of improvement, the man of goodwill need
patience ; but alas, " the hard thing but to pray, but bid fo
Patience is ! "   Birds build, yet the political peacemaker, lik
Time's eunuch, strains but fails to produce " one work tha
wakes " ; for

> " What pure peace allows
> Alarms of wars, the daunting wars, the death of it ? "

No wonder then if man in the aggregate lives, in a spiritua
sense, " hand to mouth " and increasingly falls back upon th
comfort that serves in a whirlwind :

> " all
> Life death does end and each day dies with sleep."

It may be urged that Hopkins's God, whom men have bee
gradually persuaded to abandon, gave him no more comfo
than their various idealisms (their *ersatz* gods, he might have saic
have brought the rational humanists.   But this would not b
altogether true.   In spite of his despair, the Jesuit poet's defini
faith gave him powers of recovery which many of his mo
sensitive modern readers would lack.   The exacerbating dela
amounting to failure in our attempts to establish the Kingdom
Heaven on earth is less devastating to the soul of man when th
soul's main purpose is the attainment of Christ's spiritua
Kingdom ; and this exaltation of individual personality an
salvation above the collective personality and *material* welfa
of mankind is clearly apparent in one of Hopkins's very late
works, *That Nature is a Heraclitean Fire*.   Nevertheless, the wor
" recovery " in the title of the present chapter needs justifyin
and its justification will depend upon a closer scrutiny of th
poems of 1885-9.

As we have said elsewhere, " how easy it is to draw fal
conclusions from the ' terrible ' sonnets ! " [1]   The unwarrantab
downright rejection of Hopkins's Christian optimism as ' fal
gold ' ; the sceptic's refusal to give the poet credit for knowir
himself and respecting truth when he declared that he w

---

[1] Introduction to *Poems of G. M. H.*, Third Edition.

requently " busied with God " and wished to be so more con-
inuously—such attitudes lead to misunderstanding as inevitably
is the opposite assertion, that Hopkins was so completely absorbed
n his priestly vocation that worldly interests could never have
disturbed his peace of mind.

To *Carrion Comfort*, that sonnet " written in blood " in 1885,
here could be no better introduction than a glance at the note
Hopkins made during his retreat at Beaumont in 1883.[1] His
genuine humility is revealed at once : " I remembered Fr.
Whitty's teaching." And among his papers we find many
imilar hastily jotted reminders of " lights " and " graces "
eceived through colleagues. The note continues :

> " Also, since God gives me at present no great humiliations
> and I am not worthy of them and did not accept them when they
> came, to welcome the small ones whenever such shall occur.
> " During this retreat I have much and earnestly prayed that
> God will lift me above myself to a higher state of grace, in which
> I may have more union with him, be more zealous to do his
> will, and freer from sin. . . ."

As a disciple of St. Ignatius he was in duty bound to welcome
humiliations. His self-love, however, has betrayed him into
ome degree of attachment to worldly values, the very sin against
which he had warned himself and others in so many poems.

The bitter struggle within his soul between ' Love as getting '
nd ' Love as giving ' is personified, in *Carrion Comfort*, as a
wrestling match between himself and God. The imagery of the
ctave has the vivid inconsequence, the unbelievable actuality
f a nightmare.[2] He first remembers how once, like some
Romantic decadent, he was tempted to glut himself with his
wn morbid spleen ; but no, he refused to comfort his soul with
hat dish of carrion. He would not ' eat out his own heart ',
either would he put an end to his own life, for he could still
esire and hope for the light of grace, could still cry, ' Up, my

---

[1] See above, Chapter vi. p. 315.

[2] Cf. the poet's *Journal* under Sept. 18, 1873 : " I had a nightmare that night.
thought something or someone leapt on to me and held me fast : this I think
oke me, so that after this I shall have had the use of reason. . . . I had lost all
uscular stress elsewhere but not sensitive, feeling where each limb lay and thinking
at I could recover myself if I could move my finger, I said, and then the arm and
the whole body. The feeling is terrible. . . . I cried on the holy name and by
egrees recovered myself as I thought to do. It made me think that this was how
e souls in hell would be imprisoned in their bodies as in prisons and of what St.
heresa says of the ' little press in the wall ' where she felt herself to be in her vision."
Note-books, pp. 184-5.)

soul, be doing ! ' Then suddenly and without transition he
again sees himself wrestling with an incubus, which mangles
him beneath a monstrous heel capable of wringing tears and
blood from a whole world. The one who had refused the
shameful feast seems now about to be devoured. But why
should he be forced to crouch there, petrified with fear, pinioned
by the lion-limb and fanned by the wing of an Adversary (was
it demon or angel ?) who seemed always to withhold the mortal
blow ?

The question is answered in a great climax of self-edification
he remembers that he had really wanted all this to happen ; he
had acquiesced in a process of purgation : " Why ? That my
chaff might fly ; my grain lie, sheer and clear." Turning back
to the Beaumont diary, we find an explanation of " sheer and
clear " :

> " *Sept.* 9. In meditating on the Crucifixion I saw how my asking
> to be raised to a higher degree of grace was asking also
> to be lifted on a higher cross."

Hopkins's acceptance of his own crucifixion was (as Dr. Pick
reminds us) an act of submission to the Divine Will analogous
to that of the tall nun in *The Deutschland* : " The cross to her
she calls Christ to her, christens her wild-worst Best."

Yet even in the last tercet, when the poet is turning the eye
of reason upon the bygone visitation, the similitude of dream
consciousness is maintained. He is still a little dazed. He
remembers how the feeling of being reborn, of drawing new
strength and joy from the ordeal, had made him " laugh
cheer ". But whom had he applauded ?—the Scourger ?—or
himself, the worthily scourged ? Was it " each one " ? Had
he felt some pride in his own prowess, the complacence of the
' game fighter ' who has taken his punishment ? He fears that
all the dross has not been threshed out of him, for nothing but
his own stubborn selfhood could have provoked his God to
make such an onslaught. Hence he looks back with a shudder to

                           " that night, that year
Of now done darkness I wretch lay wrestling with (my God !) my
      God." [1]

___

[1] The speaking of this line as it is written and as Hopkins intended it to be spoken
has been described as " a physical impossibility ". But Mr. Valentine Dyall the
actor, in a broadcast reading of the poem, has shown that it can be done : he reduces
the parenthesis to a whisper of horror without destroying the sequence of " wrestling
with my God."

The experience described in this poem is not a sign of achieved ' mysticism ', but it belongs to what is called ' the mystic way '. The mystics have rarely attempted to describe the " war within " (their purgative phase) in such vivid terms as these ; but they have frequently assured us that until the Self has been completely mastered no mystical ' union ' is possible. At the same time the poem describes the extreme pitch or instress of an experience which is common to a considerable number of sensitive and religious people who would make no claim to be mystics. That epithet " wring-world " is akin to the " world-sorrow " of the next sonnet (No. 41), just as the wincing and singing on the " age-old anvil " of the latter recalls the " anvil-ding " of *The Deutschland*—God's plastic stress moulding the spirit of man to its " foredrawn " shape. *Carrion Comfort* is a stark, terse, unsentimental anticipation of Francis Thompson's *The Hound of Heaven*—that great poem (whatever its detractors may say) which has almost rivalled Gray's *Elegy* in the wideness of its appeal. Yet the full motivation of *Carrion Comfort* cannot be brought out until we have examined two of its sister-sonnets, Nos. 41 and 45.

There is more than one way in which a man possessed with the idea of God may react to his experience of the numinous. One is Hopkins's way—immediate or ultimate self-surrender, whether the instress be delectable or harrowing. Another way is that of Whitman, who liked to see and caress and praise God in what Blake called " the human form divine ". *Leaves of Grass* opens with transports which are quite Hopkinsian :

> " One's self I sing, a simple and separate person. . . .
> Of Life immense in passion, pulse, and power,
> Cheerful, for freest action form'd under the laws divine,
> The Modern Man I sing."

That last line is the parting of the ways ; Hopkins does not confine humanity within ' the modern man ' or contract God into humanity. It was Whitman's obsession with the idea of freedom and happiness in emergent man which led him to resent anything, even the stress of moral law, if its immediate effect was to lower the plumes of strutting human personality, to destroy the placidity of the achieved and quietly articulate rolling earth. Still another reaction to the instress of God is that of Baudelaire—a deliberate, blasphemous rejection of the God who comes as a Lawgiver, as the principle of restraint, enforcer of the stern ' Thou shalt ' or ' Thou shalt not '. But just as Whitman was always modifying his own conclusions, so Baudelaire was continually harried by remorse, dogged and persecuted by the Principle he had rejected. In both men the vacillation was due to the fact that neither, as poet and thinker, could consistently repudiate the *total* idea of God. Both were haunted by the sensation of Immanence : in every aspect of nature—clouds, the sea, the stars—they felt the presence of a divine Spirit of Goodness which they could not permanently dissociate from the same Spirit working in and through the soul of man—a principle of judgment and restraint as well as an impulse of liberty and lust : " freest action form'd under the laws divine."

Baudelaire, with his rare power of telescoping many phases of experience, has unconsciously fused in one quatrain Whitman's exaggerated humanism and his own Satanism, with Hopkins's Christian submissiveness as the implied norm :

> " L'Humanité bavarde, ivre de son génie,
>   Et, folle maintenant comme elle était jadis,
>   Criant à Dieu, dans sa furibonde agonie :
> «O mon semblable, ô mon maître, je te maudis !»" [1]

Between Whitman's deification of man and Baudelaire's inverted Catholicism, Hopkins's picture of the lower and higher Personality was very much the right way up. Yet even his view of the two spheres of the spirit, the natural and the supernatural, was not always perfectly balanced. In *Carrion Comfort* the balance was held : that poem asserts the right of the human personality to live and expand, however justly that right may be limited from without and within. But in the sequel-sonnet, " No worst, there is none ", the balance is lost. Here we have the logical outcome of feasting on, instead of refusing, that carrion comfort, Despair. The poem is a cry of human agony, not *furibonde* but impotent ; it ends not with a curse or a benediction but with a spiritual black-out.

Some idea of the spiritual lights and reliefs that had failed Hopkins may be gained from the Beaumont diary. After the words quoted above on p. 334 he writes : " Then I took it that our Lord recommended me to our Lady and her to me." In the sonnet under discussion he appeals desperately to the Holy Ghost (the Comforter) and the Holy Mother :

[1] *Le Voyage*, vi.

" No worst, there is none. Pitched past pitch of grief,
    More pangs will, schooled at forepangs, wilder wring.
    Comforter, where, where is your comforting ?
    Mary, mother of us, where is your relief ? "

In this and other sonnets of the same period there are certain recurrent nightmarish symbols, and at this point we must refer the reader to what we have already said in Volume I concerning the Shakespearian *underthought* in these poems.[1] Our present inquiry centres in the *overthought*, in the direct religious significance of the " fury " (angel or demon) who comes yet again in a storm of wind to smite and overawe the cowering " wretch ". The violent assaults—with lulls between, the *coup de grâce* ever threatened but strangely withheld, the furry menace of darkness and the sensation of a gaping void—all these carry the poet at last to the very brink of hell ; but not beyond. In " No worst, there is none " he could imagine temporal pangs which would wring wilder than any he had yet endured—a fact which probably safeguarded his sanity, his essential hope ; and at the end of " I wake and feel the fell of dark " he can still look beyond death to a plight worse than his own—a fact which confirms his Christian faith.

If any poem, after *Spring and Fall*, could be suspected of expressing unbelief or doubt it is " No worst " ; yet the poem seems to indicate not doubt but rather an unwilling suspension of hope, like the words wrung from the dying Christ—" My God, my God, why hast thou forsaken me ? " The faith of a man inured, as Hopkins was, to self-proliferating sorrows had not been finally overthrown. Like an overwhelmed boxer who ' covers up ' and longs for the end of the fight, so Hopkins looked for a respite in sleep and death ; but the poet knew that the consequences of his own moral defeat would be as inevitable for him at the Judgment as the consequences of physical overthrow would be for the beaten boxer after the relief of the last bell. We say that Hopkins *knew* this, because in all his subsequent prose and verse, that knowledge, in the form of absolute belief, is implicit if not indeed explicitly stated. For instance, in some Retreat Notes made at St. Stanislaus' College, Tullabeg, in January 1888, Hopkins writes : " All my undertakings miscarry : I am like a straining eunuch. I wish then for death ; yet if I died now I should die imperfect, no master myself. O my God, look down on me." [2]

---

[1] Chapter v. pp. 174-9.
[2] From an unpublished MS. in the possession of the poet's family.

In a letter of 1888 Hopkins tells us that he suffered from insomnia ; but the midnight agony of No. 45 derives its poetic and cathartic force from a symbolic and not from a purely literal reading :

> " I wake and feel the fell of dark, not day.
>
> What hours, O what black hours we have spent
> This night ! what sights you, heart, saw ; ways you went !
> And more must, in yet longer light's delay."

Here again, " light " is the light of God's illuminating grace. Like Dante midway upon the journey of his life, Hopkins had awakened suddenly to the full horror of his own and incidentally the whole world's moral predicament.

> "Nel mezzo del cammin di nostra vita
> Mi ritrovai per una selva oscura,
> Che la diritta via era smarrita." [1]

So Dante had begun his great poem ; and those " sights " and " ways " to which Hopkins refers must also, like Dante's " dark wood ", have something to do with the general loss of innocence and faith, all the vice and ignorance in the world as Hopkins saw it—" Le spectacle ennuyeux de l'immortel péché ", as even Baudelaire could perceive it. As a statement of a purely personal problem this sonnet, like *Carrion Comfort* and " No worst ", is impressive enough ; but the five words which begin the second quatrain are highly significant : " With witness I speak this." Testimony as to the actuality and degree of his desolation could have been given only by God Himself, or by other men with a similar ' psyche ', environment, and world-view ; and it is difficult to find many such men outside the ranks of the accredited saints. Dante was in some ways of their kind, but he unworthily found relief from his world-sorrow in a vindictive crowding of the *Inferno* with his personal enemies. The most cogent " witness " of all was of course Christ, whose tears over Jerusalem and agony in the Garden constituted for Hopkins the prototype of all desolations. Hopkins, like his Master, was " exceeding sorrowful even unto death " ; he too had prayed : " take away this cup from me : nevertheless not what I will but what Thou wilt " [2]—

> " I am gall, I am heartburn. *God's most deep decree*
> *Bitter would have me taste* : my taste was me. . . ."

[1] *Inferno*, I. 1-3.   [2] *Mark* xiv. 34 6.

We cannot believe that Hopkins was expressing a conviction that he was being made to suffer exclusively for his own sins. It is hard to believe that his sins amounted to very much more than a failure to perform the impossible. We cannot be sure of this ; but it seems to us that his lack of balance consisted in his inability to recognize his own congenital limitations. Such a weakness may not be without merit ; for in his case a natural propensity for vicarious suffering, strengthened by intellectual bias and a continuous brooding over the spiritual decadence of man, had produced an *alter Christus* whose impersonal motives were curiously entangled or identified with the symbols of a personal neurosis.

It should be noticed that in *Carrion Comfort* (line 13) " That night " is immediately expanded to " that year ". In the present sonnet *hours* " mean years, mean life ". This poem was partly the outcome of ill-health, that " coffin of dejection in which I live without even the hope of change " ; [1] but we know that Hopkins was not all his life in such a desperately neurasthenic condition. The application of the mood of the sonnet to the whole of his life, or (as a symbol) to life generally, lifts the verse on to a higher plane than that of an impassioned egotistical valetudinarianism. The emotional climax of the sonnet is line 11, which sums up canorously the universal-personal *motif*—the total inadequacy of the body unless it is possessed by a healthy, justified, fulfilled spirit. But the next words are ambiguous :

" Selfyeast of spirit a dull dough sours."

Both the spirit *and* the body could do the souring, for as St. Paul said, " the flesh lusteth against the spirit, and the spirit against the flesh : for these are contrary one to another." [2] Primarily Hopkins meant that his bodily weakness had prevented him from " walking in the spirit " ; but there is also the suggestion that he, like most men, had culpably allowed his thoughts and actions to take on a disproportionate ' worldly tone ' : in him, as in all humanity, a deficiency in will and ' good will ' had led to spiritual degeneration. This point must, indeed, be stressed : no matter what we to-day may think of Hopkins's scrupulosity, he was always inclined to put the final blame upon himself, as we see by the conclusion of the Tullabeg Retreat Notes : " Then I went

[1] *Letters*, vol. i. pp. 214-5 (April 1, 1885).
[2] *Galatians*, chap. v. Hopkins had expressed the same view in *The Caged Skylark*.

out and I said the Te Deum, and yet I thought what was needed was not praise of God but amendment of life."

From here to the end, the last tercet follows the line of St. Paul's thought : those who give way to the weaknesses and lusts of the body will not obtain the kingdom of God :

> " I see
> The lost are like this, and their scourge to be
> As I am mine, their sweating selves ; but worse."

There is nothing ambiguous in that, as we can prove by referring to the poet's note on damnation in the Beaumont diary. And here again he was speaking " with witness ". In working through the *Spiritual Exercises* he had probably learnt by heart the words of the Ignatian " meditation on hell " : [1]

> " The first prelude, a composition, which is here to see with the eye of the imagination the length, breadth and depth of hell.
> " The second to ask . . . for an intimate sense of the pain that the damned suffer, so that, if through my faults I become forgetful of the love of the Eternal Lord, at least the fear of pains and penalties may be an aid to me not to give way to sin."

After enlarging on the fires and lamentations, Loyola proceeds :

> " The fourth, to taste with the taste bitter things, as tears, sadness, and the worm of conscience."

As we have seen, Hopkins was one of those Catholics who stress not *fire* as the instrument of punishment but rather " the strain of removal " from God : hence the " sweating selves " in the poem must signify the extremity of mental anguish.

To show that Hopkins's life, as reflected in these later sonnets, was an example of ' utilitarian ', ' epicurean ', or ' masochistic ' asceticism (to use the terms of modern psychology) [2] would be to say little indeed about its underlying motives and far less about its ultimate values—both for him personally and for us to-day. A serious consideration of the universal implications of these poems forces us to compare them with such a piece of profoundly symbolic and prophetic writing as *Isaiah* liii. : the vicarious pains of that " man of sorrows ", who by his knowledge shall justify many, seem to carry over beyond the Incarnation to include some of those who by nature and choice are cast for the ' imitation ' of Christ, for a subordinate but still redemptive mission.

---

[1] *Ed. cit.* pp. 40–1.　　　　[2] See J. C. Flugel, *op. cit.* pp. 88–92.

Carrion Comfort and " I wake and feel the fell of dark " are great poems, because although subjective in treatment they impinge upon the whole human personality. That other sonnet, which deals more particularly with the poet's reaction to the social and political aspects of his exile in Dublin, does not strike home with such terrifying force. Though strongly phrased and intensely revealing, " To seem the stranger " is almost exclusively personal, and is therefore a smaller poem :

" To seem the stranger lies my lot, my life
 Among strangers. Father and mother dear,
 Brothers and sisters are in Christ not near
And he my peace my parting, sword and strife."

If this were merely a complaint that he was obliged to live abroad and apart from his family it would be an unmanly wail, the homesickness of a schoolboy. That feeling that he was a " stranger " is partly explained in a letter of 1888 written while he was on holiday with a Jesuit colleague at Lochaber : " It appears I want not scenery but friends." [1] By this he probably meant that as an artist (poet and would-be composer) he was deprived of that intimate friendship and conversation which affords sympathetic understanding and encouragement. Correspondence with three poets was not enough : he wanted the personal contact. But the really lacerating ' apartness ' indicated in the second sentence of the above quatrain was something more spiritually urgent. As he said in another letter, religious differences " go deep " ; he could not find reassurance and permanent peace in his Catholicism unless its graces were shared by all, and especially by his own kin. [2] For him, the heresy of the world was heresy and would not let him rest.

 In the next quatrain we feel the distressing conflict in Hopkins

---

[1] *Letters*, vol. i. p. 278.

[2] His sincerity in this matter is shown in the reply sent to Bridges (Oct. 20, 1888) after the latter had reminded him that his old Oxford friend and fellow-convert, W. E. Addis, had seceded from the Church of Rome : " It is as you say about Addis. But why should you be glad ? Why at any rate should you burst upon me that you are glad, when you know that I cannot be glad ? " Between himself and Bridges there was a spiritual barrier : " It seems there is something in you interposed between what shall we say ? the Christian and the man of the world which hurts, which is to me like biting on a cinder in bread." He hopes that Addis will not marry someone he has met in his priestly life, and concludes : " I feel the same deep affection for him as ever, but the respect is gone. I would write to him if I had his address . . ." (*Letters*, vol. i. p. 298.)

between his sympathy with the Catholic Irish and his loyalty to his own country :

> " England, whose honour O all my heart woos, wife
> To my creating thought, would neither hear
> Me, were I pleading, plead nor do I : I wear-
> y of idle a being but by where wars are rife."

From being a Catholic stranger among English Protestants he had now become an English stranger among Irish Catholics. His position was similar to that of his colleague, Thomas Arnold (second son of Arnold of Rugby), a convert like himself who, in 1882, had become Professor of English Literature. In the 1860's Arnold's broadening views had led to a temporary rupture with the Catholic Church ; and we may be sure that Hopkins, who contributed an account of R. W. Dixon to the English professor's *Manual of English Literature* (1885), was not unaware of his colleague's earlier doubts and vacillations. In the unrest and anti-British ferment of Dublin during the years immediately following the Phoenix Park murders, Hopkins felt, and resented, the exasperation of the clear-sighted man who can see both sides of the question but is impotent to affect either of the con-testing parties. Worse than that, he felt that he was, in one sense, aiding and abetting an unlawful cause. Though there is little surface consistency in his political opinions as recorded at this period, the above quatrain condenses meanings which must be elucidated by reference to the poet's letters and private notes.[1]

In February 1887 Hopkins complained to Bridges that two Catholic archbishops were giving open support to the Nation-alists : Walsh of Dublin was giving financial aid to Dillon and other traversers on trial for preaching the Plan of Campaign, while Croke of Cashel had contributed " to the cause of concord and civil order " by proposing to pay no taxes :

> " One archbishop backs robbery, the other rebellion ; the people in good faith believe and will follow them. You will see, it is the beginning of the end : Home Rule or separation is near. Let them come : anything is better than the attempt to rule a people who own no principle of civil obedience at all, not only to the existing government but to none at all. I should be glad to see Ireland happy, even though it involved the fall of England, if that could come about without shame or guilt. But Ireland will not be happy : a people without a principle of allegiance

[1] *Letters*, vol. ii. p. 177.

cannot be ; moreover this movement has throughout been promoted by crime." [1]

Hopkins was right ; but he should have added that crime begets counter-crime. He takes up the same point as late as January 1888, in his Retreat Notes made at Tullabeg :

> " The question is how I advance the side I serve on. This may be inwardly or outwardly. Outwardly I often think I am employed to do what is of little or no use. Something else which I can conceive myself doing might indeed be more useful, but still it is an advantage for there to be a course of higher studies for Catholics in Ireland and that that should be partly in Jesuit hands ; and my work and my salary keep that up. Meantime the Catholic Church in Ireland and the Irish Province in it and our college in that are greatly given over to a partly unlawful cause, [2] promoted by partly unlawful means, and against my will my pains, laborious and distasteful, like prisoners made to serve the enemies' gunners, go to help on this cause."

Here, surely, his various motives—religious, political, and scholastic—have become sadly confused. He continues :

> " I do not feel that outwardly I do much good, much that I care to do or can much wish to prosper ; and this is a mournful life to lead."

Mournful indeed ! And unless this pitiful statement is regarded as the spindrift of a passing nerve-storm, it implies a pitifully low ideal for a Professor of Classics ! But although we may think that Hopkins should have applied himself to his immediate duties with more faith and fortitude, we must guard against the error of supposing that his Tullabeg self-audit was something entirely unusual and pathological : almost every conscientious and hypersensitive professional man could, at some time, set down a similar if less poignant record of failure and frustration. We must admit, however, that very few men are as honest with themselves as Hopkins was.

Immediately after the above confession comes the apparently illogical suggestion that it is not so much jangled loyalties and

---

[1] *Letters*, vol. i. pp. 251-2.

[2] G. M. H. first wrote " an immoral cause ". The change to " unlawful " makes it pretty clear that any attempt to weaken the unity and solidarity of the British Empire was, to Hopkins, a form of treason, hence politically if not ethically " immoral ". In the next line " unlawful means " is preceded by " immo " deleted.

bad conscience as indifferent health that makes him loathe his own life :

> "In thought I can of course divide the good from the evil and live for the one, not for the other : this justifies me but it does not alter the facts. Yet it seems to me that I could lead this life well enough if I had bodily energy and cheerful spirits. However these God will not give me. *The other part, the more important, remains, my inward service.*"

The italics are ours, because in that last sentence we have, as always with Hopkins, something which may be called, with theological precision, a saving grace.

To return now to the second quatrain of "To seem the stranger", we can easily understand how Hopkins must have chafed at an atmosphere of strife in and through which he was powerless to act, either as combatant or peacemaker. The splitting of "wear-y" at the end of line 7 (cf. "ling-ering" in No. 41) emphasizes the drawn-out agony ; but the somewhat querulous self-pity of this passage is not so easily modulated into the universal key.

In the sestet this peevish note is largely neutralized by words which sound greater depths of both Christian and personal feeling :

> "Not but in all removes I can
> Kind love both give and get."

He wants to correct any false impression he may have given that there was something wrong with Ireland as a field for professional duties and the normal social contacts. "Out of Ireland," he said in 1887,

> "I should be no better, rather worse probably. I only need one thing—a working health, a working strength : with that, any employment is tolerable or pleasant, enough for human nature ; without it, things are liable to go very hardly with it." [1]

As hardly, in fact, as the close of this sonnet, with its muffled inhibitions and tragic bewilderment, powerfully and tersely proclaims :

> "Only what word
> Wisest my heart breeds dark heaven's baffling ban
> Bars or hell's spell thwarts. This to hoard unheard,
> Heard unheeded, leaves me a lonely began."

[1] *Letters*, vol. i. p. 251.

In his *conscious* mind it was not the inhibition of his poetic or musical talents which worried him most. His verses he was content (or so he thought) to leave to their fate, for " they stand or fall by their simple selves " ; but he believed that what he could write on philosophical matters

> " if unsaid right . . . will be said by somebody else wrong, and that is what will not let me rest." [1]

With the greatest caution, perhaps, should be considered in this context a remark Hopkins made to Bridges in a letter dealing with one of his own musical compositions :

> " discouragement is not what my complaint, in my opinion, needs. Our institute provides us means of discouragement, and on me at all events they have had all the effect that could be expected or wished and rather more." [2]

In 1884 he had spoken of the Jesuit censorship as " a barrier which I do not know how anything of mine on a large scale would ever pass " [3] ; and this suggests strongly that he feared something too markedly idiosyncratic, if not actually unorthodox, in his own philosophical and theological speculations. Yet nothing in his writings, published or unpublished, would now justify this fear.

In the next two sonnets, " Patience, hard thing " and " My own heart let me have more pity on ", we detect a certain easement, a partial escape from the tightening band of self-laceration and despair. They are, in fact, the answer to the poet's prayers, the " comforting " so earnestly besought of the Paraclete. It requires, he says, an act of mortification even to pray for Patience ; yet the reward is worth all the pains :

> " Patience, hard thing ! the hard thing but to pray,
> But bid for, Patience is ! Patience who asks
> Wants war, wants wounds ; weary his times, his tasks ;
> To do without, take tosses, and obey.
>   Rare patience roots in these, and, these away,
> Nowhere. Natural heart's ivy, Patience masks
> Our ruins of wrecked past purpose. There she basks
> Purple eyes and seas of liquid leaves all day."

The consolation is felt in the flowing language : the syntax is not tortured as it is in, say, " To seem the stranger ". This octave is like a development or exegesis of the earlier *Peace*, for in that poem it is Patience that " plumes to Peace thereafter ".

[1] *Letters*, vol. ii. p. 150.   [2] *Ibid.* vol. i. p. 248.   [3] *Ibid.* p. 200.

Now, in an exquisite image (ivy mantling the war- and time-scarred ruins of some old abbey or castle) we are made to see and feel the whole process—the transformation from alarums, wars, and wounds to reconciliation, healing, and peace.

The sestet takes us at once down to the raw quick of the exacerbated consciousness :

> " We hear our hearts grate on themselves : it kills
> To bruise them dearer. Yet the rebellious wills
> Of us we do bid God bend to him even so."

The important words which must not be overlooked are " even so ". The poet seems to say : ' Even though we, in mastering our moods and suppressing our selfish desires, may feel at the last that we are tearing at the fibres of our very being ; even though it seems that one more pang will burst the heart, yet it is right that our wills should be orientated towards God, no matter what the cost in sighs and tears.' In the *Letters* we can hear Hopkins's heart grating on itself :

> " It always seems to me that poetry is unprofessional . . ." [1]
>
> " I wish, I wish I could get on with my play." [2]
>
> " . . . when one mixes with the world and meets on every side its secret solicitations, to live by faith is harder, is very hard." [3]

Apart from the merit gained, the immediate social purpose of this total submission to God's will is summed up in the last tercet :

> " And where is he who more and more distils
> Delicious kindness ?—He is patient. Patience fills
> His crisp combs, and that comes those ways we know."

The " crisp combs " suggest the firmness of the disciplined will of the well-planned, industrious and selfless life ; and " those ways we know " means that we must combine the familiar patience of the bee with the well known fortitude of the great martyrs and saints ; for in the total inscape of the Christian life success and failure have no separate meaning.

The sonnet is nobly and sensuously didactic, but it does not state the whole truth about suffering human nature. We gather from Hopkins's spiritual notes that what was lacking in his rigidly scrupulous or over-anxious attitude to duty had been pointed out by a Fr. Foley or Fr. Whitty, some colleague or confessor. In any case, when the poet sat down to write No. 47, " My own

---

[1] *Letters*, vol. i. p. 197.   [2] *Ibid.* p. 191.   [3] *Ibid.* vol. ii. p. 93.

heart let me have more pity on ", he appears to have realized that the man who shows no charity towards himself is eventually incapable of distilling delicious kindness or of filling his crisp combs with anything but gall. At once homely, subtle, vigorous, and pathetic, this sonnet is one of his most original and, despite the idiosyncrasy of the close, one of the most satisfying.

It is one thing to deny oneself; it is another and often a better thing to forget oneself. Excessive introspection is a form of egoism, and may be a form of cowardice; and Hopkins, who knew the truth as well as anyone, and who gave in so many directions a noble example of self-effacement, was nevertheless dogged by the introspective habit to the verge of insanity. Instead of glutting his sorrow on a morning rose, he too frequently aggravated his tormented mind by harping and brooding on its very torments. It all comes back to what we have already said about his lack of psychic adjustment, his pathetic failure to launch into the world one child of his mind which would exist in its own right, apart from himself. But in this sonnet at last he resolves to escape from the treadmill of vain endeavour, the vicious circle of self-breeding cares. The vortex into which he is being sucked is perfectly realized in the centripetal sweep of the syntax of both parts of the octave, at the end of which his whole world is swathed in cloud. [1]

With the beginning of the sestet the clouds part and a beam of practical wisdom floods the landscape. The unnatural claustrophobic tension of the grammar is broken up into short colloquial ejaculations; even the decorous dictionary seems to emit that Horatian chuckle—*dulce est desipere in loco*:

> " Soul, self; come, poor Jackself, I do advise
> You, jaded, let be; call off thoughts awhile
> Elsewhere; leave comfort root-room; let joy size
> At God knows when to God knows what; whose smile
> 's not wrung, you see; unforeseen times rather—as skies
> Betweenpie mountains—lights a lovely mile."

---

[1] The last image in the octave:

> " or thirst can find
> Thirst's all-in-all in all a world of wet,"

is, of course, a reminiscence of the Ancient Mariner's

> " Water, water, everywhere,
> Nor any drop to drink."

The " world of wet " suggests Glendower's " world of water " (1 *Hen. IV.*, III. i. 94) —i.e. copious brackish tears; it also suggests endless devotions which do not bring the expected spiritual comfort, as in No. 41, lines 3 and 4:

> " Mary, mother of us, where is your relief? "

Hopkins says in his own dramatic way what Milton had said with elegant rhetoric in the sestet of his sonnet *To Cyriac Skinner* :

> " To measure life learn thou betimes, and know
>   Toward solid good what leads the nearest way ;
>   For other things mild Heav'n a time ordains,
>   And disapproves that care, though wise in show,
>   That with superfluous burden loads the day,
>   And, when God sends a cheerful hour, refrains."

We turn away from these intensely personal and introspective sonnets to say something about the poet's powers of ' recovery '. It is significant that on the same sheet as the four sonnets we have just examined, and preceding them, appears the first draft of that unfinished ' curtal sonnet ' called *Ash-boughs*. It goes to prove that even before writing the self-admonition of No. 47 Hopkins was still capable of calling off thoughts from professional worries, of leaving comfort not only " root-room " but room also for hung-heavenward boughs, lashtender sprays, and twigs that burst pyrotechnically in the sky. The only other extant draft of *Ash-boughs* is on a separate sheet, so we are probably right in assuming that Hopkins had recovered sufficiently from the gall and heartburn of " I wake and feel the fell of dark " to return to the nature-poem in the hope of recapturing the mystical vision and pure delight of the poems of 1877.

Within the last fifty years there have been many Wordsworthian poets

> " To whom a tree seems something more than tree "—

poets who had found in trees a vague but exciting metaphysical significance. For Mr. J. D. C. Pellow they are " sacramental ". Trees that swirl and wash round and over the distraught soul of man are for poets like Whitman and Harold Monro a balm and a consolation ; and Mr. Aldous Huxley (once a pure poet) was teased by Lombardy poplars into asking :

> " Or are you all an upward agony
>   Of undefined desires ? "

In *Ash-boughs*, Hopkins had anticipated and answered Huxley's question ; and his answer was the outcome of many years of happy and precise observation. The ash, one of his favourite trees, was delicately described in the early fragment called *Richard* :

> " thinning skywards by degrees,
> With parallel shafts,—as upward-parted ashes,—
> Their highest sprays were drawn as fine as lashes," [1]

He discovered in the ash-tree the same inscape " mixed of strength and grace " as in a bluebell,[2] and in 1870 he sketched in his *Journal* " the skeleton inscape of a spray end of ash." [3]

In Marsh 1871 he found in the budding and opening of trees " a new world of inscape ". The male ashes, he says,

> " are very boldly jotted with the heads of the bloom which tuft the outer ends of the branches. . . . When the bud breaks at first it shews a heap of fruity purplish anthers . . . but these push open into richly-branched tree-pieces coloured buff and brown, shaking out loads of pollen, and drawing the tuft as a whole into peaked quains,—mainly four. I think, two bigger and two smaller." [4]

Two months later he noticed that the ashes, having opened their knots, made " strong yellow crowns against the slaty blue sky." [5] Yet at least fourteen years had to elapse, and the poet had to feel himself lying in a coffin of dejection before his spirit, casting the body's vest aside, could slip finally into the boughs of his beloved trees. Once more that outward visible beauty was the sign of an inward spiritual grace : for *Ash-boughs* implies a reading of earth and its inanimate progeny as in a mystical sense related to the nostalgic, developing, aspiring spirit in man :

> " Not of all my eyes see, wandering on the world,
> Is anything a milk to the mind so, so sighs deep
> Poetry to it, as a tree whose boughs break in the sky.
>
> Say it is ash-boughs : whether on a December day and furled
> Fast or they in clammyish lashtender combs creep
> Apart wide and new-nestle at heaven most high.

---

[1] *Poems*, Third Edition, No. 87.   [2] *Note-books*, p. 134.
[3] *Ibid.* pp. 141-2.   [4] *Ibid.* p. 142.
[5] *Ibid.* p. 147. Cf. p. 211 : " I looked at some delicate flying shafted ashes—there was one especially of a single sonnet-like inscape."

They touch heaven, tabour on it ; how their talons sweep
The smouldering enormous winter welkin ! May
Mells blue and snow white through them, a fringe and fray

Of greenery : it is old earth's groping towards the steep
Heaven whom she childs us by." [1]

The poet sees the combs or topmost crests of the ash-tree
splayed out against the sky, as fine as eyelashes ; yet the naturalist
knows at the same time what is happening up there : he seems
to feel the sticky lining of the burst bud-coats, the clammy
freshness of the bright new shoots. This poem, moreover, can
be read or apprehended differently at two levels of the mind,
the normal and the ' liminal '—the almost subliminal : at the
first the imagery is mainly *visual* ; at the second it is mainly
tactile.

When we have read and pondered the poem many times we
find that the predominant image (beginning in the second line
and culminating in the last) is physiological, progenitive. We
are made to think of a new-born child nestling against the bosom
of the mother. The tapering, talon-like fingers of the eager
suckling grope for, tabour on and clutch at the full breast
(cf. " milk to the mind ")—snow-white clouds with veins of
blue sky between—the seemingly near yet mysteriously remote
source of that heavenly milk (" heaven most high ") ; for both
the tree and the mind of man reach upwards as well as downwards for their sustenance. As the scientific rationalists would
say, man is still a mere nursling at the breast of nature ; but
Hopkins parts company with the rationalists by saying that the
human spirit must be nourished by the spurting fountains of
supra-rational instress, by that " deep poetry " which is nothing
less than intuitive ontology—the knowledge of the ultimate
essence and being of all things.

A mother can sigh lovingly over her child or can be coldly
aloof, angry and terrifying (" the smouldering enormous winter
welkin ") ; but whatever the mood of that life-giving source
called Nature, the infantile creature, be it man or tree, is partly
or wholly dependent upon her, the mighty Mother. Yet Nature
herself (or " earth ", as she is more intimately designated in the
last sentence of the poem) is not the real *fons et origo* ; for earth
herself, who yields to the male embrace of One who begets upon

[1] The version we give from line seven onwards is the one we personally prefer—
he first.

her a numerous progeny, is still like a mere babe groping up
and grasping at " steep Heaven "—the God who is at once
husband and father. The poem, therefore, is a nature-parable
based on the mystical opening theme of the fragmentary No. 73 :

> " Thee, God, I come from, to thee go,
> All day long I like fountain flow
> From thy hand out, swayed about
> Mote-like in thy mighty glow."

Indeed, *Ash-boughs* may well strike us as being a subtle poetic
embodiment of a very ancient religious concept—that God, in
His infinite Being, includes both sexes : He is both Father and
Mother, Seed and Matrix. According to the poem, " heaven
most high " is both begetter and nurse ; and when we consider
the functions of the Holy Ghost and Mary Mother of God in
Christian dogma, we can understand how the month of May
" mells " not only blue and white through ash-boughs but also
the Catholic conception of Godhead with something far more
primitive. Again, one might almost find, in the final image, a
suggestion of the Spinozist concept of God and the world as the
ctive and *passive* aspects of an all-embracing Nature (*natura
naturans* and *natura naturata*).

As we have seen in other poems, Hopkins's imagination,
when it was working freely and strongly, tended sometimes to
include philosophic or mythological elements which were pre-
Christian and pagan.[1] In his second version of *Ash-boughs*, in
which the last five lines of the first draft were expanded to seven,
he made one significant alteration : in line 11,

> " Heaven whom she childs *us* by "

became

> " Heaven with it whom she childs *things* by "—

as though he had feared the monistic or pantheistic implications
of " us ". His very first thought had been, " Heaven once

---

[1] E.g. in *Spelt from Sibyl's Leaves* and the *Heraclitean Fire*. We remind the reader
so that in his two Marian poems Hopkins boldly associates the Virgin Mother with
some aspect of nature—first with the creative energy of the Prime Good, which
brings forth *beauty* in trees and flowers and *truth* in man, then with the enveloping
atmosphere, the screening medium between the gentle Son and the awful Sun,
. between the passive worshipping soul of man and the almighty, " O thou terrible "
Father. This connexion between Mary, the " mighty mother " of *The May Magnificat*,
and Nature or Earth constitutes a link, however tenuous, between the Marian poems
and *Ash-boughs*.

Earth childed by ", which could refer equally to the creation of
Adam and ash-boughs ; so that his second thought, " us ", is
more authentic than the ugly and timid " things " ; for in a
physical sense human beings are indeed children of Earth. The
relationship of men to ' mute insensate things ' had been even
closer in *Ribblesdale*, in which the poet says that man is the " eye,
tongue, heart " of Earth ; so that when a just man knits his
brows with pain and sorrow at the sight of sin and ugliness,
then Earth too appears to " wear brows of such care, care and
dear concern."

By 1886 Hopkins had become so sensitive to the insidious
interpenetration of good and evil, of physical beauty and moral
ugliness in human life, that on looking at the portrait " of Two
Beautiful Young People "—a brother and sister—he exclaimed :

> " O I admire and sorrow ! The heart's eye grieves
> Discovering you, dark tramplers, tyrant years.
> A juice rides rich through bluebells, in vine leaves,
> And beauty's dearest veriest vein is tears."

Ostensibly this is just another beautiful lament evoked by the
destruction wrought by time on the body—the inevitable wrinkle
and hoar hair, which Hopkins foresees. But the highest and
most lovable beauty is *moral* beauty. All the " juice and joy "
of the sonnet *Spring*, though still sweet, leaves now upon the
poet's own aging palate a faint bitterness, the after-taste of
experience and disenchantment. The mood of *On the Portrait* is
the mood of *Spring and Fall* shot through with a deeper theological
note, which causes joy and melancholy to be constantly breaking
through each other :

> " Happy the father, mother of these ! Too fast :
> Not that, but thus far, all with frailty, blest
> In one fair fall ; "

Having congratulated the parents, Hopkins checks his enthusiasm ; so far, he says, physical perfection, though undermined
by moral frailty (the " fair fall " of beauty masking the ' foul
Fall ' of Original Sin) augurs well ; but who can tell how their
characters will develop ? Nevertheless their high potentiality,
nay, the very uncertainty of their future has its fascination :

> " but, for time's aftercast,
> Creatures all heft, hope, hazard, interest."

Like Cowper on his mother's picture, Hopkins now pays tribute to the art " that can immortalize "—the fixing of lineaments

> " That fleeted else like day-dissolvèd dreams
> Or ringlet-race on burling Barrow [1] brown."

There is a tender loveliness in the stanza which describes the two naturally posed figures, the Patmorean dependence of the girl on the brother whose looks, " the soul's own letters, see beyond, / Gaze on, and fall directly forth on life."   The poet suggests that they are like a bright forelock on the brow of Time ; hence Hopkins must take time by the forelock and ask them a pertinent question :

> " Where lies your landmark, seamark, or soul's star ? "

Such beauty as theirs must be matched, orientated and protected by an equivalent strength and beauty in the affective will ; and Christ is the only star by which an unerring course may be steered through the rock-strewn seas of an affluent and ' sheltered ' life.   " There's none but truth can stead you "— can serve your purpose and *steady* you, as Miss Phare has sensitively explained.[2]   And there is another expressive ambiguity in the next stanza :

> " There's none but good can be good, both for you
> And what *sways* with you, maybe this sweet maid ; "

Hopkins rightly addresses the man as the greater power for good or evil and the one more likely to go astray. The clause " what sways with you " means first of all " what is close to your heart, exerts an influence over you " ; but it suggests also that his sister's fate, like his own, is in the balance, and the stability of *her* happiness may depend upon the firmness of *his* grasp on virtue.   Hopkins fears that he may be weighed in the balance and " found wanting "—like that young man who turned away from Christ because he had " great possessions " :

> " a warning wavèd to
> " One once that was found wanting when Good weighed."

The natural bent of these young people might be towards good or evil : the election of the secret will is unpredictable : " Fast furled and all foredrawn to No or Yes." But the direction

---

[1] The river flowing past Monasterevan, Co. Kildare.   [2] *Op. cit.* p. 60.

given to the will by an intellect which knows its goal, its supreme Good (which is Christ), will in time enable the soul to operate, in a wise passiveness, by a power other than its own ; for in this state, as St. John of the Cross said, it is the Holy Spirit which moves the soul to perform its acts.[1]

Such was Hopkins's faith, but he knew the conditions of fulfilment to be difficult. In this poem he is experiencing again, though more poignantly, the mood which produced *The Bugler's First Communion*—the same mood which, before his own day, had wrung from that kindred soul, Eugénie de Guérin, the cry : " Oh, the agony of being in fear for a soul's salvation, who can describe it ? " Hopkins has done so, as few others could. He had none of Browning's easy optimism : he did not believe that " what began best can't end worst, / Nor what God blest once, prove accurst." Such a doctrine ignores the power of environment and deprives man of moral responsibility. ' No,' Hopkins warns his young friend of Monasterevan,

> " that most in you earnest eye
> May but call on your banes to more carouse."

In proportion as you are clever and attractive . . . but we have only to think of Oscar Wilde to realize the bitter truth of stanza 8.[2]

Hopkins saw clearly what Browning and Whitman were usually too robustiously ' healthy ' and hopeful to observe, namely, that there are no limits to the lust, cruelty, and destructiveness of men—those who have rejected Christ, even some of those who have professed Him :

> " Enough : corruption was the world's first woe.
> What need I strain my heart beyond my ken ?
> O but I bear my burning witness though
> Against the wild and wanton work of men."

Hopkins could not rhapsodize like Tennyson about future vistas of material progress, or bluster like Browning about man's need

[1] Cf. Fr. Bede Jarrett : " It is clear, indeed, from the Catholic doctrine of grace, that it is possible for God to move the will so powerfully as to determine not merely that the will shall act, but to determine also that it shall act freely . . . God is so intimate to the will that He can, so to say, save it from within. (*The Holy Ghost*, pp. 30–1.)

[2] The kind of experience which went to the making of this poem is related in a letter of 1888 : " There was a young man in this house in my first year, an Englishman, manly and winning too, the sweetest mannered boy. After he left us he went astray. I tried to call on him, but after many trials, finding he shunned me, I gave up trying. I hear he has made a mess of it [the medical profession] and is going to make a new beginning in Australia." (*Letters*, vol. i. p. 282.)

to drive straight for his own desire, be it good or bad. Hopkins was not constrained either by popularity or the lack of it to pander to a complacent public ; he had no public, but was confronted daily with the plain facts of man's moral delinquency. For the " hung-heavenward boughs " of infinite faculty and godlike apprehension, Hopkins, like Hamlet, entertained the deepest veneration ; but for the " havoc-pocked leaves ", for the pitiful declension of this angel and beauty of the world to " this quintessence of dust "—for these facts Hopkins knew of only one credible explanation, and that was the doctrine of the Fall— " the world's first woe ". [1]

Why therefore, he asks, should he strive to foresee the future of these two young people, and wring his own heart (perhaps needlessly) in the process ? He knows all the possibilities, good and evil : there is no perfection in man living, but only in man saved. His, as a Christian, is not to reason why, but only to pray and " lie by ", as he had said in *The Bugler*. This stanza has not an air of " hopelessness and defeat ", as one critic has suggested,[2] but a combination of righteous anger and resignation. Yet we have the feeling, too, that the poem could not have been carried further. The poet has explained why he admired and why he sorrowed. Apart, perhaps, from reiterating his faith in the Salvific Will of God, there was really nothing more to be said. Even as it stands, the poem makes a satisfying whole.

Because Hopkins was not sufficiently well acquainted with the persons in the portrait to be swayed by feelings of personal regard or animosity, he achieved in this elegy a genuine philosophic detachment. He informed Dixon that he hoped in a few days to see the hero and heroine of it, which might enable him to finish the poem—" (or quite the reverse ; perhaps that : *it is not well to come too near things*)." [3] There is a sense, then, in which a detailed, intimate knowledge of people distorts perspective ; in this sense " to seem the stranger " is the lot of every true poet.[4]

[1] There is an apposite passage in a letter to Patmore : " But why do we find beautiful evil ? Not by any freak of nature. . . . it is old, simple, and the undeniable fact. It comes from wicked will, freedom of choice, abusing the beauty, the good of its nature." (*Further Letters*, p. 159.)

[2] E. E. Phare, *op. cit.* p. 62.   [3] *Letters*, vol. ii. p. 154.

[4] In the MS. there is a deleted stanza which resembles a part of *To his Watch* (No. 70) :

> ' Ah, life, what's like it ? Booth at Fairlop Fair ;
> Men, boys brought in to have each our shy there, one
> Shot, mark or miss, no more. I miss, and " There !
> Another time I . . ." " Time, says Death, is done." '

Hopkins again achieved an unusual detachment (this time not only from his subject but also from doctrinal under- or after-thoughts) in the two Dromore sonnets of 1887. During a holiday spent in a house and grounds " once Bishop Percy's ", he wrote his two highly studied ' caudated sonnets '—*Tom's Garland : upon the Unemployed* and *Harry Ploughman*. Both works show that Hopkins was intellectually and psychically aware of the changing social world about him. It was in 1884 that the Third Reform Bill, by extending the franchise to the agricultural labourer, had given that neglected but indispensable worker a new dignity in his own and in the world's eyes—a pride which is reflected in the lissom body and dynamic beauty of Harry Ploughman ; and it was in 1886 that the march of the Unemployed on ' Bloody Sunday ' brought the great problem of late-Victorian industrialism to a lurid climax.

Concerning *Harry Ploughman* a living poet-critic has said :

> " In nature Hopkins saw the glory of God, and in himself he felt the terror of God. There is little in his poetry between these two extremes, little objective concern with ordinary human life. In poems like *Harry Ploughman*, Harry is merely a section of the physical universe." [1]

There is a general truth in the second half of this statement ; for unlike Wordsworth, Browning, Whitman, and most other modern poets, Hopkins wrote very few poems which deal directly with the actions and emotions of ordinary life. Yet the statement as a whole may be misleading. Hopkins saw the glory of God not only in nature but in man—in the Blessed Virgin (his *Ewig-Weibliche*), in the Bugler, in the lad with the " handsome heart ", in Henry the sensitive brother, in all the choice spirits who passed like lanterns in the night. And in his own struggle to emulate Christ he perceived, in ' negative ' as it were, the instress and inscape of the creative Holy Ghost—the glory of God. Again, he saw the terror of God in nature as well as in man— in the elements which smote the *Deutschland,* in the squall which overset the *Eurydice,* in the deadly swoop of the windhover and the black whirlpool of Inversnaid. Indeed, the whole " million-fuelèd bonfire " of nature forces from him the cry, " O pity and indignation ! "

In estimating Hopkins's concern with ordinary human life we must distinguish between accidents and details on the one

[1] Mr. Edwin Muir, *op. cit.* pp. 91–3. (See above, p. 322, note 2.)

hand and essentials on the other. Implicitly, and in a purely ethico-poetical sense of the word ' human ', Hopkins has a great deal to say about ordinary human nature. Our commentary hitherto should have made this clear. But to elaborate a specific instance, one has not read *To What Serves Mortal Beauty?* with anything like a full imaginative comprehension unless one perceives its wide application to common life. In the opening lines one sees (apart from Hopkins) the hedonist who may become the respondent in a common divorce case, the man who is weighing the ethical pattern and happiness of many lives linked to his own against the selfish possession of some new beauty. To our mind, the emotional stress could not be greater, the poet's solution could not be clearer, if Hopkins had padded out the poem with as much circumstance and paradox as Browning gives us in *The Statue and the Bust*. Hopkins's short poem is devoid of cheap sensation and romantic appeal ; it merely throws an intense beam of wisdom upon a score of life's common but crucial experiences.

In the process of delimiting Hopkins's achievement the same critic says :

> " The pathos of Felix Randal is the pathos of his ' mould of man ', of natural decay like that of a tree. . . . Hopkins clearly knew very little about Harry Ploughman and Felix Randal as human beings, except on this [the ' natural '] plane and perhaps cared to know very little more."

This, again, is half-truth. Did the " sweet reprieve and ransom " —the sacraments of Penance and Supreme Unction administered to the farrier mean nothing at all to the priest ? The excellent comparison with a tree is marred by the fact that a tree may be riven but hardly shriven. Hopkins the priest was not a ' hireling wolf ' : he knew far more about Felix Randal than he thought fit to set down. His knowledge is distilled into the passion of the poem. He probably knew little or nothing about the private life and opinions of Harry the ploughman, and his artistic purpose in that poem would not have been served by such details.

Harry Ploughman is a poem of ' recovery '. It has " Churls-grace, too, child of Amansstrength " ; but its very strength (as shown in the packed epithets and muscular syntax) would hardly have been possible without the poet's powerful, sensitive recoil from inhibition and frustration. It was the man who could write to Bridges " AND WHAT DOES ANYTHING AT ALL

MATTER ? " and then, " I am, I believe, recovering from a deep fit of nervous prostration ",[1] who was best fitted to prove the force of Gray's famous stanza :

> " See the Wretch, that long has tost
>   On the thorny bed of Pain,
> At length repair his vigour lost,
>   And breathe, and walk again :
> The meanest flowret of the vale,
> The simplest note that swells the gale,
> The common Sun, the air, the skies,
> To him are op'ning Paradise." [2]

It is in this sense that Harry Ploughman is a section of the physical universe—an item in the general " news of God ".

The healthy objectivity of this poem is maintained in *Tom's Garland*, which shows what may happen to men like Harry in times of agricultural and industrial depression. In previous chapters we have spoken of the form and style of this sonnet ; and speaking, in Volume I, of the subject-matter, we stigmatized a certain apparent lack of sympathy in the poet's description of the workless as " packs " which " infest the age ".[3] That criticism of the immediate, contemporary motivation still stands. We have now to consider the value of the poem for the present age and the future.

More important than the personal feeling manifested by the poet is the mystical sense of Relationship and Degree from which the whole poem springs—an adaptation to the social sphere of St. Paul's statement regarding the mystical Body of Christ's Church : " that there should be no schism in the body but that members should have the same care one for another." [4] Now the ordinary working man's real " garland " or gift of grace is " Heart-at-ease ", the state of being secure and comfortable without gnawing responsibility ; whereas the crown or special reward of those who bear the pains of government is eminence, ceremony, the pleasure of wielding power. The ideal state or society is a graded hierarchy of function ; but broadly speaking, all people fall into one or other of two classes : " earth's glory, earth's ease ". The two balance perfectly, for the degree of *real* freedom we enjoy is in inverse proportion to the responsibility we bear. There is no room for grasping ambition (*over*-participation) and there is no room for unemployment (*under*-participation) : each

---

[1] *Letters*, vol. i. pp. 192–3. [2] *On the Pleasures Arising From Vicissitude.*
[3] Chapter v. p. 159. [4] 1 Corinthians, xii. 25.

member of the state must feel that " honour " consists in working according to his ability and in being contented with his lot.

This is the Catholic view of the function of the individual in the state ' under God ' ; and *Tom's Garland* is a local and particular embodiment of the same concept. If the Church, like this poet, tends to be conservative, it is not only because it deprecates forces which threaten to destroy Christianity ; it is also because it foresees the difficulty of accommodating the inevitable social changes within the inevitable hierarchical structure of society. Already we are threatened with a considerable body of workers who are educated and conditioned above their functional status. Unless and until the social fabric is adapted to receive them, the undercurrent of discontent and suppressed fury as described by Hopkins will always obtain.

In 1887 Britain was still galvanized by the doctrine of the sacredness of Work, as preached by Carlyle. Nowadays the emphasis has shifted from Work to Leisure. Moreover, with the decline of fervid, disinterested patriotism (a decline due to the growing conviction that a more broadly international outlook is rendered imperative by economic conditions) Tom Navvy's slogan, " Country is honour enough in all us " stirs now but a feeble response. Hopkins was probably right, for the nation must remain as a social and economic unit which demands a co-operative loyalty. Nevertheless the first line of that recruiting song which Hopkins thought so necessary in 1885, " What can *I* do for the land that bred me ? ", sounds to-day with an inverted echo in the minds of a million conscripts—' What will the land I fought for do for *me* ? '

Tom's Garland is a living poem because it evokes a positive attitude towards problems which are still far from being solved ; and even if they were solved it would still remain as a warning. The very diction is an antidote to national inertia : " rips out rockfire ", " sturdy Dick ", " Lustily ", " Little I reck ho ! " " mighty . . . mainstrength ". Tom's cheerfully hobnailed ' Homeward Ho ! ' was, we feel sure, matched next morning by an equally contented and percussive ' Workward Ho ! ' The poem underrates the now general desire to attain more " level " or a higher social status, but it gives us a much-needed reminder of the compensations of humble service. Finally it suggests that if God's will is to be done on earth, that golden syllable *Work* must never return a leaden echo, whether it be the snarl of a Manwolf or the sneer of a Sybarite.

Hopkins tells us that during his Dublin years it was not so much lack of time as lack of inspiration that prevented him from writing poetry.[1] But what is inspiration but the movement of a spirit which is confident in its power *and right* to use time for a creative purpose? Hopkins did not succeed in calling off thoughts as often and as completely as the sacred fire demanded. The two Dromore sonnets and *That Nature is a Heraclitean Fire* (the only finished poem of the year 1888) were all begun when the poet was away from Dublin on vacation, at times when he felt justified in forgetting his lectures and examination papers.

The *Heraclitean Fire* is the climax of recovery, the almost exhausted poet's great counterblast to " joyless days, dejection ". On this work we have already written at some length.[2] The only serious criticism which can be levelled against it is that the objective truth of the last eight and a half lines cannot be finally denied or attested until the reader is incapable of any further ' psychological adjustment '. That is why some critics call this the greatest of the poems, while others dismiss it as " totally unexplosive ". Those last lines are a powerful appeal for faith ; but since nearly all our great motives and cues for action are based ultimately upon faith (the perfectibility of man, the abolition of war, the classless society, etc.), the dogmatic close of Hopkins's poem stands or falls by its poetry ; and that, we think, is secure. The *Heraclitean Fire* is one of the great Christian poems of all time.

Even the sceptic will sympathize with Hopkins's belief in the Resurrection when he reads, in the letters of 1888, the poet's increasingly bitter complaints about his inability to complete his literary projects. A paper of his on Sophocles had failed to appear in the *Classical Review*, and on May 25 he wrote to Bridges :

> " So I am afraid the whole will come to nought. However, to me, to finish a thing and that it should be out of hand and owe its failure to somebody else is nearly the same thing as success.
> " For instance I began an Epithalamion on my brother's wedding : it had some bright lines, but I could not get it done. That is worse." [3]

Time has added the comment that *Epithalamion*, though merely a fragment of some forty-seven lines, is one of the loveliest

---

[1] *Letters*, vol. i. p. 270.   [2] See Vol. I. chapter v. pp. 161–5.
[3] *Letters*, vol. i. p. 277. Cf. *ibid*. p. 294.

nature-poems in the language. The sprung rhythm, in irregular paragraphs and lines carrying anything from two to ten stresses, is managed throughout with the most delicate ear. The rhyme-scheme also is irregular, twenty-nine chimes being used—now together, now with long intervals in the manner of Patmore—delayed repetitions which overlap the paragraphs and enhance the effect of bird-call and boy-shout in the care-free lapse of this "echoing-of-earth" rhapsody. The twinkle of leaves, the sun-sparkle of foam and the flash of wet bodies are all conveyed in a rich phonal texture which recalls the poet's earlier Welsh days :

" Hark, hearer, hear what I do ; lend a thought now, make believe
    We are leafwhelmed somewhere with the hood
    Of some branchy bunchy bushybowered wood,
    Southern dene or Lancashire clough or Devon cleave,
    That leans along the loins of hills, where a candycoloured, where
        a gluegold-brown
    Marbled river, boisterously beautiful, between
    Roots and rocks is danced and dandled, all in froth and water-
        blowballs, down.
    We are there, when we hear a shout
    That the hanging honeysuck, the dogeared hazels in the cover
    Makes dither, makes hover
    And the riot of a rout
    Of, it must be, boys from the town
    Bathing : it is summer's sovereign good."

Hopkins probably remembered, as an object for emulation, the natural setting of Spenser's two great marriage-poems—the flowers, birds, and echoing woods. This poem, too, gives us the quintessence of summer's delights ; yet with all the brightness and movement there is also a suggestion of calm, an atmosphere mystical and consecrated, as in the background of a sacred picture by Fra Angelico or Raphael :

" . . . Rafts and rafts of flake-leaves light, dealt so, painted on the air,
    Hang as still as hawk or hawkmoth, as the stars or as the angels
        there,
    Like the thing that never knew the earth, never off roots
    Rose . . . "

The "heavenfallen freshness" of the stream, which tumbles down from the moorland "Dark or daylight on and on", is a fitting symbol of spousal love (and how significantly different from the fiery erotic symbols of a D. H. Lawrence is that "flinty

13*

kindcold element " !). Moreover the earthly glory of tha
delightful dene is a symbol of wedlock quite in keeping with th
mystical symbolism of the Catholic school of Luis de León
which owed much to the *Song of Songs*. The only weakness, a
we have said before, is the disconcerting abruptness of th
exegesis.

In the last two years of his life Hopkins completed no mor
than five poems, but even more extraordinary than this smallnes
of output is the range of feeling and mood they cover—exultan
faith, proud resignation, cynical disgust, and pathetic despai
In the sonnet on St. Alphonsus Rodriguez (1889), the selfles
objectivity of *Epithalamion* gives way to an objectivity which i
impregnated with a deeply-felt self-analysis ; in the last thre
' Miltonic ' sonnets the poet is quite unable to escape from hi
own sad self.

San Alfonso Rodriguez, in whose life Hopkins saw somethin
like a prototype or reflection of his own, died at the age of ninet
in 1617. Unlike Hopkins, however, he had been married, anc
it was the loss of his wife, daughter, and mother that made hin
give serious thought to what God was calling him to do in th
world. When nearly forty he was accepted as a lay-brother o
' temporal coadjutor ' of the Society of Jesus, and for forty-fiv
years he served as Porter at the College of Montesion in Majorca

By all who knew him he was described as a perfect example o
modesty, cheerfulness, and obedience. He seems to have attainec
to a greater degree of detachment than his English eulogist ; bu
to illustrate the affinity between the two men, and to show tha
Hopkins's spiritual unrest was not incompatible with the orthodo
Catholic conception of sainthood, we quote from Butler's *Life* o
St. Alphonsus :

> " Every minute left free by his work and what it entailec
> was given to prayer ; but though he achieved a marvellou
> habitual recollection and union with God, his spiritual path wa
> far from an easy one. Especially in his later years he sufferec
> from long periods of desolation and aridity. . . . Added to thi
> he was beset with violent temptations, just as though for year
> he had not curbed his body by fierce austerities, which now hac
> to be made even more rigorous." [1]

Such was " the war within ", that " fiercest fray " the hurtle o
which was made audible to the world at large by Hopkins'

[1] Edn. of Herbert Thurston, S.J. (1942), vol. x. Oct. 30 ; pp. 367-71.

powerful sonnet and perhaps by that alone, for *Lives of the Saints* no longer make popular reading. As Hopkins said in a letter, " Alphonsus was, it is believed, much favoured by God with heavenly light and much persecuted by evil spirits ; " and it is interesting to note that the Freudian school of critics will, in the case of Alphonsus, be harder put to it than in that of Hopkins to justify their obvious allegation, namely that the aridity and temptations and ' evil spirits ' of this elderly Spanish widower proceeded entirely from repressed sexual instinct.

The sestet of the Alphonsus sonnet is among the finest things Hopkins ever wrote ; its ' Italian ' form is perfect in the incidence of the climax (line 12) and the serene but firm lapse of the close :

> " Yet God (that hews mountain and continent,
>   Earth, all, out ; who, with trickling increment,
>   Veins violets and tall trees makes more and more)
>   Could crowd career with conquest while there went
>   Those years and years by of world without event
>   That in Majorca Alfonso watched the door."

That sestet, as we have seen throughout the present study, was Hopkins's own justification. It proved to be almost his epitaph. The last two sonnets that he sent to Bridges (Nos. 50 and 51) seem like the winding up of his literary affairs. Yet the passionate plea in the last line of the former and the keen self-knowledge evinced in the octave of the latter are not compatible with a state of complete hopelessness. No doubt the pressure of suffering, the feeling of frustration, had been so prolonged that a breakdown into apathy and dementia was at least a possibility ; but there is no feebleness in the sonnet dated ' March 17, '89 ' (No. 50), which Hopkins says " must be read *adagio molto* and with great stress ".[1]

The original motive of this sonnet would seem to have been set down just over a year previously, in the Tullabeg Retreat Notes of January 1888. But if we compare this dull, lifeless prose with the vigorous, pulsing sonnet, we shall realize the cathartic and tranquillizing effect of time upon the raw emotion of despair; we shall also realize the force of the word ' recovery ' in the title of the present chapter. In the sequel to the notes as quoted above [p. 343], Hopkins writes :

> " I was continuing this train of thought . . . when I began
> to enter on that course of loathing and hopelessness which I have

[1] *Letters*, vol. i. p. 303.

so often felt before, which made me fear madness and led me to give up the practice of meditation except, as now, in retreat and here it is again. I could therefore do no more than repeat *Justus es Domine, et rectum judicium tuum* and the like, and then being tired I nodded and woke with a start. What is my wretched life ? Five wasted years almost have passed in Ireland. I am ashamed of the little I have done, of my waste of time, although my help-lessness and weakness is such that I could scarcely do otherwise. And yet the wise man warns us against excusing ourselves in that fashion. I cannot then be excused ; but what is life without aim, without spur, without help ? "

In the sonnet, after quoting *Justus es*, etc., from *Jer.* xii, Hopkins complains to God of his crippling sterility in lines of taut and impressive poetry. His opening shows a combination of plainness and rhetorical strength :

> " Thou art indeed just, Lord, if I contend
>   With thee ; but, sir, so what I plead is just.
>   Why do sinners' ways prosper ? and why must
>   Disappointment all I endeavour end ? "

The tone is at once tender and respectful ; but in the next quatrain we detect a note of almost angry bewilderment : the poet is so carried away that he forgets to observe the usual *volta*—or rather it occurs (as often in Milton) a little late :

> " Wert thou my enemy, O thou my friend,
>   How wouldst thou worse, I wonder, than thou dost
>   Defeat, thwart me ?   Oh, the sots and thralls of lust
>   Do in spare hours more thrive than I that spend,
>   Sir, life upon thy cause."

The pleading is masterly. How, one asks, could a just God refuse to hear such a prayer ?

At this point the plaintiff seems to feel that he has gained by direct assault a position which he must now consolidate by pathetic infiltration. He drops into a more subdued but richly figurative and allusive style :

> " See, banks and brakes
>   Now, leavèd how thick ! lacèd they are again
>   With fretty chervil, look, and fresh wind shakes
>   Them ; "

This abrupt pause ushers in the climax :

> " birds build—but not I build : no, but strain,
>   Time's eunuch, and not breed one work that wakes."

Another pause, like that of a skilled counsel about to make his last appeal ; then the final plea, the clinching request :

> " Mine, O thou lord of life, send my roots rain."

One almost suspects that Hopkins would have made a better advocate than preacher.[1]

Hopkins had felt for years as even Wordsworth had felt for a certain period, that he was (in the words of the latter) :

> " Unprofitably travelling towards the grave,
> Like a false steward who hath much received
> And renders nothing back."

In the sonnet just quoted he defends himself nobly against the possible charge of having betrayed his stewardship ; and in so doing he was anticipating the Divine judgment as he had described it in a sermon of 1879 :

> " He [Christ] defended Magdalen and took means that the story of her generosity should be told for ever. And though he bids *us* say we are unprofitable servants, yet he himself will say to each of us / Good and faithful servant, well done." [2]

Hopkins must have believed this as firmly in 1889 as in 1879, and this belief in God's justice forms the pith and marrow of what we call his ' power of recovery ', evidences of which appear right up to the end. In 1888, when he seemed to be dying of a slow physical and moral agony, he was deeply engrossed in his music. In the long letter which touches on subjects as various as *Statistics and Free Will*, his " madrigal in canon," his father's book on Numbers, his own poetry, and Addis's apostasy, he recalls with glee a practical joke played on a colleague, chuckles over " ' Gifted Hopkins ' the humorist ' who died of his own jocosity ' ", jests about his own style and his own eyesight, and in the midst of this entertaining gallimaufry quietly announces : " And strange to say, I have taken up drawing again." [3] Such gusto, humour, and versatility are not the usual symptoms of a body and soul *in extremis*.

In his very last letter to Bridges, dated April 29, 1889, he says :

> " I believe I enclose a new sonnet. But we greatly differ in feeling about copying one's verses out. I find it repulsive, and

---

[1] To Baillie, in 1877, he wrote : " You see moral theology covers the whole of life and to know it it is best to begin by knowing everything, as medicine, law, history, banking. But law is what I should most like to know." (*Further Letters*, p. 95.)

[2] *Note-books*, p. 265.　　　　[3] *Letters*, vol. i. pp. 294–8.

let them lie months and years in rough copy untransferred to my book. *Still I hope soon to send you my accumulation.*" [1]

The italicized words indicate that " every impulse of creation " has by no means died in him. The poetic afflatus, whenever it stirred, could still force him to cover sheets of paper with rapid, excited, almost illegible jottings. In the sonnet just mentioned he describes this exquisite annunciation and gestation :

> " The fine delight that fathers thought ; the strong
> Spur, live and lancing like the blowpipe flame,
> Breathes once and, quenchèd faster than it came,
> Leaves yet the mind a mother of immortal song.
> Nine months she then, nay years, nine years she long
> Within her wears, bears, cares and combs the same :
> The widow of an insight lost she lives, with aim
> Now known and hand at work now never wrong." [2]

We should hardly expect the really moribund writer to give us such a perfect description of incipient life. Outwardly, Hopkins at forty-five seemed a much younger man ; in the lecture room, at a musical gathering, by the fireside of friends, he could be vivacious, charming, and virile. It was his heart and vitals, as he said, that were " shaggy with the whitest hair." So the sestet of this, his last sonnet, complains :

> " Sweet fire the sire of muse, my soul needs this ;
> I want the one rapture of an inspiration.
> O then if in my lagging lines you miss
> The roll, the rise, the carol, the creation,
> My winter world, that scarcely breathes that bliss
> Now, yields you, with some sighs, our explanation."

Where are these lagging lines ? Certainly not line 10, about which George Saintsbury said, " The poet seems to have slipped in the ' one ' out of pure mischief " ; certainly not the climax (line 12), for that is like the ghost of the murdered king occupying, in full regalia, the vacant throne. We once read this sonnet to an intelligent working man ; his immediate reaction was : " It sounds like good poetry—most of it ; but it seems to tail off at the end." It is just that feature, the apparently prosaic close, which confirms the supreme art of the whole poem—the penultimate line drooping wearily, with " Now ", into the ultimate,

---

[1] *Letters*, vol. i. p. 304.

[2] In the Third Edition of the *Poems* we have justified the restoration of the original " combs " in place of the " moulds " substituted by Bridges (l. 6).

with its three pauses and (as Miss Phare says) "a diminuendo down to the last flat dull word 'explanation'."

Had Hopkins's poetic genius been less "ill-broker'd", and had he succeeded (to use his own word) in "managing" himself better, his physical condition might have enabled him to withstand the enteric bacteria which ended his life on the 8th of June 1889. Yet even such natural regret and speculation, which arises from our deep pity and admiration for the man, seems a little unwise if not blasphemous when we consider the posthumous turn in the tide of his literary fortunes. He is reported to have died after uttering, three times, the words, "I am so happy." And if ever the consciousness of duty done, or at least nobly attempted, could console a dying man, that man was Hopkins. As we turn from one letter and poem to another (from plaint to praise, from admonition to anecdote, from diatribe to definition) we may perhaps wonder at the grace which reconciled so many different Gerards to one another and to God on that deathbed and under the chrism of the Holy Viaticum ; but those dying words were really the only logical outcome of his life : had they not been uttered all his ecstasies and pains would have seemed empty and futile. It was fitting that at the last he should glimpse those fields

> "where flies no sharp and sided hail
> And a few lilies blow."

EPILOGUE : MAJOR OR MINOR ?

WHEN this Epilogue was first written, some ten years ago, it included the following words :

> " The best of the later, deeply-pondered critical studies of Hopkins (those of G. F. Lahey, F. R. Leavis, André Bremond, D. Sargent, and B. W. Kelly) have all sought to establish the fact that Hopkins was not merely an interesting experimentalist and innovator in the technique of poetry ; they have proved that he is entitled to be acknowledged as a complete and successful poet."

That it should still be necessary to enunciate this claim points to an unhealthy state of criticism, a tendency to pay too much attention either to the manner and technique of poetry or to the matter alone—an extraordinary inability to comprehend poetry as it really is, that almost mystical *compositum* of thought, emotion, and form.

The many pages we have ourselves devoted to the formal aspects of Hopkins's verse have been justified (in as many more pages) by the clear assumption that the importance of his new and striking manner is dependent upon the supreme value of the total poetic effect. Apart from the rare and exalted pleasure to be derived from his work, the attitudes evoked are undoubtedly conducive to the social and spiritual welfare of mankind.

Too many of the critics who have written articles on Hopkins the Revolutionary Poet, the Innovator, or the Pioneer have created a false standard of assessment ; they have, in Fr. Lahey's odd but true phrase, " prescinded from the well-spring of Hopkins's poetry ". But this well-spring was not solely his religious ideals : it was that region in the subconscious mind where all the hidden tributaries of sensory experience met and mingled with his deepest intellectual convictions. To a degree not realized by many who have deplored his " frustration " and " self-laceration ", the aesthetic and purely poetic values of Hopkins were ontologically or mystically bound up with his strong religious emotions.

Hence the poetic *compositum* or total poetic effect of Hopkins's work can be known and felt only by those who acknowledge

God and the supernatural basis of life, and who at the same time appreciate the natural and traditional foundations of Hopkins's rhythm and style. All other readers may hold and cherish some *part* of this poet, but they cannot claim to comprehend and expound his complete personality, experience, and significance.

Hopkins's great work as a rhythmist has a unique absolute and historical value. Its unique absolute value lies in a variety, a subtlety, and a power of rhythmical effect which have never been surpassed and have probably never been equalled in any other poetry of comparable bulk. Its historical importance is that it proved, once for all, that the old native and popular stress-rhythms are as worthy to be considered the traditional rhythms of English poetry as the Romance syllabic metres which date from Chaucer. It is unlikely, however, that syllabic metres will be finally superseded ; for the sprung, expressional, and cumulative rhythms of Hopkins demand a greater share of " auditory imagination ", a more delicate sense of musical tone and timing, than are given to most poets. Sprung rhythm either succeeds perfectly or fails lamentably. As we have seen, Hopkins himself triumphantly avoided all the pitfalls by combining what was healthy and robust in the native rhythms with the finest graces of the Greek melic poetry and Welsh *cynghanedd*.

As a master of poetic diction and of poetic 'linguistics' Hopkins again occupies a unique historical position. In an age of diffused Romanticism, he broke through the hidebound literary tradition which, save for brief exceptions in Wordsworth, Keats, and Browning, had for nearly two hundred years divorced the diction and phrasing of poetry from the direct perceptions of everyday life and language. Carefully avoiding the prosaism of Browning, the archaism of Swinburne, and (for the most part) the awkwardness of Doughty, Hopkins restored to poetry something like the fluidity and resourcefulness of Elizabethan English ; by so doing he materially helped all later poets to reduce the gap which had always seemed to exist inevitably between the greatest master of poetic language, Shakespeare, and his successors.

Of almost equal importance is the mark left by Hopkins's powerful idiosyncrasy upon the *texture* of English poetry. The rich phonal qualities of his verse reinforce, and are themselves enhanced by, the flexible stress-rhythm ; and all these auditory elements are at the same time skilfully modulated to suit the shifting phases of closely packed thought and developing emotion.

Pre-eminently Hopkins's example has revived the tradition (long in partial abeyance) that poetry is to be read with the ear and not merely with the eye.

Hopkins, in fact, has set up a standard of poetic beauty which, for the many who now fully acknowledge its fascination, is profoundly disturbing. After an intensive reading of Hopkins, most other English poetry seems outwardly facile and in varying degrees inadequate : its harmonic pattern is too simple, too adventitious ; it seems not to have advanced far enough along the road which leads from plain utilitarian prose to the purest of literary art-forms—to the " condition of music ". This does not mean that the admirer of Hopkins can no longer enjoy other poets : his appreciation of Shakespeare, of Donne and the other early seventeenth-century poets, of Milton and Keats will probably be increased rather than diminished. It does mean, however, that the proportion of other poetry to which he can return with the old enjoyment will be noticeably smaller ; his taste, sharpened and refined by Hopkins, will demand a more exquisite amalgam of thought and emotion, a more significant concentration and point, to make up for the lack of *inscape* and *instress* in the outward form.

Gathering and retwining so many straying strands of the European poetic tradition, Hopkins was a great eclectic who was also eminently creative and original. The total complex of his style is (to use his own expression) a poetic " species " ; as such it can never recur—except by shameless imitation.

Our final estimate may in some measure be influenced by the answer we give to one outstanding question, namely, how far Hopkins can be said to reveal, through his poetry, a truly mystical vision. He knew the Purgative Life, and had glimpses of the Illuminative ; but that last calm ' possession ' of God was a consummation desired but never attained in this world. Nevertheless, his direct apprehension of the Infinite through the medium of His creation frequently assumes a mode of expression which is identical with that of the acknowledged mystics—a fact which caused the late Evelyn Underhill to signalize Hopkins as " perhaps the greatest mystical poet of the Victorian era ".

Current verdicts on Hopkins's ultimate status as a poet vary between the designations " minor " and " great ". The former points to the relative smallness of his output,—for this, and this only, can provide reasonable grounds for calling him a *minor* poet. But the deficiency is more than compensated by the absolute merit and subsequent influence of those poems which will continue to be *read*, and not merely admired, as long as the English language endures. In some age not attuned to his peculiar music and message, his reputation may suffer temporary eclipse ; but the re-emergence of his fame will be all the brighter.

Hopkins is already a ' classic '. In his poetry we recognize not only what he himself demanded—" a fine execution ", but also what Joseph Warton rightly called the two chief nerves of all genuine poesy—the Sublime and the Pathetic. By both criteria Hopkins attains the heights, though not the long sustained flights, of the acknowledged great masters—of Dante, Shakespeare, Milton. It is this fact, coupled with his unique individuality, which sets him apart from and above the exquisite *minor* poets, like Herrick, Marvell, and Christina Rossetti.

We shall attempt to justify those critics who have already pronounced Hopkins a *major* poet. Firstly, the fact that a *Times* reviewer,[1] in giving him this title, compared his achievement in " bulk and quality " with that of Matthew Arnold is significant : it would appear that Hopkins's fourteen hundred lines can make as deep an impression as the fourteen thousand of Matthew Arnold. Indeed, whether his work be considered from the point of view of matter, manner, or both, Hopkins is, for the present writer, the more important poet ; though in saying this we do not call in question the *major* status usually assigned to Arnold, Swinburne, and D. G. Rossetti.

According to Dr. F. R. Leavis,

> " Hopkins was one of the most remarkable technical inventors who ever wrote, and he was a major poet. . . . He is likely to prove, for our time and the future, the only influential poet of the Victorian age, and he seems to me the greatest." [2]

An Australian critic, D. P. McGuire, writes :

> " The genius of Hopkins comprehended, as none other has comprehended even to our own day, the characteristic features of the oncoming world : the still increasing tempo, the still increasing complexity of modern life. For the social philosopher as well as for the common reader he is the most important poet since Shelley." [3]

Such judgments will not pass unchallenged ; and it must be admitted in the best interests of Hopkins that each pronounce-

---

[1] *Times Literary Supplement*, Dec. 25, 1930.

[2] *Op. cit.* pp. 159 and 193.

[3] *The Poetry of G. M. H.* (English Association, Adelaide Branch, Pamphlet No. 2, 1934), p. 5.

ment contains an unfortunate touch of exaggeration. Surely
Browning and Whitman cannot be dismissed as less influential
than Hopkins ; and surely those two very considerable poets,
together with Tennyson, will in future times be of the highest
importance to the social philosopher and probably also to the
common reader.

D. P. McGuire's statement about the increasing tempo and
complexity of modern life suggests a further relevant observation. The growing bulk of the best European literature makes
it ever more difficult for people of culture to keep pace with it.
If we must have specialization and ample scope for personal
preferences, then Hopkins is certainly a major poet on the
showing of the above representative critics ; but if those who are
to decide the value and status of a poet are to be conversant
with all the best poetry of the modern world, then the significance of mere *quantity* in a poet's output must be held to be
rapidly diminishing. For most readers, it is obviously more
profitable to skim the cream of *two* famous poets than to imbibe
all, good and indifferent, of either one. Even Hopkins, who
urged Patmore to write more poetry for the sake of his fame,
was slightly contemptuous of his laboriously prolific contemporaries : " Just think of the blank verse these people have
exuded ".[1] And to-day Mr. T. S. Eliot is certainly not alone in
thinking that the effect of some of the nineteenth-century poets
was lessened by their bulk :

> " Who now, for the pleasure of it, reads Wordsworth, Shelley
> and Keats even, certainly Browning and Swinburne and most
> of the French poets of the century—entire ? "[2]

Who, indeed ? And why should Coleridge, Byron, Tennyson,
and William Morris be excluded from the list ? Stopford Brooke
reduced Coleridge to " twenty pages of pure gold " ; and if this
sifting and refining process were extended to all the above
poets, the result would be a series of selections each of which
would be hardly larger (if not actually smaller) than the total
output of Hopkins. Such selections are constantly being made,
chiefly for educational purposes, and the editors show no great
diversity of choice. It should therefore be frankly admitted that
only by their best can the voluminous writers of the past be
poetically and culturally active to-day. Such an admission
would bring the self-winnowed Hopkins into line with most of

[1] *Letters*, vol. i. p. 111.
[2] *The Use of Poetry and the Use of Criticism* (1933), p. 152.

the poets whose work now commands a much larger space in our libraries and academic literary manuals.

For some years to come the many alleged faults and errors of taste in Hopkins may seriously reduce the bulk of his ' active ' poetry. Meanwhile, we may go back for reassurance to Longinus, who asked himself whether the greater number or the higher quality of excellences should bear the bell in literature. The higher natures, he said, are the least faultless. Major excellences, even if not uniformly present, should always carry the election ; for their greatness of thought if for nothing else.[1]

According to Wordsworth, however, the emphasis in any assessment of poetry is to be placed not on ' thought ' but on ' sensibility '. Of genius in the fine arts, he says,

> " the only infallible sign is *the widening the sphere of human sensibility*. . . . Genius is the introduction of a new element into the intellectual universe . . . the application of powers to objects on which they had not before been exercised, or the employment of them *in such manner as to produce effects hitherto unknown*." [2]

By this criterion, too, Hopkins was undoubtedly a genius, and is certainly a major poet.

After a century of poetry in which the purely intellectual element was, to say the least, uncertain, diffused or exiguous, it is not surprising that to-day poets and critics alike are trying to redress the balance. In this respect, the scope and quality of Hopkins's work has provoked some adverse comparisons. The late W. J. Turner, for instance, said that Hopkins did not show the intellectual powers of Keats—that he had not the power of philosophic thought as manifested by Shakespeare, Milton, Donne, Keats, and Shelley.[3]

Now although this opinion is true as regards the greater intellectual range of Shakespeare, Donne, and Milton, it contains, we think, a serious fallacy. W. J. Turner, like Dr. Richards and other agnostic critics, assumes too readily a position which would require volumes to ' justify ', namely, that Christian beliefs and principles are mere emotional vagaries having little to do with intellection. It would be extremely difficult to prove that the free play of intellect in agnostic poets like Shelley and Keats has produced ideas and attitudes which are *more valuable* than those arising from the play of an intensely original mind and imagination among and around the matured tenets of Christianity.

[1] Περὶ ὕψους, XXXIII.   [2] Essay Supplementary to Preface, 1815.
[3] *Loc. cit.* See Volume I. p. 210.

To strip the subject of cant, what does the "philosophy" of Keats really amount to? Though it may have, for the speculative mind, deep implications, it is stated in such broad and vague terms that it could almost be ignored. One can find it entire in the five great odes, *Lamia*, parts of *Isabella*, and the first line of *Endymion* ; the splendid fragment of *Hyperion* does no more than promise greater heights and depths. The range of Keats's thought is best revealed in his superb *Letters* ; but it so happens that as a writer of critico-literary and autobiographical letters Hopkins is second to none in English, and to our mind shares the first place with Keats himself. As for Shelley, he is one of the greatest of poets in spite of, not because of, his "philosophy". His real strength lay in the superb lyricism of his primitive mythopoeic faculty—a faculty not primarily intellectual. The *Prometheus Unbound* will be judged by most to be greater than any single work of Hopkins ; but for those who prefer the philosophy of Hopkins, Shelley's 'thought' in that symbolic drama can be reduced to a few plain aesthetic and revolutionary tenets musically but somewhat monotonously reiterated in an endless fountain-play of foam-flowers, star-glints, and rainbow-hues.

In the exercise of a mature intellect upon the raw materials of poetry, as also in the underlying and unifying metaphysic of his finished work, Hopkins must be pronounced equal and in some ways superior to both these earlier poets. Where they are promising and sometimes successful (in the invention of character and fable), Hopkins makes no claim to excellence ; where they are really strong (in the speculative and meditative lyric), he is, we think, even stronger.

No informed critic would nowadays deny the major status of Donne, Baudelaire, and Walt Whitman. They are still living forces ; though their influence is largely refracted through the minds of other writers, they continue to modify thought and action. Now for the present writer at least, Hopkins, in the sheer power or stress of his genius, has a real claim to rank with these three poets.

His affinity with Donne derives from the play of intellect on the problems of faith and religious endeavour—the yearning of imperfection towards perfection, the desire to know and hold God more closely—together with the play of individual sensibility upon the materials of poetry and on the conventional standards of diction and rhythm. In Donne, the clash between the 'man of the world' temper and the claims of a pious and ascetic calling did not admit of a poetic reconciliation so clear and sharp as that of Hopkins ; for Donne never found, as Hopkins did in Catholicism, an interpretation of life which could be so flushed with feeling as to become a complete and illuminating experience. Although Donne has the wider range of ideas, he is often fanciful, fantastic, and inconclusive ; Hopkins, though hardly less ' cerebral ' and exciting and frequently far more troubled, expounds on the whole the more rational and realistic world-view.

Baudelaire, too, was a poet who looked at human life and the universe with almost the same eyes as Hopkins ; but the two men differed fundamentally in their interpretations of what they saw. Not always, however, in their reading of life : at times it seems to be rather a difference in the degree of will-power or moral consistency of which each was capable—the gift of grace not only of seeing what is best but of holding only to that. For instance, Baudelaire's *L'Horloge* expresses the same high and strict morality as Hopkins's *To his Watch* ; *L'Avertisseur* and many other poems show the French poet's constant preoccupation with sin and redemption. In *Le Gouffre* (where the link is Pascal) we find that overwhelming sense of the simultaneous presence and absence of God, that apprehension of ' le vide et le néant ' which only the mind capable of the fullest realization of the numinous can experience. What could be more like Hopkins than

> " et sur mon poil qui tout droit se relève
> Mainte fois de la Peur je sens passer le vent ",

and

> " Sur le fond de mes nuits Dieu de son doigt savant
> Dessine une cauchemar multiforme et sans trêve.
>
> J'ai peur du sommeil comme on a peur d'un grand trou,
> Tout plein de vague horreur, menant on ne sait où ;
> Je ne vois qu'infini par toutes les fenêtres,
>
> Et mon esprit toujours du vertige hanté
> Jalouse du néant l'insensibilité."—

and again :

> " J'implore ta pitié, Toi, l'unique que j'aime,
> Du fond du gouffre obscur ou mon cœur est tombé " ?

Nevertheless, one great difference cannot be overlooked : Baudelaire's physical and mental morbidity made him the poet of *Les Litanies de Satan* and other works which must be read (if read at all) with the strictest caution. However much we admire the artist and pity the man, the sheer diabolism of much of his verse lowers the value of his achievement. By contrast, Hopkins's moral healthiness more than compensates for his smallness of output and frequent obscurity.

In his essential sanity Hopkins was closer to Whitman, whose impetuous rhythms, dynamic style, and pervasive nature-mysticism are often so like his own. Both poets expressed the " pure wild volition and energy of nature." As Mr. Charles Madge once pointed out in an illuminating short essay,[1] there is a Corybantic strain in each one, much as the inhibited and obedient Jesuit differed from the broad-minded and broad-tongued Democrat. Hopkins's sky " all in a rush with richness " and his ecstatic " What is all this juice and all this joy ? " are paralleled by Whitman's

> " Hefts of the moving world at innocent gambols silently
> rising, freshly exuding,
> Scooting obliquely high and low. . . .
> Seas of bright juice suffuse heaven." [2]

Both were fascinated by the infinite variety and laciness of natural beauty ; as Whitman said :

> " I effuse my flesh in eddies, and drift in lacy jags ; " [2]

and Whitman, like Hopkins, knew the value of a strict asceticism in his private life. Yet here again there is a fundamental difference : it will redound, we think, to the Christian poet's credit that he shows a more pronounced " chastity of mind ", a strength to resist the glib emotional generalization. The great friendly Whitman-arm thrown indiscriminately round the shoulders of Humanity may prove, in the end, a Judas-kiss. Instead of singing :

> " None has begun to think how divine he himself is, and how
> certain the future is ",[3]

Hopkins was prophetically inclined to lament the fact that too many have arrogantly assumed divinity, while too few have begun to think how divine they might become and how desperately uncertain their souls' future may be.

---

[1] *New Verse*, No. 14, April 1935, pp. 17–21.
[2] *Song of Myself.*   [3] *Starting from Paumanok.*

We can agree with E. E. Phare when she says that the mere prose substance of Hopkins's poetry has more value than that of most avowedly didactic and philosophic poetry. The same critic asserts too that if all their respective poetical works were turned into prose paraphrases, Hopkins would have the better of Browning and possibly, also, of Wordsworth.[1] Her doubt as regards Wordsworth is reassuring ; for Wordsworth is, of course, the greater poet. But Miss Phare's opinion will not seem extravagant to anyone who sets the highest value upon the Christian faith and philosophy. Moreover her choice of Wordsworth and Browning in this context is a more extraordinary tribute to Hopkins's merit than at first appears ; for of all nineteenth-century English poets, these two have probably given an intellectual stimulus, a more constructive and hopeful orientation, to the greatest number of intelligent people.

Before drawing our final conclusion we must say a last word about Hopkins's faults. That he left so many poems unfinished was partly his misfortune and partly to his credit : he refused to substitute putty and rubble for genuine inspiration. The peculiar nature of his mind and inner experience made it necessary for him to fuse, adapt, twist and sometimes distort the elements of his native language ; and at rare times idiosyncrasy led him into oddity or extravagance. Yet the truth of Erigena's saying, that ' a vice is but a spoilt virtue and can have no separate existence ', is in this case so curiously demonstrated that the task of absolute critical discrimination becomes well-nigh impossible : what seems good to one reader may seem bad to another. All the critic can do is to expound the processes of thought and expression, indicate the general solipsist tendency, and leave the individual educated reader to form his own judgment on this word or that construction. We must repeat, however, that most of this poet's awkwardness and difficulty disappears when we have taken the trouble to master his idiom. His style is not for imitation, because it is doubtful whether the same combination of qualities will ever be found again in one man.

When the clamour of protest and approval has died down, these facts about our subject will, we believe, emerge clearly : that by his unique personality and character, merging good living with high thinking ; by his interpretation of beauty and duty, touching man to the very quick of his being ; by his power of speech at once sweet and strong, melodic and harmonic ;

[1] *Op. cit.* p. 121.

by his skill in architectonic and execution ; by the stimulus he gave to the ethical and creative purposes of poets yet to be—by these and other qualities Gerard Manley Hopkins has certainly earned the distinction of being called a *major poet* : and in his finest moments he is assuredly one of our greatest.

APPENDIX A

HOPKINS AND MUSIC

HOPKINS, in taking such an active interest in music, as he did from 1880 until his death in 1889, was not doing anything quite so remarkably odd for a Jesuit priest as might be supposed. Music, as he said himself, was " more professional " than poetry. " Jesuits," he adds, " have composed and well, but none has any fame to speak of." To-day also there are many Jesuits who are expert musicians and successful composers of church music. If Hopkins had lived longer he too might have essayed " the highest " in this kind as in poetry. The musical compositions he did attempt were mostly secular—airs for lyrics by Sappho, Shakespeare, Wm. Barnes, Bridges, and Dixon, and more elaborate settings for poems by Collins, Campbell, and Patmore.

Yet even his secular vein is not surprising when it is considered in the light of a statement published in 1937 by Dr. Peter Gradenwitz.[1] Writing on the transformations of musical style in the mid-eighteenth century, Gradenwitz points out the great influence exerted by " the characteristic spiritual schooling " of Jesuitism in Germany and Austria during that period. The Jesuits used every means in their power to lead men to their spiritual salvation, and among these means was the intensive cultivation and patronage of the arts :

> " Pomp and magnificence, ecstasy and sensuousness, all contribute their share to man's preparation for a spiritual life, and all this is effectively supported by art and music." [2]

Those words might have been written expressly about Hopkins.

The Jesuitic training which many of these Catholic artists underwent made them acutely aware of the fundamental conflict between sensualism and asceticism, between worldliness and spirituality ; and these conflicts are reflected even in the development of the sonata and symphony. The same spiritual forces which later moulded Hopkins had helped to produce those admirable musical contrasts between storm and calm, between a turbulent wrestling with the tragic elements in life and a subdued religious meditation, between these two again and the rollicking burlesque of the *scherzo*—the calling-off thoughts awhile and leaving comfort root-room on the earthly as well as on the transcendental plane ; and lastly the triumphant paean of the *finale*.

Although in Hopkins the love of music was innate, the earlier

---

[1] *Music and Letters*, July 1937 ; pp. 265–75. [2] Gradenwitz, *loc. cit.* p. 269.

letters contain relatively few allusions to this art. In 1865 he asked Baillie :

> " What in music answers to realism in painting ? The other arts seem to depend on truth (no : Truth) as well as Beauty. What answers, I mean what is, Truth in music ? . . . Is not Wagner something to do with it ? " [1]

The above aesthetic question was later combined with a moral question. In the unfinished poem *On a Piece of Music* we see that music, by reason of its ideality and freedom from the problems of applied moral law, was for Hopkins, though almost against his will, a liberation of the spirit. The purest form of Art (*homo additus naturae*), it was a further rich example of God's plenitude : it was " news of God ". Through the inscape, instressed pattern, or individuated beauty of music, Hopkins had immediate contact with the universal Nature, the unified mystical substratum of all existence flowing from and back to God (see the rubric to the sonnet on *Henry Purcell*).

Yet the material ways and means also held their fascination. In 1873 he lovingly made notes on the old musical instruments in the Kensington Museum.[2] As he walked in the little wood near Stonyhurst College, a bluebell reminded him of a wind instrument.[3] Later, in his commentary on *The Spiritual Exercises*, he compared " the ranks of the angelic hierarchies " to the notes of a scale and a harmonic series, and found assurance in such equating of music and astronomy as " the Music of the Spheres and the morning stars singing for joy ".[4] Music, in short, was never far from his thoughts.

It was not until 1880, when he had been a Jesuit for thirteen years, that Hopkins began to take himself seriously as a composer. In June of that year he told Bridges that he had written airs for the latter's *Spring Odes*[5] ; there were accompaniments by Grace Hopkins, but these did not satisfy him :

> " I sorely wish I knew some harmony . . . I wish I could pursue music ; for I have invented a new style, something standing to ordinary music as sprung rhythm to common rhythm ; it employs quarter tones. I am trying to set an air in it to ' Summer ends now ' [*Hurrahing in Harvest*]." [6]

This suggests the " freer musical time " which he desiderated in conjunction with " a stricter verse prosody "—some form of music derived from the Greek modal style and medieval plain-chant and anticipating modern syncopation and the barless music of Stravinsky.

Writing to Bridges again in September of the same year, he says :

> " I am happy that you (and that Woolrych [7] . . .) like my music. Your poetry is very songful and flies into tunes."

[1] *Further Letters*, p. 78.　　[2] *Note-books*, p. 184.　　[3] *Ibid.* p. 146.　　[4] *Ibid.* p. 348.
[5] The air to the first Ode, preserved in autograph at Amen House, is reproduced in fascimile opposite, p. 391.
[6] *Letters*, vol. i. p. 103.
[7] Mis-spelling for ' Wooldridge '.

Speaking of his setting (now presumably lost) to Bridges's " I have loved flowers that fade ", he says of the musical rhythm of one line

that it is, to imitate it in vērse, " Betráying the héart's desíre, betráying

the héart's desíre, O ". And some further remarks in the same letter show how closely music and verse-prosody were associated in his mind :

> " In the setting I should have been glad if Grace had been bolder. The accompaniment should have a shower of semiquavers or demisemis, with great chords at certain places. On the words ' And where the bare trunks ', where a note is four times repeated, the chord should have been varied four times, rising or descending, an obvious and beautiful effect of counterpoint, and not been repeated, as she has done. If I could make my own harmonies much of the expression of the piece could be conveyed in the accompaniments of course." [1]

The required shower of short notes punctuated by great chords has its approximate prosodic equivalent in the rapid polysyllabic and weighty monosyllabic feet of *The Wreck of the Deutschland, The Windhover*, etc.[2]

Hopkins believed that verse-prosody should have only a few rules, which should be rigidly respected. Yet in practice his own system allowed of far more licences and variations than the conventional syllabic versification. So in music he always hankered after freedom, range, variety—plenty of scope for incidental, inspirational effects. In him the classicist was always at war with the inveterate romanticist.

As an example of this we may take his tune to Bridges's " I love my lady's eyes ".[3] He calls the air " rather trifling, but not more so perhaps than the words." Though not unpleasing, it is remarkable only for the *rubato* effect given by a plentiful use of pauses, as in the following passage :

A - bove her shad-ed hair a - bove her feat-ured f o r m   And her lips daint-y-warm

We remember the *tempo rubato* stipulated for the correct reading of *Spelt from Sibyl's Leaves*. It was this affinity between poetry and music which inspired the tenth line of *The Windhover*, where, with the aid of a typographical device (" AND "), an extra stress is slipped into the line, the special effect being that the potential of the other five legitimate stresses is considerably raised.

---

[1] *Letters*, vol. i. pp.105–6. Cf. his remarks on the harmonies of Chopin (quoted below, p. 387).

[2] See Volume I of the present work, chapters ii and iii.

[3] *Letters*, vol. i. p. 118.

By 1880 Hopkins had begun to study Stainer's *Primer of Harmony* and by 1883 was patiently—or perhaps rather ' impatiently '— working through elementary exercises in counterpoint. His work was corrected by Sir Robert F. Stewart, Professor of Music at Dublin University. Amid slashing criticisms, the kindly tutor occasionally interjects " Very good " or " Nice sequential work ". Of these exercises, which some experts have pronounced to be quite ordinary, Mr. John F. Waterhouse says :

> " They have the usual beginner's faults—motionless parts, great gaps between alto and tenor, hidden octaves, even strange confusion of scales ; but they are strewn with indications of his enterprise and enthusiastic impatience." [1]

Such a rebuke as the Jesuit's imperfectly informed stubbornness earned from Sir Robert was not altogether to the pupil's discredit :

> " I saw, ere we had conversed ten minutes on our first meeting, that you are one of those special pleaders who never believe yourself wrong in any respect. You always excuse yourself for anything I object to in your writing or music so I think it a pity to disturb you in your happy dreams of perfectability—nearly everything in your music was wrong— but you will not admit that to be the case. . . ." [2]

Even Hopkins the poet (like Van Gogh the painter and many other highly original artists) was at the outset looked upon as a wrong-headed amateur.

The case of Hopkins as the would-be composer in a new style is unusual, because all his life he complained of being unable to play any instrument or even to read music with any fluency. Through his studies in Greek prosody he had gained some knowledge of Greek music, and as a priest he was familiar with the ecclesiastical modal systems. He knew enough about musical terminology to pronounce it " full of confusion " and to theorize with some complacency about the false fifth and Didymus's comma.[3] Yet " there was no hint of the charlatan or of the iconoclast in Hopkins's eagerness to be an innovator." [4] He had a genuine urge to composition, and seems to have possessed in no small measure that type of musical imagination which, because it is based upon an understanding of the principles underlying all art, is in some measure independent of technical skill ; but he knew that in the composer this latent or receptive imagination must be activated by sound knowledge and extensive practice.

In music, as in poetry, he worked on the principle that the art must be constantly renewed or rejuvenated by a revolt against convention (even against its own perfection) and by a return to primitive modes. Thus he frequently set passages from Greek odes and choruses

[1] " G. M. H. and Music ", *Music and Letters*, July 1937, p. 231.
[2] *Further Letters*, p. 279. [3] *Letters*, vol. i. p. 249. [4] Waterhouse, *loc. cit.*

to "fancy music" or plain-chant, and delighted in effects which he called "more curious than beautiful, but very flowing in a strange kind"; such was his air to Sappho's Ode to Aphrodite "barred as for Dorian Rhythm" (1886) [1]; and his feeling for Church plainsong (with an extended range) may be gauged by the following setting for the opening words of Pindar's second Olympian: [2]

'A- να-ξι-φόρ-μιγ - γες   ΰ - μνοι

Again, of his air for "Get you hence, for I must go", from *The Winter's Tale*, Dr. J. Dykes Bower has said:

> "This attractive tune . . . shows very clearly the influence of Greek modal music. It seems almost to be single-toned music, defying all attempts to harmonize it." [3]

Hopkins shared with Bridges an enthusiasm for the sixteenth-century madrigalists ("Would that I could hear some madrigals!" he exclaimed when in Dublin), and one of his ambitions was to write unaccompanied polyphonic songs. In 1872 he had gone to *Macbeth* not to see the play but to hear the "beautiful music" of Matthew Locke (d. 1677). Since the latter was the most eminent predecessor of Purcell in the composition of stage music, Hopkins's passion for Purcell himself is partly explained.

Yet there was an unaccountable, capricious element in his tastes. Of Weber's music he said, in 1880:

> "For personal preference and fellow-feeling I like him of all musicians best after Purcell. I feel as if I could have composed his music in another sphere. I do not feel that of Handel or Mozart or Beethoven." [4]

This preference is interesting in view of the fact that Stravinsky, in his recent American lectures, has proclaimed Weber a greater composer than Wagner. About the latter Hopkins was writing again to Baillie in 1880:

> "What do you think of Wagner? I heard a concert of his music in the winter. He loses greatly, I fancy, off the stage. The Germans call him the Master of the Masters and Hartmann the greatest of philosophers and the last new thing everywhere the greatest that ever was. This is a barbarous business of greatest this and supreme that that Swinburne and others practise. What is the thing that has been? The same that shall be. Everything is vanity and vexation of spirit." [5]

[1] *Letters*, vol. i. p. 239.   [2] *Ibid.* p. 123.   [3] *Ibid.*, vol. ii. p. 170.
[4] *Ibid.* vol. i. p. 98.   [5] *Further Letters*, p. 99.

Nevertheless, the attraction of the new music was irresistible :

> " *Ah ! you will have heard* the Nibelungs' Ring. You must tell me your impressions." [1]

Despite his almost boyish delight in novelty, he always retained his sense of basic values. At times, admittedly, his self-assurance is breath-taking :

> " I am sometimes surprised at myself how slow and laborious a thing verse is to me when musical composition comes so easily, for I can make tunes almost at all times and places and could harmonise them as easily if only I could play or read music at sight. Indeed if I could play the piano with ease I believe I could improvise on it." [2]

This passage smacks a little of Lady Catherine de Bourgh puffing her clever but delicate daughter ; but it would be rash to assert that Hopkins was entirely mistaken.

By 1883 he seems to have read the history of plain-chant in Helmore's *Primer* (Novello's Music Primer Series). He realized, however, that a simple revival and secular application of modal music without harmony was at that date hardly thinkable ; hence he worked away at counterpoint " as the solid foundation of harmony ". But though urged by Wooldridge to be " very contra-puntal ", he soon began to suspect that counterpoint

> " was only an invention of the theorists, a would-be or fancy music, for what is written in it ? Not even the Preludes to Bach's fugues." [3]

He declared that he or another ought to tabulate Bach's practice and principles.

His first elaborate setting was mentioned in a letter of 1884. Patmore's " The crocus, while the days are dark " (from *The Year*) had been set as a three-verse madrigal and sent to the Professor of Music at Oxford [5] " for censure ." The harmony of this piece, Hopkins says, " came in the end to be very elaborate and difficult " : the second and third verses " were a kind of wilderness of unintelligible chords ", but the first verse seemed to the happy composer to be " very good ". The work has not survived, but we know that for the next four years he strove to give it more " variety " and in 1888 announced, with almost a shout of glee, that he had enriched it with a " complicated canon ". " Success in canon," Hopkins wrote, " beats the other successes in art ; it comes like a miracle, even to the inventor." From his new peak in Darien he declared :

> " I see a whole world of canon and fugue before me. I do not say I am going there. But one madrigal in canon I will finish and then I hope one in fugue. No accompaniments ; and the human voice is

---

[1] *Further Letters*, p. 104. [2] *Letters*, vol. i. p. 136.
[3] *Ibid.* p. 182. [4] *Ibid.* p. 199.
[5] The Rev. Sir Frederick A. Gore Ouseley (1825-89).

immortal. You [Bridges] said nothing would come : I hope you may have been wrong." [1]

His attempt at a harmonic treatment of modal music is more clearly explained in his references (1884) to " some music, Gregorian, in the natural scale of A, to Collins's *Ode to Evening*." Of this he says :

" What came out was very strange and wild and (I thought) very good. Here I began to harmonise it, and the effect of harmony well in keeping with that strange mode (which, though it is, as far as notes go, the same as the descending minor, has a character of which the word minor gives you little notion) was so delightful that it seems to me . . . as near a new world of musical enjoyment as in this old world we could hope to be. To the novelty of effect the rhythm and a continued suspense natural to the mode and easy to carry further contribute too. It is meant for a solo and a double choir singing in unison, the organ or a string band bearing all the harmony. It is in three movements, something like a glee, the third returning to the first." [2]

This was his " great light on the matter of harmony . . . new, I need not say (framed on the model of Mr. Pecksniff's ' pagan, I regret to say ') ; true, I hope." Whatever we might now think of this work and the " Crocus ", if they still existed, there is some reason to believe that imaginatively at least Hopkins was moving in the same general direction as that taken by Debussy and others after 1884. Like the French ' father of modern music ', Hopkins saw that music must develop along lines parallel to those along which poetry or painting develop. Hopkins called his setting for the *Ode to Evening*

" a new departure and more like volcanic sunsets and sunrises in the musical hemisphere than anything ye can conçave." [3]

There we have a hint of that direct interpretation of feeling, that subtle investigation of colour, light, tone, and pattern which gave rise to Debussy in music and, in painting, to both the ' realistic ' and the ' luminist ' schools of Impressionism. Mallarmé and Rimbaud could also be fitted into the broad movement ; and when Hopkins speaks of music which is wild, strange, and a wilderness of unintelligible chords, he seems almost to have blundered upon the challenging atonal world of Schönberg and Hindemith.

Writing to Bridges four months later (March 1885) about the setting for Collins's *Ode*, Hopkins shows a confidence similar to that which made him refuse to alter a single word in *The Deutschland* :

" It seems to me like a new art, the effect is to me so unlike anything I ever heard. The air is plain chant where plain chant most departs from modern music ; on the other hand the harmonies are a kind of advance on advanced modern music. The combination of the two

---

[1] *Letters*, vol. i. p. 278. Bridges admired the " Crocus ", and Sir Robert Stewart gave it " a very good mark (and he does not flatter) ".

[2] *Ibid.* pp. 199–200.   [3] *Ibid.* p. 202.

14

things is most singular, but it is also most solemn, and I cannot but hope
that I have something very good on hand. It is so very unlike everything
else that I am independent of and do not hold myself in abeyance to
the judgments of musicians here ; for in fact they know no more than
I do what right I have to employ such and such chords and such and
such progressions." [1]

True, all the great composers have broken traditional laws of harmony,
and have been severely rebuked for their pains ; but they always
knew exactly what they were doing.

A friend of Bridges (whose name is deleted in the *Letters*) had
found one of Hopkins's tunes " plain, far too plain ", and either he
or Bridges had complained of the absence of modulation.   But that
omission, Hopkins replied, was deliberate :

> " I look on modulation as a corruption, the undoing of the diatonic
> style.   What they call the key of the dominant, viz. one in which the
> fourth of the tonic is sharpened, I say is not the key of the dominant
> (which is another mode than the key of the tonic and has no leading
> note) but the key of the tonic misplaced and transposed. I believe that
> * * * * and I would give diametrically opposite names to the same
> things : what he calls variety I call sameness, because modulation reduces
> all the rich diatonic keyboard with its six or seven authentic, not to
> speak of plagal, modes, to one dead level of major ; where he finds
> tameness I find variety, specific quality (not of key, which is not specific,
> but) of mode." [2]

Later he anticipates a certain modern school by affirming :

> " All keys are the same to me and to everyone who thinks that music
> was before instruments and angels before tortoises and cats." [3]

He was not unaware of the difficulties inherent in his " new art ",
for in the letter quoted above he continues :

> " Here, however, I must allow, is the hitch.   For if I am right in
> theory, in practice I am bound to give that variety by my own methods.
> I find a difficulty in doing so and I am obliged to resort to devices of
> counterpoint (would I knew more of them !).   Still I do hear plenty of
> variety which pleases me in that piece, and I hoped others would ; there
> is the mischief." [4]

Bridges sent Hopkins quotations from his favourite, Purcell, to illustrate
the variety which that master could command by the modern system.
Hopkins replied that he knew quite well what could be done with
modulation ; he could produce and had produced the simpler effects
himself, " and in fact modulation even to remote keys and so on is
not difficult to do ; it may be to explain."

For Hopkins, plain-chant melody had " an infinite expressiveness
and dramatic richness.

---

[1] *Letters*, vol. i. pp. 211-12.   [2] *Ibid*. pp. 213-14.
[3] *Ibid*. pp. 289-90.   [4] *Ibid*. p. 214.

> The putting in or leaving out of a single note in an 'alphabetical'
> passage changes the emotional meaning : all we admirers of plain chant
> feel this, the rest of the world . . . do not."

He contrasts the sobriety of plain-song with the intoxication of rich romantic harmonies :

> "When I hear one of Chopin's fragmentary airs struggling and
> tossing on a surf of accompaniment what does it matter whether one or
> even half a dozen notes are left out of it ? its being and meaning lies
> outside itself in the harmonies ; they give the tonality, modality,
> feeling, and all." [1]

Yet we feel that Hopkins might have envied Chopin those rich harmonies. Although he himself tried to produce melodies which had the bold " *charpente* " and dramatic feeling of the Old English airs, at the same time he wanted harmonies which would be characterized by a certain complexity—a mystery and 'mystical' value.

In one sense therefore it is strange that towards the end of his life Hopkins was struck more and more by the greatness of Handel. True, that master's " Renaissance " style in recitative was deplored (" so spiritless and mean, with vulgar falls and floundering to and from the dominant and leading note ") :

> "The only good and truly beautiful recitative is that of plain chant ;
> which indeed culminates in that. It is a natural development of the
> speaking, reading, or declaiming voice, and has the richness of nature ;
> the other is a confinement of the voice to certain prominent intervals
> and has the poverty of an artifice." [2]

There is truth in that ; and it comes with grace and persuasiveness from the poet who established " sprung rhythm " and to whom plain-chant was ' second nature '. But after hearing Handel's violin sonata in A he could exclaim :

> "What a genius ! what a native language music was to him ; such
> sense, such fluency, such idiom, and such beauty ! " [3]

He supposed that the " immediateness of impression " received from Handel was due to his power being conveyed into smaller sections of his work than other men's and not needing accumulation for its effect. (This is probably no more true of Handel than of Bach or Beethoven ; in poetry such " immediateness of impression " is certainly common to Shakespeare, Keats, and Hopkins.)

Firmly and with good humour (despite his moods of despair) Hopkins held his own against Bridges and the experts. We can imagine the surprise of the friend when, on being asked to study the setting to the *Ode to Evening*, he was told :

> " if you do not like it it is because there is something you have not seen
> and I see . . . and if the whole world agreed to condemn it or see

[1] *Letters*, vol. i. *loc. cit.*   [2] *Ibid.* p. 280 (Aug. 1888).   [3] *Ibid.* p. 290 (Sept. 1888).

nothing in it I should only tell them to take a generation and come to me again." [1]

No wonder Bridges asked him whether he meant to rival Purcell and Mozart. Gerard's reply was wise enough to counterbalance his former pretensions :

" No. Even given the genius, a musician must be that and nothing else, as music now is ; at least so it has been with all the great musicians. But I did aim at two things not in themselves unattainable, if to me far easier things were not now unattainable." [2]

Unfortunately Hopkins attempted too much to accomplish any one project as well as he might have done.

At about this time (May 1885) he was engaged on his setting to Campbell's *Battle of the Baltic*. It was originally intended " for choir and orchestra " but later " for two choirs [British and Danes] singing in unison, with pianoforte accompaniment." In the two completed verses (which have survived) he wanted to see how long he could go without modulations, because

" Palestrina and the old madrigal writers and others did produce masterpieces—and Hullah says actually final in their kind, that is which you cannot develope by modern science ; you can only change the school and kind—without modulation, but employing the modes. . . ." [3]

Of *The Battle of the Baltic* setting Dr. J. Dykes Bower has said :

" The second stanza is in the form of a ground bass (misnamed by Hopkins Basso Continuo) on an excellent subject :

which undergoes skilful rhythmical variation on each of the ten repetitions. This composition has many ideas, but Hopkins's inadequate knowledge of harmony prevented his making really effective use of them." [4]

In 1886 Hopkins wrote airs (" very suitable to the words and as if drawn out of them ") for two poems by the Dorset lyric poet,

---

[1] *Letters*, vol. i. p. 214. Cf. *ibid*. p. 253 (March 1887) : " I feel pretty sure the matter never struck Rockstro nor perhaps anyone else and that I have the key to the history of modern music in what my inquiry points to, viz. that modern harmony could not arise till the old system and its tuning was got rid of and that it was goodness, not dulness, of ear which delayed its growth." (Cf. N. Suckling, below, p. 390, note 1).

[2] *Ibid*. p. 220 (May 1885).   [3] *Ibid*. p. 220.   [4] *Ibid*. vol. ii. p. 170.

William Barnes. One he harmonized, " with plenty of modulation " ;
but, he adds :

> " I can never succeed with piano music, for the piano cannot really
> execute independent parts, as I make mine ; indeed my pianist said to
> me, Your music dates from a time before the piano was invented.
> However two schoolboys sang the air ; which went well." [1]

By general consent, his most successful air is the one composed in
1881 for R. W. Dixon's *Fallen Rain* ; it was first printed in the third
Appendix to *Letters*, Vol. II, and is reproduced in the present volume
opposite p. 389. Dr. Dykes Bower has already called attention to
its many interesting features ; but the following notes by another
skilled musician will not be superfluous :

> " The song is very interesting and unusual in many points. There
> are, of course, several details which could be criticized adversely ; for
> instance, the long run of twenty-one continuous quavers occurring first
> in D minor, then repeated in F minor, in the middle section and coming
> again at the end. Perhaps this feature could be excused on the ground
> that similar passages occur in the songs of the great masters, but un-
> fortunately the passage is marred by incorrect accentuation and by such
> words as ' of ' being unnecessarily prolonged.
> " To lessen the effect of the rather abrupt key changes, the middle
> section in F minor seems to want to be separated from the first and last
> sections by a longer break than the mere half bar given by the composer.
> Nevertheless, this melody shows Hopkins to have worked with some
> originality ; the curious cross-accents and somewhat unexpected mixture
> of semi-modal and (for his day) modern type of melodic structure seem
> to indicate an adventurous mind looking forward to effects in music
> which were not used on any wide scale until some time later. The
> interval marked ' to be sung as a quarter-tone ' is certainly something
> of a surprise, but hardly one to achieve much popularity among singers." [2]

The quarter-tone was probably suggested by ancient Greek music,
and (as Dr. Dykes Bower says) " in view of present-day experiments
in quarter-tones this passage is interesting ".
The present essay makes no pretence at being an exhaustive
account of all the technicalities, lights and confusions of Hopkins's
" new art " as far as it was known to himself and shown to us in his
extant compositions and writings : those who seek precise knowledge
on these points will naturally turn to the musical scores and the
Letters. Our purpose has been merely to reveal the general trend of
his activities in a sister art which in this case bore a specific and not
simply a generic relationship to his main art, which was poetry. It is,
however, a matter of interest that although many musical critics may
be sceptical about Hopkins's theorizing, and indeed about the whole
question of a harmonic treatment of Gregorian music, Mr. Norman

---

[1] *Letters*, vol. i. pp. 229–30, and *Further Letters*, p. 223.
[2] Mr. L. H. Baggarley, L.R.A.M., F.R.C.O.

Suckling, in his recent authoritative monograph on Gabriel Fauré, has stoutly defended Hopkins's contention that modulation " reduces all the rich diatonic keyboard with its six or seven authentic, not to speak of plagal; modes, to one dead level of major." [1] He also affirms what was virtually the Jesuit's belief, that plain-chant implies its own harmonic background :

> " I cannot agree with Dr. R. P. Morris that ' there is no such thing as modal harmony ', because I do not believe either in the existence of melody which implies no harmony or in the inevitability of cadential progessions." [2]

Fauré (1845–1924) was Hopkins's contemporary, and it is significant that M. Koechlin and Mr. Suckling stress the influence upon his work of the ecclesiastical modes. As Koechlin says :

> " His tonalities, clear as they are, sometimes are established very quickly and for a passing moment only—a practice observable in the sixteenth century and favoured by familiarity with the ancient modes, because they allow greater flexibility in modulation." [3]

So Mr. Suckling observes :

> " One may see how right Hopkins was in his contention (for this is what it amounts to) that what we have called ' modulation ' in the ' tempered ' sense is better described not as modulation at all but as transposition—transposition of the same tonal-and-semitonal succession to a different level of pitch ; and how great an enrichment of the art would derive from the newly acquired freedom to range over a real variety of scales in which modulation should really involve a different order of degrees." [4]

[1] See *Fauré* (Dent, 1946) : " . . . the discovery of plainchant helped to convince sensitive musicians of the gratuitous impoverishment of their art for which the tonic-and-dominant obsession and its ubiquitous leading-note had been responsible " (p. 53). And again :
" But though the motive of the diatonic evolution [including modulation] may have been the search for variety, its ultimate effect was one of the flattest monotony, as was observed with varying degrees of consciousness by numerous composers from the mid-nineteenth century onwards, especially French*, and stated in so many words by Gerard Manley Hopkins in a protest against the ideas of ' official ' musicians in his time."
* And one might add, Russian ; but in *their* musical background the modal tradition had not been so completely lost as to require deliberate revival " (p. 54).
[2] *Op. cit.* p. 53 (note).
[3] *Gabriel Fauré*, pp. 162–3 (quoted by Suckling). Cf. Suckling (*op. cit.* p. 185) : " It frequently happens that a practice deriving from the harmony implicit in one of the modes is precisely what accounts for the ' modernity ' of Fauré's writing. Foremost among such practices is that of dispensing with the leading-note and its too emphatic pointing towards the tonic of a scale, as also with other items of musical syntax based on a similar principle, and thus avoiding the ' dead level of major ' which so wearied Hopkins. Successive applications of this method may be traced through an early but mature work, the C minor piano Quartet."
[4] *Ob. cit.* pp. 54–5.

Mr. Suckling may perhaps be overstating the possibilities of " enrich-ment " ; but he obviously believes that Hopkins the musician was something more than a blindly-groping, amateur enthusiast.

In the very last of his letters to Bridges (April 29, 1889), Hopkins comments on what seems to have been his latest handling of his three-verse madrigal on Patmore's " Crocus " :

> " My song will be a very highly wrought work and I do hope a fine one. . . . This is how it stands. I tried at first to make the air such that it should be rigidly the same in every note and rhythm (always excepting the alterations to save the tritone) in all its shifts ; but I found that impracticable and that I had reached the point where art calls for loosing, not for lacing. I now make the canon strict in each verse, but allow a change, which indeed is besides called for by the change of words, from verse to verse. Indeed the air becomes a generic form which is specified newly in each verse."

This priest, who was already languishing in health prior to being stricken down with his last illness—typhoid, continues in the following confident strain :

> " It is like a new art this. I allow no modulation : the result is that the tune is shifted into modes, viz. those of La, Mi and Sol (this is the only way I can speak of them, and they have a character of their own which is neither that of modern major and minor music nor that of the plain chant modes, so far as I can make out). The first shift is into the mode of La : this should be minor, but the effect is not exactly that ; rather the feeling is that Do is still the keynote, but has shifted its place in the scale. This impression is helped by the harmony, for as the third is not flattened the chord appears major. The chord at the beginning of every bar is the common chord or first inversion ; the $\frac{6}{4}$ may appear in the course of the bar and discords in passing or prepared. Perhaps the harmony may be heavy, but I work according to the only rules I know. I can only get on slowly with it and must hope to be rewarded in the end. Now I must lie down." [1]

As Mr. Waterhouse has pointed out, Hopkins

> " does not seem clearly to have realized that a mode which bears ' the feeling that Do is still the keynote ' is not to modern ears established as a mode at all ; nor that the power of modulation depends not on the new key but on the process of establishing the new key." [2]

Again, Hopkins seemed not to be aware that under the modern system each key has, for many musicians, as much " character " or specific quality as any of his ancient or personal and peculiar modes had for him. On the other hand, he does seem to have realized that the elaborate modern processes of key-change tend to become stereo-typed ; that although he might not, by his own methods, produce a variety which was *richer* than that of Wagner or Brahms, he might at least create a music which was *different*—odd at first, but with familiarity subtle, refined—a legitimate phase in the evolution of an art which has so far proved to be inexhaustible in its resources.

[1] *Letters*, vol. i. pp. 304–5.　　　　[2] *Loc. cit.* p. 234.

Mr. Waterhouse concludes his sympathetic article with the following words :

> " Might he, perhaps, granted a longer life, have turned consistently to his own verse and become a neo-Greek poet-musician, creating simultaneously with the words a barless, unaccompanied enharmonic music ? Whether his music could ever have matched his verse is doubtful, or at least beyond conjecture."

Although Hopkins might often have essayed the little tried art of the unaccompanied solo song, he would not, we believe, have been entirely satisfied with single-toned music : *The Leaden Echo and the Golden Echo*, for instance, seems even now to be crying out for a free modal setting, with harmony borne by stringed instruments and oboe. He might have lost or considerably modified his ' modal ' obsession. Listening recently to the first broadcast performance of Sir Arnold Bax's " Five Greek Folk Songs, for unaccompanied chorus," we felt that here, perhaps, was a type of that music " wild and strange " which Hopkins heard when he " groped in his soul's very viscera " and " thrummed the sweetest and most secret catgut of the mind "— a vaguely apprehended new world of musical delight which a wider technical accomplishment would have enabled him to objectify and make audible to others.

APPENDIX B

(See Chapter II)

Translation into Greek Dorian Rhythm

THE following translation into Greek of the song " Orpheus with his lute made trees ", together with the metrical scheme, are reproduced from MS. " A " (pp. 173–4), by kind permission of Mrs. Robert Bridges.

" Dorian rhythm, syncopated, and with triplets in resolution."

σχῆμα (στροφή) [1]

ἀντιστροφή

χιόνος κρύος μεσούσας. πόντιον δε κῦμα
τῶν τ' ἐριβρόμων ἀίοντ' ἀνέμων πνεύματα γαλάνα πέσεν.
κιθάρᾳ δὲ ταῖς τε Μούσαις ὡς ἔνεστ' εἰπεῖν τὸ παυσίλυπον
'ἀδύνατον· κατεκοίμασ' αὐτίκα πάντα λάθα.

APPENDIX C

(See Chapters II and III)

Sidney C. Lanier (1842–81)

IN a letter from Dublin of April 16, 1884, Hopkins says :

" The Century is an interesting serial. There is in it a saddening account of a young American poet called Sidney Lanier, who had good notions about poetical form, scansion, etc., and died young, in struggling circumstances. The samples of his own were something like E. A. Poe,

---

[1] In the autograph, the scheme and the verse are given separately.

14*

something like Whitman, and shewed, I thought, some genius, but not of a high order ; but there was little to judge from."

The prosodic theories of Sidney C. Lanier (1842–81) [1] show that his approach to the rhythms of poetry by way of music and popular verse was in many ways similar to that of Hopkins.

Lanier's chief work, *The Science of English Verse* (1880) is among the best books of its kind and gives a more complete and sensitive account of the aural effect of good verse than is usual with prosodists. Besides showing how the sounds of verse differ in Duration, Pitch, and Intensity, he has an interesting section on Tone-Colour, under which he includes Rhyme, Vowel- and Consonant-distribution, and Alliteration.

His main thesis is that the rhythm of English verse is based upon Duration or Time and not, as was usually supposed, upon Accent or Stress ; and his main corollary is that to some forms of verse, as to music, *rests* are just as important as the sounds thereof. Indeed, he went too far in maintaining that there is no difference between the sound-relations used in music and those used in verse. Discarding the old metrical terms—iambic, etc., he adopted the terms of music and the musical notation of time, rests, etc.

Lanier was an enthusiastic admirer of Old English poetry, the rhythm of most of which, he says, is to be described in terms of $\frac{3}{8}$ time. Thus the beginning of *The Wanderer* :

| Oft him | an-ha-ga | a-re ge- | bi-deth, |

| met-od-es | milt-se | theah-the he | mod-cear-ig |

The irregularity of approximating a bar like " metodes " to others like " ānhaga " and " ðeahðe hē " with their long syllables is elsewhere accounted for by Lanier. In such lines, he says, as

| | Byrhtnoth | mathelode, | bord | hafenode |

and

| " All in the | valley of death | rode the six | hundred " |,

the bars " mathelode " and " valley of death " are to be written thus : $\frac{3}{8}$ 𝄚 ; though, he adds, they might be written $\frac{3}{8}$, the line above indicating, as in music, that the four eighth-notes are to be played in the time of [2]

---

[1] A good biographical and critical study of Lanier is Aubrey Harrison Starke's *Sidney Lanier* (1933 ; University of North Carolina Press).

[2] *The Science of English Verse*, p. 157 and *Sidney Lanier* (Starke), p. 340.

That way, of course, lies Sprung Rhythm—which requires only the additional " instressing " of Stress.

We are again reminded of Hopkins when Lanier first praises the stirring rhythm of *The Battle of Maldon* (" often boldly opposing a single syllable in one bar to three or four in the next ") and then laments the timidity of English poetry " during the last two hundred years "—its fear of venturing out of the round of its strictly defined iambics, of varying bar with bar and employing rhythmic breaks as in " Mother Goose " rhymes :

These rhythms, " though complex from the standpoint of our customary rhythmic limitations, are instantly seized and co-ordinated by children and child-minded nurses ". Like the *Maldon*, in short, they depend upon the sense of rhythm " which is well-nigh universal in our race " to account properly for the time-measure in reading.[1]

On this principle he presents " the great diversity of bars " in Tennyson's " Break, break, break " :

Incidentally, this analysis of the three-stress line agrees with Patmore's statement (in *English Metrical Law*, 1857) that the line of three feet is really one of four feet with the last foot silent.[3] The objection to Lanier's notation, however, is that it confuses the musical with the prosodic system, and suggests a syncopated rhythm which does not in fact exist.

[1] *The Death of Byrhtnoth*, A Study of Anglo-Saxon Poetry (Essay X in *Music and Poetry*, 1909), pp. 143-4.

[2] *The Science of English Verse*, p. 138.

[3] In *Letters*, vol. i. pp. 119–20, Hopkins refers to Patmore's theory and shows how in his own verse he never protracts the four-stress line (or gives it a " heavy ending ")

Using the pure musical notation, Hopkins might have demonstrated the diversity of bars in *The Wreck of the Deutschland* as follows :

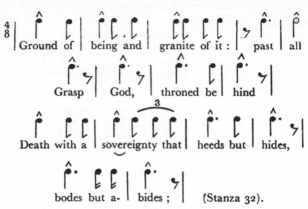

(Stanza 32).

In the penultimate foot or bar of the first line we have real syncopation. Such timing, however, can only be a variable approximation ;
for Hopkins realized that owing to the uncertainty of *quantity* in
English syllables the rhythm of verse is much less absolute and regular
than the rhythm of music. Hence, perhaps, his desire for " a freer
musical time and a stricter verse-prosody ".[1]

Reacting against the abuses of the chromatic tone in nineteenth-
century music, Lanier says :

> " Now, as music has reached a point where it must pause and re-
> establish the dominancy of the whole tone, fortifying it with whatever
> new tones may be found possible . . . so must our tongue recur to the
> robust forms, and from these to the underlying and determining genius,
> of its Anglo-Saxon period." [2]

---

without strict overreaving, i.e. beginning the next line with a " sprung head " or
falling cadence, as in :

> " Márgarét, aré you gríeving
> Óver Góldengróve . . . (No. 31).

[*and not* e.g. Concérning Góldengrove] unléaving." But when he uses the three-
stress line, " the heavy ending or falling cadence of one line does not interfere with
the rising cadence of the next, as you may see in the *Brothers* " :

> " By méanwhiles ; máking mý play
> Turn móst on ténder býplay."

All this is because, as Patmore had pointed out, " we carry mentally a frame of
fours, which being filled allows of no more ".

[1] *Letters*, vol. i. p. 120 : " Now this principle of symmetry and quadrature has, as
I think, been carried in music to stifling lengths and in verse not far enough and
both need reforming ; at least there is room, I mean, for a freer musical time and
a stricter verse-prosody."

[2] *Music and Poetry*, Essay X. pp. 144–5. Cf. G. M. H.'s musical theories, in
Appendix A.

While Lanier was thus theorizing, Hopkins was actually putting these ideas into practice, as we have shown in Chapter III of the present volume.

Finally, it is interesting to note a certain spiritual affinity between the Hopkins who gazed long and metaphysically at a bluebell and the Lanier who wrote :

> " I know that thou art the word of my God, dear Violet.
> And Oh, the ladder is not long that to my heaven leads.
> Measure what space a violet stands above the ground."
>
> (*Poems*, 1892, p. xxxix).

APPENDIX D

(See Chapter III)

The ' Onomatopoetic Theory ' in Hopkins

THE words in -sh employed by Hopkins are mostly native monosyllables of (probably) imitative origin : *crash, crush, lash, gush,* etc. (*plush*, however, is from the French). Passing over the almost unlimited number of adjective compounds in -ish (O.E. -isc), we find that the majority of the words in -ish taken from French (from verbs in -ir, -iss-) denote likewise *either* destruction, violent action, *or* fullness, richness, brightness : e.g. (1) *abolish, astonish, banish, blemish, brandish, demolish, famish, punish, ravish, vanquish :* (2) *burnish, embellish, flourish, furnish, garish, garnish, lavish, planish* (beat *and* polish), *replenish, varnish.* (Some of these French words seem to have acquired the connotation of speed and/or violence under the influence of the English imitative -sh : *vanish, perish, finish, planish.*)

That Hopkins realized the general native significance of -sh is proved by an exhaustive survey of his use of these words. First there is a passage in *The Woodlark* (64),[1] in which the idea of rich colour is strikingly combined with the ideas of speed and violence : even a relatively neutral word like *sash* is brought into the prevailing notion of richness :

> " lush the sash
> And crush-silk poppies aflash,
> The blood-gush blade-gash
> Flame-rash rudred
> Bud shelling or broad-shed. . . ."

Here -sh occurs nine times, and the effect is perhaps ruined by excess. Perfect beauty is achieved in the *Heraclitean Fire*, where *flesh, trash,* and

[1] The number in brackets is the number of the poem in the 2nd edn.

ash form an apt compound symbol of the mortal body which is suddenly changed :

" In a flash, at a trumpet crash ".

Other examples of neutral words which are imbued by their contexts with one or more of the aforementioned ideas are : " That guilt is *hushed* by, hearts are flushed by " (4·6) ; " lives were *washing* away (4·15) ; " azuring-over greybell makes / Wood banks and brakes *wash* wet like lakes " (18) ; " down dazzling *whitewash* " (48) ; " *thrush*'s eggs . . . *thrush* . . . leaves and blooms, they *brush* / The descending blue " (9) ; " *flesh* and fleece " (18) ; " *flesh* filled . . . the curse " (45) ; " *dragonish* damask " (32 : here there is a subtle fusion of " violence " and " richness ") ; " long *lashes* lace, lance, and pair " (48) ; " *ash*-boughs . . . *clammyish lashtender* combs " (56). The following references complete the list :

Fullness and/or Richness.	Speed and/or Violence.	Both Ideas Combined.
silk-ash (24)	crash (4·10 ; 48)	bush-browed (53)
blushed (30)	crush (86)	crushes (77, p. 133)
burnish (57)	crushed (4·17 ;	Crushed (7)
fresh burnish (58, p. 76)	76 ; 86)	flashed (49, 58)
bushy-bowered (72)	dashed down (58)	flashes (38 ; 72)
flesh (37, line 55)	fashed (36)	flashing (37)
flesh-flowers (77)	flash (4·34 ; 77, p. 133)	flesh-burst (4·8)
heart-fleshed (4·34)	flashed (58, p. 76,	flush (*ibid.*)
flush (85)	twice)	flushes (66)
flushed (80)	fresh (58, p. 77)	gash (12)
flushing (*Note-books*, p.31)	Gnashed (4·21)	gashes (77, p. 130)
sun-flush'd (77, p. 133)	gash (49)	gush (4·8)
fresh (vb. *Note-books*, p. 41)	deathgush (17)	froliclavish (72)
fresh (adj. 3 ; 16 ; 19 ;	Hush there ! (36)	plashes (77, p. 133)
37, l. 56.; 58, pp.	lashed (43)	pushed (23)
76 and 77)	pashed (32)	rash-fresh (11)
fresh-firecoal (13)	perished (76)	rushy (58, p. 78)
lush (75)	*perishing* (4, 25)	
lush-kept (4·8)	plash (77, p. 133)	
plush-capped (*ibid.*)	rash (4·19 ; 58, p. 79)	
plushy (3)	rush (76, 5)	
	threshing-floor (78)	
	washing (77, p. 134 ;	
	79, p. 138)	

We may compare with the above the following everyday words *not* used by Hopkins : brash, clash, hash, mash, quash, slash, smash, splash, squash, swish, swash, thrash, and the vulgar but equally relevant " bash " and " posh " (cf. ma*sh*er).

The same principle of classification reveals the naturalness and spontaneity, as of a universal linguistic impulse, in such alliterative and rhyming groups as "quelled or quenched "¹ (19)—cf. *quash, quieten* ; "stanching, quenching" (4·32)—cf. *clench, wrench, pinch* (pressure) and *stop, stem, squelch, clinch* (finality) ; "havoc-pocked" (54), "hack and rack" (19)—cf. *hawk*, "hell-rook" (23), *peck, crack, sack, wrack* ; "gropes for, grasps" (56)—cf. *grip, grapple, grab, group* ; "the turmoil and the torment" (58)—cf. *tumult, torture, turbulence, terror* ; "Is strung by duty, is strained to beauty" (17)—cf. *strong, stride, stress, strict, strenuous,* and "O brace sterner that strain" (27).

In 1863 Hopkins had written : " In fact I think the onomatopoetic theory has not had a fair chance " (*Note-books*, p. 6). Later he made ample amends by breathing poetic life into the dry bones of philological research.

APPENDIX E

(See Chapter III)

HOPKINS's *cywydd*

CYWYDD

ANNERCH i'r tra pharcedig D. Th. Brown esgob yr Amwythig, wedi cyrhaedd o hono ei bummed flwyddyn ar hugain, yr hon a elwir y Jubil ; a chwyno y mae'r bardd fôd daiar a dŵr yn tystiolaethu yn fwy i hên grefydd Gwynedd nag y bydd dŷn, a dywed hefyd mai gobeithia fod hyny gael i ei gyfnewid o waith yr esgob.

> Y mae'n llewyn yma'n llon
> Â ffrydan llawer ffynon,
> Gweddill gwyn gadwyd i ni
> Gan Feuno a Gwenfrewi.
> Wlaw neu wlith, ni chei wlâd braidd
> Tan rôd sydd fal hon iraidd.
> Gwan ddwfr a ddwg, nis dwg dŷn,
> Dyst ffyddlon am ein dyffryn ;
> Hen ddaiar ddengys â'i gwedd
> Ran drag'wyddawl o rinwedd ;
> Ni ddiffyg ond naws ddyniol,
> Dŷn sydd yn unig yn ôl.
> Dâd, o dy law di ela
> Fardd a lîf â'r hardd brîf dda ;
> Tydi a ddygi trwy ffŷdd
> Croyw feddygiaeth, maeth crefydd ;
> A gwela Gwalia'r awr hon
> Gwîr saint, glân îr gwyryfon.
>
>> Brân Maenefa a'i cant
>> Ebrill y pedwerydd ar hugain
>> 1876.

For a translation and notes on the text, see *Poems of G. M. H.*, Third Edition (1948).

Commenting on the *cywydd* in a letter to the present writer, Sir H. Idris Bell wrote, in 1938 :

> " This is a most interesting discovery you have made. I feel no doubt in view of what you tell me that the poem is by Hopkins. There are mistakes in Welsh, and the *cynghanedd* is most incorrect, indeed it hardly exists except in one or two lines. On the whole, the structure of the Welsh seems to me remarkably better than the *cynghanedd* ; the two lines
>
> > Gwan ddwfr a ddwg, nis dwg dŷn,
> > Dyst ffyddlon am ein dyffryn,
>
> are quite in the spirit of the *cywydd*, though the *cynghanedd* of the second is all wrong."

We have to thank Mr. M. Harries, of Dynevor School, Swansea, for pointing out a possible allusion, in " gwyryfon " of the last line, to the eleven thousand virgins of St. Ursula, who are mentioned in a passage of Tudur Aled's *Cywydd i Wenfrewi Santes* :

> Y ferch wen, fu'r ychwaneg
> Fel yr oedd un fil ar ddeg
> Gweryddon, a gâi raddoedd,
> Gwenfrewi deg, un fryd oedd.

As the present writer has pointed out in the Third Edition of *Poems of G. M. H.* (p. 267), the Welsh bardic signature, " Brân Maenefa ", is the one used by Hopkins at the end of the MS. " A " copy of *The Wreck of the Deutschland*, which was completed in the same year, 1876. Again, " Bran " was the pseudonym over which Hopkins published two triolets in the *Stonyhurst Magazine* in 1883 ; moreover the highly characteristic tone and substance of the prose and verse place his authorship beyond doubt. The focal point bright with the streamlet of " weak water " (gwan ddwfr) is reproduced in the last fragment of *St. Winefred's Well*, where the poet is describing the breaking out of the miraculous fountain at Holywell :

> " This Dry Dene, now no longer dry nor dumb, but moist and musical
> With the uproll and the downcarol of day and night delivering
> Water, which keeps thy name, (for not in rock written,
> But in pale water, *frail water*, wild rash and reeling water) . . ."

With this we may compare an allusion to the famous Well in a letter to Bridges of April 3, 1877 : " [St. Beuno] was St. Winefred's uncle and raised her to life when she died in defence of her chastity and at the same time he called out her famous spring, which fills me with devotion every time I see it and would fill anyone that has eyes with admiration, the flow of ἀγλαὸν ὕδωρ is so lavish and beautiful. . . ."

Moreover, the fifth couplet of the *cywydd* :

> Hen ddaiar ddengys â'i gwêdd
> Ran drag'wyddawl o rinwedd ;

    ("The old earth, in its appearance, shows an eternal share of virtue ; ")

is not unlike

> "it is old earth's groping towards the steep
> Heaven whom she childs us by."
> (Ash-boughs.)

And this feeling for Earth informs the whole of the sonnet called *Ribblesdale* :

> "Earth, sweet Earth. . . .
> strong
> Thy plea with him who dealt, nay does now deal
> Thy lovely dale down thus and thus bids reel
> Thy river, and o'er gives all to rack or wrong."

Equally pertinent is a comparison with *In the Valley of the Elwy*, which points the same contrast between the lack of religious enlightenment among the people (this time the Welsh) and the beauty of their country. As the *cywydd* puts it (lines 7 and 8) : " Weak water brings faithful testimony to our vale, but man bears no such witness." The same thought occurs in the prose dedication.

    It should be noted that Hopkins addressed two other poems, one in English and the other in Latin, to this same Bishop of Shrewsbury on the occasion of his jubilee. See *Poems*, Third Edition, No. 30 and 136.

APPENDIX F

TABLE OF REFERENCE

IN both volumes of the present work, all *numerical* references to the poems of Hopkins follow the numbering in the Second Edition, since most readers, at present, are likely to have access to that volume. For the convenience, however, of those who have access only to the new Third Edition the following key has been compiled. Below that will be found a similar key to the early poems and fragments quoted in Chapter I and now reprinted, from the *Note-books*, in the Third Edition.

No. in Second Edition.			No. in Third Edition.		No. in Second Edition.			No. in Third Edition.
1	.	.	19		46	.	.	70
2	.	.	20		47	.	.	71
3	.	.	24		48	.	.	72
4	.	.	28		49	.	.	73
5	.	.	29		50	.	.	74
6	.	.	30		51	.	.	75
7	.	.	31		52	.	.	98
8	.	.	32		53	.	.	101
9	.	.	33		54	.	.	119
10	.	.	34		55	.	.	120
11	.	.	35		56	.	.	111
12	.	.	36		57	.	.	113
13	.	.	37		58	.	.	105
14	.	.	38		59	.	.	118
15	.	.	39		60	.	.	112
16	.	.	40		61	.	.	102
17	.	.	41		62	.	.	103
18	.	.	42		63	.	.	104
19	.	.	43		64	.	.	100
20	.	.	44		65	.	.	99
21	.	.	45		66	.	.	108
22	.	.	46		67	.	.	110
23	.	.	47		68	.	.	109
24	.	.	48		69	.	.	122
25	.	.	49		70	.	.	114
26	.	.	50		71	.	.	115
27	.	.	51		72	.	.	121
28	.	.	52		73	.	.	116
29	.	.	53		74	.	.	117
30	.	.	54		75	.	.	4
31	.	.	55		76	.	.	1
32	.	.	62		77	.	.	2
33	.	.	56		78	.	.	18
34	.	.	57		79	.	.	21
35	.	.	58		80	.	.	22
36	.	.	59		81	.	.	23
37	.	.	60		82	.	.	25
38	.	.	61		83	.	.	3
39	.	.	63		84	.	.	26
40	.	.	64		85	.	.	27
41	.	.	65		86	.	.	107
42	.	.	66		87	.	.	106
43	.	.	67		88	.	.	133
44	.	.	68		89	.	.	131
45	.	.	69		90	.	.	132

POSTSCRIPT

(to Chapter I)

Since the proofs of this volume were passed, three more early verse-fragments by G. M. H. have come to light—in a letter dated " Sept. 3rd 1862 " and addressed to E. H. Coleridge.[1] Speaking of " a good many poetical snatches " he had then been writing, Hopkins adds : " The best thing I have done lately is *Il Mystico* in imitation of *Il Penseroso*. It is not finished yet. . . ." Of this poem he copied out 142 lines. The imitation is competent, but the Miltonic style is copiously shot with ethereal lights and rainbow-hues from Shelley ; and in the same letter he tells E. H. C. that he has just been reading " Shelley's *Prometheus Unbound*, which is as fine as, or finer than, the *Prometheus Bound* of Aeschylus—though perhaps a little too fantastic." The fragment of *Il Mystico* begins :

> " Hence sensual gross desires,
> Right offspring of your grimy mother Earth !
> My spirit hath a birth
> Alien from yours as heaven from Nadir-fires : "

Earthly things are bidden not to foul and cumber " The shaken plumage of my spirit's wings." The Spirit he invokes is a combination of the Holy Ghost and Shelley's Spirit of Nature : he wishes—

> " like a lark to glide aloof
> Under the cloud-festoonèd roof,
> That with a turning of the wings
> Light and darkness from him flings ;
> To drift in air, the circled earth
> Spreading still its sunnèd girth ;
> To hear the sheep-bells dimly die
> Till the lifted clouds were nigh,
> In breezy belts of upper air
> Melting into aether rare. . . ."

Two other fragments given in the same letter are entitled " A Windy day in summer " (10 lines) and " A fragment of anything you like " (9 lines). Neither piece calls for special comment.

[1] Published in the *Times Lit. Supplnt.*, Sept. 25, 1948.

INDEX

Note.—All references to the prose works and poems of Hopkins are indexed under ' Hopkins, Gerard Manley '.

All matters relating to the technique of poetry are indexed under ' Versification '. Musicians and musical critics are indexed under ' Music '.

21/17